Economics as Ideology

Economics as Ideology

Keynes, Laski, Hayek, and the Creation of Contemporary Politics

Kenneth R. Hoover

ROWMAN & LITTLEFIELD PUBLISHERS, INC.
Lanham • Boulder • New York • Oxford

ROWMAN & LITTLEFIELD PUBLISHERS, INC.

Published in the United States of America
by Rowman & Littlefield Publishers, Inc.
A wholly owned subsidary of The Rowman & Littlefield Publishing Group, Inc.
4501 Forbes Boulevard, Suite 200, Lanham, Maryland 20706
www.rowmanlittlefield.com

PO Box 317
Oxford
OX2 9RU, UK

Distributed by National Book Network

British Library Cataloguing in Publication Information Available

Library of Congress Cataloging-in-Publication Data

Hoover, Kenneth R., 1940–
  Economics as ideology : Keynes, Laski, Hayek, and the creation of
contemporary politics / Kenneth R. Hoover.
      p. cm.
Includes bibliographical references and index.
  ISBN 0-7425-3112-0 (hardcover : alk. paper)—ISBN 0-7425-3113-9
(pbk. : alk. paper)
  1. Economics—History—20th century. 2. Keynes, John Maynard,
1883–1946. 3. Laski, Harold Joseph, 1893–1950. 4. Hayek, Friedrich A.
von (Friedrich August), 1899–1992. I. Title.
  HB87.H67 2003
  330.15—dc21

                                                            2003004954

∞™ The paper used in this publication meets the minimum requirements of American
National Standard for Information Sciences—Permanence of Paper for Printed Library
Materials, ANSI/NISO Z39.48-1992.

For Benjamin Kim Hoover
May his century do better. . . .

Contents

Preface

LEFT, RIGHT, AND CENTER IN THE TWENTY-FIRST CENTURY

At the opening of the twenty-first century, politics in the West have come to a curious pass. The partisans of the market are everywhere heard, while the partisans of government are muted and defensive. A half century ago, political discussion was quite the opposite. Then government was the wave of the future, and the evils of the market were widely advertised. In between, during the century's third quarter, the dominant belief was that the wise regulation of relations between government and the market could end depressions and open the path to a more progressive society. By the end of the century, the pendulum had swung nearly all the way in the market's favor.

On a moment's reflection, it is clear that governments do good things, as well as bad. And markets likewise are Janus-faced, sometimes provident, other times the wastrel. Similarly, for the behavior of the elites who run the regulated society: occasionally they are wise, and often they are quite out of touch with the masses whom they rule. The ways that people think about government, the market, and ruling elites are deeply influenced by ideologies.

We know that ideologies are the work of ideologues and politicians, those who take complicated ideas, resolve the ambiguities, and render them fit for mass consumption. Who are these ideologues, and where, in turn, do they draw their material from? This book is about three powerful thinkers who shaped the foundations of the left, right, and center of the political spectrum in the twentieth century.[1] John Maynard Keynes (1883–1946), Harold Laski (1893–1950), and Friedrich Hayek (1899–1992) did more than any of their contemporaries to define the center, left, and right of the political spectrum in Western industrial democracies.

Harold Laski was the tribune of democratic socialism in the thirties and forties. He argued for a democratically responsive state that would replace capitalism with a socialized economy. Maynard Keynes (rarely John) became the architect and impresario of the regulatory state of the post–World War II era. Keynes thought that intelligent policy makers could bring the state and the market into harmony and rescue them from the "stupidity" of the less enlightened. Hayek was to be the evangelist of the market in the century's closing decades. Hayek celebrated the market and deprecated governmental regulation. At first dismissed, Hayek finally came to eminence as the founder of the conservative revolt against the welfare state in the 1980s and 1990s.

The tale told here might be read for reasons other than its analytical value. Each of these three personalities has a life story with developmental dimensions that are intertwined with historical moments of great consequence. The fact that they knew and worked with, and against, each other for more than twenty years adds no small measure of drama to the narrative.

Similar in age, colleagues in academic life, and participants in the century's defining political events, the story of these three men is also the story of how we in the West came to define politics as the choice between government and the market, between regulation and "freedom," and between the classes and the masses. Doctrinal fights over the primacy of the market, or of government, are the essence of partisan politics. Populist complaints about elitism are the stuff of much political discussion. Newspapers, books, magazines, websites, and the airwaves are filled with the combative verbiage of libertarianism, populism, and egalitarianism.

The spirits, and sometimes the very words, of Keynes, Laski, and Hayek, infuse these scripts. They are among the principal dramatists whose ideas animate contemporary political theater. Their lives were quite distinctive: Hayek, the émigré bearing a continental legacy; Laski, a Jewish prodigy and rebel against his class; and Keynes, the doyen of a commune of intellectuals and artists. They knew each other, carried on public and private disputations, and worked as colleagues in the same institutions. In searching the lived experience of each one, we will see how their ideas became the catalysts for powerful movements that reshaped the political universe.

The kernel of each legacy lay in the orientation to the basic institutions of modern society, to the market and the government, and to the regulators that shape relations between them. As the twenty-first century begins, the legacy of their conceptions is everywhere. The dismantling of Laski's socialist state spreads around the globe, and Hayek's market becomes the yet more dominant institution, while Keynes's creation, the regulatory regime symbolized now by the International Monetary Fund that he established, is the focus of popular resistance to elites and their globalizing project.

How these orientations came to be is the subject of this analysis. Yet we are interested in more than documenting the history of ideas, in more than biography, and in something beyond the human interest story of the relations between these three seminal personalities. While the book goes into detail on all these matters, the point is to gain a perspective on the process of ideological formation and change. The question at the heart of the book is, What are the relationships between identity development and ideological beliefs? What is illustrated in the book is the nexus between identity, ideas, and ideology.

How can we extract the salient aspects of identity formation in these three complex and fascinating lives and then draw the connections to ideologies and political change? I look at each figure in a developmental perspective. That is, I examine how each personality was formed in confronting the challenges that shape a sense of identity. These developmental turning points are matched with the emergence of the ideas that characterized each person's political views. The analysis concludes by drawing some lessons about the relations between identity formation and ideology that may shed light on our contemporary political situation.

In particular, I show how opposition to social and political institutions and practices, derived from identity needs, propels the shift from ideas to ideology. The oppositional bind of ideology arises from an analytical blindness that permits the resolution of contested ideas in ways that are more reflective of developmental needs than of careful consideration. The link between identity and ideology turns out to have more to do with what people are against than with what they are for. In the course of these explorations, we may learn something about why socialists are seen to have trouble figuring out the economy, why libertarians appear to be confused about governance, and why elites so often misread the masses. The book concludes by linking the analysis to the ideologizing of institutions that characterizes contemporary politics. This demonstration of the importance of understanding the relationships between identity and ideology opens the way to the consideration of progressive policies for addressing identity needs and other aspects of developmental freedom.

ACKNOWLEDGMENTS

The quest to understand the origins of contemporary political economy has occupied me intensively for the last seven years and, more broadly, for four decades—ever since my junior year abroad at University College, London, and the London School of Economics and Political Science. The play of ideas on political consciousness, witnessed in political activism and in countless discussions about identity and ideology with students and colleagues, is the principal fascination that lies behind this work.

The list of acknowledgments for all those who made this intellectual journey possible must necessarily be rather long and still quite inadequate. This book originated with a sabbatical in 1996–1997 at the University of Washington and, in the spring term, at the London School of Economics and St. Catherine's College, Oxford University. Lord Plant, then Master of St. Catherine's College, was instrumental in arranging several key interviews for the project. Among those interviewed for the book were Tony Benn, M.P.; Anne Bohm, the London School of Economics; Peter Clarke, St. John's College, Cambridge; Lord Dahrendorf, formerly Director of the London School of Economics; Michael Freeden, Mansfield College; Lord Hattersley, formerly Deputy Leader of the British Labour Party; Jack Hayward, Professor and Director of the Centre for European Politics, Economics, and Society, Oxford University; Lord Harris, Institute of Economic Affairs; George Jones and Ken Minogue, the London School of Economics; Michael Newman, North London University; Mark Perlman, University of Pittsburgh; and Lord Skidelsky, Warwick University and the Social Market Foundation. Archives consulted include collections of the British Library of Political and Economic Science, the Modern Archives of King's College Library, the Modern Politics collection of the Bodleian Library, the British Library, and the Hoover Institution at Stanford University.

Professional colleagues too numerous to mention contributed significant comments on papers given at meetings of the American Political Science Association, the British Columbia Political Science Association, the European Society for the History of Economic Thought, the International Society for the Study of Political Psychology, and the Pacific Northwest Political Science Association.

A spring term at Nuffield College, Oxford, in 2000 provided the perfect environment for concluding this research, and I am deeply indebted to the Politics Group at Nuffield and particularly David Miller and Alec Stone Sweet, Official Fellows in Political Theory and Comparative Politics, for making this possible. Comments received from the Nuffield Political Theory Workshop, the C. T. Studd Society at Balliol, and the Interdisciplinary Seminar in Economics at London City University helped to shape the final manuscript. The expert assistance of Jacqueline Cox, Modern Archivist at King's College, and of Carol Leadenham at the Hoover Institution is gratefully acknowledged, as are the labors of my research assistants at Western Washington University: Bill Biebuyck, Mary Harvey, Johnny Peel, and Ann Vetter-Hansen. Throughout, the work has been supported by Western Washington University's leave program and the Bureau for Faculty Research directed by Geri Walker and Dean Mohab Ghali. To them, Deans Elich and Kleinknecht, and my colleagues in political science, many thanks. Thoughtful readings by Rodney Barker of the London School of Economics, David Miller of Nuffield College, Sanford Schram of Bryn Mawr, Carl Simpson of Western Washington University, James Scott of Yale, Erik Olsen of Seattle University, Raymond Plant of King's College, and David McIvor contributed considerably to the clarity of the argument. Charlotte Cubitt, secretary and translator for Friedrich Hayek for the last fifteen years of his life, permitted me to research her files of correspondence (now placed with the Hoover Institution) and read her remarkable memoir of their work and friendship.

This work stands on the shoulders of a marvelous body of biographical, analytical, and critical literature, the citations of which are noted as exhaustively as possible. The bibliographic database of all the sources involved covers over eight hundred books, articles, letters, manuscripts, interviews, and commentaries. Readers who would like to see the complete bibliography or who would like to offer comments may contact me at Ken.Hoover@wwu.edu. For permission to quote from correspondence and other sources, I am indebted to Bruce Caldwell, Jean Cornuelle, Mary Cranston, Charlotte Cubitt, Milton Friedman, Michael Newman, Robert Skidelsky, and Harold Laski's grandchildren: Andrew, John, and Pat Mathewson, as well as the Society of Authors, the Provost and Scholars of King's College, Cambridge, and Curtis Brown, Ltd., on behalf of the estate of Winston Churchill.

My principal debt, and warmest appreciation, must be recorded to a leading British citizen, scholar, peer, and public intellectual, Raymond (Lord) Plant, who encouraged these efforts and did so much to make them possible. To all of these, I offer gratitude and absolution.

Judy Hoover, who shared and assisted in this exploration every step of the way, learned with me that love and work sometimes complete each other.

1

Of Identity, Ideas, and Ideologies

It is a cliché of psychohistory that in each great person's life there must be some turning point that defines identity and shapes destiny. The paradigmatic case is Luther's call to the monastery in defiance of his father's wishes and his subsequent confrontation with the Holy Father in Rome as the catalytic moment of the Protestant Reformation.[1] Less dramatic, but perhaps as powerful, were the forces that shaped the lives and minds of Maynard Keynes (née John Maynard Keynes), Harold Laski, and Friedrich Hayek.

There are critical moments or phases where destiny does its work. We will look for the turning points that shape the direction of future ideas and beliefs. By understanding these episodes, we can seek out the themes that make sense of their lives. We can see ideas emerging from identity formation. And, in these three cases, we can find patterns that suggest something revealing about the genesis and limitations of ideologies. Each person played a powerful part in responding to the historic challenges that beset England and the industrialized world as the twentieth century unfolded. With this understanding, the points of departure for the politics of the twenty-first century come into focus.

Ideas come from people. Keynes wrote famously that

> Practical men, who believe themselves to be quite exempt from any intellectual influences, are usually the slaves of some defunct economist. Madmen in authority, who hear voices in the air, are distilling their frenzy from some academic scribbler of a few years back. I am sure that the power of vested interests is vastly exaggerated compared with the gradual encroachment of ideas.[2]

The three figures to be examined are the relevant "academic scribblers" of our age. They created many of the ideas that made "slaves" of the practical folk and of their political leaders. Contemporary ideologies surrounding the role of governments, markets, and elites borrow heavily from the works of Maynard Keynes (1883–1946), Harold Laski (1893–1950); and Friedrich Hayek (1899–1992). Born at the end of the nineteenth century, this trio would largely define the ideological spectrum of the West as it appeared at the beginning of the twenty-first century. Their legacies structure political discussion as globalization intensifies.

Where earlier forms of ideology centered on values such as individualism, justice, community, and class or nationalist solidarity—these theorists targeted the role and mission of institutions as the essence of politics.[3] These three became the intellectual icons around whom were gathered many of the West's major political actors. While communism and fascism comprised the extremes of the ideological spectrum, neither survived the century, and neither maintained itself by democratic means. The versions of socialism, liberalism, and libertarian conservatism defined by these three became mass movements of enduring power. The decades from the 1920s through the 1940s have been termed the "age of Laski" by historian Max Beloff. Economist Milton Friedman labeled the 1950s through the 1970s the "age of Keynes," and the remainder of the century the "age of Hayek."[4] And now political scientist Kenneth Minogue has named Hayek "the man for the century ahead of us."[5]

The fascinating fact about this trio is that they all knew each other well. Keynes, Laski, and Hayek were colleagues and rivals from the 1920s through the 1940s. Keynes died in 1946, Laski in 1950, and Hayek outlasted his two contemporaries by living to the age of ninety-two, but the contest with their ideas accompanied him to the end of his long life. They interacted personally, in policy-making arenas and in the public media. The interplay interactions make the story all the more intriguing.

The movements they promoted in Anglo-American politics came to center stage in successive decades from the twenties through to the eighties. The eras of socialist advocacy, the regulatory state, and the market comprise the main phases of twentieth-century politics in the Western democracies. There was the upsurge of socialist advocacy in the twenties, thirties, and early forties culminating in the Labour Party's victory in England in 1945 and of reform liberalism as the dominant postwar movement in American politics. The institution of "cradle to grave" social security measures, along with the nationalization of principal industries, set off a new era in relations between the state and the economy.

The socialist impulse contended with a milder rival, the effort to coordinate the activities of market and state through intelligent intervention. Interventionist government on the model offered by Maynard Keynes achieved worldwide significance with the Bretton Woods agreement on the postwar financial order and the creation of the International Monetary Fund in 1945. The regulatory state rose to prominence as the socialist phase wound down and became dominant in the West in the sixties and seventies. By 1980, a third phase appeared: a reaction against government and a celebration of laissez-faire capitalism with the advent of Margaret Thatcher and Ronald Reagan. Hayek was Thatcher's avowed intellectual mentor. He was a hero to Reagan, a college economics major. Hayek received the Medal of Freedom from Reagan's heir, George Bush.

So there are three phases and three "scribblers." The task of explaining the ideas of these scribblers is well advanced, with large literatures and voluminous collected works in place for all three—and many of them will be cited here. For those whose understanding comes to rest in the details and particularities of each individual contribution, there are rich materials to be read and digested.

But there remain larger questions to be answered. What about the relationships between individual thinkers, the era they lived in, and the construction of ideologies that shaped political economy? Are there no themes that structure the assessment? Can we find patterns in all three cases? Is there a link between developments in their personal lives and the ideas they generated that came to dominate public opinion?

What we are looking for are the tendrils that connect *identity*, *ideas*, and *ideology*. This is where intriguing patterns are to be found. Here one can see the themes that make sense of the past, reveal the present more clearly, and illuminate the future. We can hope to approach the twenty-first century with an understanding of how politics came to its current pass.

1.1 – FROM IDEAS TO IDEOLOGIES: OF CONTESTATION AND RESOLUTION

What are political ideologies? In his pathbreaking study of ideology, Michael Freeden claims that "ultimately, ideologies are configurations of *decontested* meanings of political concepts"[6] What does this mean?

As was suggested at the outset, concepts of the market or of government are morally ambiguous. Good and bad can be found in both. The friends of each do battle over defining such concepts so as to include what they think is good and screen off what they see as bad. The definitions are caught up in the values of their definers. "Markets allocate scarce resources among conflicting demands." Sounds benign. "Governments (democratic ones at least) protect rights and translate the will of the people into public policy." Not bad. Or "Markets serve wants more than needs, and waste resources thereby." Not so good. "Government is dumb, the market is rational!" So it goes.

The disputes over meanings occupy scholars and, sadly, render their works dull and difficult. But practical people need to decide. Someone has to form up each side in the struggle. The three figures we will learn about did this. Freeden observes that ideologies try to settle contests over meanings:

> In concrete terms, an ideology will link together a particular conception of human nature, a particular conception of social structure, of justice, of liberty, of authority, etc. "*This* is what liberty means, and *that* is what justice means," it asserts.

Each ideology discussed in this book asserts specific meanings for such contentious concepts as equality, justice, freedom, and so forth. The act of settling the conflict over these meanings leads directly to decisions about political action. Michael Freeden continues:

> Ideologies need, after all, to straddle the worlds of political thought and political action, for one of their central functions is to link the two. The political sphere is primarily characterized by political decision-making, and decision-making is an important form of de-contesting a range of potential alternatives.[7]

The question for this book is, Why did these thinkers decontest ideas about government and the market in the way that they did? What mix of motivations and ideas led them to their conclusions? Why did their versions catch on? Why did mass publics and their leaders respond to these "voices in the air"?

1.2 – IDENTITY RELATIONS: A DEVELOPMENTAL PERSPECTIVE

Each of these three personalities has a life story with developmental dimensions that are intertwined with historical moments of great consequence. In probing the development of identity, I will consider the three critical markers of identity formation and change: the kinds of *competencies* or skills each came to have; the *communities* they were part of; and the interpersonal ties and *commitments* that defined their private lives. These are the critical arenas within which people come to be who they are.

The selection of these markers is neither accidental nor casual. This analysis draws on the rich stream of theoretical formulations and empirical research by Erik Erikson, John Bowlby, and Carol Gilligan, as well as the verification and refinement found in three decades of work by James Marcia and other social psychologists.[8] The intention is not to invoke detailed psychiatric evidence, but rather to see the contours and major features of each personality in a historical context. Rather than speculating about psychic impulses, the focus will be on what can be known from their writings, their behavior, and the impressions they created on their colleagues, contemporary observers, and the public. My sources are biographies, memoirs, scholarly articles and books, archival materials, and interviews with those who knew them or who studied their lives in great detail.

Systematic research on identity formation tells us that each aspect of identity involves *relations* between the inner constitution of the self and the pressures and responses of the society. Identity formation is a two-sided transaction between self and society, between psychosomatic endowment, and sociopolitical environment. The ability, discipline, and motivation each person brings to the formulation of a particular *competency* requires, for its full emergence, the recognition, legitimation, and certification that society provides.

A poet who publishes nothing faces a hard road to acceptance by peers. Similarly, the *communities* that sustain an identity, whether of region, religion, race, ethnicity, gender, class, or voluntary affiliation, all interact in a web of relations that create patterns of acceptance and exclusion, of affirmation and discrimination, and of domination and resistance. And finally, the private struggle over fidelity and duty that undergirds interpersonal *commitments* can be aided or frustrated by one's surroundings. The productive relations and civil practices in society have fateful consequences for all the elements of identity.

The emergence of these relations and the struggle over them defines a person's identity. Identity is, as extensive empirical research reveals, a three-legged stool. Competencies, communities, and commitments support identity. When one is firmly seated and well grounded, identity is strong. When the legs are stabilized by solid relations between individual characteristics and a supportive society, identity is achieved.

Paradoxically, the research also tells us that identities built on solid relations correspond with more tolerant personalities. Insecure identities correlate with authoritarianism.[9] Thus, the achievement of identity carries with it a civic benefit. Consequently, our analysis has particular relevance to the larger issues of the sustainability of democracy.

When the three-legged stool begins to tip, the stronger legs take the load. People whose sense of competency is undermined, as for example when a job is lost, tend to place stress on their familial and community relations. When the legs are weakened, the self is summoned to seek strength in new and more

durable relations with elements of society. New vocations, personal relationships, and social affiliations become more significant.

I have titled this approach *identity relations analysis* to distinguish it from
identity politics or the assertion of fixed characteristics, such as race or gender, as the basis for identity. The position taken here is that identity is neither
given by one's personal characteristics nor an artifact of an exercise of power
nor of social construction, but rather a dynamic set of relations in which both
self and society play an inescapable role.

It is particularly the changes in these relations that, as we shall see, precipitate the formation of intellectual convictions. These turning points are also
where complex political concepts are transformed into ideologies. Ideological
convictions, by decontesting complex notions, can provide a way of buffering
the tensions of identity formation and change.[10] Ideologies are taken up by
identity-affirming affinity groups such as political parties. Ideologies also provide scenarios for identifying heroes and villains. Ideologies invite allegiance
to abstractions rather than to living, breathing "others" whose complex and
ambiguous responses are less reassuring in the struggle to form an identity.
What factors in the development of each of these remarkable personalities
shaped the convictions that made them articulators of potent political ideas?
For some, an identity-defining moment will be as dramatic as a sudden conversion; for others the "moment" will last a decade or more.

Erik Erikson, the pioneer of the identity relations approach to understanding
ideology, observed that

> identity and ideology are two aspects of the same process. Both provide the nec-
> essary condition for further individual maturation and, with it, for the next
> higher form of identification, namely, the solidarity linking common identities
> in joint living, acting and creating.[11]

I will explore the relationships between personalities, ideas, and political
change. What led to ideologizing the institutions of society in the particular
way that characterizes contemporary politics? Why did Laski become the theorist and advocate of socialist government, Hayek of the capitalist market,
and Keynes of the wise elite that could mediate between them? Along the
way, readers are invited to test the explanatory power of *identity relations
analysis* by comparing what the story of these lives has to offer with what
they know from a more powerful authority—their own experience.

2

The Prewar World: Seeds of Struggle

All three of these personalities were brought onto the stage between the acts of a huge historical drama. The developmental scenarios of childhood and early adulthood were acted out in cultures that were being disassembled by conflict and disintegration. Each man would respond differently and give voice to powerful themes that would ultimately alter and redefine the relations of peoples, their governments, and the economies in which they lived.

Maynard Keynes, Harold Laski, and Friedrich Hayek arrived in a world that resembled an overripe melon ready to split apart. Keynes and Laski were born to the world's greatest empire at the height of its power, and Hayek was the child of an empire no less magnificent in its adornment, even if its rivals had steadily diminished its primacy in Europe. England's Queen Victoria ruled for sixty years and brought the British Empire to its apogee, while Austro-Hungarian Emperor Franz Joseph died in 1916 after sixty-eight years of imperial aggrandizement and decay.

When Queen Victoria celebrated her Diamond Jubilee in 1897, Maynard Keynes was fourteen and Harold Laski was four. The Pax Britannica had, since Lord Nelson's victory at Trafalgar in 1805, produced for England a century of security from foreign invasion. Victoria's realm circled the globe, encompassing 372 million people. The treasures of myriad cultures flowed to England creating unparalleled wealth and power. Commercial savvy and supreme self-confidence, bolstered by a formidable navy, gave England an intellectual and economic pre-eminence out of all relation to her size and population.

England's hegemony was as much cultural as it was commercial in nature. The university town of Cambridge was Keynes's birthplace, while the industrial city of Manchester was the childhood home of Laski. Each embodied a potent aspect of empire. Cambridge and Oxford nurtured the ideas and the confidence that emboldened generations of Englishmen to visit their culture on far-flung outposts. Keynes, raised on the doorstep of the university, absorbed an ethos of intellectual adventurism.

The cities of Cambridge and Manchester resemble each other very little, but they had in common the distinction of lying at the fault line of portentous changes in the culture of England and of the West generally. The commercial dynamism of Manchester, with its mills and factories, supplied the means and the mode of a new industrial civilization. Manchester is where the forces of transformation from an agricultural to an industrial economy were most keenly felt. The workers who came to the city from the fields and hamlets of northern England and Ireland brought with them communal traditions that were not easily undone by the routines of factory work. Using their labor, the commercial foundations of the empire were built by a new class of entrepreneurs who worked through this epochal transition.

The textile mills of Manchester attracted an émigré businessman and intellectual, Friedrich Engels, just as it had the grandfather of Harold Laski who arrived from Poland in 1831. Nathan Laski, Harold's father, worked his way up to partnership and then ownership of a cotton export business built on extensive contacts with Indian merchants. The imagination of his son Harold was fired by utopian writers drawing on a budding protest movement that took the form of idealistic experiments with cooperative mills in the Yorkshire dales.

The security of another empire was the womb of Friedrich Hayek. By the time of Hayek's birth in the last year of the century, Austria-Hungary occupied the crossroads of Europe, from Switzerland in the east, to Romania and Russia in the west; and from Serbia and Italy in the south, to Germany and Poland in the north. Vienna, Hayek's birthplace, evinced the magnificence of European culture. The Hapsburgs erected a show city with a *ringstrasse* at its heart to display the wealth and elegance of a monarchy that ruled over polyglot peoples of differing ethnicities, languages, and temperaments.

Symbolic of this eminence, the University of Vienna had entered into a period of distinction among all the academies of Europe. Hayek's father was a medical doctor and teacher attached to the university, and his lineage permitted the attachment of "von" to Hayek. Hayek's father and mother provided a home where study took precedence over play, and visitors were often academicians—as all three of their sons would become.[1]

Within the Austro-Hungarian and British empires, the world of the mind could grow and expand without the fears for survival that constrain more threatened peoples. A surplus of wealth afforded security for the creation of family commercial dynasties, as with the Laskis, and for the cultivation of the scholarly life among those such as the Keyneses and the Hayeks, who found meaning in the precincts of the university. The convergence of art, music, theater, and letters upon themes of high culture provided coherence and sense of purpose that impelled precocity and ambition. Their location in the professional classes exposed them to ambition and status, while their family's position depended at least as much on cultural positioning as on wealth.

Yet the security of their childhoods was to be threatened and disrupted as the great empires were to blunder into conflict. As the cosmopolitan logic of capitalist commercial relations swept through the German duchies, the ethnic enclaves of central Europe, and the fractious islands of Great Britain in the nineteenth century, so these forces expanded to the globe as the century closed. Conflicts over imperial ambitions between and among England and the continental nation-states deepened.

These two great empires, their cultures, and the public expectations of a generation were tied to the prestige and power of vast aggregations of force, power, and trade. Karl Marx gave voice to those left out or victimized by these combinations of capital, and Keynes was born the year Marx died. The entanglements, the buried resentments of ethnicity and race, the bursting energies of rapid industrialization, the pretensions of rulers, and the massed ground and naval forces all comprised a rich and simmering stew that would turn toxic in the second decade of the new century.

Each young man was to come to adulthood amid shattering change. World War I was a cataclysm of empires, and for these three, a crisis of maturation. This chapter will take us through to the outbreak of World War I. As these three childhoods unfold into young manhood, three quite distinctive personalities emerge: a prodigy, a rebel, and a seeker after pattern and meaning. Here will be found the making of identities: the nurturing of competence as political economists, the formation of distinctive and shifting communities, and the beginnings of intense personal commitments to others.

2.1 – KEYNES: THE PRODIGY OF POLITICAL ECONOMY

We begin with Maynard Keynes, born ten years before Laski and sixteen years before Hayek. Keynes offers a more complicated picture than either Hayek or Laski. There are enough turning points and other events in Keynes's life to supply Donald Moggridge with material for nine hundred pages of biography and Robert Skidelsky with nearly twice that number. Yet there is agreement between these and other biographers, as well as the acquaintances and experts I interviewed, that Keynes's identity development was deeply shaped by a constantly reinforced sense of the superiority of secular intellect over faith, custom, conventional sources of authority, and even morals.

From a home life in a family immersed in Cambridge's academic culture, to youthful triumphs at Eton, to undergraduate stardom at King's College, followed by distinction in his examinations and in his first posting at the India Office, there is an unbroken record of attainment based on intelligence and a distinctive charisma.[2] Keynes's home was a kind of laboratory for the transformation of a culture. Located on the edge of Cambridge University's grounds with their greens, commons, and exquisite gardens, Keynes was raised on Harvey Road in a solid brick Victorian home.

Reared by doting parents who were deeply involved in the intellectual and political life of Cambridge, Keynes drew stores of learning from Neville Keynes, his donnish father, and political ambition from Florence Keynes, his activist mother.[3] Neville Keynes was a logician and a pioneer in the emerging field of economics, authoring texts in logic and economics. In recognition of his eminence, he was offered the editorship of the journal of the newly formed British Economics Association.[4] Instead, Keynes's father became the chief administrator of Cambridge University. Florence moved from volunteer activities to become an alderman and, later, Cambridge's first woman mayor.[5] She went on to help found the National Union of Women Workers and to become President of the National Council of Women. Both survived their son and were close companions to him throughout his life.

Keynes was a child prodigy. An aunt once told him that Keynes rhymes with "brains."[6] The prophecy was fulfilled not only by Maynard but by his siblings, Margaret and Geoffrey, born at two-year intervals after him. His sister became a social worker, in the model of her mother, and married a Nobel laureate, A. V. Hill, a fellow of Trinity College. His brother was to become the husband of Charles Darwin's granddaughter.[7] Geoffrey Keynes distinguished the family further as a surgeon, Vice Marshal of the Royal Air Force, and noted bibliophile.[8] The family was a perfect expression of Cambridge values—of what Roy Harrod, Maynard Keynes's student and biographer, terms "the presuppositions of Harvey Road" about the primacy of "an intellectual aristocracy" in directing Britain's course.[9]

Moggridge, who closely researched the Keynes family, reports that his father spent hours with his sons sorting stamp collections. On Sunday mornings, a pile of his father's duplicates and castoffs would be available for Maynard and Geoffrey to alternate in choosing. Maynard learned the economics of prices from researching the value of stamps his father would offer to his boys.

His father was also the disciplinarian; Keynes was "smacked, slapped, and even whipped" as a consequence of his willfulness. Though this fostered an early preference for his forgiving mother, diaries and letters reveal that as a teenager, Keynes found the companionship of his father most enjoyable and stimulating.[10] Later on, it was his mother's political sensitivity and passion for progressive causes that drew him closer to her.[11]

Comfortable, high-minded, and stimulating to an adventurous mind, the Keynes's home and family were also materially secure. The mundane preoccupations of less-endowed families were not to interfere with Keynes's upbringing. This was a world where a child might build a castle in his imagination and proceed to live in it, not noticing the hovels at the gates. Were it not for the active political involvement of his mother, Keynes would not have had reason to be concerned about "the social question." Even so, it was to be a less than immediate concern to this rapidly developing prodigy.[12]

Young Maynard was temperamentally precocious, a bit conceited, and very quick witted. Skidelsky reports that he practiced his conceit on his sister, Margaret, at the age of six, by convincing her that she was a *thing* rather than a more exalted entity. He was rewarded by her tears.[13] His conceit did know bounds; he suffered from the conviction that he was ugly.[14] His appearance was always rather arresting, and perhaps, to a boy, distinctiveness is ugliness at an age in which conformity becomes a matter of urgency.

Florence Keynes snapshots a word picture of her prematurely self-possessed son:

> Maynard especially enjoyed coming down to lunch and listening to grown-up conversation. Sometimes it was necessary to remind him that he would not be expected to join in the talk himself. He accepted the situation but remarked sadly that it would be "a great drawback."[15]

His family, with roots traceable to a Keynes who came over with William the Conqueror in 1066, was poised to launch another conquest—this one of an intellect let loose in the world of political economy.[16] As a child of post-Victorian Cambridge, Keynes was destined to become a principal actor in the attempt to replace Christianity with a secular ethics based in a kind of intellectualism that was pragmatic and progressive, romantic, and idealistic.[17] In the cosmology of Cambridge, as Keynes later observed, the problem with Christianity was its dubious historical claims and the "strict principles" that flowed from these claims. "Why can an age only be great if it believes, or at least is bred up in believing, what is preposterous?"[18] It was for Keynes to attempt the practical reconciliation of a culture built on traditional morals with a world where values were of a decidedly more secular origin.[19]

Keynes's early achievements in boarding school at Eton provided the legitimation that a developing identity, particularly a precocious one, requires. Entering in 1897, he took care that his style of dress was at the top of the register with a new white tie every day and a fresh buttonhole flower from the village florist.[20] Living with all the other scholarship boys in the same house, Keynes was in his element from the start. Insulated in that company from some of the more philistine values and practices of the regular clientele, Keynes could work his way into Eton's culture with assurance. The intensity of boarding school life at Eton propelled an emotional drive. His superior attitude did not go unnoticed, but he was clever enough to avoid the hazing and casual violence that were part of public school life. Skidelsky suggests that

> He neither wanted to beat or be beaten. Intellect offered a way out. He had already used it to get his own way at home. Later he would use it to offer the world an alternative to rebellion or submission.[21]

Not that he lacked courage; he was even good at football. Neville Keynes, closely following his son's progress, had every reason to be pleased with his propensity for winning prizes for scholarship.

Keynes went up to King's College, Cambridge, in 1902, to read classics and mathematics. King's was the counterpart to Eton in fostering the development of a prodigy with a bent toward playing the *enfant terrible.* Keynes's distinctively long nose, which earned him the nickname "Snout," gave him a cachet that meshed well with his superior intellect, small moustache, and lively countenance.[22] Surrounded by young men of similar inclinations, Keynes and his friends could attempt to construct an alternative to the ugliness, monotony, and pretentiousness of late Victorian society. They also lived in a social cocoon apart, very largely, from the company of women. Women would not be admitted to full membership in the university until two years after Keynes's death.

With his early recruitment to the Apostles, a brilliant coterie of mostly homosexual dons and undergraduates, the stage was set for an unconventional personal life.[23] The modal conflict of the era, between traditional morals and the pursuit of mundane pleasures, presented itself to the young Keynes and his male companions in immediate form. The Apostles' practice of gathering in some member's rooms and giving papers on ethical and metaphysical topics on Saturday nights provided a forum for working through the conflict. Noel Annan describes the methodology of the hearthside debater noting that:

in their assault upon the bourgeois citadel, the modernists rediscovered the most effective method of demolition. One method is to use invective and destroy the enemy's fortifications by the sheer weight of bombardment. Another is to use reason to shell first one redoubt and then another until your enemy is left without defences. But the most devastating method is to undermine his Maginot line by burrowing under it. You tunnel first with ridicule, then with mockery, insinuation, derision, flippancy and satire; and suddenly the defences of bourgeois society collapse. . . . Before mockery religion quailed, respect dissolved and faith failed.[24]

They might have settled the conflict of the sacred and the profane by dignifying their physical pleasures. Fortunately, perhaps, they had proper guidance that led them to a more elevated perch from which to view the contest. They had G. E. Moore, philosophy don and Angel (senior Apostle), who published that year his *Principia Ethica.* Here was a recipe for resolving, however abstractly, this dilemma.[25] Keynes reminisced about its impact three dozen years later: "Its effect on *us*, and the talk which preceded and followed it, dominated, and perhaps still dominate, everything else."[26]

Moore's argument amounted to a kind of idealist's utilitarianism. Rather than centering on physical pleasure, Moore located the ideal in the realm of intuited "goods" such as beauty, friendship, and aesthetics. In such a realm, the speculations of the Apostles acquired the halo of ethical inquiry. Physical indulgence was subsumed in the pursuit of a discernible set of aesthetic standards. As possessors of especially keen faculties of intuition, Keynes and his friends could see themselves as the vanguard of a proletariat seeking liberation from the ossified strictures of the Victorian establishment.[27] They knew beauty, they thought. The good life could be envisioned, and lived, in a realm beyond convention. Keynes recalls:

Nothing mattered except states of mind, our own and other people's of course, but chiefly our own. These states of mind were not associated with action or achievement or with consequences. They consisted in timeless, passionate states of contemplation and communion, largely unattached to "before" and "after." . . . The appropriate subjects of passionate contemplation and communion were a beloved person, beauty and truth, and one's prime objects in life were love, the creation and enjoyment of aesthetic experience and the pursuit of knowledge. Of these love came a long way first."[28]

What remained of utilitarianism in the Cambridge experience was the presumption that actions should be judged by their results rather than their intentions. But Moore pulled Keynes toward an introspective morality based in aesthetics, "a purer, sweeter air by far than Freud cum Marx."[29] The young Keynes was launched on this lifelong pursuit armed with a vocabulary originating in Moore's speculations. Keynes, looking back from 1938, remembered "it was exciting, exhilarating, the beginning of a new renaissance, the opening of a new heaven on a new earth, we were the forerunners of a new dispensation, we were not afraid of anything."[30] It remained for him to find a way to practice Moore's injunctions.

Progressive politics might have been the natural vent for such motivations. The young Keynes's politics were reported to be "free trade Liberal" in common with most advanced thinkers of his day. In time he became President of the Cambridge Union and of the Liberal Club. But there were also flirtations with the Fabian socialism of Beatrice and Sidney Webb, whom he joined on the side favoring "Collective Socialism" in a debate before the Cambridge Union.[31] Just how far Keynes went toward the left is disputed by his interpreters.[32] He went far enough to cause his father to conclude that he favored the "confiscation of wealth," but not so far as to actually join in the class-based agitation of the militant socialists. The Liberals, after all, were led by figures such as Lord Rosebery, who declaimed in 1906: "Socialism is the end of all, the negation of Faith, of Family, of Property, of Monarchy, of Empire."[33]

Keynes clearly was searching among the available alternatives for some way of generalizing, if not democratizing, the intuition of the good that was so vivid among the Apostles. As Keynes later reflected, the tool was to be *words*: "The instrument of impeccable grammar and an unambiguous dictionary." "If it appeared under cross-examination that you did not mean *exactly* anything, you lay under a strong suspicion of meaning nothing whatever."[34] Verbal combat was the test of character, rather than the more physical sports that absorbed so many of his peers. Words, but not exactly deeds. "There was not a very intimate connection between 'being good' and 'doing good'; and we had a feeling that there was some risk that in practice the latter might interfere with the former."[35] Within this sphere of intense personal commitments, there was not yet room or energy for social activism. That would come later.

Keynes had learned to prize intellect above all, and the "all" included conventions of morality, behavior, political ideology, and deference. His apostasy from conventional morals was the fulfillment of his upbringing. Intellectual competence trumps community values.

> We entirely repudiated a personal liability on us to obey general rules. We claimed the right to judge every individual case on its merits, and the wisdom, experience and self-control to do so successfully. This was a very important part

of our faith, violently and aggressively held, and for the outer world, it was our most obvious and dangerous characteristic. We repudiated entirely customary morals, conventions, and traditional wisdom. We were, that is to say, in the strict sense of the term, immoralists.[36]

The point here was not just self-indulgence, it was the realization of a philosophy devoted to "good feelings" and the "fit objects" that evoke these mental states. These feelings respond to the beautiful parts of nature and creation and displace the ugliness, stupidity, and banality of ordinary existence.[37] Good feelings are not the same as "pleasant feelings" necessarily, for Moore loaded the concept of good with ethical intent and with classical qualities of harmony and rightness.[38]

If this theory bespeaks the insouciance of Keynes and his friends, it also expresses a notion of altruism that was to be visited on a range of human endeavors. For Keynes, the mundane discipline of economics was never to be remote from the other arts and sciences, but an aspect of them. As he came to see it, economics is about the practical task of reorganizing society to produce a composition of forces that will improve life.

Moore taught that, as Skidelsky summarizes it, "the best achievable states of affairs are bound to be 'complex wholes,' the value of which do not add up to the sum of the value of their parts."[39] There is a near mystical quality to Moore's view that led Keynes throughout his life never to be content either with theorizing on the basis of a trend built on a single indicator or with the existing arrangement of "parts." Keynes firmly believed that some better composition awaited realization if only the right practical measures were put in place. In later life, when he could be found moving among a dizzying array of responsibilities and tasks, he was fashioning the various pieces of an improved "complex whole."

In Keynes's emerging view, what is perceived as traditional or "old" is not necessarily bad so much as misaligned. At the same time, movements of transformation such as revolutions or irrevocable trends struck him as ignorant of the immanent purpose of various elements of the social composition.[40] While he could be cantankerous about the rightness of his departures from traditional policies, he was never a revolutionary; while he would be a self-advertised "Cassandra," he would never be a Marxist—or a fascist.

There had come to be at Cambridge a vocational possibility apart from philosopher, humanist, or classicist. The modern vocation of economist had been invented by Alfred Marshall, Keynes's great predecessor at Cambridge, for the purpose of establishing a secular morality. By opening decisions about the use of resources to analysis, rather than leaving them to the impulses of the self-interested, there would be the possibility that ethics, moral principle, and even a sense of duty could enter in to such calculations.[41] The discipline of economics promoted the reordering of the elements of society around the rational, and hopefully morally justifiable, allocation of resources.

In a pedantic sense, Keynes would never be a formally trained economist. He had taken the Mathematics Tripos in 1905. Instead of finishing his degree with the Economics Tripos, in preparation for which he had taken about eight weeks of study under Alfred Marshall and others, he decided instead to take the Civil Service Examination that involved a section on economics, among other topics. The economics discipline was relatively new at Cambridge and had only the beginnings of a literature, whereas the civil service beckoned as a well-established path to, among other places, London, and the center of affairs—both political and personal. A visit to Lytton Strachey, who had taken up residence in London, and with whom Keynes had been romantically involved, helped settle his decision.[42]

Keynes understood the manners and temperament of his time and would operate with consummate artistry to shape public opinion, but he was never "of" the establishment. These tensions manifested themselves in the theater of Keynes's personality. Michael Holroyd, viewing Keynes through the eyes of Strachey, soul mate, and prophet of the Apostles, paints this portrait:

> His [Keynes'] mind was so restless and quick that his more turgid, watchful emotions never caught up with it, were never quite in step. The brilliant sparkle of his writing is not superficial, but rather icy. Like a barrister, he was often bent on putting over a point of view at one remove from himself, and his stated opinions seemed on occasions to be oddly vicarious. His retrospective exposition of an initially false premise was sometimes brilliant, extending his ingenuity to the full; and round this central untruth the satellites within his orbit would spin brightly and with incredible velocity.[43]

His path to greatness opened immediately on graduation. He placed second in the Civil Service Examination among 104 candidates, dragged down a notch, to his rage, by his scores in economics and mathematics. The reward for first place was a post in the Treasury. Coming second in the exams, he entered the India Office, where he was brought into the center of the fateful experiment in imperial governance known as the British Empire. The differences between India and Britain, most especially the stark contrast between a customary rural economy and a laissez-faire industrial economy, gave to the experiment an almost surreal quality.[44] The classic issues of protectionism and free trade and of monetary stabilization were everyday fare for the freshly minted prodigy who never had, and never would, set foot on the subcontinent.

The India Office was an excellent tutorial in the practical dimensions of economics. Keynes could work at specific problems and, by intellection, reach further and further into the basis of economic theory. This became the style of his progressively greater competency in the field. The accoutrements of expertise were picked up along the way—Adam Smith's *Wealth of Nations* was not read until 1910. His fluency with the classics of the field was never outstanding.[45]

Keynes saw the uses and abuses of governmental regulatory activity and acquired an intimate familiarity with the varieties of expertise, as well as manifestations of stupidity in the highest councils of government. He complained to his friend Strachey, "I am bored nine-tenths of the time and rather unreasonably irritated the other tenth whenever I can't have my own way. . . . It's maddening to have thirty people who can reduce you to impotence when you're quite certain you're right. . . . [The] dread of taking any responsibility is almost pathetic . . . it prevents any original or sporting proposal ever being made."[46] But it was not bureaucrats alone who attracted his ire: he published articles on the mishandling of the monetary crisis by City of London bankers just prior to the war.

While he left the India Office for Cambridge after two years, he stayed long enough to become deeply involved in the management of Indian monetary policy and even to write a short book on it entitled *Indian Currency and Finance* (1913). A defense of government policy, it would open the way to other policy books of a far less conventional sort.

At the tender age of twenty-five, he had become a fellow of his old school, King's College, Cambridge. Reporting to his friend Bernard Swithinbank, the move was met by the admonishment of his friends that he would never have the money for "legitimized copulation" on his meager stipend.[47] Two years later, in 1911, he became the editor of the distinguished *Economic Journal*. With this appointment and the editorship, he filled his father's shoes. He was to remain editor for thirty-three years, dispensing crisp judgments and incisive comments to the accepted and rejected alike.

One of the earliest reviews he wrote was of a book on gold and the monetary system by an Austrian economist, Ludwig von Mises, whom he characterized as lacking originality and "in a sense, decadent. Dr. Mises strikes an outside reader as being the very highly educated pupil of a school, once of great eminence, but now losing its vitality."[48] It was a school he would hear a great deal more about when the star pupil of von Mises, Friedrich Hayek, became one of his principal antagonists a decade later.

His personal life was a tangle of crosscurrents. Duncan Grant, a young artist and his principal paramour, would remain a close friend for the rest of his life. Roy Harrod describes Grant. He was "restless and volatile . . . strongly original, and had abounding interests and an eager flow of spirit."[49] He and Grant lived together and traveled to France in 1913. Keynes's mother records her recollection of traveling to the Riviera to minister to a diptheria-stricken Keynes. She and Duncan spent a night at the gaming tables where, she notes, "my companion won rather more than I lost and remonstrated at being dragged away."[50] Keynes's familial and amatory commitments were apparently not at odds.

Maynard Keynes in 1911, age 28. Courtesy of Milo Keynes.

However, Grant's cousin, Lytton Strachey, looked on the liaison as a jealous rival. Feeling rejected, Strachey penned an acerbic portrait of the youthful Keynes in his diary:

> He wallows in secret cynicism, I really do believe the only subjects in which he takes any interest are what he calls "fie-nance" and lechery—and they certainly don't seem to make a nice combination. He throws a cloak of itching satisfaction over both—oh terrible! terrible! He brings off his copulations and speculations with the same calculating odiousness, he has a boy with the same mean pleasure with which he sells at the top of the market, and he can hardly tell the difference between pocketing fifteen per cent and kissing Duncan.[51]

Whatever these crosscurrents may have been, his private pursuits did not interfere with a rising social eminence. He was taken up by the gadfly hostess Lady Ottoline Morrell who introduced him to the Prime Minister. His paramour, Duncan Grant, was invited to a party at Downing Street. The British respect for privacy kept the question of orthodoxy in personal relations outside the pale.[52] Indeed, Harrod's biography, published in 1951, would not mention a word about homosexuality.

Brought back to the government in 1915 by World War I, this time to the Treasury Department, he became a key staff member in managing the financing of the war effort. Within a year, he was in charge of all questions on the external financing of the war effort. Here he got his first glimpse of the financial power of the Americans. Their response to him took the form of a reproof at his rudeness in negotiations.[53] In the next war, he would try charm.

For all of his skepticism, the few years in the Treasury let him see the utility of an institution that could confront "wickedness" and "enthusiasm," even if it did so unimaginatively.[54] For imagination, he had another venue: London's Bloomsbury district. Just as his ferocious intellect insulated him from the banalities of ordinary discourse, the financial independence and cultural apostasy of Bloomsbury set him and his friends apart, and deliberately so, from the homely, prosaic, ingrained realities of life around them.[55] His participation in the semicommunal arrangements of the famous "Bloomsberries" began with his employment at the Treasury in 1915 and extended for more than two decades. His companions included the artistic and literary avant-garde of London.

Cambridge provided a cultural link between these disparate souls. London's contribution was the ambience of Bloomsbury, the site of the British Museum and the University of London, and the adjacent, slightly more raffish and cosmopolitan "Fitzrovia" district, not to mention the proximity to Soho. Seldom has civilization afforded such a lush garden for the flowering of intellect and the indulgence of the senses.

Among those gathered in Bloomsbury were the artists Clive and Vanessa Bell née Stephens, her novelist sister Virginia, and brother Adrian; "aspiring critic" Lytton Strachey and his cousin, the painter, Duncan Grant; Desmond and Molly McCarthy, both writers; and two civil servants, Sydney Waterlow and Saxon Sydney-Turner; a Liberal M.P., Hilton Young; and a Cambridge mathematician, H. T. J. Norton. Leonard Woolf joined the group about the time Keynes did and was to marry Virginia Stephens, who, as Virginia Woolf, would become Bloomsbury's most famous writer.[56] The tribal character of the commune is noted by Quentin Bell, a child of the commune. Half of the twenty he lists were Apostles, seven were members either of the Strachey or Stephens families, and Cambridge claimed all but five.[57]

There was a tribal aspect to Keynes's set. The youthful community of the Apostles shaded into the adult commune of Bloomsbury and an even more tangled web of personal commitments. Bloomsbury provided a kind of communal medium in which artists, essayists, dancers, poets, politicians, and one economist could test their creativity without the constraints of convention. The free flow of ideas, of sentiments, and of romantic and sexual turmoil within and among genders and marriages kept an edge on daily life. Wit ruled the day, and the night.

The denizens of Bloomsbury were, to be sure, at odds with conventional social mores and quite experimental in their artistic endeavors, but they were also disinclined to radical militancy and poor candidates for the rigors of socialist agitation. As art critic Richard Shone notes, "Bloomsbury was not organized; it did not come together to form a club, worship a god, found a movement or inspire social action."[58] What they did do was harbor new creative impulses and disparate intellectual tendencies.

The Bloomsbury revolt, so far as it went, was against "cant" rather than against the economic or political institutions of the society. Skidelsky notes that "the particular form of their revolt 'against the Victorians' depended on other aspects of Victorian life remaining in place.... Bloomsbury was as hostile to any notion of a 'proletarian culture' as it was to 'capitalist culture.' Both were symptoms of a degraded industrial system."[59] In a way, this partially vindicates the suspicion the British have of their intellectuals, seeing them not so much as critics, let alone revolutionaries, but more as "insiders with a stake in the status quo."[60]

Even at that, the communards violated not so much the practice as the politesse of elite culture. The Prince of Wales, after all, was widely observed carrying on affairs with married women. As Robert Massie notes, "The essential rule underlying the entire structure was discretion; everything might be known, nothing must be said."[61] But the Bloomsberries said what they felt and thought or, better, wrote it down in letters and relentless memoirs that sooner or later were published.

Quentin Bell, writing sixty-five years later of his childhood, recalls life in a house shared with Keynes, his parents, Clive and Vanessa Bell, and occasionally others:

> Other people, proper people, had front doors which were black, or very dark grey or navy blue; ours was bright brilliant glaring vermilion so that the world could know that we had the wrong ideas. . . . It was not until later that I discovered that other people had family arrangements with the usual number of fathers and mothers and not our ill-defined but manifestly chaotic plurality of parents.[62]

By sheer brilliance and in the intensity of his friendships with those similarly in pursuit of new truths, Keynes hoped to find the answers to the great ethical questions of the ages.[63] In setting forth on this path, he left behind guideposts of custom and religious wisdom—and ultimately orthodox political economy. In the shifting romantic commitments of his impulsive lifestyle, he found moments of both inspiration and depression. In the exploits of his social life lay the personal side of an experimentation with the orthodoxies of political and economic life that would beguile the West in much of the rest of the century.

A collision between the divergent worlds of Bloomsbury and the realities of a society steeped in custom and tradition arrived quickly. The inevitable break appeared first as a disjunction between this precious personal world and his everyday experience of life. He could seek refuge from those realities in his coterie at Eton and in the Apostles of the Conversazione Society at Kings, then in Bloomsbury. He could practice his homosexuality within these close circles, and, when outside of them, by the occasional use of male prostitutes.[64] While tolerated at Cambridge, the official view of homosexuality within British society was codified in the law that made sodomy a felony punishable by up to a life sentence.[65]

The web of identity relations with which developing personalities surround themselves was, in the case of Keynes, a communal as well as an individual exercise—and his community was quite distinct from the surrounding society. The tug of war between Bloomsbury and British society was to have intriguing consequences for his developing competence as a theorist and policy maker. Meanwhile, the unsettled nature of his intimate commitments left him restless and tentative in his connection to the surrounding society. The war would finally break open the tie that bound him to the conventions of the political establishment.

2.2 – LASKI: OF FAMILIES AND REBELLION

While Keynes was sharpening his wits at Eton and Cambridge, Harold Laski was entering a world of privilege, chauvinism, and sharp differences of class and status. Six decades of Victoria's reign had brought prosperity to the English merchant class and to Laski's family in England's industrial heartland, Manchester. Harold was the second son of a prominent family active in the Jewish synagogue and in the affairs of the Liberal Party. In all three realms, work, religion, and politics, the Laskis were leaders among a close and well-connected Jewish community.

Fortified against English racism and snobbery by intense communal solidarity, England's Jews had seen Victoria's greatest Prime Minister, Benjamin Disraeli, bring official legitimacy to the position of Jewry with his ascension to office in 1868. The Prince of Wales had, in founding the Marlborough Club for his cronies in 1869, permitted Jews to join. Yet even Disraeli's verisimilitude and the prince's broad-mindedness could hardly dent the chauvinism of an island race that had its own reasons for fearing people of differing religions and rival commercial interests. Over 96 percent of the population of England and Wales were native born, as was Laski. However, his ancestors were Polish, and his race set him apart in an overwhelmingly homogenized community.[66]

From within the Manchester Jewish community, the very sense of solidarity that buffered the Laski children from the suspicions of their environs were, to an imaginative and sensitive youth, a kind of enclosure of the spirit. His older brother, Neville, modeled himself neatly on the orthodox values of Jewish family life. The curly-haired younger sibling was impelled toward new expressive possibilities. He found them in the teachers who shaped his education, in the utopian literature he read as a boy, and, as we shall see, in the more palpable form of a striking young woman, eight years his senior.

For Laski, the revolt against his parents has been widely remarked on by his principal biographers: Michael Newman (1993); Isaac Kramnick and Barry Sheerman (1993); and Kingsley Martin (1953). His was a two-edged revolt: directly against the authority of his father in a patristic cultural and familial environment, and no less directly, against the privileged circumstances of his upbringing.

Laski's prominence came on the heels of a religious and social rebellion against a powerful and determined father. While brother Neville exhibited the virtues that his father believed in, Harold was torn by the class differences in his surroundings. Doubtful of the verities of his faith, his intellectual impishness was fed by books and endless conversations. Reason must challenge faith, tradition must withstand critical appraisal, and exploitation must be exposed.[67]

A sickly and bedridden Harold read William Morris's *News from Nowhere* in 1908. That, along with the writings of the Sidney and Beatrice Webb, introduced him to the hidden world of the poverty stricken. The book was given to him by his schoolmaster, J. L. Paton, a "liberal humanitarian" and frequent visitor to the Laski home.[68] Another friend of the household was Manchester University Professor Samuel Alexander, a noted moral philosopher and "ethical socialist." Alexander was the first Jew to be a fellow of Oxbridge.[69] Paton and Alexander represented the twin traditions of the left, liberal progressivism and socialism. There at Smedley House, the Laski family home, they found an eager lad filled with curiosity about the world beyond the comfort of his surroundings.

Thus invited to think for himself, the youthful Laski cast his searching eye upon the liberal Jewish establishment of which his parents were an integral part. He found in it a mask for injustice, and he set out to remove the curse of inequality from the larger society. Though he earnestly accepted the ritual of the bar mitzvah, Laski abandoned his religious faith in his early teens. Laski was repulsed by the strictures of religion and the snobbery of the class system that he saw everywhere around him.[70]

Laski's baptism to politics came in distinguished company—company with whom he would dramatically part in later life. As a boy of eleven, he was introduced to a political acquaintance of his father, Winston Churchill, a rising young Liberal politician. Churchill, who ran for parliament from Manchester, stayed in the Laski home off and on from 1904 to 1908. The young Laski would watch fascinated as Churchill practiced his speeches in front of the bedroom mirror. Churchill's opponent, William Joynson-Hicks, made an issue of Churchill's cultivation of the "Jewish vote." Taken along on the hustings, young Laski developed an early instinct for the cut and thrust of political debate—and its portentous consequences for his own circumstances.[71]

Laski learned early to distinguish sharply between the mundane, imperfect world of his Manchester surroundings and "the more rational and just world that could be attained."[72] This visionary idealism was complicated by the tensions of the Jewish experience in England. The youthful Laski made these tensions the subject of his first book, *The Chosen People*, an unpublished analysis accompanied by chapters of painfully self-reflective short fiction.[73] He wrestled with the twin pressures of religious patrimony and youthful rebellion while simultaneously constructing a version of democratic authority that would confront the class privilege he detected behind the appearances of the Liberal establishment.

The young Laski may have left aside the mandates of religious authority, but he also learned from the Jewish experience in British society the meaning of dissent and difference. While the strictures of his received religion were, in his view, not rationally defensible, the role of resister to religious oppression was nonetheless appealing to an intense and idealistic adolescent.[74]

At the age of sixteen, Laski, recuperating from appendicitis at a clinic near Birmingham, heard a lecture on eugenics by a Fabian physical culturalist named Frida Kerry. Frida was neither Jewish nor conventional in her beliefs and behavior, and she was eight years older than Laski. Of solid English stock, she had gone off to Sweden to study massage and gymnastics to the great dismay of her family, who feared it might be a cover for some sort of prostitution.[75] She returned to teach anatomy and medical gymnastics in Birmingham. The rapport between the beautiful liberated young woman and the sickly precocious boy was, for some reason, instant. Laski, sixteen, told her he was eighteen, though she had thought by his manner that he was twenty.[76]

Laski immediately embarked on a two-year courtship that wore down her reluctance. In one fervid letter a year after they met, he rated himself her intellectual equal, compared her favorably to his mother "as my ideal of womanhood," and averred that "you belong to the small band of women who make for the progress of the race."[77] Letters of that sort continued for the next forty years whenever the couple was apart.

Charmed by his wit and engaged by his responsiveness to her own fascination with eugenics and feminist causes, she consented in the summer of 1911 to a sexual relationship. Her independence of mind and will gave young Laski a focal point for the rebellion of son against father, youth against the strictures of religion, and idealism against tradition.[78] When Frida's parents learned of the affair and "sort of engagement," they threatened to go to the senior Laskis. After the passage of Harold's eighteenth birthday on June 30, he and Frida eloped to Scotland. As she recalled years later, they were married at the Glasgow City Hall "among all the drunks."[79]

The marriage was a severe shock to his family. Kingsley Martin describes the uproar that awaited them at the Laski home in Manchester:

> One of Harold's uncles descended upon the newly-wed pair and swept them back to Smedley House, where Sarah Laski took the wedding ring from Frida's finger, and put her to bed like a naughty girl with Harold's sister. Harold, the married man of eighteen, was deprived of his cheque-book and shut up in a room at the top of the house.[80]

Laski's father suffered a mild heart attack. He arranged for Laski's books to be sold. His parents were concerned lest Frida already be pregnant. Frida was sent back to Glasgow where she had a job. Frida's refusal, with Laski's support, to convert to Judaism further alienated his parents. Laski, already accepted at Oxford, had to agree to live separately from Frida until his degree was completed.[81]

Difficult as it was, their passion was confined to letters: "I must have you to hold in my arms and to kiss with a gorgeous passion thousands of times on your dear lips and your throat and your breast."[82] They decided to reserve their sexual relations for procreation when that would be possible. This discipline gave their relationship an idealistic quality that apparently suited both temperaments.[83]

This fervid combination of ardor and intellectual fascination formed the basis for a lifelong commitment. Their marriage was, by all accounts, the emotional foundation of Laski's ability to manage a huge volume of writing and his involvement at the highest levels of British, and often American, politics. For Frida, the marriage served similarly as the basis for her life of political activism on behalf of working-class movements.

What Frida gave him from the outset was refuge from his own inner turmoil, as well as the practical sense to make daily living workable. Feminism and eugenics took up his intellectual and political energies. The thought that careful breeding could obviate the world's social problems captivated progressive intellectuals in the prewar period—among them, for a time, Keynes.[84]

Laski carried his enthusiasm for Frida's progressive causes to Oxford. He dropped his other interests to take the requisite science courses to qualify him for university-level work in the field most closely allied to eugenics. However, science was not for him. He failed his science exams and turned from eugenics to the study of politics and history under the tutelage of H. A. L. Fisher and Ernest Barker. Fisher, mentor to a generation of Labour politicians, brought together idealism and a commitment to political involvement. Fisher's rationalist skepticism about religion and his commitment to Fabianism led Laski further along the path of progressivism. The path was marked as well by the liberal convictions of Barker, the great scholar of Locke and Hobbes. Laski found himself in a political community struggling with the contrary tensions of socialism and liberalism.[85] He joined the Fabian Society and began to work toward a rethinking of the basis of the political system.

His first dramatic engagement with politics came on behalf of women's suffrage. A bookworm, to be sure, Laski was a man of action as well. He undertook a mission of militant protest involving a pipe bomb to be planted at the Oxted train station. Laski got away more by chance than guile from the bungled attempt. The lavatory took a direct hit, and he escaped, though leaving a slip of paper with his mother's name on it, and fled for a time to France until the incident blew over.[86]

Laski had heard the great labor champion, Keir Hardie, declaim on the sacrifices of miners in their struggles to form a union.[87] His evolving view led to an advocacy of syndicalism as a way of empowering workers against a paternalistic state controlled by capitalists. Syndicalists believed that unions could generate centers of political power based on associations of workers who would then work out ways of cooperating on the basis of mutual interests. He joined a delegation of dons and activists who visited Lloyd George to press for better treatment of workers. One participant recalls that Laski "set upon the unhappy Minister with the fury of a little gamecock." [88]

After all the struggles for democracy, the vote, Fabianism's tool, seemed unlikely to suborn the capitalist state.[89] After the train station debacle, however, direct action held no further attraction for him. The violent excesses of the militant Pankhurst faction of the suffragettes caused him to turn away in "mental sackcloth and ashes" after 1913.[90] His skepticism about his culture, and his increasing commitment to class politics, were soon to be tested in the controversies over the meaning and consequences of World War I.

The young Laski took his First Class degree from New College, Oxford, in the fateful year of 1914. Now reunited with his wife, but cast off from his family's financial support, he took up a journalist's position at the *Daily Herald* in London. Opposed to the movement toward war, he editorialized for working-class resistance. With the descent into hostilities, Laski voiced his paper's commitment to a nonaggrandizing peace. His resistance notwithstanding, he volunteered to do his duty and join the army. A weak heart led to his rejection.[91]

Clearly destined for the academic life, Laski was called by the Warden of New College and asked if he would take up a sudden opening at McGill University in Montreal. With money grudgingly lent from his parents, he made his way there. In asking for help from home, the supplicant Harold had to contend with a comparison to his older brother, the model Jewish son, Neville. Neville, now a captain in the Lancashire Fusiliers, was engaged to the daughter of one of Britain's most eminent rabbis.[92] An ocean's separation was welcome on both sides.

On arrival in Montreal, the young couple settled in as best they could. Frida became pregnant. The birth of their daughter, Diana, who was very sick for a time, led to huge debts and a good deal of strain for both parents. Laski found a paying outlet for his political ideas in various magazines and was able to begin establishing a reputation as an acute observer of political trends.

Frida Laski was the perfect complement to Harold. Kingsley Martin describes her:

> Frida was eight years older than Harold, good-looking, intensely practical, enthusiastic about Women's Suffrage, birth-control, and Socialism. She scorned finesse, was suspicious of all compromise, liked shocking elegant or conventional

people, and tended to regard any form of tact as insincerity. She instinctively sided with all underdogs and espoused advanced causes. Her enthusiasm in those days was not yet clouded by experience of fellow enthusiasts . . . at this period it was Frida, rather than Harold, who had the reputation of being a firebrand.[93]

The young lecturer found McGill University ill suited to his vaulting ambitions. He had tasted the heady brew of intellectual idealism and practical politics in his brief role as journalist and editorialist for the *Daily Herald.* Writing for political magazines while at McGill University gave him more exposure, though the stale routines of his less-engaged colleagues left him disgruntled with his situation. A fortunate encounter with a friend of Harvard Law School's Felix Frankfurter led to an immediate friendship with the young professor, and an appointment to Harvard's faculty in 1916 followed.[94]

There was no better place for such a person than Harvard in 1916 and no better time than the transition between the prewar progressive movement and the wartime forging of a new left. Laski was attracted to the gospels of Darwin and Marx. The radicalism of their rationalist views formed an overlay on the deeper roots of his own cultural identity in the experience of the Jewish ghetto endured

The Laski family in the 1920s. From left to right; back row: Cissie, (older brother) Neville, Mabel, Harold, and Frida; middle row: Sarah and Nathan; bottom row: Philip, Marghanita, and (daughters) Diana and Pamela. Reprinted by permission of the Manchester Jewish Museum.

by his Polish ancestors. Kingsley Martin, his close friend, read Laski's early writings, and saw him reaching for a new humanism that would remain faithful to Jewish moral values, while accepting the secular visions of the progressive scientists of society.[95]

Laski's childhood had given him both the cultural tools and the motivation for a rebellion against society. Situated now in his professional development and supported by a passionate commitment to his wife, Harold Laski was ready to immerse himself in the great causes of the times.

2.3 – HAYEK: THE PATRIMONY OF A BOTANIST

Born in 1899, Friedrich Hayek was, like Laski and Keynes, a child of the end of the nineteenth century. The family had been ennobled a century earlier. Both father and mother came from a line of accomplished civil servants, teachers, and professors. They were a family of comfortable means. His father's modest salary as a municipal physician for the poor was supplemented by an equivalent amount from his mother's inheritance. His father preferred a steady rise in the ministry of health to the uncertainties of a private practice.[96]

The oldest of three brothers, Hayek benefited from a doting father and a strongly supportive homelife. He reminisced that

> We probably had an ideal family life. Three meals together every day, talking about every subject under the sun, always left free by our parents to roam, to think, even to commit minor peccadilloes.[97]

Hayek's youth had its social side as well. He reports that his family's flat at Kartnerstrasse 25 was at "the dancing centre of Vienna's upper academia."[98]

His father, Dr. August von Hayek, a published authority on Alpine botany, cultivated young Hayek's interest in the natural world. The fascination of scientific inquiry provided for father and sons a private preserve of camaraderie and reflection. All three sons would become professors, thus vindicating a father whose own desire to give up medicine for a chair in botany at the University of Vienna was unsuccessful.

Roman Catholicism held a brief appeal for him; however, by the age of fifteen "I had convinced myself that nobody could give a reasonable explanation of what he meant by the word 'God' and that it was therefore as meaningless to assert a belief as to assert a disbelief in God."[99] His imagination was occupied by drama instead, and he experimented with writing tragedies in the classical style.[100]

In moving from the study of botany to paleontology, Hayek reports being intrigued more by evolution than by classification. While the natural world provided initial fascination, as a sixteen-year-old, he found his interests turning to the study of human behavior out of "a desire to comprehend the world in which I was living."[101] The evolution of the natural world similarly became the template for a generation of intellectuals who were looking for consistent patterns in human society. Hayek noticed the socialist discussion around him and began to learn about economics to which he was introduced as a branch of morals in the Aristotelian scheme of analysis.[102]

Looking back half a century later, Hayek characterizes the decade of his childhood:

> To us that first decade of our century may seem a far away period of peace; and even in Central Europe the majority of people deluded themselves about the stability of their civilization.[103]

His mind just opening to currents of change in Vienna, Hayek's anchor in the patrimony of Austria's imperial culture was about to let go. In May of 1914, he turned fifteen. In June, the Austrian Archduke was assassinated at Sarajevo. In the next year, Hayek would confront the disaster of World War I in person.

The fertile soil of the British and Austrian empires had nurtured three distinctive identities. As the Great War engulfed Europe, these three young men found themselves in very different communities. Maynard Keynes lived in a commune, but worked in the lair of the establishment. Harold Laski, expatriate in Canada and now at Harvard, entered a community of progressive intellectuals at odds with their patrimony. Friedrich Hayek, still in his teens, matured along with his cohort, notable for his intellect and diverse interests, but lacking a clear theoretical or ideological focus.

Keynes and Laski were educated university men by now and launched upon their professions as economist and political scientists. Both were activists, Laski as radical journalist and Keynes as policy maker and budding critic. For Hayek, the shape of things to come could be seen in the cosmos of the botanist, but the path would lead to the seemingly quite dissimilar field of economics.

As for intimate commitments, Laski, married as a teenager, was settled in a lifelong partnership with Frida, a woman as renegade to her upbringing as Laski was to his. Keynes was embroiled in a web of amatory relations, illicit by his society's standards. Hayek was, as young Viennese men were meant to be, fond of the waltz — and not yet ready for commitment.

The decades to come would see these identities strengthen, even while being molded by the vicissitudes of the times. The war would divide each one from childhood and youth and imprint forceful lessons about governments, economies, and human failures.

3

World War I: Unresolved Conflicts

Harold Laski saw World War I as the confirmation of deep-seated fears about the triumph of evil motives. Disposed to radicalism, he could now identify the malefactors and culprits among the blundering ministers and titled heads of Europe. For Friedrich Hayek, the war illustrated the feebleness of human efforts at constructing a rational world. He saw his own country nearly disintegrate. The illusion of progress was the war's first casualty. For Maynard Keynes, the war and particularly the peace negotiations supplied a theater for displaying the stupidity that he saw to be dominant in the conduct of public affairs. Far from the idyll of his communal utopia, the real world was not only ugly, but terrifying.

Each of these three took it as his mission to apply the lessons learned from the war to the reformation of society. How a person comes to decide that it is up to them to address the leading issue of their time will always be something of a mystery, though we shall attempt to penetrate some of its secrets. These three lives illustrate the force of such a redemptive presumption.

For Keynes, there was the preparation of a prodigy in the academies of his family, Eton, and Cambridge. At each step, he was at the center of a private world of high aspiration and burgeoning self-confidence. Laski's debut on the stage of history passed through the realm of youthful rebellion. He came out of it propelled by a ferocious intellect and riding a stream of cultural and political criticism that would carry him to notoriety among intellectuals, political observers, and activists.

Hayek, by contrast, rebelled not against his family, but against the forces controlling Austria's destiny at the time of his maturation. Less the public figure, but

implacable in the force of his convictions, Hayek would launch himself on a trajectory of analysis that would unsettle and ultimately change the direction of the
political economy in the West. For each of the three, as for millions of their com-
patriots, World War I would be the catalyst for the formation of new beliefs and
new political movements.

3.1 – KEYNES: COMMUNAL EXPERIMENTS
AND DYSTOPIAN REALITIES

Maynard Keynes was excused from the most onerous of the grim realities of
the war, the draft, by virtue of his work in the Treasury Department. Though
not a pacifist, he attempted to register as a conscientious objector nevertheless, feeling quite sincerely that no government had the right to dictate so personal a decision as whether to fight. The Tribunal rejected his registration, observing that it was moot in view of his exemption for government work.[1]

This odd bifurcation as resister and collaborator illustrates most dramatically the split between Keynes the person and Keynes the citizen and leader.[2]
His friends were nearly all critics of the war. Disillusionment simmered
barely below the surface. As the carnage mounted, so did Keynes's inner anxiety. The consequences were to emerge explosively from his participation as
a Treasury representative in the Versailles peace negotiations.

The war's losses came home by letter and telegram to Bloomsbury as Cambridge friends fell. The poet Rupert Brooke lost his life, and with him went
one of the fairest blossoms of prewar literary intellect. He was an idol of
Keynes's commune. Virginia Woolf née Stephens had scandalized Cambridge
by swimming naked with him in Byron's pool.[3] Quentin Bell remembers the
realization that his household was "separated from the great decent majority
of our countrymen in one matter of vital importance; we dissented from the
great religion of war; it was this that really put us beyond the pale."[4]

Some of the Bloomsbury set retreated to the country. In 1916, Vanessa and
Clive Bell bought a home named Charleston in Sussex. Duncan Grant lived
there as well, and a room was maintained for Keynes. Here those of their
friends who were exempted from the draft and classified as agricultural
workers could be seen gardening and tending the grounds.

The collision between the intellectual and social eyrie of Bloomsbury and
the mundane realities of actual politics became vividly apparent as Keynes
moved into a position of real responsibility in the Treasury. Keynes's friends
queried his work for the war, preferring pacifism. He replied that the fascina-

tion of the work kept him going. Even so, he agonized over whether to resign. By using his position to gain credibility in testifying at his friends' draft hearings, he assuaged his conscience.[5]

Keynes was now installed close to the center of affairs. He shaped the Treasury's opposition to general mobilization, thus helping to defer the draft until May 1916. His aversion to violence was abetted by a careful estimate of the damage that would be done to war production by the loss of manpower. His ambivalence about the war found public expression in a published call for a negotiated peace, written under a pen name.[6] His Treasury chief was involved in back-channel communications that hinted at just such a result.[7] Meanwhile Keynes turned his talents to the supervision of England's currency position and gold reserves.

Had Keynes not done so well in managing Britain's foreign borrowing, Robert Skidelsky speculates, England might well have been driven to the wall by economic collapse. In February 1917, Keynes estimated that the gold would run out within the month. As it was, the Allies remained solvent just long enough for the desperate Germans to launch unrestricted U-boat warfare, thus bringing in the Americans on April 6.[8] The war to the finish was on.

Keynes's workweek at the Treasury would bring him into contact with many sectors of British leadership including Prime Minister Asquith. On the weekends there would be country-house parties with Britain's elite. His home life in Bloomsbury or at Charleston was of a more bohemian style. When the Russian ballet came to town, they were feted by Keynes and his friends. Among the corps was a particularly striking personality, Lydia Lopokova. An acquaintance began that would take several years to blossom, to the amazement of his friends, into an enduring tie.

As the war dragged toward its bitter conclusion, Keynes rose in the estimation of his Treasury colleagues. His competency as an analyst came to the fore and opened a new community for him, this one in the world of public policy. The next responsibility placed under his purview was the question of reparations to be paid to the Allies by the defeated Germans and Austrians. After due analysis of the capacity of postwar Germany, his department reported a range of figures depending on the degree of destruction. The Treasury put forward the highest figure. Prime Minister Lloyd George, remembering the Treasury's timidity on conscription, handed the problem over to the members of a more politically attuned special committee who proceeded to multiply the figure by *twelve*.[9]

Keynes, now the Treasury's chief representative to the Supreme Economic Council at the Versailles Peace Conference, threw himself into the task of moderating the terms of the settlement. The recovery of a stable Europe depended on sensible measures and the suppression of revenge. Keynes put forward an audacious plan that involved minimal reparations geared to productive capacities and the recovery of Germany within the context of a union of European powers. He proposed that revenge be subsumed by the need to "seek the recovery and the health of Europe as a *whole*."[10] Indeed, he foresaw the possible extension of a revitalized Europe eastward into Russia by economic leverage. It would take World War II and the resolution of the Cold War to reopen such a possibility.

At Versailles, Keynes's moderate counsel failed utterly to stem the fury of the Allies. Wilson's good intentions did not extend to the moderation of reparations. The granite obduracy of France's Clemenceau and the political opportunism of Britain's own Lloyd George—all conspired to eradicate a rational solution. Keynes's grand application of probabilistic analysis to the complex issues of economic recovery fell to pieces. In despair, he quit the delegation three weeks before the agreement was signed—exhausted, embittered, and, in some sense, relieved of his complicity in the deeply flawed result.[11]

His notes on the travesty became the basis for a published tirade, *The Economic Consequences of the Peace* (1919). With a well-sharpened pen, Keynes skewered the leaders of the West, vented his now tragic view of its destiny, and secured his own fame. As with the Apostles, derision and defamation were the companions of cold logic, and the result was pure brilliance. The book also created a new public identity, "a new breed of economist-politician" in Skidelsky's words, and an immodest exemplar to fill it.[12] United in one text were the competent analyst and the denizen of a dissenting commune looking askance at convention and the official view.

Keynes saw Versailles as the triumph of political passion over economic reason. In words that would echo down through the decades, he predicted that

> If we aim deliberately at the impoverishment of Central Europe, vengeance, I dare predict, will not limp. Nothing can then delay for very long that final civil war between the forces of reaction and the despairing convulsions of revolution, before which the horrors of the late German war will fade into nothing, and which will destroy, whoever is victor, the civilisation and the progress of our generation.[13]

The book was an instant best-seller with more than one hundred thousand copies sold in half a year.[14] Here was a story, not about abstractions of class warfare or historical forces, but of characters, malignant when not mindless, whose great doings could now be seen and felt by every citizen. In an age before television, Keynes's word pictures laid hold of the public imagination:

> If the European civil war is to end with France and Italy abusing their momentary victorious power to destroy Germany and Austria-Hungary now prostrate, they invite their own destruction also, being so deeply and inextricably intertwined with their victims by hidden psychic and economic bonds.[15]

The fury of his attack on the leaders of the settlement was the dominant chord, but the *leitmotiv* was the threat of the masses aroused by economic collapse and willing to deliver themselves to a demagogue. The rise of fascism would be seen to illustrate the point.

There was a message for moderate regimes, as well as for those who resorted to dictatorship. Keynes was keenly aware of the intimate connection between currencies and regimes. The great trade-off between the privileges of the rich and the toil of the working classes involves the use of wealth to invest in a better future for all. Keynes believed that, before the war,

> The greater part of the population, it is true, worked hard and lived at a low standard of comfort, yet were, to all appearances, reasonably contented with this lot. But escape was possible, for any man of capacity or character at all exceeding the average, into the middle and upper classes, for whom life offered . . . conveniences, comforts, and amenities beyond the compass of the richest and most powerful monarchs of other ages.[16]

The war, and the settlement, threatened this happy state of affairs. "The war has disclosed the possibility of consumption to all. . . . Thus the bluff is discovered; the laboring classes may be no longer willing to forgo so largely, and the capitalist classes, no longer confident of the future, may seek to enjoy more fully their liberties of consumption so long as they last, and thus precipitate the hour of their confiscation."[17] Keynes was not enamored of the rich, but he was acutely sensible of the advantages of a civilized society. A quarter of a century later, following another disastrous war, the Labour Party would come to power and validate Keynes's prediction by nationalizing basic industries, thus beginning the direct redistribution of capitalist wealth.

Keynes foresaw that weakening economies by inflating currencies undermines the whole basis for the political order.

> [Inflation will] confiscate *arbitrarily*; and, while the process impoverishes many, it actually enriches some. . . . Those to whom the system brings windfalls, beyond their deserts and even beyond their expectations or desires, become

"profiteers," who are the object of the hatred of the bourgeoisie, whom the inflationism has impoverished, not less than that of the proletariat.[18]

The threat came, he thought, not from the nature of democracies unleashed from fiscal restraint, but from willful leaders who ignored sense and gave in to emotion when better advice was at hand. Destiny in these matters is not blind. Though he would later come to be vilified as the high priest of inflationary government spending, Keynes had no illusions about its dangers.

The young prophet concludes with a warning that, failing remedial action, the fate of Russia provides the exemplar "that catastrophes can still happen, and that modern society is not immune from the very greatest evils."[19] While radicals might be heartened by the Russian revolution, Keynes was no radical. He was intent on navigating a course for England between two whirlpools: the one of an atavistic communist revolution from below, and the other of fascist tyranny arising out of economic collapse.

The bitter break with the powers that shaped the settlement and the trenchant and supremely self-confident critique of them and their work in *The Economic Consequences of the Peace* were the drum rolls of an apostasy that would take Keynes into battle against the received wisdom on political economy throughout the twenties and thirties. Keynes had arrived on the stage of public affairs and would not leave it until he became, as an economist of all things, a star.

3.2 – LASKI: THE RADICAL IN THE ESTABLISHMENT

Harold Laski's move from McGill to the Harvard faculty at the beginning of America's involvement in the war may be attributed to his uncanny appeal for eminencies such as Oliver Wendell Holmes, who came to regard him as a son. Their correspondence, itself a considerable contribution to English literature, filled volumes. This distinguished patronage was to be augmented by two other notable Supreme Court justices: Felix Frankfurter, likewise a foster son to Holmes, and, later, Louis Brandeis.[20] They were to become the icons of the progressive reform of the court and, with it, the remodeling of the U.S. Constitution to permit a vast expansion of the reach of government. Because Laski was part of the conversation of this potent circle, it is doubly important to understand the evolution of his political views.

In part to pay his daughter's medical bills, Laski began to do paid writing for progressive magazines and journals of opinion. In the summers of 1915 and 1916, he became closely involved in the editorial work of the *New Re-*

public. The flagship of progressive thought, the inner circle comprised the brain trust of a movement that combined science, good intentions, and a passion for social reform. Here John Dewey, Walter Lippmann, Herbert Croly, and occasionally an English economist named Maynard Keynes could express the themes that they hoped would guide the West through the war and, after, to a better world.[21] Here, too, Oliver Wendell Holmes could view the flowering of a new political generation.

Before the war, as Alan Ryan observes, "the state was enjoying a midsummer of high glee."[22] As the war ground on, the props of its unquestioned legitimacy were to be kicked apart by muckrakers, dissidents, and the disillusioned. Moderates among the dissidents set themselves variously on the side of guild socialism, as with Dewey, or the unions in Laski's case, and against the emerging statist orientation of the socialist left. In this vision of progressive politics, the focus was firmly on the democratic will of the people, rather than on the customs of the state.

Laski's distinctive contribution began to take shape. The debut of "pluralism" as a strategy for blurring loyalty to the state and opening up other allegiances to the service of the community came in a *New Republic* article in 1916 titled "The Apotheosis of the State." As a conceptual basis for this effort, Laski formulated a view of pluralism as a kind of democracy of natural selection whereby the best talents among the people would be brought to the service of society.[23] In 1917, citing Ernest Barker as his authority, he writes:

> It is from the selection of variations, not from the preservation of uniformities, that progress is born. We do not want to make our State a cattle-yard in which only the shepherd shall know one beast from another. Rather we may hope to bring from the souls of men and women their richest fruition. If they have intelligence, we shall ask its application to our problems. If they have courage, we shall ask the aid of its compelling will. We shall make the basis of our State consent to disagreement. Therein shall we ensure its deepest harmony.[24]

The rationale for this pluralist view involved detaching the notion of sovereignty from the state as a political organization. Laski argues that sovereignty is a matter, not of legality or of institutional primacy, but of will—the will of the people. It is here that the moral basis of sovereignty resides, and it is to the people that the state should look for creativity and practical wisdom.

In Laski's emerging perspective, the state can be adverse to the will of the people and a threat to morality.[25] Laski inverts the conventionally conceived relationship between sovereignty, the state, and the law. Biographer Michael Newman has Laski arguing that "states should be bound by morality," and therefore, "if they were answerable to law, they could not be the source of it."[26] There are reflections here of the naturalistic thinking underlying the evolutionary paradigm found in eugenics. Hayek will later make a similar argument, though with much more conservative implications.

But how is this sovereignty expressed? For Laski, the answer lay in the various institutions of society, including but certainly not limited to the state. Thus, institutional pluralism becomes the practical expression of popular sovereignty in action. So far, he is not far from appropriating Edmund Burke's "organic" conservatism of institutions for liberal purposes. Burke thought of society as a congeries of interdependent, yet distinct, institutions that together comprise the complex unity of the society.

While Burke theorized about how institutions accommodate and control individual differences, Laski had a different purpose in mind. As one of his contemporaries observed, "Mr. Laski's use of pluralistic theories advances the church and other institutions and associations in the state as stalking horses for the unions of the world of labor."[27] Laski was trying to achieve a political objective without letting go of a tradition of legitimation important to democratic governance. Clearly, he wanted to retain a conception of sovereignty that would support the rule of law. He wanted to retain as well the notion of a moral will in society at large. At the same time, he also desired to create an opening for labor unions, among other associations, as agents of sovereignty. Political entities such as unions, schools, and trade associations acquire thereby a role in governance broadly conceived. Laski's pluralism was meant to open the door to mass participation in forming the moral will of the people.

A critic of the state, Laski aspired to be a friend of morality and of sovereignty too. In 1939, Laski lectured at the University of Washington and reflected on his views of that era:

> I concluded that the sources of authority were not monistic; they did not come invariably from a single place; the ultimate source of authority was not unified in a single group except as that group was the expression of all the elements within the society. The sources of authority were in fact multiple. And the more that the orders issued were built upon the consent of those to be affected—the more the will of individuals and voluntary bodies entered into the constituent matter of the orders issued—the more likely was the sovereign power to remain sovereign.[28]

His experience in America influenced Laski's reconceptualization of sovereignty. As distinct from Britain's unitary state, America's federalist system embodied a sovereignty both dispersed for certain purposes and collected for others. The states, with their separate constitutions holding together a variety of jurisdictions, and the nation, with its preeminence in certain functional areas of governance, comprise a complex structure for effectuating the variously expressed will of the people.

This emerging pattern of reconciling apparent opposites becomes characteristic of Laski's work. Laski's theory of pluralism is meant to overthrow the prevailing theory of the state, not in the name of rebellion, but of morality and even sovereignty rightly conceived. While contemporary observers would have seen union strikes as a threat to law and order, Laski places nation-states and unions on something like a par. The state is to be replaced as the guarantor of sovereignty with a higher, albeit more diffuse, moral will. His first step was to ensure equality of treatment and consideration so that all might be able to participate in the formation of such a will.

As an educational focus for their political efforts, Laski and his colleagues at the *New Republic* founded the New School for Social Research in New York on the model of the Webb's London School of Economics and Political Science (LSE). Ayn Rand, hearing him lecture there, found his commitment to egalitarianism so totally offensive that she made him the prototype for Ellsworth Toohey, the socialist antihero of *The Fountainhead*.[29] Her description of Toohey is a satire of Laski:

> A great forehead dominated the body. The wedge-shaped face descended from the broad temples to a small, pointed chin. The hair was black, lacquered, divided into equal halves by a thin white line. This made the skull look tight and trim, but left too much emphasis to the ears that flared out in solitary nakedness, like the handles of a bouillon cup. The nose was long and thin, prolonged by the small dab of a black mustache. The eyes were dark and startling. They held such a wealth of intellect and twinkling gaiety that his glasses seemed to be worn not to protect his eyes but to protect other men from their excessive brilliance.[30]

She did not like his looks. Though Jewish herself, she preferred the Aryan ideal of masculinity with a touch of violence that made the heroes of her novels such heartthrobs.[31] Nor did she like the customary self-abasement that was a standard feature of Laski's lectures. So in *The Fountainhead*, Rand visited on Laski the role of nemesis in the shape of Ellsworth Toohey. She gives him lines that expressed the opposite of her passionately held convictions: "'Identity' — it's an illusion you know. . . . We are poisoned by the superstition of the ego. . . . That is why the mind is so unreliable. We must not think. We must *believe*."[32] Hardly the credo of one of Harvard's and LSE's greatest teachers. However, Rand touches a nerve, especially for college students, when she points to the demands of the socialist cry for solidarity upon their individualistic egos.

Self-abasing about his class as Laski was, he was neither antirational nor cynical. His convictions were deep enough to lead him to political agitation. His advocacy of the Boston Police Strike, as well as his erstwhile antiwar polemics, gave a sharply political edge to his pluralist theory. His militancy in support of the strike nearly cost him his position at Harvard. The crisis over the Boston Police Strike blew up at a time when U.S. Attorney General Palmer was arresting thousands of socialists with a mind to deport them, and the *New Republic* was a candidate for closure under the sedition laws.[33] After an "inquisition" by the Harvard Board of Overseers, he was saved by the administration's resolute defense of academic freedom. The same sort of uproar had happened after a speech critical of the wartime British government at McGill. There would be another such incident in the 1930s at the LSE when Keynes among others came to his public defense.

Laski's pluralism underlay his opposition to the German cause in World War I. He would have none of the "state worship" prevalent in Germany and argued that the Allied governments were much more likely to gravitate toward true pluralism.[34] Though he was deeply suspicious of the forces motivating the war, he did not see the two sides as moral equivalents. When asked by Frankfurter, Laski accepted an offer to work for the U.S. Department of Labor on a project to define the "American case as to labor matters that will arise at peace."[35]

All in all, his American experience led him to discover "an enormous welter of local habits and problems that were entirely unfamiliar to me. . . . I discovered a society the nature of which was essentially federalistic."[36] The grassroots populism of the American experience, the jostling between state and federal constitutions, and the plethora of local jurisdictions, all challenged the intellectual framework of a scholar of politics raised in the European and British traditions of centralized governance. Distracted by this exposure from the easy equation of the good state as the key to the good society, his intellect went to work on the great questions of political philosophy: What is sovereignty? What are rights? How may democracy and justice be brought together?

Here Laski was drawn to the great mission of political theory. In the words of a distinguished practitioner, Hannah Pitkin, the political theorist "delineates . . . 'what has to be accepted as given' from 'what is to be done.'" The task of political theory is, then, to answer the political question of "how and where with whom we might take action, given our present circumstances."[37] Laski's answer was to open up the practice of politics to bring in excluded and marginalized classes and interests. His professional contribution lay in reexamining the "givens" of sovereignty, moral will, and the constitution of the state. If sovereignty is diffused in the will of the citizens rather than concentrated in the majesty of the state, then we might "act" by bringing the citizens in more directly than British institutions allowed.

These were the lessons a very young academician learned as he ran up against the activism of the World War I era. As he confronted the power realities evident in the war and its aftermath, the state increasingly took center stage in his thoughts about politics. The age of laissez-faire was, he claimed in 1918, over. His early enthusiasm for displacing the state was now waning; in its place came the idea of the democratized state as the active voice of mobilized citizens. The age of the positive state had arrived.[38] Movements might put forward a view of moral will, but their followers were not always disposed to reason. While unions could present their claims to justice, they rarely could see beyond their own particular desires. The state can focus the will of the people; properly constituted it can give meaning to their moral sensibilities.

While the state was responsible for inequality, inequality could not be eliminated without the exercise of public power. A young scholar imbued with rebellion needed a resolution of this tension. Newman suggests that these factors combined to produce the distinctive mix of radicalism by persuasion and incipient statism, which came to characterize his thought.[39] Clearly, for Laski, the democratized state is increasingly where the de-contestation of his ambiguous theory of sovereignty comes to rest. Sovereignty rests directly on the will of the people rather than on the mediation of institutions. Government is to register the wishes of the masses rather than to direct the course of the state by its own lights. The reconstructed state becomes the pivot of his theory. Theory here begins to be transformed into ideology. With the transition, Laski's tenuous grasp of the other half of political economy, the realities of markets and enterprise, slips away.

As the hostilities drew to a close, Laski saw the war as

> [a] transition period from capitalism to industrial democracy which . . . is bound to involve far-reaching change. If it fails, an organized labor will confront an organized capital with the knowledge that the immense sacrifices it had made in the last four years were made for a lie; for if the result of the war is not an improvement in the internal conditions of the western democracies, the unrest of the period before 1914 is bound to be repeated on a far larger sale. If it is successful, it is bound to go further; for no experiment in democratization that is successful can stop short of completeness.[40]

There is, here, a striking parallel to Keynes's prediction of impending disaster arising from the Versailles settlement. The difference is that Keynes's analysis was built on demonstrable calculations of the carrying capacity of economies, along with a surmise as to the political implications of economic collapse. By contrast, Laski bases his analysis less in systematic observation than in suppositions based on theories about political transformation. The theme of inevitability in history and of the perils of attempting to derail it becomes an intellectual substrate to Laski's thought. In this, he was prompted by his experience amid a community of intellectuals disabused of any lingering illusions about the majesty of the prewar nation-state.

The notion that there are "periods" of history and "experiments" as well as "transitions" to new phases is the underlying metaphor of much political thought. Such dynamics, real or imagined, are also appealing to a mind in search of deliverance from conditions disappointing to a person of high ideals. For Laski, and certainly for Hayek, history involves the movement of forces that have their own trajectories. While orthodox economists visit the metaphor of equilibrium on the market, there is no equilibrium in this view of the polity. Classes rise and fall; intellectual currents are constantly on the move; interests become forces that act on the body politic.

Casting about for a way to reconcile the deeply felt need for radical change in society and the all too apparent shortcomings of the state of his era, Laski's inventive mind was led to the works of Leon Duguit, a French syndicalist theorist. Harold and Frida Laski together translated Duguit's *Law in the Modern State* (1919). They read into Duguit's work a way of reconciling democracy and the realities of political power in a class-based society. What Duguit's syndicalism seemed to offer was a conceptualization of authority based in movements of workers, artisans, and other associations that could, in the aggregate, redirect the state toward a more humane society. The Laskis were moving toward a vision of "socialist pluralism."[41]

The problem was that Duguit was approaching syndicalism from a desire to stabilize, not to displace or even reform, the state.[42] By harmonizing the organized interests of society from the top down, Duguit thought the state could bring badly needed coherence to French politics. He was an elitist in search of a frame to contain the masses. This misreading of Duguit reflects the pressure of the Laskis' political desires on their theory as well as on practice.

The other book Laski published that year suggested by its title what his aim was: *Authority in the Modern State,* a variation on Duguit's title that substitutes *authority* for *law*.[43] Morality and will, Laski argued, were the properties of individuals, not states. States as instruments of free people can be benign, but as oppressors of conscience, they could also be the inhibitors of progress and justice.[44]

Rather than the unitary state, associations could be seen as the foundation of a new authoritative order favoring the most numerous class of society. Laski offered the federalist experience of the United States as evidence that a society of associations existing within a national polity could work. Having observed the inventive governmental arrangements of the Americans, as well as their rich associational life, Laski took fresh inspiration for his vision of socialist pluralism. Dedicated to Holmes and Frankfurter, Laski's sophisticated pluralist formulation found its way into the thinking of America's most controversial jurists. He also had acquired patrons and confessors who would sustain him in turbulent times.[45]

Laski now had achieved a certain style: politically radical, yet conventional in his social tastes, with an appearance that neatness and dapper dress made arresting.[46] Although Laski was diminutive at not much over five feet six inches, his spoken and written word carried an authority that articulated an increasingly influential strain of dissidence in the postwar world. And those who might be offended by his political views were nearly always charmed by the vigorous warmth of his personality. Laski's experience at Harvard from 1916 to 1920 in particular provided lessons in the house rules for an establishment radical, and he was shortly to return to England primed to play the role on a grander scale in his homeland.

3.3 – HAYEK: OF GOVERNMENT LIES AND ECONOMIC TRUTHS

While Keynes and Laski were coming of age in major academic and political institutions, Friedrich Hayek was making his way in Vienna as a young student from a privileged home. The comfort and tranquillity of Hayek's upbringing were sharply disrupted by his World War I service in the Austro-Hungarian army. Just sixteen years old when he entered in the spring of 1917, the young cadet was charged with coordinating communications within his unit of field artillery. He was placed amid the disaster of the Italian front. Hayek later suggested that this experience redirected his intellectual and vocational interests. As a very young officer, he saw at first hand the inefficiency and confusion of a multinational army engaged in trying to save a decaying empire. He commented on having seen "the great empire collapse over the nationalist problem. I served in a battle in which eleven different languages were spoken. It's bound to draw your attention to the problems of political organization."[47]

Hayek's ironic remark only hints at the deep sense of loss he suffered when the only close friend of his childhood years, who had been stationed nearby but whom he had not bothered to visit, died in a military hospital. He was filled with guilt and sadness and could barely bring himself to visit his friend's mother. He would not find close friends again until many years later and, then, as colleagues rather than intimates.[48]

In a respite from battle, the studious young soldier began to read more about economics and psychology. Carl Menger's treatise on economics, *Grundsätze*, was "such a fascinating book, so satisfying."[49] Returning from combat in the fall of 1918, Hayek entered the University of Vienna as a "raw youth fresh from the war."[50] He found an intellectual world as chaotic as the battlefields he had just left. As Stephen Kresge comments in his introduction to Hayek's autobiographical memoir:

> If the legitimate dominion of empire was now under attack, even less secure was the dominion of the mind. Relativity, quantum mechanics, Freud, Proust, the post-Impressionists, were altering once and for all our notions of physical existence and how we perceive it.[51]

Hayek came back from the war interested in economics and psychology and chose the former because it offered the possibility of a university degree. Simultaneously, he began his studies in an academy for future diplomats. With the collapse of the diplomatic academy in the postwar chaos, Hayek looked toward the law, in which he gained the first of two doctorates in 1921, as a course of study that would combine economics with the prospect of civil service employment.

The freewheeling world of Viennese intellectual and social life invigorated Hayek, and he found himself immersed in many subjects of study and discussion. Politically, he worked with friends to establish a German Democratic Party "in order to have a middle group between the Catholics on one side and the socialists and communists on the other side."[52] His rising interest in politics led to a second doctorate in 1923, this one in political science. A career in the family tradition of civil service seemed a likely prospect but for the gathering chaos of Austria's domestic situation.

This mix of intellectual and vocational objectives directed Hayek's youthful search for meaning from botany into economics. Many years later, he would return to the natural world through his metaphor of the "sensory order" derived from his early interest in nature's spontaneous evolution.[53] The path he followed was determined on one side by the false directions Hayek saw in the new paradigms of his time, Freudianism and Marxism, and, on the other, by his reaction to the kind of science that students of society were attempting to practice. Hayek was satisfied neither by the dissidents nor by the practitioners of conventional methodology.

Hayek's problem with the fashionable twin *enfants terribles* of the intellectual world, Marxism and Freudianism, was the stipulated nature of their assumptions:

> It seemed to me then and has so appeared ever since that their doctrines were thoroughly unscientific because they so defined their terms that their statements were necessarily true and unrefutable.[54]

Hayek approached the science of society as one oriented to the observational discipline of a botanist. He could not appreciate the kind of thought experiment that lay at the root of Karl Marx's methodology and thus dismissed his understanding of human nature. Marx's conceptual system revolves around a core premise: that the ability of humans to consciously direct their creative activity distinguishes humans from lower order creatures. Marx makes the transition to philosophy by asserting that the perfection of this creativity is the *purpose* of human life. As Bertell Ollman points out: alienation, exploitation, class, even revolution are all defined in relation to Marx's philosophical premises concerning the powers and purposes of human labor.[55] Hayek saw this methodology as placing Marx's ideas beyond refutation. The terrorism of Stalinist Russia would reveal the prescience of his insight: that there was no recourse against the will of a revolutionary vanguard empowered by a vision of human purpose whose vindication lay in the future.[56]

Neither could Hayek comprehend Freud's inductive leap from the analysis of dreams to the positing of an energy field of psychic forces.[57] Freud's imagery of energy displacement and discharge, let alone the linkages to mythology and eroticism, must have seemed far-fetched to a young botanist recently returned from a disillusioning experience with the most practical of all endeavors: combat at close quarters.

The end of the war decade cast Hayek adrift on a stormy sea of intellectual contestation, cultural collapse, and economic disaster. Left to construct an identity out of the remains of his surroundings, the young man came of age as he began to assemble a distinctive understanding of culture, politics, and economics. The twenties, promising little, held in store a time of challenge and bold response.

Wars destroy, but sometimes they also clarify. While World War I undid the illusions of proud civilizations, it provided an emerging generation with the chance to challenge the foundations of society. The blundering of leaders, the horrible consequences of imperial rivalries, the inequities of tottering monarchies, and the fecklessness of government policies all supplied targets for young intellectuals eager to remake the world.

Maynard Keynes, his public competence now established and his personal life secured by a band of friends and lovers, was ready for prominence among the rising generation. Harold Laski, broken free of his upbringing and welcomed by leading activists, had completed his time of exile and was now to return to an England receptive to new voices. Friedrich Hayek at an early age had seen war's horror. His sensitive intellect was now in search of a new certainty to replace the verities of his culture that had been shattered in the defeat.

4

The Twenties: The Government and the Market in Combat

The forces of havoc unleashed by World War I were apparent everywhere in Friedrich Hayek's Austria as well as in the England of Harold Laski and Maynard Keynes. The Austro-Hungarian Empire was mortally wounded; England, the ostensible victor, was wobbling forward on borrowed crutches. The search for regeneration revealed the fault lines in the relations between governments and economies.

With Austria's defeat, the voices of skepticism, such as Hayek's, had their chance. In England's victory, however, there were conflicting messages. The English establishment acquired a sense of self-confidence in victory that was neither shared by the decimated working class nor justified by the situation of the postwar economy. Laski became a voice of working-class protest. Keynes became, in his own phrase, "the Cassandra of the establishment."

The major events of the decade were set in motion by the outwash of the war's settlement. For Hayek, the collapse of Austria's economy, and the struggle of its political system to survive, was the crucible for the formation of his views. For Keynes and Laski, the rising tide of unemployment formed the backdrop for the battle over the Gold Standard in 1925 and then the anticlimactic General Strike in 1926. Each would have a distinctive view of these crises, and it would shape their future course.

4.1 – KEYNES: OF GOLD, UNEMPLOYMENT, AND THE LIBERAL WAY

By the early 1920s, Maynard Keynes was famous in his own right as a critic of the war, economic analyst, and political gadfly. Having turned down the

directorship of the London School of Economics and Political Science
(LSE), he turned to more worldly pursuits.[1] Now in his late thirties, Keynes
gave up his stipend as a Lecturer at King's, and while retaining his duties as
college bursar and journal editor, he began to focus on making money in the
City of London and on writing for journals of opinion.[2]

The popular don still gave a few lectures and supervised selected undergraduates, but he was free to be the man of affairs—both professional and
personal. He traveled with a new companion, Sebastian Sprott, to Algeria
and Tunisia. Sprott was also an Apostle and lecturer in psychology at Cambridge. The Bloomsbury set was becoming interested in Sigmund Freud.
James Strachey, Lytton's younger brother, would become the editor of his
Collected Works. There was time as well for a long visit to the Orkney Islands with Duncan Grant, who painted Keynes's portrait while Keynes
turned to writing philosophy.

The partial transition from scholarly preoccupations was made easier when
he finally finished the greatest philosophical work of his career, *A Treatise on
Probability* (1921), which he saw as the key to a new form of ethics that
would link probability with moral judgment.[3] Originating in the papers he
gave to the Apostles as an undergraduate at Cambridge, Keynes's views of
probability had advanced in a manner that permitted him to claim at least a
semiobjective validity for his approach to policy making under conditions of
uncertainty. It was a treatise with something of the manifesto about it.

Keynes argued that if causal knowledge is not available to mere mortals,
then somehow there must be a way to link the "probable" to the "ought."[4] The
key lay in developing an *epistemic* approach to probability. Mathematical
probability is an exercise in giving odds based on the incidence of chance oc-
currences, and it does not tell us anything useful about whether a policy is
good or bad. As an alternative, Keynes developed a view of probability as the
likelihood that a policy innovation will have better *consequences* than continuing a course of action on the basis of received wisdom. As Robert Skidelsky summarizes Keynes's position:

> Probability statements were judgments about the bearing of evidence on con-
> clusions, not forecasts of results . . . probability was concerned with the logical
> relation between the premise and conclusion of an argument; it was a branch of
> logic, not of statistics.[5]

From this perspective, Keynes concluded that a policy innovation could be
justified "if we have reason to think that of two actions, one produces more
good than the other in the *near* future, and if we have no means of discrimi-

nating between their results in the *distant* future [italics added]."[6] Probability as a basis for action is removed from the realm of mathematical analysis and placed amid considerations of the quality of evidence available for a decision.

What this formulation accomplishes is to reverse the customary advantage that uncertainty gives to tradition. Keynes is suggesting that if rationally defensible evidence tells us a course of action is beneficial and if we cannot know with certainty about future consequences, whether benign or adverse, then the probabilities are on the side of change. Traditionalists had held sway by arguing that custom embodies experience in a measure that is beyond human calculation. Keynes turned the argument around, suggesting that tradition embodies forms of ignorance as often as intelligence. It is for analysts to distinguish one from the other by penetrating appearances and bringing to bear the rational assessment of consequences. Neither a determinist nor a demagogue, Keynes here severs his ties to cultural conservatives such as Edmund Burke.

Yet Keynes does not equate probability with certainty. He adopts a wry sort of fatalism about whether any strategy of knowledge will show the path to the ultimate good. He concludes:

> The importance of probability can only be derived from the judgment that it is *rational* to be guided by it in action; and a practical dependence on it can only be justified by a judgment that in action we *ought* to act to take some account of it. It is for this reason that probability is to us the "guide of life," since to us, as Locke says, "in the greatest part of our concernment, God has afforded only the Twilight, as I may so say, of Probability, suitable, I presume, to that state of Mediocrity and Probationership. He has been pleased to place us in here."[7]

This sort of "epistemic" probability falls short of certainty, but has a rational, and therefore factual and objective, aspect that lifts it to the level of a justification for action.[8]

As Skidelsky points out, Keynes added two other considerations to the list underlying his theory of action: "the weight of argument" and "moral risk." The first refers to the amount (as opposed to the quality) of evidence available. The burden of persuasion, if proof is not possible, must be met. As for the second consideration, moral risk, Skidelsky notes:

> The principle of "moral risk" suggests that it is more rational to aim for a smaller good which seems more probable of attainment than to aim for a larger one which seems less, when the two courses of action have equal probable goodness.[9]

Taken together, Keynes's system forms a foundation for the thinking of a reformer who wishes to address the problems of society. Keynes's political intent was to justify statesmen of a liberal bent such as himself in making the world a better place to live.[10]

These adventurous ideas helped to produce a great upsurge of playfulness that gave to the twenties, and especially to Bloomsbury, its distinctive social climate. As Robert Skidelsky, his most exhaustive and intriguing biographer, comments, Keynes's views "expressed a mood of scientific and moral optimism, much at variance with the 'original sin' notions which underlay adherence to the automatic rules of the gold standard and conventional morality."[11] However, as Donald Moggridge points out, Keynes's epistemological approach was primarily about practicality.[12] The same Keynes who wrote *Probability* was deeply involved with questions such as currency reform in India, reparations from the Great War, monetary policy, and the business cycle. He was an inveterate seeker of an improved society, though never a Pollyanna about the human condition. Armed with an analytical framework, Keynes rapidly came to be seen as a uniquely competent critic of public policy making.

In the 1920s, Keynes begins to synthesize in his public and personal lives the contending forces of innovation and conventionality. This distinctive blend of policy radicalism and wary respect for orthodoxy would lead, in the next decade, to the writing of the *General Theory*, a recipe for the reordering of politics and economics. Along the way, Keynes found the vehicle for translating these developing views into practical politics.

Cambridge permitted Keynes to combine his political activities with his scholarly pursuits. By the early 1920s, the postwar boom had collapsed, the number of unemployed soon surpassed one million, and conventional policies were inadequate. Infuriated by the settlement of the war, Keynes formed an alliance with other progressives to address postwar problems. This alliance included the future architect of Britain's social service system, William Beveridge, an erstwhile reformer steeped in the grim realities of London's East End. Together they created Liberal Summer Schools in which rising young intellectuals and influential policy makers were brought into the stimulating presence of Keynes and his colleagues. These were meant as an alternative to the Fabian summer schools that had been established to promote the views of such socialist intellectuals as the Sidney and Beatrice Webb and George Bernard Shaw.

The year 1922 brought portentous changes to Europe and England in particular. Benito Mussolini seized power in Italy. There was a change of regime in Germany that elevated an acquaintance of Keynes to the Prime Minister-ship. Lloyd George, the Liberal wizard, fell to scandal and foreign imbroglios to be replaced by a Conservative, Bonar Law, for whom Keynes had worked in the Treasury.[13] Seizing the pervasive concern with the drift of postwar politics, Keynes put together a distinguished group of essayists, including the new professor at LSE, Harold Laski, to address the theme, "Reconstruction in Europe."

In working with him, Laski came to think that Keynes had "a badly swollen head," though others would have found it hard to choose between the two on that score. With a logo designed by Vanessa Bell and Duncan Grant, the nine-month-long series was launched in the *Manchester Guardian Commercial* in the fall of 1922. Keynes's own contributions reflected an increasing fascination with the notion of using economic "barometers" developed at LSE and Harvard as statistical indicators for the management of the macrolevel economy. On this foundation the manipulation of credit through government agencies could be attempted.[14]

Not content with educating the few, Keynes and his colleagues acquired control of a well-known journal of opinion called the *Nation*, defeating a rival maneuver by Harold Laski and his socialist friends.[15] On another front, Keynes worked to establish the London and Cambridge Economic Service to survey statistics and recommend scientifically defensible economic policies, a move that would bring him into contact with a young Austrian economist, Friedrich Hayek. Adding to his standing as a leading economist such assets as a magazine to broadcast his views, an economic survey series, and even a summer camp, Keynes was now an independent force in British politics.

The next step would have been a candidacy for Parliament. Beginning in 1922, Keynes was an active campaigner in three elections. In the election of 1923, he turned down the offer of a safe seat from the Cambridge Liberal Association. The election was occasioned by a huge increase in unemployment to over 20 percent. The Liberals had expected to win since the issue was the Conservative government's announced intention to impose tariffs and violate the dogma of free trade. In fact the Liberals came second to Labour. Labour's Ramsay MacDonald was asked to form the first Labour government. There was a working agreement for a while with the Liberals, but no formal coalition, so it was a minority government. The MacDonald premiership lasted only from January to November of 1924. MacDonald was replaced by Stanley Baldwin after the 1924 election provided a margin of 210 for the Conservatives. The Liberals, surprised by their relatively poor showing through all of this, were in search of a fresh program.

Keynes now began to articulate more boldly just how much initiative was required to lead the way to better times. Automatic solutions to Britain's gathering problems, such as resorting to laissez-faire, were just as foolish in view of modern circumstances as a reliance on the "forces of history" or the dialectics of revolution. In a 1924 Oxford lecture later published as *The End of Laissez Faire* (1926), Keynes assailed the simplemindedness of faith in the market. And in *Laissez Faire and Communism* (1927), he served the same kind of notice on economic determinism. Neither Adam Smith nor Karl Marx would do.

It is in *The End of Laissez Faire*, obligingly published by Keynes's friends Leonard and Virginia Woolf in their Hogarth Press, that the link between Keynes's philosophical position and his views on political economy begins to be made clear. Keynes's first attack on laissez-faire undercuts its claim to be "natural" and to result in liberating the forces that will lead to a spontaneous harmony of interests:

> Let us clear from the ground the metaphysical or general principles upon which, from time to time, laissez-faire has been founded. It is *not* true that individuals possess a prescriptive "natural liberty" in their economic activities. There is *no* "compact" conferring perpetual rights on those who Have or on those who Acquire.

So much for any natural-rights basis for laissez-faire—or for an inviolable right to private property. Having cleared away the underbrush, Keynes proceeds to discard the deity and the mechanics implicit in the *deus ex machina*:

> The world is *not* so governed from above that private and social interest always coincide. It is *not* so managed here below that in practice they coincide. It is *not* a correct deduction from the Principles of Economics that enlightened self-interest always operates in the public interest.

Over the side go the fondest assumptions of those who would let market forces play at will on the theory that beneficial consequences will emerge. But what about the merit of leaving the individual to decide matters autonomously?

> Nor is it true that self-interest generally *is* enlightened; more often individuals acting separately to promote their own ends are too ignorant or too weak to attain even these. Experience does *not* show that individuals, when they make up a social unit, are always less clear-sighted than when they act separately.[16]

Hayek will challenge Keynes on that last point a decade later, but for the present, Keynes, having reduced the opposition fort to rubble, proceeds to construct his own revetment. Here we find the tie between the philosopher and the man of affairs:

> Many of the greatest economic evils of our time are the fruits of risk, uncertainty, and ignorance. It is because particular individuals, fortunate in situation or in abilities, are able to take advantage of uncertainty and ignorance, and also because for the same reason big business is often a lottery, that great inequalities of wealth come about; and these same factors are also the cause of the Unemployment of Labour, or the disappointment of reasonable business expectations, and of the impairment of efficiency and production.

So it is Keynes's old enemies, ignorance and uncertainty, compounded by the risks that people take in dealing with them, that produce economic disarray. These are the "natural" conditions of society. They cannot be dismissed. To leave them unaddressed, or to underplay their significance, condemns us to periodic chaos both as individuals and as societies. So what is to be done?

> Yet the cure lies outside the operations of individuals; it may even be to the interest of individuals to aggravate the disease. I believe that the cure for these things is partly to be sought in the deliberate control of the currency and of credit by a central institution, and partly in the collection and dissemination on a great scale of data relating to the business situation, including the full publicity, by law if necessary, of all business facts which it is useful to know. These measures would involve Society in exercising *directive intelligence* through some appropriate organ of action over many of the inner intricacies of private business, yet it would leave private initiative and enterprise unhindered. [italics added][17]

This remarkable formulation suggests that there is a universal interest in regulation and transparency: the business community will find its operations more consistently profitable, the workers will be steadily employed, and all may proceed more equitably and surely to their own prosperity if only intelligence can be permitted to combat ignorance and uncertainty. Keynes makes an overture to central control of credit and currency and of the overall proportion and disposition of savings as between domestic and foreign industry. However, he also accords considerable weight to private decision making operating on data made public by the government.[18]

As for the economic crisis, Keynes began to see the problem and the remedy. It was the unreasonableness of people's attachment to their savings that needed to be undone by the rational alteration of their uncertainty.[19] A convincing clairvoyant, able to see ahead to the next upturn, would have done the job just as well. There being no such creature available, government needed to allay fears by proffering some substantive reassurance. The nature of the assurance Keynes proposes to offer would change from monetary manipulation, even to tariffs, and then to demand management. The underlying rationale for action would remain the same.

In all of this, Keynes, while trying to remove the *sources* of inequality, was far from an egalitarian. It is one thing to reduce the advantages that arise from an oftentimes lucky confluence of economic factors, or to address the minimal needs of those at the bottom of the order. It is quite another to override legitimate distinctions between individuals. The point is not to "level individuals," because the differences in "effort, ability, courage, and character" are responsible for productivity and creativity. The class structure that results is, in good part, a result of these differences. Keynes finds himself at odds with the leveling passion of doctrinaire socialists. He is, rather, on the side of the "educated bourgeoisie" as the practitioners of skills essential to an improved society.[20]

Keynes's manifestos and texts were informative, but not politically adroit. The problem was, as David Felix observes, "Keynes had no sense of everyman's politics. He had written a scenario for the Liberal party to talk itself to death."[21] In the summer of 1925, Keynes addressed a Liberal summer camp on the topic of whether he was, himself, a liberal. He arrived at a tentative yes largely by eliminating Conservatives and Labourites on the grounds of the inadequacies of their credos. Labour believes in class confrontation. Keynes recognizes that he is on the wrong side as a member of the bourgeoisie. Conservatives, he decides, are simply against whatever Labour is for. "They offer me neither food nor drink—neither intellectual, nor spiritual consolation."[22] Neither credo seems worthy of serious consideration.

However, it is the quality of the leadership that Keynes also disparages. The Conservatives are undermined by the heredity principle, leaving them with a large faction he labels as the "Diehards." Labour, on the other hand, has its revolutionaries and radicals—the "Party of Catastrophe." Neither organization can contain the instincts of these factions.[23] At the end of the day, he observes wryly in a speech that "possibly the Liberal Party cannot serve the State in any better way than by supplying Conservative governments with Cabinets, and Labour governments with ideas."[24]

In other words, Liberals can be the party of ideas, but only if they resist the blind impulse to democratization. Donald Moggridge found a fascinating passage in the text of Keynes's Liberal Summer School talk that was not included in the published version. In it, Keynes frankly states that economic policy questions are essential to politics, and that they "must be above the heads of the vast majority of more or less illiterate voters. . . . Recently there have been *ill-advised* [the word was crossed out in the text] movements in the direction of democratising the details of the party programme. . . . With strong leadership the techniques, as distinguished from the main principles of policy could still be dictated from above."[25] The distinction between the "techniques" of policy as opposed to the "main principles" is crucial to Keynes's technocratic approach to the reform of politics. It is the distinction on which the difference between progressivism and populism depends. As we will see later, contemporary politics is still driven by that distinction.[26]

A quintessential Cambridge man, Keynes knew the stupidity he was against, but it was not quite clear what he was for. He told a government committee probing the economic crisis that he would be in favor of "all sorts of unsound ways" of stimulating the economy so as get "a cumulative wave of prosperity which would lap up the slack." He hoped such moves would bring into play the unused capacity in the economy. This beats trying to "get straight by depressing things."[27]

What he needed to do was become the leader of a movement toward a more coherent alternative to the dogmas of left and right. But what to name his centrist alternative? His biographers and critics are not of a single mind about how to characterize the menagerie of policies that came forth. Classical liberalism makes a showing evident in Keynes's retention of the main elements of property and individual rights. Reform liberalism is represented by the presumption in favor of the less well-off. Conservatism appears as the fear of grand schemes. Throughout, there is the manifestation of the Cambridge rationalist with an unshakable confidence that a corps of well-motivated policy makers could manage it all. But there was no passion for equality, no radical desire to topple the captains of industry, and no demagogue's desire to displace institutions. There was, however, an abiding love for the core values of an enlightened sensibility.

Keynes knew the web of constraints that kept financiers and politicians in line; he just wanted to equip the decision makers analytically, and inspire them morally, to use their power to make the world a better place.[28] Regulation in a well-functioning system of political and economic institutions need not be feared as antidemocratic. Incompetent cabinet ministers could be removed from office by the parliamentary party, parties could lose elections, and bankers could lose the confidence of investors.[29] Keynes's commitment to regulation was built not on his faith in the omniscience of the regulators, but on the checks and balances of the market and government in a British-style democracy. Countervailing influences, rather than a belief in altruism, was the mechanism Keynes relied on to keep society on a progressive path.

The rising young economist was about to confront the forces of tradition on the fateful question of returning to the gold standard. Here Keynes's campaign against ingrained stupidity became personal. The personification of the opposition was the only student to best him in the Civil Service exam: Otto Niemeyer. Keynes was particularly irritated at his placing second to Niemeyer in the economics section of the Civil Service Examination. Keynes suggested it was because he knew more about economics than his examiners. In any event, Niemeyer passed up the India Office for the Treasury Department, thus opening the way to Keynes's assignment there. Niemeyer became the quintessential advocate of the "Treasury view" against which Keynes fought in the 1920s and 1930s. Niemeyer's rise to the position of Controller of Finance in the Treasury in 1923 precipitated the fall of Keynes's influence just as the struggles to maintain the pound became serious.[30]

At a famous dinner party in 1925, Winston Churchill, then Chancellor of the Exchequer, put before his five guests the question of whether Britain should attempt to restore the pound's prewar value against the dollar by going back on the gold standard. The debate pitted Keynes against Niemeyer. Keynes was unsentimental about gold, having written years earlier that "money is the measure of value, but to regard it as having value itself is a relic of the view that the value of money is regulated by the value of the substance of which it is made, and is like confusing a theatre ticket with the performance."[31]

Keynes thought the real point was to stabilize prices, and that the gold standard, with its independent fluctuations in value, would compromise that goal. Furthermore, attempting to restore prewar parity would be strongly deflationary in its impact on employment and consumption, and expensive in raising the ante for debt repayment.[32] As the dinner table debate unfolded, Niemeyer was a voice of caution and of the verities of British tradition. Keynes's side lost the debate in Churchill's view, and the government took the fateful step that seriously aggravated the unemployment problem.[33] From this bitter experience, Churchill would learn an indelible lesson about the Treasury's fixation on the conventional.

The gold standard lived in a curious liaison with the belief in free trade. The gold standard ostensibly promised fixed value or at least tangibility, and the mantra of free trade suggested fluidity free of artificial constraints. Perhaps in the nervous twenties, each enabled the other in the British psyche. Gold had a settling effect in an inflationary world awash in paper currency and fluctuations in trade. It was "knave-proof" in that politically motivated meddling was supposedly not possible. As Skidelsky notes, "adherence to the gold standard . . . was viewed as a sign of collective virtue."[34] If that was all that was at issue, Keynes might not have objected.[35] The establishment of pre-war parity (of $4.86 versus the then current value of $4.44) with the dollar was observably irrational in his view considering how much had changed after 1914. Yet he was working against the tradition that had, since 1719, *never* seen a peacetime devaluation of the pound.[36] That is what engaged the politicians—the question of prestige. As at Versailles, he had no *riposte* that could penetrate such an instinct.

As a result, British credit policy was once again imprisoned by the dictates of the gold standard, a standard that was insensitive to the political reality of more than a million unemployed workers. Credit expansion and public works or protectionism were all forbidden by the regime of maintaining parity. Policy at the Treasury and at the Bank of England was in the hands essentially of Niemeyer and three other men, all trained at Cambridge in fields such as classics and mathematics, fields not noted for producing flexible thinkers. All were, as Peter Clarke points out, "largely self-taught in economics, but owing intellectual deference to nobody."[37] Churchill, fifteen years later and in the middle of a much greater crisis, recalled having been misled by the Treasury mandarins. He subordinated their role and sought advice from Keynes directly on the financing of the second war.[38]

The other two tenets of the "Treasury view," balanced budgets and free trade, were, in these circumstances, equally insensitive to the plight of the working class. The chancellery's leadership thought a depression was no time to raise taxes even for public works projects. Tariffs to protect noncompetitive British industries and their workers were assumed to be, in the long term, counterproductive.[39] Wages would just have to be adjusted downwards until prewar values were redeemed from the artificial inflation of the Great War. The workers could be pardoned for labeling the Treasury view as class warfare dressed up as economic doctrine. Real wages, thanks in part to the unions, remained high relative to the international competition.

Keynes simply refused to accept wage decline as a necessity.[40] He took up his pen and adapted a favorite title to the new dispute, publishing an essay on *The Economic Consequences of Mr. Churchill.* Attacking the other side of the dinner party debate, he argued that Churchill had been misled about the consequences for labor of a readjustment to the gold standard. In the mold of his "vengeance will not limp" forecast, he declared that "our present policy of deliberately intensifying unemployment by keeping a tight hold on credit . . . is a policy which the country would never permit if it knew what was being done."[41] The workers got the message and were shortly to act in fulfillment of his prophecy.

Tensions boiled over in the General Strike of 1926, abortive though it was, and in the much longer coal miners strike that followed. Keynes laid the crisis at Churchill's door, noting that the disparity in coal prices versus the United States was a direct result of the return to gold. Keynes supported the strike and was thus on the losing side of both the debate on gold and the strike it occasioned.

Niemeyer and his allies were at first rewarded by a modest decline in the unemployment rate that they were happy to attribute to a return to "sound" money. However, by the end of the decade, unemployment was back up over 10 percent.[42] The political outfall of the General Strike meant that wages could not be adjusted downward for political reasons, so Britain's economic position remained difficult with noncompetitive wages, overpriced products, and an overvalued currency.[43]

Keynes's personal life in the mid-twenties was as eventful as his professional existence. Never at rest in the diversity of his pursuits, Keynes's cultivation of the aesthetic was nearly as intense, even quixotic, as his devotion to better policy. He and his Bloomsbury friends were patrons of Covent Garden where Diaghilev's Ballets Russes, "the art form which defined the age," melded the intellectual and cultural revolutions of the teens and twenties.[44] Diaghilev's expressive, romantic, vigorous style was, in the view of Leonard Woolf, of a piece with the artistic revolution of Cézanne, Matisse, and Picasso. Scores by Ravel, Stravinsky, Strauss, and Debussy propelled the sensational Nijinsky and a striking ballerina named Lydia Lopokova to stardom.[45]

The synthesis of innovation and conventionality occurs on an intimate level during this period. Keynes's male Bloomsbury friends had, during the war, discovered women and even a version of domesticity. Several had married or at least settled on shared accommodations, occasionally without quite letting go of former liaisons among their own sex. Keynes was seen from time to time with a lively socialite, Barbara Hiles, with whom he sampled heterosexuality.[46] He was also involved with Sebastian Sprott. However, his evenings at Covent Garden led to a new interest. He became a frequent guest at after-performance parties. Lydia Lopokova, the Diaghilev star, became the center of his attentions. In 1925, Keynes perplexed his friends by marrying Lopokova. In attendance at the civil ceremony were a few close friends, including Duncan Grant.

Maynard and Lydia Keynes at Tilton in Sussex, United Kingdom in 1935. Courtesy of Milo Keynes.

The ballerina with the broken Russian–English argot tripped into Bloomsbury and Cambridge to the general dismay of the communards and dons. A
diminutive dancer of enormous self-confidence and robust technique, she was
not about to be intimidated by this new audience. Lopokova brought her own
professional and personal idiosyncrasies to the union and to Keynes's remarkable coterie.[47]

Keynes undertook her education and that of Quentin, the son of Clive and
Vanessa Bell, by hiring a Daimler on Saturdays and touring them around London's great historical sights, giving lectures along the way. Young Quentin
heard a subtle change in tone as "the impishly irreverent side of him seemed
to be giving way to something more stately, more urbane and more senti-
mental although, certainly, this slight modification . . . of his stance did not
make him any less amusing."[48]

As Skidelsky sees it, Keynes's "sexual and emotional fancy was seized by
free spirits. The two great loves of his life, Duncan and Lydia, were both *uneducated*, their reactions were spontaneous, fresh, unexpected." Skidelsky
speculates that Keynes was looking for a "complement, or balance, to his own
intellectuality."[49] It is also possible to argue that Keynes found in Lydia an expression of life consistent with his own ambivalence between orthodoxy and
experimentation and between the probable and the improbable. Ballet is an
aristocratic art form expressive of stylized and mannered expression. Yet Diaghilev could make of it a raffish display of energy, wit, and physicality.

For all of its peculiarities, Keynes found in his marriage an emotional
center and a source of cultural partnership that sustained a hugely active
career as don, politician, writer, and not-very-gray eminence in the cabinets and boards of successive governments of Britain and the councils of
the West. Lydia's liveliness and humor bridged the social divide between
Bloomsbury and the social world of financiers, businessmen, and government leaders that Keynes was moving into.[50] To their regret, they were not
successful at having children. However, they confounded their old friends
by the happiness, wit, and doting sentimentality of their close and loving
relationship.

Skidelsky muses that 1924 and 1925 were decisive years in Keynes's life.
Now just over forty, Keynes had stepped clear of his former associations:

> He broke decisively with *laissez-faire*; by attacking the return to the gold stan-
> dard, he burnt his boats with the Treasury and the Bank of England; and he mar-
> ried Lydia Lopokova. Events and the processes of his own thoughts radicalised
> him, so that he emerged the self-conscious champion of a new economic and
> political order.[51]

In terms of our frame of identity relations analysis, the shifts in Keynes's professional community from skeptical insider to assertive outsider, and in his personal commitments from homosexual paramour to heterosexual husband, were the complement of a broadening of his competency to the realm of politics. He was poised to begin the formulation of an original set of ideas and of an ideology that would transform the political economy.

Keynes's political activities were showing promise of practical effect. He broke with his ally Herbert Asquith, the leader of the Liberals and went over to his old nemesis, Lloyd George, in 1926. Ever the opportunist of power, Lloyd George was in search of a program to revive Liberal Party fortunes and thought he had found it in the nostrums of Keynes, the professor of policy. With Keynes as policy strategist and Lloyd George as evangelist, the Liberals went into battle in the election of 1929 and were rudely rejected by an electorate bent on class interests. So much for a promising program. The reflationist cause was lost, and the Treasury view retained its hold on the electorate.[52]

The Liberal Party's great losses in 1929 ended Keynes's enthusiasm for direct participation in party politics, though he teamed with Lloyd George to inspire a plan for addressing the gathering unemployment crisis. The plan was bruited in Parliament, but was soundly rejected. Chancellor Churchill declared to Parliament that "whatever might be the political or social advantages, very little additional employment and no permanent additional employment can in fact, as a general rule, be created by State borrowing and State expenditure."[53] Churchill parroted the orthodox view that borrowing to finance public works would weaken the currency, displace better uses for capital as determined by the market, and therefore undermine economic recovery.

Thus rejected, Keynes cast about for new avenues, even trying his hand at drafting a "Prolegomena to a New Socialism." In a brief sketch, Keynes was trying to reconcile such disparate elements as risk taking, the uses of avarice, the relative difficulties of small and large units of production, and the role of profit. The unfinished draft remains in the archives at King's College, Cambridge.[54]

By the end of the twenties, Keynes became less a partisan activist than an independent force engaged on all fronts, though his loyalties were with the advocates of change. He wanted to amplify the system for assisting the unemployed set up in 1911 at the behest of Beveridge and the Liberal Party. The hard realities of economic instability so apparent to the Conservatives confronted the restiveness and militancy of labor that so consumed Labour.

Liberals such as Keynes were in the middle, proposing modest improvements and complex modifications.[55] They were caught with the difficulty of reconciling social justice with economic efficiency. Keynes did not yet have a clear answer as to how this could be done.[56] Meanwhile, at Cambridge, even among the Apostles, there were the beginnings of Communist organizing efforts. The British polity was heading toward a fracture based on class mobilization.[57]

The twenties gave way in a welter of conflicting strains and movements to the polarizing climate of the thirties. Keynes emerged bent on battle over the greatest issues of the times. His every step was dogged by the militants on the left and the right. In the thirties, he would armor himself with the logic of a new macroeconomics of his own devising, the better to engage the nostrums of right and left.

4.2 – LASKI: THE FALL OF CAPITALISM AND THE RISE OF THE RADICAL

From 1920 on, Harold Laski's base was LSE. Laski had become a candidate for the faculty at the invitation of Sidney Webb and with the assistance of another founder, Professor Graham Wallas. Both recommended him to William Beveridge, the newly appointed Director. Beveridge had already accumulated a strong record as a reformer of British social policy, and the appointment of Laski, fresh from Harvard, would bring to LSE a rising progressive intellectual.

The Laski family arrived back in England without the funds to secure a suitable house. Harold, now twenty-eight, returned to Manchester hat in hand. Negotiations were reopened with his family. Finally Frida came to the rescue by agreeing to convert to Judaism, a decision Laski had never pressed on her, but which resolved a great tension in his familial circle. His father opened his arms to his daughter-in-law, and Harold was restored to grace.[58]

From the beginning, Laski provoked strong feelings of affection from students, ambivalence from colleagues, and distrust from much of the establishment.[59] He upstaged the more conventional and conservative economists on the faculty. The target of Laski's rebellion was the power of capital to control the lives of the working class. Laski's professional career encompassed the agitation against capitalism that characterized the late stages of the British Empire, the catastrophe of World War I, the stock market crash, the Great Depression, and World War II. Each of these historical crises intensified the demand for class-based explanations, and each gave impetus to government-led reforms. The establishment stoutly resisted progressive reforms, let alone any serious institutional change. A succession of timid governments pointed Laski ever more directly toward the left end of the political spectrum.

Laski saw World War I as a tragedy of capitalism, fought by regimes of discredited aristocracies and capitalists at the expense of the working class. The reality was more complex. The Governor of the Bank of England, on behalf of his colleagues in the City, had vehemently opposed England's entry into the war. Lloyd George later claimed: "I saw Money before the war . . . I say that Money was a frightened and trembling thing: Money shivered at the prospect. It is a foolish and ignorant libel to call this a financier's war."[60] Many industrialists expressed a similar view. Their interests were tied to trade and to England's position as a financial center, much of which was jeopardized by the bellicose posturing of the rival dynasties.

Yet Lloyd George and the dominant faction of the cabinet felt keenly the obligation to defend France, and saw the deployment of Germany's formidable navy as a threat to all that sustained Britain and the empire.[61] These obligations, and the navy to meet them, were the creation of the political leadership more than the capitalist class. However, business and finance were visibly enriched thereby, and the slaughter of 30 percent of the young men between twenty and twenty-four buried the fine distinctions about which sector of the elite had pulled the trigger. The middle and professional classes had done at least their share of the fighting, if not more. But the staggering losses were even more shattering to the rank and file who, brimming with patriotism, were dependent on their leaders for safety and security.[62] No one of any class was prepared for the savagery of bayonets, machine guns, trench warfare, poison gas, and mass slaughter.

The returning veterans soon were victimized by rising unemployment, escalating prices, and a slumping economy. The harsh times called forth more demands than the Conservatives could tolerate or than a Liberal like Keynes could ameliorate. From the struggles for suffrage through to the strikes and socialist upheavals in Britain, Europe, and the United States during the twenties, Laski saw the working class on the rise against an increasingly inept, cynical, and pro-fascist power structure.

Fascinated but not wholly taken in by the Bolshevism of Russia, he worked at building a democratic socialist movement in Britain, first in the form of guild socialism, later on the trade union lines of the British Labour Party, and occasionally in the militant mode of mass mobilization. His academic and journalistic writings set out a theoretical justification for the advancement of egalitarianism, along with strategic and tactical guidelines, even while trying to save liberal commitments to individual freedom of expression and affiliation. He agitated these issues through regular newspaper columns, opinion pieces of great passion and clarity, and speeches at union halls and socialist meetings throughout Britain.

By 1921 he was writing that one could not assume "that the government is fully representative of the community without taking account of the way in which the characteristics of the economic system inevitably perverts the governmental purpose to narrow and special ends." Capitalist democracy cannot be trusted, but neither can "the average voter be said to transcend his own interest by merging himself into a larger whole with the result that a 'general will' is secured."[63] Here was a dilemma for a believer in individual rights and constitutionalism. He was for democracy on principle, but the practice of government was decidedly under the control of capitalists. Laski became a premier spokesperson for the ever-larger sector of the public caught up by the dilemma of democracy and capitalism.

The Marxist solution was to resolve the dilemma of capitalism and governance by turning all questions of politics into issues of class and economics. From there, it was a short step to Marx's analysis of the economic collapse of capitalism and the advent of revolution by the proletariat. In a pamphlet on Marxism for the Fabian Society, Laski lauded Marx's identification of the oppressiveness of business elites, but he stepped away from economic determinism and from revolution, in particular. Laski was averse to giving up on morally inspired leadership, and he was suspicious of the force and power involved in revolutions. His prediction was that a revolution in the twentieth century, unlike the idealistic revolutions of the past, would lead to repression—a prescient observation.[64]

Pluralism, for Laski, was a better way of addressing the problem. He was, by this time, in transition from a faith in union-based syndicalism to a broader conception that would be inclusive of a range of groups within society. The engagement of ordinary people not only in their conditions of employment but in the affairs of state was the desideratum of his view.

Laski's version of pluralism addressed another problem as well—the best use of the knowledge and insight of all elements of society. Here he moves the issue beyond the nexus between human dignity and conditions of work to the question of obtaining the best and most productive use of human talents. He observes in 1921 that

> Once, at any point, work is divorced from responsibility the result is a balked disposition of which the consequence is to diminish the creativeness of the worker concerned. The hierarchical structure of the present state maximizes this loss. Nothing is clearer, for example, than the existence of a law of diminishing administrative returns. An official cannot be charged with business over a territory beyond a certain size without administering less efficiently for each addition to his work; and no amount of efficiency at a central office will morally

compensate for the inferior interest in the result obtained of those who have had no effective share in making it.[65]

The practical and moral values of participation are mingled in this analysis. Centralized administration is viewed as an inefficient means of enlisting popular engagement. These themes will reappear a decade later in the work, not of Laski, but of his conservative antagonist, Friedrich Hayek.

Laski developed the theory of pluralism as a way of bowing to the intractability of various interests without giving up on democracy. However, there is an inevitable conflict between freedom and the kind of power that is built on the institution of private property:

> Liberty, in short, is incompatible with the present system of property; for its result is a concentration of power which makes the political personality of the average citizen ineffective for any serious purpose.[66]

The freedom to accumulate meant the loss of freedom of the propertyless to participate in any meaningful way. These ruminations seemed to lead straight to Marxism. However, Laski feared the abandonment of personal agency and the role of consent, which revolution would bring. Still, he could not quite shake the attraction of Marx's analysis, nor could he dismiss the achievement of the Russian revolution.[67]

The Laskis were becoming noted figures on the left in London. Beatrice Webb, a socialist doyen now in her mid-sixties, noted in her diary for May 1922:

> Laski is the most brilliant of the lecturers and his little wife is as restless and critical as he. He attracts me by his lively talk, witty epigrammatic gossip, not distinguished for accuracy, and his extraordinary range of intellectual interests and book knowledge. He knows, or says he knows, everyone of importance; his sympathies and likings are volatile; he scoffs at the Labour leaders, dismisses the Asquith-Grey combination with scorn and hates Lloyd George.

Laski's religion and his marriage are fixed in Webb's crosshairs in the same entry: "He has a strong Jewish racial feeling and his scoffing little sceptic of a wife has become a Jewess to bridge over the displeasure of the family at his marriage to a gentile."[68] Beatrice Webb saw Laski as part of a younger group of socialist intellectuals whose "philosophy is psychological and its method is strictly scientific: a controlled and modified capitalism is to be the 'next step' in its practical programme."[69] Of psychology and science in a contemporary sense, there is not much that today's reader would recognize in Laski.

However, his views must have struck the political class of the time as motivated by something besides socialist doctrine and class solidarity.

By 1923, Laski's writings, among those of others, offended the owners of the *Nation*, an increasingly leftist journal of opinion, and caused them to sell off the magazine to Maynard Keynes and his associates who used it to promote the reformist agenda of the Liberal Party.[70] Laski quit writing for the *Nation*.

Laski also left the Liberal Party. The agenda of moderate reformism congenial to figures such as Keynes, which once seemed consonant with Laski's pluralism, was no longer as attractive as the union-based politics of the Labour Party. Laski became a Labour Party activist. Now focused on his theme, he set out to persuade public opinion of the desirability and practicality of a "revolution by consent."[71] Writing scores of Fabian Society tracts that sold for twopence to the masses, Laski found a style and voice that appealed to workers and progressives of all classes. Rather than working as an insider Liberal critic, he now cast his lot more directly with the Labour outsiders.

The pressures were building rapidly. Mass unemployment, unprecedented in living memory, afflicted the war-ravaged working classes. By 1926, rising union militancy, particularly in the coal mines, erupted in the worst year for strikes in British history. The miners struck themselves to starvation and capitulation. The disastrous miners strike set the stage for the signal political event, the nine-day General Strike of 1926. Like the miners strike, it was an ignominious defeat for labor.

The miners strike and the brief and ineffectual General Strike called in support of it led Laski to champion the cause of the workers directly as he got involved in the negotiations between the strikers and the government. He and Frida camped at the headquarters of the Trades Unions Congress (TUC) and made themselves useful to the leadership.[72] However, the General Strike was called off very quickly on the belief that the miners were going to settle.

The failure of the settlement and the bitter months of confrontation that followed wore down the unions and galvanized the reactionaries. In 1927, the Conservative government put through a law substantially limiting the power of unions. Laski concluded that Britain's democracy was clearly reversible: "The experience of Tory democracy is valuable if only for the knowledge that it ends in Toryism without democracy."[73] He hinted that a more militant approach might be needed.[74]

Yet the Conservatives learned enough to moderate their policies, Labour pulled in its horns, and the Liberals reached back to Lloyd George to reinvigorate the party at the end of the decade.[75] As for Laski, the General Strike was the end of any lingering faith that syndicalism could generate a coherent movement to oppose the capitalist state. His youthful idealism was, by the late twenties, giving way to a practical assessment of the strength of capitalism's forces.

At LSE, he rose quickly to prominence among his colleagues. In 1926 he was appointed to the chair of Graham Wallas, his patron at LSE. Now firmly situated, Harold and Frida bought the home that they would live in until Harold's death. An unadorned, solid, three-story house of eighteenth-century origin, it sits in a middle-class neighborhood near the railroad tracks of the District Line in west London, close to Earls Court and the Olympia Exhibition Hall. Neither working class nor bourgeois, the Laskis lived as urban Londoners in plain, but comfortable circumstances.

Not all of Laski's colleagues were unalloyed admirers of LSE's increasingly visible star. The young economist Lionel Robbins observed later of Laski:

> Judged as a very precocious boy with the bewildering mixture of good and bad impulses which usually go with precocity, he had much in him that was positively lovable. . . . I shall remember from time to time his unpleasing qualities, his swank, his unreliability, his occasional vindictiveness and the curious feeling of the factitious about many of more characteristic emotional declamations. But I shall more frequently think of his . . . quick apprehension and sense of fun that so often . . . would cause our eyes to meet in mutual relish at the absurdity of some pompous colleague or some preposterous academic formality.[76]

The fault in his style was a relentless need to impress that led to a reputation as one of the century's great name-droppers. Estimates vary as to the accuracy of his tales of direct contact with the prime ministers of England and, later, "Frank" Roosevelt. There is correspondence to validate his phenomenal access at the highest levels—even if he was not, as one historian characterized his claim, "the hidden hand which guided the faltering step of British statesmen in nearly every crisis from 1920 onwards."[77] Perhaps the exaggerations were a compensation for his uniqueness among the leadership of the British left. He was the one Jew of consequence among Labour intellectuals for several decades.[78]

Institutional politics at LSE took on an increasingly bitter cast. Laski set himself in opposition to the rising power of economists and of the empirical turn in methodology occasioned in part by major support from the Rockefeller Foundation, with its emphasis on practical approaches to social problems, rather than philosophic attacks on the capitalist system. Laski encouraged students to be critical of the school, and this aroused the ire of its imperious director, William Beveridge.[79] Thus, both within LSE, and the larger polity around him, Laski was becoming ever more the professional rebel.

Laski's initial hostility to the state as the agent of capitalism was mediated by his conceptualization of pluralism as a means of democratic control.[80] His most famous book, *A Grammar of Politics* (1925), established a claim to relevance in defining a socialist form of pluralism that could be seen as a full-scale alternative to conventional institutions of political power. His writings on pluralism remain as the most enduring element of his professional work.[81] *A Grammar of Politics* is dedicated to LSE and its founders, the Webbs.

Laski made the case for socialist pluralism as the key not only to equality, but to the achievement of individual liberty as well. "A society, in fact, in which there are freedom and equality has already divided power."[82] Government alone, thought Laski, had the institutional capacity to form public policy through the systematic consultation of working-class interests. But the problem remained: how to orient the state away from its narrow focus on the interests of capitalists. Laski envisioned a harmony of interests, based on complementarity of functions and underlain by a more equitable distribution of rights and even of property. He theorized that this would resolve class tensions and lead to an ever more participatory and progressive society. In one way or another, this remained Laski's aspiration even while events led him toward the endorsement of more radical experiments.[83]

Nationalization was presented in *A Grammar of Politics* as the cure for the private monopoly of essential industries. In other parts of the economy, a network of industrial councils would work out production targets, wages, and standards. Liberated from the corrosion of competition, the economy would prosper far beyond present levels.[84] While Laski was intent on political equality, economic equality was viewed in less than draconian terms as mainly a matter of opportunity. Inequality of result could be justified by its utility for social welfare.[85]

Property, however, was suspect. Private ownership had utility for self-development. Beyond that minimal amount, however, Laski saw the accumulation of property as an excuse for gaining power in a form that should not be allowed. Redistribution, in this sense, was less important than a limitation on ownership and the power to control the fates of others. Full political equality and constraints on economic inequality are critical to liberty properly understood.[86] These views immunized Laski and much of the British left against the siren song of Leninism. More effectively than any other, Laski would guide his fellow citizens along the divide between the totalitarianism of Joseph Stalin and the democratic socialism of an evolving Labour Party.

Unlike Keynes, Laski could take at least some comfort in the progress of his favored party among the voters. In the spring election of 1929, Labour won the largest number of seats, but not quite a majority, and was asked to form a minority government with the Liberals. But there was not the strength to advance Labour's main program or to address the deepening crisis in the economy. The possibility of socialism by democratic means was yet distant.[87] The Prime Minister and his Chancellor of the Exchequer, Philip Snowden, were wedded to balanced budgets and the Treasury's dim view of public works.[88] The decade ended for Laski with a deepening sense of crisis, Labour nominally in power, and a widening rift within the faculty of LSE over the policies that should be pursued to deal with the faltering economic and political structure. Laski's star would ascend as the night darkened in the thirties.

4.3 – HAYEK: MONETARISM AND TAMING OF GOVERNMENTS

At the University of Vienna in the 1920s, Friedrich Hayek's dilemma lay in choosing between the arbitrary exaggerations of Marxism or Freudianism, on the one side, and the superficiality of empirical social science on the other. On one side of the path lay mountains with disappearing peaks; on the other side, a desert of myriad grains of sand. Neither promised a vantage point for sorting through the chaos of Austrian political economy in the postwar years.

To turn from these revolutionary new paradigms toward the practice of social analysis revealed another problem that caused Hayek unease in his university years. The migration of scientific methodology from the natural world to the study of society had produced, as might be predicted, an initial enthusiasm for a "positivist" social science. The quantification of experience through the analysis of data on behavior seemed, in a physics-driven concept of science, to be the way to attack the abstractions of an overly philosophical approach to social understanding. The physicist Ernst Mach and his followers deeply influenced the young student, even while Hayek began to wonder whether economics could be understood at more than a surface level by such an approach. Hayek had an aversion to theorizing based on abstractions, yet he wanted to understand the deeper forces behind appearances.

He was attracted to the kind of economics developed by a powerful teacher, Carl Menger (1840–1921). Menger's *Grundsätze* and particularly his *Methodenbuch* placed economics at the center of "the spontaneous generation of institutions."[89] Here, for Hayek, was the link between his interest in political economy, in psychology, and in the style of thought he had acquired from his father. The confluence fit with the emergence of a young intellectual of uncommon power and determination.

Clearly, a science along these lines was called for. Institutions of government were no longer in control of the wild gyrations of the postwar economy. The collapse Keynes had forecast was soon visited on the hapless Austrians. Hayek was, like Thomas Hobbes in the seventeenth century, to come to manhood amid collapsing institutions and a return to "the state of nature." As Hobbes turned to geometry for a style of thought, Hayek was searching for the right form of science to apply to the chaos of his surroundings. But on what premises would this science proceed?

Another Austrian, Karl Popper, was to give form in 1934 to what Hayek claims to have sensed in the early twenties: that refutation, not verification, was the key to scientific methodology. It was the ultimately nonfalsifiable character of Marxist conceptions of human purpose, or of Freud's cosmology of energy fields, that repelled Hayek. While science may not be able to verify ultimate truths or deliver us to certainty, and thence to ideology, it could show us the error of our mental constructions. By contriving tests, whether of logic or observation, to probe the falsifiability of theories, science makes its most reliable contribution to human knowledge. When dealing with human experience, where the line between tangible and intangible is sometimes hard to draw, science must become the skeptic's tool rather than the visionary's.

The result for Hayek's formation as an intellectual was a substantial skepticism of received theory, a contempt for atheoretical observation—and freedom from the challenge of verification. The style of his thought was set: he would make his mark not as the builder of new systems, but as the critic of most other intellectuals and the defender of skeptics. Hayek was comfortable with the role. As he commented a decade later in his inaugural lecture at LSE:

> it is probably no exaggeration to say that economics developed mainly as the outcome of the investigation and refutation of successive Utopian proposals— if by "Utopian" we mean proposals for the improvement of undesirable effects of the existing system based upon a complete disregard of those forces which actually enabled it to work.[90]

Hayek's original contributions to economics would be few, though important. Rather, he would become one of the century's most significant intellectuals by mobilizing insights from the past or from related fields, to challenge fashionable new theories of political economy. He was now disposed to go on the offensive.

As will be seen, Hayek's style of refutation was so successful as rhetoric that it distracted attention from the unverifiability of his own alternatives—and of the dangers of ideology found in his own work. He became the spokesperson for spontaneity rather than directed order, for evolution rather than construction, and for indeterminacy rather than certainty. What he did not see is that the common characteristic of spontaneity, evolution, and indeterminacy as concepts is that they are beyond ultimate verification. These concepts would come to be intellectually attractive alternatives to the disprovable certainties that mobilized the militants of his age.

Hayek's education in classical liberal economics took place against a political background of some complexity. As Kari Polanyi-Levitt and Marguerite Mendel observed:

> Hayek was born in Vienna at the turn of the century (1899) as the brief era of the liberal constitutional order established in the 1860s—which privileged the rising class of bankers, manufacturers, and merchants and found its social support base among middle-class urban Germans and German speaking Jews—was challenged by anti-capitalist populist movements of the Right and the Left.[91]

Hayek received his doctorate in law in 1921 and his doctorate in political economy two years later. He created a discussion group of largely Jewish students with tastes in economics, the arts, and philosophy. Among them were putative professors at Vienna, Harvard, Princeton, and the New School for Social Research, as well as two future presidents of the American Economic Association, and a member of the U.S. Federal Reserve Board. Erik Vögelin and Alfred Schutz, destined to be distinguished philosophers, were participants as well.[92]

Along the way he was introduced by Friedrich Wieser, his adviser in economics at the university, and to Ludwig von Mises. He became an avid member of von Mises's private seminar on economics. Von Mises, the intellectual successor to Menger as the premier voice of Austrian economics, published a highly influential economist's critique of socialism in 1922. Hayek was thus weaned from Wieser's "mild Fabianism" and introduced to a lifelong mentor and patron who would reorient his thinking to the virtues of the free market.[93]

Von Mises had hoped to take over the Ministry of Finance to stem the rampant inflation that was ruining the economy. He was never called, though he later advised the League of Nations commissioner who was appointed for the same purpose.[94] Von Mises' trenchant critique of socialist statism as the cause of Austria's downfall ran counter to all of the self-protective reflexes of the Austrian government. He based his critique on the impossibility of mastering sufficient information for the statist direction of the economy to better the performance of market processes. It was an argument that was widely noted at the time, and it would form the basis for his young protégé's attack on similar proposals in Britain two decades later.[95] In 1923, von Mises had Hayek appointed to a position as his assistant in an office charged with carrying out the postwar settlement. Hayek had a ringside seat for the crushing monetary disaster of the era, and the ear of one of its most astute economic analysts.

Hayek took leave to travel to the United States in 1923 to burnish his credentials as a rising young economist. Now sporting a beard, he was given introductions by the eminent Austrian economist and bank president, Joseph Schumpeter, to prominent academicians. He was promised a fellowship in New York for further research.[96] Hayek ventured from the old world to the new. The fellowship did not materialize, and he took a job as a dishwasher at a Sixth Avenue restaurant. Before scrubbing a single pot however, he was rescued by a research assistantship at New York University.

Hayek's own youthful agnosticism, as well as his skepticism about the philosophical basis for Marxism and Freudianism, left him without a system of thought. A young man, disillusioned by his wartime experience and bewildered by the intellectual disarray of the university, arrives at a moment where the abstraction of ideas provides for identity what a confusing communal reality will not permit: a resolution that points the way toward further growth and maturation. As Hayek reflected in later years, he had become a man "in search of a theory, but didn't know yet what a theory really was."[97]

Hayek took advantage of his opportunity in New York to read foreign newspapers. There he saw exposed the lies his government had told him and his fellow citizens about the Great War. If Hayek had any remaining faith in the efficacy of governments, it dissolved in the reading rooms of the New York Public Library.[98]

The falseness of Austrian propaganda about the war also removed any remaining illusions about his national patrimony. The dawning realization that Austrian intractability had precipitated the calamity must have wiped away the last vestiges of pride in his home culture.[99] While English diplomats had worked feverishly to avert the war, the Austrians and their quixotic patron, the German Kaiser, had made war inevitable. Asquith, the English Prime Minister, had referred privately to the Austrians as "quite the stupidest people in Europe."[100] As for the impact on young Hayek, Stephen Kresge concludes,

"We can date Hayek's skepticism toward the actions and motives of government from this point."[101]

This was the turning point in his relationship with the cultural community of his youth that would lead him to reconsider the role of government and of the validity of its pretensions to rationalizing society. Erik Erikson remarks in *Life History and the Historical Moment* that we need to be able to see "a 'great' man's crises and achievements as communal events characteristic of a given historical period."[102] Hayek's detachment from the intellectual and cultural universe of his upbringing was of a piece with the experience of other postwar Austrian intellectuals who came under the influence of Darwin, Freud, Marx, and Hayek's cousin, Ludwig von Wittgenstein.

On returning to Austria, he published an attack on the pretensions of American economists who advocated an extension of the Federal Reserve's power so that it could attempt to eliminate the business cycle. He feared that such hubris would lead to failure and, with it, the intervention of government and an even worse result.[103] If he needed any further stimulus to probe the relations between politics and economics, the hyperinflation he saw around him was as dramatic as any in recorded history. In a letter to the editor of the *New York Times*, Hayek pointed out that between February and August of 1923, the German mark fell to less than 1/500 of its already depreciated value. Fully apprised of the dangers of inflation, Hayek wrote a short article on the folly of trying to balance both prices and foreign exchange rates simultaneously. He then discovered that an economist named John Maynard Keynes had already made the argument in print and the article was never published.[104]

Hayek resumed his work with Ludwig von Mises, who was to become director of the Austrian chamber of industry, and he was admitted to von Mises' inner circle. This coterie was to help spark the eventual revival of classical liberalism amid the ashes of postwar collapse. However, in the crises of the twenties, von Mises was to become an increasingly isolated figure because of his regard for what others saw as a vanishing past and the anomaly that he was a Jewish defender of capitalism. While there were many Jews on the faculty of the University of Vienna, they were nearly all partisans of the left. Hayek would later recall that

a Jewish intellectual who justified capitalism appeared to most as some sort of monstrosity, something unnatural, which could not be categorized and with which one did not know how to deal. His undisputed subject-knowledge was impressive, and one could not avoid consulting him in critical economic situations, but rarely was his advice understood and followed. Mostly he was regarded as somewhat of an eccentric whose "old-fashioned" ideas were impracticable "today."[105]

Hayek was intrigued and increasingly won over to von Mises' position. Hayek remarked that von Mises, "during the great inflation . . . was the only person in Vienna, or perhaps in the German speaking world, who really understood what was happening."[106] Von Mises was virtually a lone holdout for nineteenth-century classical liberalism as summarized in a famous passage from the works of Thomas Babbington Macaulay, an English historian and literary philosopher:

> Our rulers will best promote the improvement of the nation by strictly confining themselves to their own legitimate duties, by leaving capital to find its most lucrative course, commodities their fair price, industry and intelligence their natural reward, idleness and folly their natural punishment, by maintaining peace, by defending property, by diminishing the price of law, and by observing strict economy in every department of the state. Let the Government do this: The people will assuredly do the rest.[107]

It is interesting that the link between Austrian and English political economy developed with von Mises' generation. Among others, von Mises found common ground in England with Edwin Canaan, an economist and formative influence at LSE. The path that was opened for cooperation between classical liberals in Austria and England would be decisive for the development of Hayek's influence.[108] His identification with a mentor, von Mises, who was an outsider in his intellectual context doubtless suited Hayek's own sense of alienation from Austria's political culture.

Hayek was at the same time involved in a fateful turn in his personal life. According to the explanation he later offered for the eventual failure of his marriage, Hayek had fallen in love with his cousin Helene Bitterlich prior to leaving for America and had wished to marry her. Apparently misunderstanding his intentions, she accepted the proposal of Herr Warhanek, a rival suitor favored by her family who had become involved with her during Hayek's absence in America. Disappointed, Hayek turned to a secretary in the office where he worked, Helen Berta Maria von Fritsch, who reminded him of his first love.[109] They were married in 1926.

This unsettled commitment came about amid the economic pressures of the twenties. As Hayek observed later, inflation had undercut the basis of middle-class life.[110] The hyperinflation of the early twenties and the scarcities that undermined the economy led to a drastic currency revaluation in 1923. The government was forced to dismiss eighty-five thousand civil servants.[111] Given the disarray of the Austrian government, a desired career in the diplomatic service was no longer a possibility. In 1927, with von Mises' backing, he set up an institute to analyze economic cycles.

Now established with an intellectual framework, a marriage, and a vocation—each of them formed from disappointment and fresh initiative—Hayek had achieved a hard-won coherence for his own sense of identity. He could see himself as a self-made man, even if his achievements were assisted by his mentors. It was an identity of particular importance to his times and his surroundings. The very chaos of the Austrian economic experience of the twenties made Hayek's newfound competence as an economist all the more critical.

Hayek began to integrate his extensive knowledge of trade cycles with his view of monetary theory. The vision that would integrate this knowledge was built on a commitment to classical economics, as he understood it, and to nineteenth-century German legal theory. This meant that recourse to verities of the past became his guiding star rather than the popular belief that the future required changes of a fundamental nature.

The following year his work took him to London, where he met the famous director of a similar institute, Keynes. Entering into an immediate conflict over a question on interest rates, Hayek reports that Keynes, failing in his attempt to "steamroller" the younger man, then acknowledged him as someone worthy of being taken seriously.[112] They were to be colleagues and oftentimes rivals for nearly two decades. Hayek later acknowledged Keynes as an early hero of his, and he took pains to dispute Laski's contention that Keynes once described Hayek as the "most distinguished muddlehead in Europe."[113]

For Hayek, the indelible lesson of the business cycle was that intervention, *by its nature*, was far more likely to be damaging than helpful. In the Austrian view, there was a natural underlying set of relations, specifically a natural rate of interest at which savings and investment would reach equilibrium, that can only be worked out in practice because it is reflective of the mood of the public at any given time. The difference between the *market* rate of interest offered at any given moment and the *natural* rate is the cause of speedups and slowdowns in the cycle. These differences or distortions come about for many reasons, among them the changing expectations of businesspeople acting in a world of imperfect information. Left alone, the interaction of the credit system and myriad other variables serves to sort out justifiable confidence from false hopes.

For government to interfere in this interaction distorts even further the search for equilibrium. The government acts by borrowing money in order to spend it—or by just printing money—or by the manipulation of demand or supply for policy reasons. In doing so, government reacts to the visible part of the dynamic; it cannot see, nor can anyone, the natural rate at which savings and investment will come into balance. As Bruce Caldwell notes, "the problem is that no one knows what the natural rate is; only the market rate is observable."[114] Furthermore, the unobservable natural rate is not fixed; it is relative to a community's changing desires for savings and consumption. Were there no credit, the adjustment would be quicker; given credit, the cycle is inevitably uneven.

Because the macroeconomic cycle was beyond comprehension, Hayek did not believe that the answer to the cycle would ever be found in statistics. Unlike other practitioners of business-cycle analysis, Hayek was wary of being mesmerized by data. Perhaps the relation between the unseen force of evolution and the varieties of botanical life that he observed in the Alps predisposed him to a more sophisticated conception of nature's dynamics.[115] Still, to refute what can be determined from simple observation is not to verify that any particular unseen force exists.

Hayek began to work toward a grander explanation of the "successive phases of the business cycle."[116] For seven years in the twenties, this was his main preoccupation. His search would ultimately take him both backwards, to the classical liberal tradition that was increasingly being abandoned by English economists, and forward, to a variation in the conventional justification of the market. His search for a new rationale would ultimately bring into question the ways that knowledge is used in the service of productivity and invention. Along the way, insights inspired by his early fascination with the natural world would serve as a counterpoint to the turn toward rational analysis and government intervention that came to dominate the English approach.

The efflorescence of his theoretical position proceeded apace with the disillusionment with his native culture that would lead to his departure for England in 1930. Hayek, looking back over his life, told W. W. Bartley III, his intended biographer, that he had become "somewhat estranged during the conditions of the 1920s." He found on arrival in England that "English ways of life seemed so naturally to accord with all my instincts and dispositions," such that "culturally, I feel my nationality is British and not Austrian." The migration reached deep into his personality: "It was really from the first moment arriving there that I found myself for the first time in a moral atmosphere which was completely congenial to me and which I could absorb overnight."[117] The untimely death of his father due to blood poisoning at the age of fifty-seven in 1928 further weakened his ties to home. Hayek emigrated to England and there commenced a crusade to save his adopted country, and Europe more generally, from the pernicious fallacies of state intervention in the economy.

Friedrich Hayek (ca. 1930). Reprinted by permission of Corbis.

Unsettled times provide those who are coming of age with opportunities for innovation. For younger men in their twenties and thirties, there were manifold openings as old institutions, their foundations cracked by the war, struggled to regain control. The national communities that had so proudly gone to war were now fractured and, in Austria, shattered by defeat. The political regimes that governed them forged ahead amid a deepening skepticism about their legitimacy. The intellectual movements that had sponsored the illusions of Western "civilization" would never recover their hubris after the realities of a world war proved their evanescence.

In practical terms, the burden of public concern shifted from the imbroglios of empire to the necessities of economic revival. In the prior century of limited governments and laissez-faire economies, the idea of government responsibility for prosperity had not yet taken hold. After the war, governments could not evade the crisis set in train by the massive dislocation of the war effort. A new problem demanded new competencies, and a new profession of economist was created to answer the call.

Maynard Keynes advanced in public esteem by writing a trenchant economist's critique of the war's settlement. The twenties were a time of experimentation as he moved to marry his economic analysis to political activism. A string of losing causes persuaded him that he needed stronger ammunition. One can see in the twenties the restless preoccupation with bringing the values of Cambridge to bear on England's destiny. For Keynes, the thirties would become the decade of opportunity.

What Keynes saw as a problem of redirecting the judgments of elites, Friedrich Hayek, forming his ideas amid economic collapse, came to see the crisis as a much larger challenge: reorienting public opinion about the fundamental institutions of politics and the economy. Austria was on the periphery now and discredited. He needed a posting of more prominence.

Politics before the war had been largely the province of politicians. Universities entered politics only elliptically through the spread of ideas and the preservation of critical discussion and debate. The twenties demanded voices less beholden to interests and better equipped to reach deeper into questions of legitimacy and meaning. Harold Laski settled into LSE and proceeded to fashion the role of public intellectual—half academic, half political commentator, and, increasingly, another half of rhetorician. It was an outsized role for any normal person, but not for a dynamic young professor with a photographic memory, immense self-confidence, and the experience of a successful personal rebellion against the patrimony of his Manchester upbringing.

The communities each man lived among in the twenties made distinctive contributions to the consolidation of their identities. Bloomsbury gave Keynes a sanctuary and a hothouse in which an imagined society of enlightenment, art, and beauty could be seen to flower. The entanglements of his shifting personal commitments were resolved on Bloomsbury's edge, by marrying an artist in her own right—but one practiced in appealing to both the demimonde and the establishment. Keynes's personal life was at last secure.

Hayek threw off the familiar community of his youth as his national patrimony fell into disgrace and came into the company of a powerful mentor, Ludwig von Mises, who would launch him on the search for a new community built on distinctive premises. Married, but not fully committed, the search would be the more urgent for not proceeding from a settled base. He heard the call of destiny and left for England.

Laski's genius for attracting favorable attention to ideas, and to himself, enabled him to maneuver adeptly among political and intellectual rivalries in the twenties. In a time when others on the left were experimental in their personal commitments, Harold and Frida teamed together bonded by love, temperament, and political solidarity. He was poised to move from dilettante to actor in the political dramas of the worldwide depression.

5

The Thirties: Duel of Allegiances

The cracks in Western societies that opened in the war widened in the twenties and became chasms in the thirties. For Harold Laski the thirties were an unfolding drama, and he became one of its most notable scenarists. His attempts at bringing together the conflicting scripts of moderation and revolution were resolved into an ever more determined radicalism.

Less conspicuously, Friedrich Hayek entered the seam of English intellectual life at the London School of Economics (LSE). He set about deepening the foundations of a reaction to the progressive intellectual movements that were contending for public favor. Maynard Keynes, meanwhile, was consolidating his own work in fashioning a new rationale for political economy — and a plan for saving the fundamental institutions of his society.

As the depression worsened and the rival forces of fascism and socialism mobilized in the streets of Europe, academicians, too, rallied in their less conspicuous, yet quite consequential way. The thirties were for Keynes, Hayek, and Laski a time of definition. Their writings would reveal an ever-bolder profile of their drive to alter the terms of politics and economics.

5.1 – KEYNES: ARENAS OF CONFRONTATION

Maynard Keynes's growing competence as a policy adviser and his affiliations with the Bloomsbury community, along with his new personal commitments, must be seen as the developmental impetus for his works on political economy. Keynes was now the fully credentialed public intellectual with a supporting cast of friends, protégés, and admirers. Equipped by temperament and strengthened by his spirited wife, Keynes could forge ahead in his quest for progressive approaches to Britain's crises.

The context for these developments was a new form of economic challenge. Almost immediately after World War I, there had appeared in Britain an economic phenomenon that would define the challenge to the capitalist system: persistent high unemployment. At 10 percent or above through the twenties, and much higher in the Great Depression, it became an impetus to left-wing politics—and to the reexamination of economic orthodoxy.[1]

The conventional view had been that unemployment in England would be resolved when lower wages returned the labor market to equilibrium. But normality of this sort would have acknowledged the subordination of England, and Europe, to American financial power; and it would have the gravest consequences for domestic politics.[2] The economist's equilibrium was the nationalist's recipe for decline, and the socialist's for the immiseration of the working class.

The political consequence of this dilemma was that all three parties were thrown into crisis. The Liberal leadership buckled under the strain of rising unemployment, and the Conservatives only managed an occasional gesture toward reform. There was, in any event, no great difference between them. Laski, tabulating the class origins of cabinet ministers in governments of the two parties, could find little to differentiate them as to affinity for the aristocracy and the old school tie.[3]

Keynes saw the leadership of the Labour Party as caught between its fear of economic experimentation and its commitment to utopian ideas of class justice. For there to be a compelling scenario of exploitation, the class warriors of the Labour Party needed the fixed target of oppressive capitalist relations of production. This entailed a commitment to the orthodoxies of supply and demand. Karl Marx had no disagreement with conventional analyses of how capitalism worked, even while he forecast a radically different result. Labour's leaders were caught in this mindset and were "totally unsympathetic with those who have had new notions of what is economically sound."[4] As the decade opened, the Labour Party's annual conference specifically rejected a proposal to ameliorate the worsening slump by Keynesian measures, preferring instead to see it as the final crisis of capitalism. Only a structural change to socialize the means of production would, in this view, make any real difference.[5]

Undaunted by such apocalyptic scenarios, Keynes persisted in refining his moderate approach. The fruit of Keynes's economic labors had first seen the light of day with the publication of his *Treatise on Money* (1930). He looked into the question of managing the relationship of savings and investment and came up with the idea that bank policy could be used to manipulate the two so as to stabilize prices.[6] Since bankers decide how much of savings will be lent for investment and have discretion over the percentage of cash reserves, they have a powerful lever for influencing the amount of investment. Rather than responding to estimates of what would achieve some arbitrary conception of desired savings (and therefore investment), the policy should be managed with a specific investment outcome in mind.

Friedrich Hayek, in a review, wrote that this approach was misguided and futile, and that the market would rectify the situation more efficiently.[7] Keynes dispensed with Hayek's critique by dismissing his faith in the "automatic mechanism" of market interest rates for reconciling savings and investment. Keynes argued that the public and entrepreneurs, not to mention bankers, changed their attitudes toward savings and investment for reasons other than interest rates, per se.[8]

Keynes's view riled the conventionalists because it suggested a role for deliberate regulation of the interchange between savings and investment, rather than relying on the invisible hand to sort out the relationship. Von Mises and Hayek wanted to remove the possibility of meddling by requiring 100 percent reserves so that there would be no such thing as credit, and the link between savings and investment would be complete.[9] For Keynes, the problem was not the elimination of meddling, but the provision of an inducement to invest and thereby generate growth.

In addressing this objective, Keynes's *Treatise* also distanced him from the program of the socialists. By way of casting doubt on the presumed benefit of saving and the virtue of abstinence from consumption that underlay it, Keynes wound up celebrating the socialist's *bête noir*, profit.

> If enterprise is afoot, wealth accumulates whatever may be happening to thrift; and if enterprise is asleep, wealth decays whatever thrift may be doing. Thus, thrift may be the handmaid and nurse of enterprise. But equally she may not. And, perhaps, even usually she is not. For enterprise is connected with thrift not directly; but at one remove; and the link which should join them is frequently missing. For the engine which drives enterprise is not thrift, but profit.[10]

Keynes commended profit seeking not out of some Puritan theory of the value of striving or even an economist's love of macrofunctionality. In fact, he saw it as a rather base activity, in ways a socialist might find congenial. It is just that where there is a need to build up productivity to fulfill basic needs, as opposed to aspirations for positional goods such as the best educational and employment opportunities, profit served the socially useful purpose of facilitating investments and new techniques of production.[11]

That said, like Adam Smith before him, Keynes understood that materialism for its own sake is morally indefensible. Adam Smith's system was based not on material self-interest directly, but on the human desire for respect:

> To deserve, to acquire, and to enjoy the respect and admiration of mankind, are the great objects of ambition and emulation. Two different roads are presented to us, equally leading to the attainment of this so much desired object; the one, by the study of wisdom and the practice of virtue; the other, by the acquisition of wealth and greatness.[12]

Adam Smith did not approve of every stratagem for gaining respect. The best stratagems from Smith's point of view are those of "a select, though, I am afraid, but a small party, who are the real and steady admirers of wisdom and virtue."[13]

In the fullness of life, Keynes agreed with Smith that materialism is a bad strategy for salvation. In a remarkably sunny essay published in 1930 titled "Possibilities for Our Grandchildren," Keynes looked forward to increases in productivity and the workings of compound interest on the resulting capital accumulations bringing the world to general prosperity. At such a time,

> The love of money as a possession—as distinguished from the love of money as a means to the enjoyments and realities of life—will be recognized for what it is, a somewhat disgusting morbidity, one of those semi-criminal, semi-pathological propensities which one hands over with a shudder to the specialists in mental disease.[14]

At that time, all the unjust aspects of wealth distribution that serve only to inflate egos can be dispensed with. Sounding remarkably like Marx, Keynes speculates on a three-hour workday. The difference, of course, is that Keynes thinks society can get there by managed capitalism, and Marx by its revolutionary overthrow.

In the more immediate political situation, the Labour leadership's dithering led to its downfall in 1931 and the replacement by a National Government coalition with a Labour Prime Minister, James Ramsay MacDonald.[15] Britain went off the gold standard within a few months and then implemented an austerity budget to address a crisis in the balance of payments. Keynes was gratified by the abandonment of gold and appalled at the cuts in unemployment compensation and other austerity measures that he thought would only worsen the situation.[16] He had preferred even tariffs to such a remedy.[17]

Keynes's negative judgment of government leaders came from a bitter experience with a commission formed to address the issues of the gathering depression. Keynes had begun in the twenties to develop an argument for extracting the linchpin equation of the Treasury Department view.[18] The Treasury accepted the orthodoxy that, for practical purposes, every pound saved was effectively a pound invested. So long as savings and investment were seen as equivalents, there was no room for government intervention that would decrease savings without also decreasing investment. The dictum applied to easing credit as well as to raising taxes. Both would depress savings, thus investment, and consequently economic activity. But what if they were not equivalents? What if they were affected differentially by variations in government policy?

As the storm clouds gathered over the economy, Keynes was called to testify before, and participate in, various commissions and committees. One of his suggestions was to form an Economic Advisory Council to see Britain through the crisis following the U.S. stock market collapse. The government obliged and went one step further at his request in the summer of 1930, forming a small Council of Economists to formulate policy proposals. This initiative marked the arrival of the discipline of economics as a scientific approach to policy. For the rest of the century, economists would never be far from the centers of power in the counsels of the West.

While most of the committee members were at least congenial to Keynes's ideas for policy, one was not: Lionel Robbins, a believer in the emerging Austrian school of economics.[19] Robbins's intervention on the council was fateful for England. Keynes had hoped to smoothly orchestrate the conclusions by a masterly analysis that would lead to a unanimous report. Robbins objected to the majority's recommendation of an active policy to stimulate demand. He was supported in this by Otto Niemeyer, testifying to the council in Keynes's absence, who, while he was at it, defended Britain's return to gold and a high rate of parity. Keynes was furious. Even the Treasury chiefs had muted their opposition to an activist approach, yet here was Robbins throwing a spanner into the works.[20] Worse, he was complicit with Keynes's dedicated enemies.

In the course of the deliberations, Keynes picked up an argument from colleagues, Richard Kahn and James Meade, to the effect that the primary increase in employment due to government spending on public works might well generate a secondary increase of the same magnitude because of increased consumer spending. The workers on the road projects would put their wages into food, clothing, and other goods and services, until the "leakages" to imports and the dole caused the effect to disappear. This came to be called by Keynes "the multiplier" and would henceforth play an important role in the substance, and the rhetoric, of the case for activist government.[21] It was a useful counter to the argument that public investment from taxes would simply displace private consumption and investment. In effect, by creating money from deficit financing and with the added effect of the multiplier, there would be a net stimulus to economic activity. Given the presumption that there was unused productive capacity in the economy due to the slump, the argument acquired fresh legitimacy. That the multiplier magnified the effect meant that the piper needed less pay for his happier tune.

As a result of the division in the council's deliberations, however, the government declined to follow its recommendations for a hike in tariffs and expanded public works, and England had no immediate New Deal to combat the depression.[22] As it happened, the policy that was followed eventually came around to the same remedies. First came cheap money and budget cuts, the classical remedy; then came the introduction of tariffs, which did work to the extent that unemployment was cut in half in the mid-thirties; and then, finally, the government proposed additional public spending in 1935.[23]

Robbins later admitted that he was wrong in his dissent and that his error was the result of his becoming

> the slave of theoretical constructions which . . . were inappropriate to the total situation which had then developed and which therefore misled my judgment. . . . The basic theory from which these unhappy conclusions seemed to flow . . . had recently been given much greater coherence by the work by . . . von Mises and Hayek, in which the coming into existence of this "real" disproportionality was explained in terms of a failure of money rates of interest to reflect adequately the relation between the disposition to save and the disposition to invest. Presented in this way, the explanation acquired much greater appearance of completeness and logical force.[24]

Robbins concluded that the policy prescriptions that resulted from this error were "as unsuitable as denying blankets and stimulants to a drunk who has fallen into an icy pond, on the ground that his original trouble was overheating."[25]

After the 1931 victory for the conservative elements of the National Government, Keynes offered selective assistance to members of the Labour Party and a good deal of intellectual patronage to those who were shaping its agenda. He reproved Labour's leadership for ignoring the new economic insights available from himself and others in favor of taking socialist orthodoxy at face value, the better to sharpen the distinction of interests based on class.

He told them in person at a socialist gathering in 1932 that most of their goals could be reached by redistributive policies and capital controls without the need for all out class warfare.[26]

Retreating a bit from direct action in politics, he returned to his base area of competence: economics. Keynes and Hayek debated the monetary and other aspects of the crisis over a series of exchanges in the journal *Economica* from 1931 to 1933. The realities of the depression came home again after a brief improvement consequent on the devaluation of the currency and the retreat from the gold standard in 1931. By 1933, the economy was even more seriously distressed.

Keynes stepped again into the debate, this time in public rather than behind the doors of the committee room, with a pamphlet "The Means to Prosperity." Notable as much for a change in tone as for its specifics, Robert Skidelsky captures the new style: "Bloomsbury wit, digs at stupid bankers, mad politicians and so on were put aside in favour of a wholly serious, unadorned development of his case. . . . At fifty, the *enfant terrible* was acquiring gravitas."[27]

The advent in America of the New Deal in March of 1933, under the charismatic leadership of President Franklin Delano Roosevelt, sparked a fresh optimism in Keynes. He penned an "open letter" to the President that was published in the *Times*:

> Mr. Roosevelt has made himself the trustee for those in every country who seek to mend the evils of our condition by reasoned experiment within the framework of the existing social system. If he fails, rational change will be gravely prejudiced throughout the world, leaving orthodoxy and revolution to fight it out. But if he succeeds new and bolder methods will be tried everywhere.[28]

Keynes goes on to probe the question as to whether the President is spending too much political capital on "reform" of the underlying capitalist system and not enough on "recovery." He proposes that a successful recovery would propel the reform of basic institutions, but that reform attempted before recovery might well fail by undermining the confidence of the business community. Recovery would require an even greater stimulus to demand than Keynes observes presently.

Others among Britain's intellectual pantheon were not so sure about Roosevelt. William Beveridge, according to his biographer Jose Harris, thought that Roosevelt's program amounted to a mass of contradictions between "inflation and deflation, expansion and contraction" that would undermine the foundations of capitalism. The hard-lining Beatrice Webb, who had become convinced that only Soviet-style planning could tackle such fundamental systemic problems, joined him in this view.[29] Roosevelt, for his part, was deeply suspicious of the British Empire and of the aristocracy that ran it.[30] The President's affinity for Laski no doubt owed something to the professor's establishment-baiting rhetoric. With Keynes, he could not be so sure whether the don's clever rationales were not just another excuse for propping up the overextended empire.

These conflicting views among the elite aside, Keynes was becoming a hero to his students. The style was captivating. Sir Alec Cairncross remembered him as the brilliant lecturer:

> He had a resonant and melodious voice, lecturing conversationally in a matter-of-fact way without gestures. The argument was developed lucidly and systematically, assisted by an occasional witticism, doses of what he called "symbolic arithmetic" and once in a while by reflections on one of his predecessors or by a flight into philosophic speculation. . . . Keynes mistrusted intellectual rigour of the Ricardian type as likely to get in the way of original thinking and saw that it was not uncommon to hit on a valid conclusion before finding a logical path to it.[31]

The notoriety of Professor Keynes, the economist, earned him a meeting with President Roosevelt when he visited the United States in 1934. His work had been recommended by his acquaintances from an earlier visit in 1931, Felix Frankfurter and Walter Lippmann. Frankfurter arranged the Roosevelt appointment as a way of counteracting the vitriol about the New Deal that Keynes had encountered in a 1931 visit to Wall Street.[32] David Felix in his *Biography of an Idea: John Maynard Keynes and the General Theory* records that the President and the English economist were rather "baffled" by each other. Keynes spent the hour reciting figures and summing up key variables that he noted Roosevelt seemed not quite to grasp. Roosevelt was observant of the man and his usefulness politically, even if his economic analysis was not particularly comprehensible. As it was, they were headed along the same path, and their reputations became steadily more intertwined.[33]

Keynes was in fact quite taken with the New Deal. He returned to England filled with the sense that in America

> not in Moscow, is the economic laboratory of the world. The young men who are running it are splendid. I am astonished at their competence, intelligence and wisdom. One meets a classical economist here and there who ought to be thrown out of [the] window—but they mostly have been.[34]

The depression revealed to all the fecklessness of conventional economic analysis. Keynes, the outlier in the profession, was now consolidating his personal and professional resources to meet the great crisis of his era. The depression summoned forth all the ingenuity and character he could muster and seated in his persona the qualities that would prepare him for the even greater crisis of World War II. In 1933 and 1934, he formulated the critical ideas that would become known with the publication in 1936 of *The General Theory*.[35]

Clearly, a systematic rethinking was called for. Keynes, who had grown up with Alfred Marshall, the lion of economic orthodoxy, literally at the dinner table in Harvey Road, took it as his mission to find a new path for Britain and then the West.[36] His disputes with Marshall were not just arid academic debates or personal skirmishes but also confrontations with the authorities of his youth. It was as if intelligence could conquer everything—even the verities by which he had been raised.

Rejected by capitalists and socialists alike for tampering with the orthodoxies underlying conventional economics, yet vindicated by his prophecies on the consequences of Versailles and of the gold standard, Keynes was driven to an all-out assault on orthodoxy itself. High unemployment and the depression, in Keynes's view, followed from the Versailles Peace Treaty and from the ineptness of capitalists and party leaders alike in responding to new conditions. The division among economists prevented a unified intervention. In 1936, Maynard Keynes responded with his masterpiece, *The General Theory of Employment, Interest, and Money,* detailing a system of macroeconomics that would permit the regulation of the economy so that massive unemployment would never again become a problem.

He set out to uproot orthodoxy and, with typical bravado, informed his reader of the attractions of the policy he was about to attack:

> That it (economic orthodoxy) reached conclusions quite different from what the ordinary uninstructed person would expect, added, I suppose, to its intellectual prestige. That its teaching, translated into practice, was austere and often unpalatable, lent it virtue. That it was adapted to carry a vast and consistent logical superstructure, gave it beauty. That it could explain much social injustice and apparent cruelty as an inevitable incident in the scheme of progress, and the attempt to change such things as likely on the whole to do more harm than good, commended it to authority. That it afforded a measure of justification to the free activities of the individual capitalist, attracted to it the support of the dominant social force behind authority.[37]

The orthodox doctrine made everything but sense. Keynes proposed to redeem the discipline from this devastating folly.

Remember the policy problem placed before him. The higher wages consequent on war spending could only be sustained without raising unemployment if investment could be supplied in sufficient quantity to bring up the level of demand. But the means to increased investment seemed to involve plundering savings through taxes—a contradiction of orthodoxy. The key was to unlock nonproductive savings either by regulatory schemes or by substituting government spending on public goods paid for through borrowing and taxation, until prosperity itself would right the balance.

The answer lay in a refutation of the equivalence of savings and investment. Keynes did this by pointing out that equivalence functions only at full employment. By inventing the concept of "effective demand," he opened up a disjunction between savings and investment. Given a certain amount of available savings, effective demand drives the proportion of savings that will be invested. Noninvested savings increase when effective demand is low. Low demand creates a psychology in which savers pull back from investment. Uncertainty, the ubiquitous adversary of rational calculation, undermines the equilibration of supply and demand. Unless effective demand changes, the market can become stabilized at a level below full employment.[38]

In fact, as Donald Moggridge makes clear, Keynes had gone through four steps to get to his conclusions in the general theory. First, he observed that consumption generally rises faster than income, since the psychological effect of increasing income is to reduce the incentive to save, leading people to use credit more freely. Second, he came to the notion of effective demand and the salutary effect of the multiplier in conditions of suboptimal production. By redistributing purchasing power from those with less propensity to consume, the cautious rich, to those who are eager to spend, the underemployed poor, effective demand will be increased.

Third, Keynes rethought the economic meaning of interest. Conventional economists see interest as "the price of credit." Raised interest rates reduce borrowing, and lowered interest rates encourage it. Keynes conceptualized interest as "the measure of liquidity preference." Interest rates rise when people would rather spend than save, and rates fall when savings are more desirable. Since this happens somewhat independently of the level of employment, underinvestment can be the result of low interest rates—a contradiction of convention with considerable policy consequences.[39]

Finally, Keynes worked out the idea of "the marginal efficiency of capital." Without engaging the technical details, his point was that capital is invested based on *prospective* rates of return, not current rates. It is, therefore, heavily influenced by expectations that are shaped by a variety of economic conditions more than they are by the present interest rate.[40]

All four of these points lead in the direction of intervention to shape the allocation of resources so as to activate unused capacity and to bolster expectations and therefore stimulate private spending and investment. Keynes's policies would take from the rich, who save too much and prefer liquidity to investment in difficult times, and give to the poor, who would like to consume, but cannot.[41]

Keynes rejects the notion that falling wages would right the economy. The complex trade-offs between falling wages, reduced demand, the differential propensity to consume on the part of workers and bosses, and the effect on real wages of the numerous factors influencing prices—all add up to a case for dismissing the simple laissez-faire view. The only demand factor he concedes might be improved would arise from a falling rate of interest consequent on lower wages, and this same result could be achieved by expanding the money supply. Wage deflation had not worked in the United States from 1929 to 1933, so as Mark Blaug reports, the ground was well prepared among professional economists for the reception of Keynes's alternative view.[42]

Paradoxically, the only system where there would be a direct trade-off between reduced wages and increased demand arising from lower prices would be in a closed, authoritarian system. Keynes wryly observes that "is only in a highly authoritarian society, where sudden, substantial, all-round changes could be decreed that a flexible wage policy could function with success."[43] In any event, by 1936, nobody except Hayek was seriously proposing that workers be further disadvantaged.

The political situation, meanwhile, had become a bit clearer. The 1935 election nearly finished off the Liberals to the benefit of the Conservatives who added 10 percent to their vote. The Labour Party was restored to its 1929 position in terms of vote share, but not of seats. The result was the continuation of a Conservative-dominated National Government coalition led by Stanley Baldwin.[44] The 1935 election was to form the governing coalition for the next decade because of the exigencies of World War II.

What was to be fortified by *The General Theory*, the political economy of the "middle way," was in eclipse as a governing alternative after the 1935 election. The big losers were the Liberals whose leader, the indefatigable Lloyd George, was now a public advocate of Keynesianism. They received only twenty seats. A smart young conservative named Harold Macmillan had stolen their thunder. Macmillan crafted a conservative manifesto that embraced the middle way of moderate regulation allied to traditional authority.[45]

The die was cast for a system of two-party politics. But the clarification of British politics along class lines meant that the next crisis, the war, would involve more serious compromises for Britain's ruling elites. Baldwin, a conservative who understood noblesse oblige, recognized the need to appeal to the working class. His successor as Prime Minister in May 1937, the rigidly orthodox Neville Chamberlain, did not.[46] The coalition government was to become a jousting ground for divergent and rival tendencies that were to weaken the Conservative cause in the 1945 election.

Keynes, now in his fifties, was operating at peak level and engaged in a massive overhaul of the discipline of economics amid a deepening crisis in the political and material fortunes of his age. What the mind was willing to attempt, the body was not able to support. In May 1937, having felt several warning symptoms, he suffered a major coronary thrombosis. The weakness of his heart forced him to withdraw at least partially on all fronts: less business activity, fewer lectures, and a more limited role as editor and writer. Lydia became his guardian, protector, and manager.[47] His eminence assured, he would now focus only on the most essential activities, with his followers often picking up the slack as the Keynesian revolution in political economy took hold and spread.

As war approached, the intellectual formations that would bolster the ideological combatants in the postwar world were forming up in the economics profession. Keynes and his followers were a rising force. In opposition there was the remnant of classical liberals who would regroup around Friedrich Hayek. He became their designated leader as the war engulfed Europe.[48] However, the more obvious political movement of the thirties was the increasingly militant socialism articulated most persuasively by Harold Laski.

5.2 – LASKI: THE MODERATE MILITANT

In Harold Laski's scripted view, World War I was the tragic revelation of the greed and violence that flows from capitalism. In the thirties, he came to visualize the state as the only entity powerful enough, if directed by the working class, to contain the power of capitalists. The depression demonstrated the instability of capitalism, and the inability of its patrons to confront the need for reform. Yet he initially demurred on the question of outright statist control of the economy.[49]

Increasingly radical in his politics, Laski became a powerful polemicist, confidant, and nettlesome critic of prime ministers as well as of President

Roosevelt. A leader among British Labourites, he was on stage for all the major political dramas of the 1930s. As the American historian Carl Becker observes, Laski is "omnipresent and omnivocal" on the left.[50] Max Beloff established the legend that the thirties were "the age of Laski."[51] As Norman Birnbaum comments, Laski is "the dramaturge of the left" who decried the sins of capitalism, even while holding out hope for a more humane, democratic, and sensible future.[52]

The defining element of Laski's story in the thirties is his uncertain progress toward a Marxist stance—a position he was to embrace, in a significantly tempered form, by the end of the decade. An enthusiast of the Russian revolution, he was still sufficiently critical of Stalinism that his endorsement of the regime was qualified and hesitant. On the home front, however, he pressed ever more stridently for direct government intervention to resolve the economic crisis.

Faith in conventional democracy was wearing thin. Ingrained inequality was eating at its foundations. "Our inegalitarian system corrodes the conscience of the rich by extracting ransom from them; and it destroys the creativeness of the poor by emphasizing their inferiority in the very conference of benefit." It is a declining system no longer "supported by the authority of religion." The system of allegiances is hostage to "the growth of education [which] is increasingly destructive of deference."[53] Still, he is not bereft of faith. "We must rather have faith in the power of reason to direct the human spirit to the prospects of concession and sacrifice. We must rather seek to persuade our masters that our equality is their freedom."[54]

Laski's attitude toward private property and profit moved in the direction of a socially defined justification. Writing in 1930, in an essay called "The Dangers of Obedience," he states his view:

> Property, we are beginning to say, is justifiable where it results from effort made for ends and in ways of which the community approves. We are beginning to look upon it not, as in the American Constitution, as a sacred right, but as a return made to one who performs a function that society regards as beneficent. We are seeking, that is to say, such a regulation of the profit-making motive as will make the business man the servant, and not the master, of the state.[55]

While Keynes and Hayek were inclined to see profit, and the institution of property that underlay it, as a bolster to productivity, Laski was looking for a way of reconciling notions of rights with concepts of need and justice. For Laski property was an economic "return to function," and the function was its contribution to meeting social need. Keynes and Hayek are more diffident about what would motivate someone to accumulate profit, though Keynes, as we have seen, was unimpressed by those who fail to use their capital productively.

Along the way, Laski, perhaps unwittingly, paraphrases Rousseau who famously remarks about inequality: "Wealth should never be so great that a man can buy his neighbor, nor so lacking that a man is compelled to sell himself."[56] In Laski's words, "it [wealth] must never be so large in amount that its possessor exercises power merely by reason of its magnitude; and it must never be so small that its possessor is bound hand and foot to material appetite."[57] Perhaps remembering the class differences in Manchester and the winters in Montreal with a sick child and doctor's bills, Laski points toward the compulsion of material need as the key element, rather than psychological subordination per se.

The slide toward the left in Laski's thoughts also has to do with his weakening attachment to notions of benign, class-based authority and his increasing belief in the ability of scientifically trained intellectuals to manage society in an equitable fashion. As early as 1919, he was puzzled about the problem of "centralized authority." "It is so baffled by the very vastness of its business as necessarily to be narrow and despotic and over-formal in character."[58] At times he expressed a certain faith in the power of extraordinary individuals, even aristocrats, to manage well. As Kramnick and Sheerman report, he gravitated toward a kind of proxy democracy:

> Laski would ultimately . . . opt for a third alternative: government by the working class or at least government for them by their intellectual sponsors. This meant, in others words, government by people like himself, in whom he began to see all the best qualities of the aristocracy, charm and altruism, but mediated by a thorough-going twentieth-century scientific education.[59]

The problem of self-interest is not directly addressed here, except to suggest that "scientific education," together with certain qualities of character and intellect, would enable decision makers to operate in an accountable and democratic manner.

Laski's solution, at this point, was to use the methods of political democracy to change the power relations involved in the production of goods and services. He wanted "to introduce representative institutions both into socialized industries and those which remain under private management."[60] Fixated on the unequal power relations involved in production, Laski would not grasp a key distinction. A method designed to facilitate deliberation may have its uses in business, but it is not the same as a method to elicit and direct the forces of production efficiently. Governance and enterprise proceed by differing logics and by making distinctly separate claims on people's time and energies.

The debate was growing less and less theoretical and becoming quite real with unemployment skyrocketing. In the United States the depression arrived with Republicans in power, and the electorate could visit their outrage on the party of business. In Britain, a Labour-led National Government bore the brunt of the collapse at the end of the twenties. Laski was convinced that the bankers were behind it. There was a run on the pound, and the *Times* in particular placed the blame on the refusal to lower social benefits, namely the dole. Laski believed he had the evidence that the run was precipitated by the Bank of England as a deliberate attack on Labour's majority in the Parliament and the coalition cabinet.[61]

Unable to agree to cuts in unemployment insurance, the minority Labour government fell in 1931. In a complex set of maneuvers, MacDonald suddenly resigned and was immediately reappointed by the king as the head of a coalition dominated by the Conservatives. A month later, Britain abandoned the gold standard and implemented an austerity budget. Laski saw these moves as the result of hysteria set up by the bankers and the media to displace Labour. The pound lost more than a quarter of its value in three months.[62]

As Laski's friend, Kingsley Martin, notes, "the defection of MacDonald . . . hit the rank-and-file with all the impact of treachery. [These events] only proved to convinced Socialists that Labour would meet with backstairs opposition from bankers if it sought to overcome the capitalist's financial crisis without reducing the workers' standard of living."[63] The loss of face for Labour partisans was profound, but there was no reliable alternative. The leader of the government, Labour's MacDonald, called an election in October and led the coalition to victory over its critics on the left. Laski had hoped for 240 Labour seats in the election, and the result was a disastrous 46.[64] The voters had wreaked havoc on the Labour Party and given the Conservatives a huge increase in seats, thereby continuing the National Government as a puppet of the right. The British electorate, in the face of economic crisis, was not ready to trust the socialists.

Any remaining illusion that Laski's pluralist utopia might be feasible in England was dashed by the 1931 election. A divided Labour Party and a discredited Liberal Party were demolished by the Conservatives. Austerity measures were implemented as a means of restoring Britain's international credit. Thereafter, Laski claimed that the depression proved for all to see the bankruptcy of capitalism and the cynicism of the ruling class. The value of the pound was hostage to the financiers who demanded cuts in benefits to

the working class as the price of recovery, and this in the face of an unemployment rate that escalated to 22.5 percent. Rather than democratic socialism advancing through government, even a government led by a Labour
Minister became the agency for enforcing capitalism's priorities.[65] At this
point, George Bernard Shaw proclaimed himself, in a letter to Laski, a
Communist.[66]

While Lenin and Stalin beguiled intellectuals, the fascination of British
elites for Benito Mussolini—including Winston Churchill who put up his picture at Chartwell for a time—confirmed Laski's despair about the decline of
democracy.[67] Laski had referred to Churchill as a "pinchbeck Mussolini" in a
commentary on the General Strike.[68] That Churchill himself was arguing for
a retreat from full democracy to an electorate "weighted in favour of the
'more responsible elements,'" suggests that Laski's pessimism was at least
partly justified.[69]

Jettisoned along with moderation was the theory of the pluralist state. Laski
had come to see that according participative sovereignty to groups within society was effectively to confer legitimacy on entities such as the Nazi Party
in Germany. Traveling in Germany, "my views began to change. My answer
to the question, 'Whoever knew truth worsted in a free encounter' became a
two-fold answer. First, I had known truth worsted; and second, rarely was the
encounter a free one."[70] He decided, on a reading of the *Federalist*, written in
defense of the newly drafted U.S. Constitution, that property relations were at
the heart of the ostensibly pluralist federal system. He became persuaded that
"the Marxist theory of the state was unanswerable, and that a pluralistic theory was only valid when a society had attained approximate equality within
itself." Genuine pluralism could not arrive until "the broad interest of the
members was an equal interest."[71]

Struggling to define his conception of socialism, Laski set down a view
that turned on the relative significance of individual claims and social need:

> I understand by Socialism the deliberate intervention of the State in the
> process of production and distribution in order to secure an access to their
> benefits upon a consistently wider scale. From this angle, it is clear that no
> theories are entitled to be regarded as socialist which are not distinguished by
> at least two features. They must admit the right, and duty, of the State to sub-
> ordinate individual claim [*sic*] to social need, not as an occasional incident of
> its operation but as a permanent characteristic of its nature; and they must, in
> the second place, seek the deliberate and continuous reconstruction of social
> institutions to the end of satisfying social demand upon the largest possible
> scale.[72]

Among the various grounds on which socialism has been defined, Laski's definition is distinctive for what it emphasizes and for what it leaves out. The question of individual versus collective claims and needs is, as Rodney Barker points out in cataloging the various strands of socialist argument, only one issue among many. Other principal issues include the relative importance of labor and property, the matters of equality and justice, a belief in cooperation and fraternity, and the commitments to the transformation of work—and to social democracy via working-class political power. There are also distinctively socialist beliefs about rationalization and efficiency, working-class culture, the politics of personal relations, and, finally, the relationships between plans, liberty, and markets.[73]

The theme of self-subordination has an almost psychological cast to it. However, Laski seems to want not to *subordinate* the individual person's psyche so much as to *enable* as many individuals as possible to share in the bounty that is possible through rationalized social production. The subordination of personal claims to collective need is not an end in itself, but a means toward the end of satisfying social demand. The reasons for this subordination are not the unworthiness of individuals and their claims, but rather the fact that production arises out of complex interdependencies in society and, therefore, has a social character to start with.

That said, there is no real explanation of how individuals are to be brought around to working productively when their work is directed from above, how the disposition of their work product is determined by a process of social control, and how the payback received is apportioned by a determination of need rather than effort. Laski could be inventive about the institutional arrangements involved in these transactions, but his explanation never quite reaches the motivational sources of human behavior.

As with many socialists, he hopes to achieve by persuasion a transformation of attitudes that will bridge the discontinuities between personal aspiration and social consciousness, and between the privileges of the rich and the powerlessness of the working class: "We must rather have faith in the power of reason to direct the human spirit to the prospects of concession and sacrifice. We must rather seek to persuade our masters that our equality is their freedom."[74]

Projecting his views onto the international stage, Laski wrote a tract in 1931 for the Fabian Society that envisioned the steady growth of world government. Reflecting the "one-world" mentality of many contemporary intellectuals and political progressives, he predicted that expertise would displace the politics of sovereignty and self-interest. Expert panels would feed data to statesmen skilled in balancing the considerations of principle, practicality, scientific analysis, and political realities. What is interesting in view of later developments is his argument that

> The expert, in short, remains expert upon the condition that he does not seek to co-ordinate his specialism with the total sum of human knowledge. The moment that he seeks that co-ordination he ceases to be an expert. . . . The Wisdom that is needed for the direction of affairs is not an expert technic [*sic*] but a balanced equilibrium. It is a knowledge of how to use men, a faculty of judgment about the practicability of principles. It consists not in the possession of specialised knowledge, but in a power to utilise its results at the right moment, and in the right direction.[75]

Rather than situating governance in a pyramid of ascending knowledge with the expert at the top, Laski sees that there are differing realms of activity, of which the accumulation of facts is but one, and that the essential task for government is to bring these varying influences into harmony with social goals. Technical organizations, representative assemblies, and statesmen would each play a part in responding to the logic of necessity and rationality in planning the use of the world's resources. For Laski and Keynes, if not for Hayek, political judgment is an essential element, distinct from knowledge per se, in the art of governance.

As the fateful decade proceeded, Laski became convinced that democracy and capitalism could no longer coexist, and he saw the rise of fascism as a symptom of their incompatibility.[76] He became an antagonist of the existing British state and an advocate of a new regime with strong powers to override property relations. He was creating a tide of sentiment that trended to the radical left. A public opinion poll at the time indicated that if forced to choose, three-quarters of the public would take communism over fascism.[77]

At this point also, the split in the Labour Party between its militant and moderate wings took institutional form. The moderates led by Hugh Dalton and Herbert Morrison took control of the party's National Executive Committee (NEC) and brought in young economists influenced by Keynes as well as by Hayek. Among them was Hugh Gaitskell, destined to be a postwar leader of the party.[78] Laski and his Socialist League allies pressured the Labour Party to move left.[79] Publications under their name, including a manifesto written by Laski, agitated for a radical alternative to existing politics. He published a frankly political book, *Democracy in Crisis* (1932), to make the point in detail. Reacting to the split with the NEC, Laski prophesied: "In the long run it is going to mean the break-up of the Labour Party."[80]

The battle lines were clearly drawn, and Laski would spend the rest of his life engaged in skirmishes as much internally within the movement, as externally with the forces of reaction. The combat between capitalism and socialism and between socialism and communism would now spread to all fronts. Laski continued improbably to hope that a socialist victory would come through the ultimate acquiescence of capital rather than revolutionary violence.[81]

Maynard Keynes wrote to him that year to express sympathy with his aspirations for world government, but to take exception to his view that overcoming capitalism was a prerequisite. "I find it hard to conceive any civilization without capitalism, i.e. without private property and interests." He assured Laski that "international financiers, as far as I have come across them, [are] perfect lambs."[82] For Laski, by contrast, world government required the establishment of democratic socialism as a precondition. He had become persuaded that capitalism was the cause of war and that capitalists were people of evil intent, a reductionist argument that edged him ever closer to a Leninist position on the imperative of revolution.[83]

Laski's lectures and weekly newspaper columns in the *Daily Herald* raised his public visibility to the point where there were comments in Parliament and a dustup with the LSE administration. His columns were often witty pen portraits of the notables of the day; though there was a sharp edge to his political remarks. The acquisition of a mass following was to have mixed consequences. On a trip to Russia with Frida in 1934, the LSE professor lectured his Soviet hosts on democratic socialism and the requirement that freedom of thought always be permitted. While this part of his talk was denounced by his sponsors as a criticism of the Communist Party, Laski also alluded to how, in England, the "gentlemen of England" were given to changing the rules of democracy when their side appeared in danger of losing.

This reference to the 1931 election, in the context of some exaggerated media accounts of his talks, led King George V to seek an account of Laski's views from the LSE administration.[84] Questions in Parliament and letters to the editor led to an LSE inquiry. As a consequence, Laski, though unrepentant, agreed to give up his paying relationship with the *Daily Herald*. Support for Laski on academic freedom grounds was forthcoming from, among others, George Bernard Shaw and Maynard Keynes.[85] Laski wrote Keynes saying that his letter had "moved me greatly."[86]

Notwithstanding his support, Keynes was becoming a threat from Laski's point of view. His views were attractive to middle-class intellectuals as an alternative to class warfare and the strong state. Laski took on

Keynes directly in 1934 in the unlikely venue of the American *Redbook* magazine. They took opposing sides on whether America could "spend its way to recovery." Keynes made the arresting point that nobody produces anything if someone is not spending to buy it. Governments inevitably go into debt during depressions because they pay the social costs of poverty. Why not spend the money stimulating production instead and get the benefit of lowering unemployment?

Laski's response is a curious amalgam of orthodoxy in economic analysis and of militancy in the cause of socializing the means of production. Government spending might produce an uptick in employment for a while, but "it raises grave financial problems; it may mean inflation, or heavy taxation, or wasteful expenditure, or all of these things; it may mean an unbalanced budget *with the disturbance of confidence* [italics added]."[87] Thus accepting the conventional view of how the economy would respond, Laski sees the costs of such a policy ultimately being visited on the working class through a reduction in social welfare expenditures. The only real answer, he says, is a planned society and this could only be achieved by public ownership of the means of production. Thus, he dismisses Keynes's moderate approach without really supplying a convincing account of the economics of socialism.[88]

Democracy had a meaning rooted in Laski's particular kind of class consciousness. He essayed the role of the gentleman in a short piece written in 1932. Here one can find a kind of visceral animosity to the upper classes that leads him even to attack the virtues that a friend of democracy might wish to praise: "The gentleman's tenacious hold on power has given him something like an instinctive knowledge of when compromise and concession are desirable." These virtues are laid at the door of cunning rather than wisdom or virtue. It is the attitude of superiority that appears to drive his animus: "Until, at any rate, the outbreak of the War, the gentleman had persuaded the world to believe that he was the final term of human evolution." A mix of Puritan and aristocrat, the gentleman possesses "a certain mature graciousness."[89]

He proceeds to find gentlemen wanting in the skills of innovation, rigorous analysis, scientific discipline, and organizational mentality. They are, above all, overconfident. Though better masters than the Gradgrinds and Bounderbys of Coketown, the gentleman remains "a public danger to England" who no longer, in view of the challenges England faces, "has a useful function to perform."[90] One can see, in a mirror so to speak, the traits Laski prefers and, indeed, would like to ascribe to himself. Bold, logical, intrepid analyst, icon of solidarity, and humble. Others did not see Laski that way, and for many besides gentlemen, the willingness to throw overboard attributes of faith, doing one's duty, piety, and loyalty to others might seem self-indulgent.

Laski was not attracted to this sort of moderation. In 1935, reaching a new height in his militancy, he published an attack on reformism of the Keynesian variety. In his *The State in Theory and Practice*, he declaimed:

> I believe that we have reached a phase in the history of capitalism when this contradiction between class-structure and potential productivity is insoluble in terms of the present social order. . . . I do not . . . believe, as Mr. Keynes believes, that there is an inherent tendency in all large-scale public enterprise to develop an ethical practice in which private interest is subordinated to an abstract and objective social good.[91]

Laski here footnotes a discussion in Keynes's *The End of Laissez-Faire* (1926) in which he notes the tendency for large public corporations to divorce stockholders from managers and for the latter to become more sensitive to public criticism and the complaints of customers than to the need to aggrandize stock value beyond a conventional rate of return.[92]

Laski also derided Hayek's and Robbins's views of the limited state as the complement to capitalism, arguing instead that it was state coercion that maintained capitalism. The real functioning of the capitalist state needed to be exposed so that it might be transformed in the service of socialist goals. The transformation, he forecast, would come either by consent or, far more likely, by revolution.[93]

Most especially since 1932, Laski had been controversial at LSE. By the mid-thirties he had become, in the mind of Beveridge, LSE's strong-willed Director, responsible for a historic violation of the school's mission. He urged Laski, Robbins, and the other political activists to refrain from partisan disputes "as inconsistent with the scientific outlook."[94] In his parting shot as he left the directorship in 1937, Beveridge pointed to Laski, present on the stage, as responsible for undermining the detachment essential to the social sciences. But Laski was not his only target; Beveridge turned on Keynes, not present, for forsaking observation for theory. Neither approach, he thought, would serve the best purposes of the social sciences.[95] Politicization of the study of politics was as likely to bias inquiry as the theorization of economics. Both politics and economics were, in Beveridge's view, eminently practical pursuits that demanded the rigorous discipline of trained observer, the skepticism of a scholar, and the dispassionate analysis that empiricism could offer.

"The effect was shattering—and saddening," according to Lionel Robbins, who took the attack as directed at himself and Hayek as much as Keynes and Laski.[96] Beveridge's successor as Director, a youthful Alan Carr-Saunders, arrived from Liverpool to find, as he reminisced years later, that he was in the position of a newly appointed vicar in a parish where the curates were the prophets Jeremiah and Ezekial, referring to Hayek and Laski.[97] Born of ideological fervor, yet with intentions of academic professionalism, LSE seemed now to be driven by partisan encampments.

Yet ideology did not blind Laski to the possibilities on the other side of the Atlantic. In Roosevelt's New Deal, he initially found the outlines of an attainable socialism that was prevented from being born in Britain by a ruling class that was alternately reactionary and ineffectual. In 1935, Laski, through his friend Frankfurter, arranged to see Roosevelt during his visit to the United States. There were to be four more meetings in the late thirties and a series of letters that received cordial responses.

Laski became an advocate for the New Deal and helped dispose public opinion favorably toward Roosevelt's experiments in governmental activism. Roosevelt was the first leader of the West who was willing to take on capitalism and laissez-faire directly. However tentative and experimental the New Deal might have been and however strong the counterattack from the minions of business, it was a courageous assertion of the need for a new kind of politics. His bitterness at the rejection of leftist solutions at home gave impetus to his endorsement of experimentation in America. Laski's prewar book on the American presidency is little else than a celebration of Roosevelt's bold leadership and a plea for its continuance.[98] Here was a leader up to the task of a "revolution by consent."

The British political scientist could now reach public opinion through another channel. His friend, Edward R. Murrow, was the newly appointed head of CBS News in Britain. Murrow was invited to a cottage the Laskis had acquired in 1935 in the village of Little Bardfield, and Laski charmed Murrow with a visit to the "most democratic" of all institutions in Britain, the village pub. Murrow brought a radio crew to the "local" and broadcast the songs of a village bard to his international audience. Laski, a regular at the pub, never, according to a colleague, "played the great man" in those environs.[99]

Roosevelt's New Deal provided one marker in the spectrum of progressive responses to the Great Depression; the revolutionary regimes of Lenin and Stalin provided the other. Laski had positioned himself on the left of the British Labour Party. However, the defining question soon became where one stood on the strategy of establishing a "popular front" that would join the efforts of the Labour Party, the Communist Party, and other like-minded movements. Initially attracted to the idea, Laski argued for the Popular Front in various venues from 1935 to 1937. However, in 1938, the matter came to a head, and the leadership of the Labour Party came out against collusion with the Communist Party. In a decision that Laski would never take back, he agreed with the leadership. His commitment to consensual change remained intact.

On the right, important segments of the British establishment, including Prime Minister Neville Chamberlain, pursued appeasement with the fascists. Yet there were powerful exceptions, as the Churchill case exemplifies. On the left, many influential figures kept a vital degree of distance from Stalinism. Both the Churchill faction of the Conservative Party, immunized by Churchill's rhetoric from participation in appeasement, and Laski's Labour Party were positioned to discredit conventional conservatives for complicity in the disaster that followed. As Laski saw it, Chamberlain's appeasement had little to do with peace and much to do with the business interests of capitalists.[100] Yet he could not be accused of taking a pro-Soviet line.

Though he retained ties with his friends on the communist left, Laski finally resisted the call for a popular front because, as Michael Newman points out, Laski realized there could not be an alliance unless "a totally new relationship with the Soviet Union had *already* been established. For he now realized that the external control of the CP meant that, in the final analysis, the interests of Stalin would prevail over any considerations of the British party leadership."[101] This signal event testified to Laski's bedrock faith in democratic politics.

The turn away from the Popular Front strategy was, for the British left, a major divide that would set Britain aside from the continental trend toward an increasingly ruthless communist movement dominated by Stalin and his agents.[102] As bitterly anticapitalist as he had become, Laski was not willing to join forces with an alien power intent on its national interest. His tactical position thus diverged from his intellectual stance. While the logic of the Marxism to which he was now attached seemed to lead straight to revolution, Laski remained an advocate of socialism by means of a democratically controlled mass movement.

The Labour Party, which had wandered in search of a coherent view ever since the 1931 debacle, was now coming together. Laski's militant line appears in the 1937 party program with its endorsement of nationalization for a limited number of basic industries and utilities. However, the manifesto was far from its namesake of 1848. The nationalization program stopped well short of the expropriation of the capitalists and the "ameliorative" and "prosperity" proposals that accompanied the "socialization" section were extensions of existing measures.[103]

While resistant to the Popular Front strategy, Laski's advocacy of leftist ideas on domestic policy through the Socialist League set him at odds with the leadership of the Labour Party. At the insistence of the leadership, the Socialist League was disbanded in 1937, but the principals continued their agitation for a broad-scale alliance among the working class, if not a Popular Front. In 1939, matters came to a head when the National Executive Council of the party expelled his League allies, Stafford Cripps and Aneurin Bevan, though not Laski himself.

While Laski steered clear of entanglement with the Communist Party per se, his intellectual position was now in camp with Marx. In 1939, he proclaimed himself a "Marxist socialist," and therefore neither a Keynesian nor a "Marxist communist."[104] He positioned himself with the doctrinaire left, but not with its premier political party. Nevertheless, the sudden announcement of Stalin's nonaggression pact with Hitler stunned Laski, who heard the announcement on the radio at a dinner party that included Hayek. Hayek reported years later that Laski had spent the preannouncement part of the dinner extolling the virtues of Russia, only to go into rhetorical reverse on receiving the news. At that moment, said Hayek, he decided Laski was not sane.[105]

Laski's declaration of his commitment to a Marxist perspective played predictably badly in the United States. On leave for a year in the United States, he was appointed amid great controversy, as a lecturer at the University of Washington in Seattle. At the urging of the Daughters of the American Revolution, Republicans in the legislature contemplated a resolution of denunciation, but settled for voting against, by a 2 to 1 margin, an invitation for him to address the solons.[106] Roosevelt, informed by his daughter Anna who was living in Seattle with her publisher husband, took delight in the contretemps. In a note to Laski, he quipped, "May the furore increase in furiosity. Come and see me as soon as you get back."[107]

The intellectual, personal, and political journey that had led Laski to the far edge of the democratic left was completed by the outbreak of war in 1939. His theory was now infused with a passion made coherent and radical by the economic and political calamities of the 1930s. A historic opportunity for climactic class struggle now appeared—not as revolution, but as another world war.

Harold Laski. Courtesy of Art & Visual Materials, Special Collections Department, Harvard Law School Library.

5.3 – HAYEK: THE FOUNDATIONS OF DISSENT

The thirties would clarify Friedrich Hayek's message as well. The steps in his journey would take him through the same events in the same country as Laski and Keynes, but from a far different perspective.

Hayek's academic work in the twenties was intended to secure what had eluded his father, an appointment to the faculty of the University of Vienna. With the publication of his first book on monetary cycles and a successful defense of his thesis, Hayek became a Privatdozent in 1929 with the right to teach at the university. This recognition amounted to a license to set up shop for tuition-paying students, though without any guarantee of income. He awaited the opening of one of the three chairs in economics at the university, a distinction usually not achieved until relatively late in life.[108]

His inaugural lecture as Privatdozent gave Hayek the chance to attack the theory he heard while in New York that recessions and depressions were the results not of overproduction, but of underconsumption.[109] The obvious policy implication pointed to the stimulation of consumption through some kind of manipulation of credit or of demand itself. In Hayek's view, this was an invitation for government, pressured by the observable decline in production, to go blundering in and upset the unseen forces of monetary adjustment. Here was a preview of what would come with greater force and sophistication in the 1930s from Keynes. As it happens, the lecture Hayek gave on his appointment to the lectureship was read by Robbins, the ambitious young head of LSE's Economics Department.

At this time, Robbins, the self-made son of English puritan parents, was involved in a portentous standoff with Keynes on the Council of Economists. Robbins tried unsuccessfully to get permission for Hayek to testify as an expert before the council. Failing that, Robbins arranged for Hayek to give a lecture at LSE. Hayek noted that "he (Robbins) pounced on my subject: This is the thing we need at the moment, to fight Keynes. So I was called in for this purpose."[110] Robbins was fascinated by Hayek's approach. Robbins recalled that "the lectures were at once difficult and exciting. The Marshall Society at Cambridge, on hearing Hayek, were much less impressed. His elaborate explanation of production streams was met with puzzlement and silence."[111]

However, at LSE Hayek "conveyed such an impression of learning and analytical invention" that Sir William Beveridge, LSE's Director, proposed Hayek for the Tooke Professorship in Economics. Robbins and his colleagues unanimously agreed.[112] Hayek's calling card just prior to taking up the professorship was a harsh critique of Keynes's *Treatise on Money* published in *Economica*, a journal edited by Robbins.[113]

Hayek and Robbins thereupon became close colleagues.[114] The two men, both in their early thirties, became neighbors raising their young families on a little square nestled in Hampstead Garden Suburb. Hayek's second child, Laurence, was born there in 1934. Ironically, the community was a planned development initiated by a social reformer, Henrietta Barnett, who thought that good living circumstances would generate good character.[115]

Later that year, Hayek traveled alone to Carinthia and visited his first love, Helene Bitterlich Warhanek. They stayed up long into the night talking of their feelings for each other and, according to her, decided then to seek a way of being together for the rest of their lives.[116] Up until the outbreak of the war, they saw each other three or four times a year, however a divorce never seemed to be within reach. The stage was set, however, for a personal crisis that would have a profound impact on Hayek's behavior after the war.

Robbins may well have been motivated in his enthusiasm for Hayek's appointment not only by his antipathy to Keynes but by his rivalry with the other young doyen of the faculty, Harold Laski. Laski, increasingly an outspoken socialist, was to political science what Robbins hoped to be for economics: a premier teacher, a creator of new styles of thought, and a public intellectual of the first rank.[117] Robbins and Laski got along together as colleagues and book collectors, even sharing the editorship of LSE's journal, *Economica*, for a time. However, their contending political views led to a divergence as the thirties wore on.[118]

Hayek and Laski became rivals, according to Beatrice Webb, and took to denouncing each other as "unrelenting propagandists."[119] Laski had foresworn such a role in the inaugural lecture for his chair in political science: "My object as the occupant of this chair is not to create a body of disciples who shall go forth to preach the particular and peculiar doctrines I happen to hold. It is rather that the student shall learn the method of testing his own faith against the only solid criterion we know—the experience of mankind."[120] Robbins never believed Laski's intentions were so pure. With Hayek aboard, Robbins now had reinforcements.

The manner and style of Hayek and Laski as two contenders for intellectual supremacy could hardly have been more distinct. A student who recorded impressions of them both described the politically outspoken, charismatic Laski as "by far the most fascinating, and as a human being he had probably the softest heart."[121] The same observer saw in Hayek a man who "wore a perpetually benevolent smile, a trait which did not belie his nature. But his English was thick and his thought appeared tangled."[122] A more partisan view is that of John Kenneth Galbraith, who participated in Hayek's seminar, though he called him "a gentle man of comprehensively archaic views." Laski, Galbraith noted, was "in notoriety . . . easily the equivalent of a dozen or so less ostentatious conservatives."[123]

A mitigating factor in the struggle, however, was that Laski stayed away from the Hayek–Keynes economic disputations—mainly because he was tending toward a Marxist analysis that bracketed both positions as inadequate attempts at stabilizing capitalism. Economics were not, in any case, his strong suit.[124] On policy matters, however, Laski did support Keynes's early proposals for revenue tariffs as a way of stabilizing the British economy.[125]

In later years, Hayek recalled that book collecting was all he and Laski could amiably discuss—"but apart from this we had nothing in common at all. We hardly spoke the same language. Don't ask me to begin to tell you stories about LSE—because of this extraordinary person Harold Laski, it was a most peculiar place." He was, Hayek thought, a "pathological liar" whose stories of amazing book finds and, later, of miraculous escapes from Hitler's bombs, were entirely made up. Nevertheless, they saw each other daily in the senior common room and "got on quite well together."[126]

Hayek's willingness to engage in public political combat quickly emerged. He was animated in part by the sense that his homeland had lost its way among the bitter extremes of left and right. These divisions would eventuate in the brief, but bloody, Austrian Civil War of 1934. England was, as he saw it, the home of the liberty that classical liberalism had promised. As an émigré carrying a burden of disappointment in his native land, Hayek had some of the zeal of the convert to a new community of faith who then takes up arms against the forces that would weaken it from within as well as without.[127]

Hayek weighed in with a scathing review of Keynes's *Treatise on Money* (1930). Hayek's put-down of the work was that "the *Treatise* proves to be so obviously—and, I think admittedly—the expression of a transitory phase in a process of rapid intellectual development that its appearance cannot be said to have that definitive significance which at one time was expected of it."[128] Keynes had jumped into the question of the divergence of savings and investment without taking into account Austrian theories of capital and interest.[129] This much was true, and Keynes would ultimately respond by outflanking the discussion with a reconceptualization of the whole cast of economics.

In the interim, Keynes responded to Hayek in kind, though not by attacking the review's substance, but by attacking Hayek's earlier work on capital theory. Keynes noted sourly in his annotated copy of Hayek's review:

> Hayek has not read my book with that measure of "good will" which an author is entitled to expect of a reader. Until he can do so, he will not see what I mean or whether I am right. He evidently has a passion which leads him to pick on me, but I am left wondering what this passion is.[130]

While the duel of reviews is mired in technicalities, a principal bone of contention was the relationship between savings and investment, Hayek's favorite sparring ground. Keynes, whose ideas at this point were still in their formative stages, could not quite find a way out of the confines of conventional theory. So long as that constraint held, Hayek had a credible critique that, perhaps, explains Keynes's petulance.[131]

But Hayek had a problem too. While his view of savings and investment had a symmetry that conveys certainty in the manner of a ticking watch, important parts of Hayek's clock are invisible to the naked eye. His formulations, such as the key notion of the natural rate of interest, belied empirical validation. Keynes, though less sure of his conceptual base, would become adept at serving up his ideas in forms that permitted statistical testing.

The result was that the controversy is replete with elliptical struggles over definitions, jousting on shifting ground, and claims of point dodging and ill intent. Hayek charges that Keynes's "exposition is so difficult, unsystematic, and obscure, that it is extremely difficult for the fellow economist who disagrees with the conclusions to demonstrate (the) exact point of disagreement and to state his objections."[132] Keynes avers that as Hayek is "finding himself being led down strange and distasteful paths, he tries to prevent himself from being dragged along any further by representing the molehills in the pathway as mountains."[133] As Ralf Dahrendorf observes, "'Nature's cure' versus the State, as it were: here were the first rounds in a bout that would last half a century."[134] It would take Keynes's *General Theory* (1936) to shift the debate to new ground. The larger battle would last for decades.

The culmination of Hayek's work in the twenties was published in 1931, entitled *Prices and Production*. Though he revised the work in view of criticisms and republished it in 1935, he later conceded that he had failed to satisfactorily account for the ways that capital is developed and deployed over the course of the business cycle.[135] Nevertheless, his efforts marked him as an economist of note. The book was introduced by Robbins and drew the fire of

Keynes who called it "one of the most frightful muddles I have ever read, with scarcely a sound proposition in it."[136] Keynes asked Piero Sraffa, a close friend and colleague, to review Hayek's book, and Sraffa did so by devastating a main argument concerning the relative unreliability of credit as a basis for economic recovery and by attacking Hayek's notion of a "natural" rate of interest. The bitter confrontation set in motion the marginalization of Hayek's economic work that would result in his isolation by the end of the thirties.[137]

The tangle with Keynes had its inauspicious beginnings with Hayek's critique of Keynes's *Treatise on Money* (1930). Given that Keynes was bent on government intervention and that Hayek was opposed, it was not likely that they would ever have sorted out their differences. As it was, the strategy of replying by attacking Hayek's book, rather than defending his own, brought the judgment from one of his old mentors, A. C. Pigou, that Keynes had engaged in "Body-line bowling. The methods of the duello."[138]

On a more immediate level, the debate was over what to do in response to Britain's depression. The Keynesian forces rejoined the debate in the summer and fall of 1932. Hayek, Robbins, and others stated the opposing view that further public spending was not called for.[139] The rival teams were established, with Keynes leading the Cambridge and Oxford forces, and Robbins and Hayek as captains of the LSE contingent.[140] As Richard Cockett notes, it was

> the crucial intellectual debate of the century in the democratic West. It clearly divided economists—and ultimately politicians—into two distinct camps; the borders set down between these two camps were to run through British politics, across party boundaries, and out into the wider democratic world, as the century unraveled."[141]

Hayek staked out his ground with an unapologetic defense of competitive markets amid the chaos of the deepening Great Depression. In 1933, his inaugural lecture at LSE foreshadowed the themes that would characterize the rest of his career. Addressing the "waste" by capitalists who replace obsolescent machinery that still has useful value with more modern technology, Hayek argues that the factors entering into such a decision involve a complex of related markets, not just the utility or cost of the machinery per se. There are the relative uses of capital as investment elsewhere; there are considerations of labor cost, maintenance, and overall productivity: "The new machinery will be introduced *not* in order to do the work of machinery which is already in existence, but because it does that work *plus* the work of a quantity of other factors which will produce elsewhere more than the new capital could have done." Only the custodian of that capital is sufficiently motivated and informed to make the choice. For these reasons, with regard to governmental efforts to protect against adverse consequences of modernization, "it is not possible to be very optimistic about the outcome."[142]

What Hayek had experienced so painfully in Austria in the twenties, namely the inability of government to calibrate its responses to economic crisis, was transposed to the situation of the West in the thirties. Hayek's contribution to the evolving discussion was to adduce economic reasons why it would be very difficult for government to play such a role, and, later in the decade, a rationale based in the uses of knowledge about why this was, in fact, an impossible task.

Seminars offered by Robbins and by Hayek at LSE became the workshops for economic theories and policy proposals. Keynes, meanwhile, had his own Cambridge "Circus" at work responding to his developing arguments, entertaining critiques, and rival ideas. Ultimately, after the publication of Keynes's *General Theory*, there would be a "Joint Seminar" between LSE and Cambridge for the purpose of narrowing the divide between the two schools.[143]

The debate over activist policy was much more than an intellectual's disagreement. Powerful financial forces were at work in the background. During the thirties, the Rockefeller Foundation played a central role in supporting LSE. The same foundation also supported L'Institut Universitaire des Hautes Etudes Internationales at Geneva that became, with von Mises on its staff, the center of the European resistance to socialist and Keynesian approaches to governmental intervention in the marketplace. William Hunold, the Director of that Institute, an ally of Hayek's, organized two conferences in the thirties specifically to refute the validity of Keynesian economics.[144]

To be convincing as a critic, however, Hayek needed more than the abstruse contentiousness of economic theory on his side. There were, indeed, many other economists who had technical reasons for doubting Keynes's views, among them Beveridge. Many of these critics were to be won over to Keynes's side as his school of thought was modified, elaborated, and popularized in the ensuing years. Certainly there was a strong political appeal in a brand of economics that promised an activist approach to the obvious crisis of the thirties, while retaining protections for property and individual freedom against the socialist program of nationalization.

There was also Keynes's restless intellect at work testing ideas, putting them out in written form, then revising his approach to take account of his own or other's reflections and critiques. Where Hayek saw his own views as unfolding along a consistent line to higher levels of sophistication, Keynes thought of himself as a pragmatist working within a framework of general assumptions and modifying specific elements as required by new evidence and insight.

Hayek was increasingly becoming a self-styled ideological gladiator. He, along with Robbins, put a stop to Beveridge's plan to acquire the library and faculty of the Frankfurt Institute because of its ties to Marxist and Freudian influences. Beveridge's reasoning was that the outstanding reputation of some of its faculty and the jeopardy some of them were in as Jews in Nazi Germany created a prima facie case for the acquisition. But for Hayek and Robbins, the intellectual orientation of the Institute's faculty was the determining consideration.[145] The advocate of freedom, it seems, had reservations about extending a lifeline to those whose views he disliked.

What is puzzling, even to Hayek years later, was his failure to respond directly to Keynes's *The General Theory* (1936). Hayek's explanation was that Keynes's announcement that he had changed his mind on a critical point had undermined Hayek's review of Keynes's earlier work. Hayek claimed to have concluded then that there was no point in investing time and energy in keeping up with Keynes's shifting positions However, later, Hayek suggested that the real reason was his own sense that Keynes had really gone beyond particular issues into a transformation of economics from the micro to the macro level.[146] Skidelsky's view is that Hayek did not want to risk the kind of attack on his own reputation that resulted from his hostile review of Keynes's *Treatise on Money*.[147]

What was at stake in the move from micro- to macroeconomics, from the economics of particular exchanges to the conceptualization of the economy as the interplay of statistical aggregates? For Hayek, it was the subordination of the significance of prices in the market. *The General Theory* "took the whole structure of relative prices for granted and provided no tools to explain changes in relative prices of their effects."[148] For Keynes, the economy reacts more to expectations concerning aggregates of supply and demand than to variations in prices, per se. Keynes had, in effect, dismissed the central element of Austrian economics and attempted to outflank his antagonist.[149]

Keynes treated prices, not as reliable indicators of underlying dynamics, but as the dependent variable in a series of equations. Each independent variable was an aggregate of factors, several of which might be distorted by human miscalculation—and corrected by clever intervention. The simple fact is that prices respond less to the interplay of supply and demand, which are equivalent taken together, but more to the *motivation* of individuals to produce and consume. Such motivations rely on changes in income and output, as well as to psychological moods and states of mind. For Keynes, prices were as likely artifice as reality. They might well be messengers, not of an immanent reality, but rather of disarray and confusion.[150]

The contrasting Austrian view was that prices are the language of economics, and their variations are to be understood according to a natural syntax of meaning and grammar. Prices sum up the whole complex interchange between knowledge, material realities, and intentions in such a way that these elements may not efficiently be separated, let alone manipulated. *Natural* prices, as opposed to manipulated prices, are the vital indicators of the economy as an organic system. *The General Theory* dismantles this system, and, in Hayek's view, lays it open to the violation of its essential function.

Though Hayek did not acknowledge the point, there was another fundamental element to the transformation precipitated by *The General Theory*. Keynes had produced a masterly application of his method of ethical probability to the problems of the depression.[151] The whole cast of the book was toward clarifying the known relationships among aggregate economic factors in such a way that action could be justified. While we cannot know for sure the prospects for, say, a given investment, we can make well-informed judgments about the likelihood that the public will react in predictable ways to its value. Armed with the knowledge of patterns of behavior seen in economic statistics, the decision maker can improve the chances of being correct to the point where the risk is acceptable in view of the observable dangers of doing nothing. Keynes cleared away a sufficient number of mysteries, in his view, such that the path to intervention was open. He placed the probabilities on his side.

Hayek, ill at ease with the translation of the scientific method into the study of society, had no alternative to offer to the faith that Keynes's progressive form of science seemed to provide. He could neither mount the systemic challenge that a refutation of Keynes required nor invoke such a powerfully attractive political solution for his side of the debate. Hayek's complex views admitted of no easy metaphor. The prescription of withdrawal from manipulation of the economy ran counter to the intuitively obvious realities evident across the economy. Individuals and companies made decisions every day that advantaged the "haves" over the "have-nots." Could these decisions not be overridden by ministers in the public good?

While *The General Theory* invited technical debate, it really changed the whole framework of discussion. Hayek had indeed been outflanked. He needed breakthroughs of his own. For Hayek, the path to a new understanding of the case for spontaneous market forces lay not in the formulas of economics but in an analogy from nature. Hayek had begun to think about how society comprised a spontaneous network of transactions as early as 1933. In

his inaugural lecture at LSE, he cast the history of political economy since
Hume and Smith in this mold:

> In short, it showed that an immensely complicated mechanism existed,
> worked and solved problems, frequently by means which proved to be the
> only possible means by which the result could be accomplished, but which
> could not possibly be the result of deliberate regulation *because nobody un-*
> *derstood them.* [italics added][152]

This passage foretells much about the premises that would guide Hayek's developing views. There is the imitation of biological evolution as the main
metaphor—adaptation solving problems that the species could not have overcome by deliberation. Finally, there is the skeptic's method of *disjunction* at
work here: reduce a complex social phenomenon to its elements and recom-
bine the elements without resorting to will or purpose or similar abstractions.
If neither Marx nor Freud would serve, there was indeed Darwin. Finally,
there is the turn toward the fundamental role of knowledge in the formulation
of deliberate action.

Hayek's remaining problem was what to do with the difference between
the *unconscious* evolution of plants and animals and the *conscious* activity of
human beings. Clearly, human intellect, knowledge, and choice *do* play a role
in the development of economic systems, among other cultural formations.
The key was to separate out intention from intellect. We do indeed apply intelligence to our choices. Nonetheless, the impossibility of having sufficient
knowledge to foresee all eventualities means that the intentions behind our
choices run afoul of happenstance and even perverse consequences. Intellect
can only be applied where there is knowledge, and knowledge is necessarily
limited. However good our intentions, they are constrained by how little we
can know.

Hayek gave voice to the economic implications of these insights in 1936 in
a speech to the London Economic Club.[153] He reached into the same foundational discussion of the nature of knowledge that prompted Keynes's progressive innovations. Keynes saw the job of intellect as weighing probabilities in an indeterminate world in order to discover the best option for action.
In his perspective, what cannot be known is beyond the pale of calculation
and therefore must yield to that which can be known. Hayek was moving in
the opposite direction. For Hayek, what one person knows is necessarily different than every other person's knowledge. Knowledge cannot efficiently be
summed up by a single mind or subset of minds. The greatest mobilization of
knowledge will occur when everyone is able to act on what they know best.

These are not diametrically opposed positions, which may be the reason why the dispute between Hayek and Keynes has never really been settled. The burden of Keynes's view rests on the necessity for choice at the boundary between the knowable and the unknowable. Rather than presuming that the unknowable necessarily holds the greater part of wisdom, Keynes, as we saw earlier, reverses the point and claims for the knowable the privileged position. With that, the skilled analyst becomes the key figure.

Hayek, by contrast, focused not on the observable, but on the observer. He saw each person as a uniquely qualified contributor to the totality of knowledge. Where Keynes stressed the role of ratiocination in extending the reach of knowledge through the estimation of probabilities, Hayek relied on a plurality of viewpoints brought into spontaneous interaction to illuminate the path society should follow. Whether such a path leads anywhere that makes sense becomes an issue that Hayek would spend the remainder of his life attempting to figure out.

Keynes never rebutted Hayek's epistemological position directly. In one respect, he did not need to. One can imagine operating on both Keynes's and Hayek's insights without finding them in conflict. In determining the best choice, it would be elemental wisdom to obtain the best-considered views of the widest possible number of directly knowledgeable individuals. To say that such knowledge cannot be aggregated by the skilled decision maker, as an economist does in estimating market behavior, is to belie all examples of expertise in whatever the field—not just in economics.

Conversely, nothing in Keynes's view requires decisions to be made by a "planner" who substitutes the judgment of one person for that of many. His preferred mode of action was to find the least intrusive form of intervention and to act on it when there was clear evidence of likely benefit, though with the possibility of changing course as new information became available. The existence of a problem was the prod to action, rather than an indication of an imbalance of "natural" forces. Keynes disliked stupidity whether it was the stupidity of failing to act when the evidence showed likely benefit *or* of acting on mindless adherence to doctrine or on irrational impulses. The latter was characteristic of the parties to Versailles, and the former of the British government when confronted with the depression. Similarly, relying on automatic, or even spontaneous, forces as a corrective to a failing economy was, in his view, just as stupid.

Hayek, on the other hand, had found his weapon. The 1936 speech was the "decisive event" that shaped his future course.[154] With the publication of Karl Popper's *The Logic of Scientific Discovery*, also in 1936, Hayek had the other tool he needed: a basis for attacking Keynes's appropriation of science and statistics for his cause. For Popper, the point of a social science was not the construction of certainties. In a world of complex phenomena, observation is too limited for that. Rather, the best application of the scientific method is in the refutation of hypotheses. Observation can tell us what is not true, but not the reverse.

But once again, Hayek had overreached the argument. Keynes never presumed that he was demonstrating a catalog of certainties. Consequently, he focused on probabilities as a basis for action. The data that underlay his calculations were used to assert relationships, but both data and relationships were testable through observation. Keynes's system met Popper's test, and indeed the modification of Keynesian economics has proceeded on this basis ever since. Hayek's metaphysical turn of mind led him to see Popper as categorically opposed to the construction of rationales for action, but he missed the heuristic value of Popper's progressive pragmatism.

The attack on rationalist "constructivism" became the dominant theme of Hayek's work as he moved further and further away from economics in the conventional sense. He broke with his mentor, von Mises, on just this point. In 1937, he published a critique of von Mises' work on the ground that it relied too much on the supposed rationality of the marketplace and not enough on the benign effects of spontaneity arising from varieties of dispersed knowledge. Hayek by now saw himself as a defender neither of the equilibrium model of the economy nor of its affinity for rational choice making, but rather of the market as a process of discovery operating through incessant trial and error to secure the survival of the species.

His apostasy from the conventions of the economists' frame of reference may have been driven in part by his increasing isolation at LSE. His principal sympathizers, even the translator of one of his books, were falling in with Keynes. Doctoral students defected. His one remaining disciple, Ludwig Lachmann, makes the plaintive observation that Hayekians were everywhere at LSE in the early thirties and, by the end of the decade, gone but for him and his master.[155]

Meanwhile, subtlety was rapidly disappearing from the political scene. Austria had become immersed in the swirling politics of fascism and communism to the point of civil war in 1934. Choosing sides became a social necessity. Hayek learned that his mother had been converted to Naziism by a friend.[156] He was in Vienna in 1938 and saw Hitler's enthusiastic reception at the Heldenplatz. The subsequent *Anschluss* and the enthusiastic participation of Austrians in Naziism ended any hope that Hayek might have had for the political salvation of his native land. Hitler, a son of Austria, now triumphed over the left, the old state, the establishment, and even the churches, with a new faith based on race, nationalism, and authoritarianism. Austria was now in the grip of a new *Reich* that would make the state the arbiter of every aspect of life.[157] Hayek departed his cultural patrimony for good and became an English citizen in 1938.

In England, as the depression ground on and war clouds darkened over Europe yet again, there was predictably little sympathy for a defense of the market. Rather the issues were played out against the background of class analysis. The dominant strain of intellectual commentary saw fascism and communism as the two opposed excesses: the one of the capitalists and their reactionary allies, and the other of the mobilized working class. Democratic socialism became, in this Laskian perspective, the centrist position.

Hayek dissented and joined in an effort to rally the defense of classical liberal ideals. A group of intellectuals met in Paris in 1938 and styled themselves *Le Colloque Walter Lippmann*. Lippmann, acknowledging the influence of Hayek and von Mises, viewed all three ideologies as symptoms of rising collectivism.[158] Lippmann's formulation placed him and his colleagues on the side of freedom and as the antagonists of equality. They framed the issue as one of individual choice versus rule by government. *Le Colloque* never met again, but it set the precedent for what would become, in the postwar years, a powerful new impetus in the form of the Mt. Pelerin Society to be assembled in Switzerland by Hayek from some of the same participants. The movement proceeded on the basis of an alliance with conservative foundations that would ultimately finance a recapture of the intellectual initiative from the intellectual forces of the left.

At the 1938 conference, the role of public expositor for the pro-market forces was suggested to Hayek. Richard Cockett reports that this is when Hayek began thinking of writing *The Road to Serfdom* (1944), which was to become the manifesto of the self-styled "liberals" as they arrayed themselves against "collectivism and Keynesianism."[159] The objective was from the outset to show that the Keynesian middle way was not an *alternative* to, but rather a *version* of, socialism.

In the company of like-minded European and American intellectuals, Hayek could begin to work out a way to recoup his position. As an economist in the Robbins camp at LSE, Hayek saw that the battle was being lost. Younger faculty members were turning to Keynes, as was the profession more generally.[160] An analysis by one of Hayek's own students demonstrated the contribution of deflation to the rise of Hitler, as opposed to the more benign results of Sweden's Keynesian approach to their crisis. This thesis contributed to defections among economists.[161] On the political front, however, there was a new salient open to attack.

Hayek returned to LSE to find that not only the socialist, Laski, but the Director who had hired him, Beveridge, had been persuaded of the benign qualities of socialism and the reactionary nature of fascism. He wrote a memorandum to dissuade Beveridge of this position by linking socialism to the abuse of reason and establishing its commonality with fascism. In Hayek's view, fascism was "a sort of lower-middle-class socialism."[162] For Hayek, this memo was the beginning of a book project that would detail the historical decline of reason—and the basis for a "popular version . . . aimed at the British socialist intelligentsia" that would emphasize the illustration presented by the rise of collectivism in its several forms.[163] As Keynes popularized government regulation, Laski and the left gravitated steadily toward the nationalization of the means of production as the central tenet of socialism. Even the Conservatives were embracing ideas of regulation and the nationalization of railroads. Hayek's targets merged into one that loomed large and clear in his mind. The book became his wartime focus. Hayek would dedicate *The Road to Serfdom* to "the socialists in all parties."

As 1940 commenced, Hayek was completing his last major attempt at settling the fundamental issues of economics. He finished *The Pure Theory of Capital* in June. But the world was at war, and nobody paid any attention. As Bruce Caldwell, editor of Hayek's *Collected Works*, observes, "Few in the profession even noticed the book. Furthermore, it was clear to Hayek that even after a prodigious effort he had not gotten very far . . . he had made no further progress towards building on this new foundation a fully dynamic theory of the cycle. Hayek never returned to this task, hoping that it would be completed by others. It remains unfinished."[164]

Along the way, Hayek carried on his scrap with Keynes. He claimed that Keynes's *The General Theory* leaves the reader with the impression that "no real scarcity exists," rather that "the only scarcity with which we need concern ourselves is the artificial scarcity created by the determination of people not to sell their services and products below certain arbitrarily fixed prices."[165] It seems unlikely that such a contention could be taken at face value. It is rather a polemical thrust at Keynes's preoccupation with freeing up, by government manipulation, resources that could contribute to economic growth.

More convincingly, Hayek brings together in his new work the implications of his economic theory and of his view on how knowledge is used in the market. Andrew Gamble points to the reordering of economic thinking that follows from Hayek's innovation:

Hayek abandoned the assumption that the correct starting point for analysis was the concept of a general equilibrium, arguing instead that it was necessary to begin with the plans of individuals and the distribution of knowledge in society. The achievement of order and equilibrium were the end result, not the starting-point, for the analysis. The correct procedure was to see by what institutional mechanisms co-ordination was achieved and maintained.[166] Thus, there is no such thing as macroeconomics.

From this perspective, Hayek took apart Keynes's treatment of capital investment as an "aggregate" by demonstrating the variability of decision making about investments depending on foreseen and unforeseen events.[167] The complicated structure of his argument was, in one sense, an illustration of his major point—that investment decisions are microdecisions that are buffeted by more considerations than Keynes and others had conceptualized. These decisions cannot be broken into discrete elements without distorting what is really happening.

The argument of complexity is a hard one to refute. It is even harder to accept a refutation if one is not trained to pay attention to complexity in the first place. Caldwell highlights the sense in which economists are attuned to equilibrium theory and marginal choice analysis. This makes them insensitive to an argument based on the complex uses of knowledge. Where economists fixate either on restoring "equilibrium" of such aggregates as supply and demand by some kind of policy or on nudging economic behavior along a desirable trajectory, Hayek increasingly placed the discovery of information at the heart of economics.[168]

Whatever its appeal to economists, Hayek's argument for complexity was also less likely to be honored in a crisis-driven world where policy choices need to be made. For these reasons, Hayek had an additional impetus to turn from economics to politics, for that was where the pressures would build to find an end, in the postwar world, to the chaos that characterized the thirties. To break through to those who could communicate with a mass audience, Hayek needed to turn from the arid world of economic theory to the pungent discourse of ideological confrontation.

All three—Maynard Keynes, Harold Laski, and Friedrich Hayek—entered the thirties primed with new ideas, though not yet focused on the practicalities of change. By the end of the decade they had clarified their messages and acquired significant followings. The times had called forth all the competency they could marshal, and their published works, especially those of Keynes and Laski, were now widely read. All three were actively bridging the divide between the university and politics, and they were forging new public understandings of the relationship between the government and the market.

Keynes and Laski proceeded from settled commitments in their personal lives that reinforced their energies. Frida and Harold struggled as comrades in the radical movements sweeping through England. Keynes, weakened by a heart attack, relied on Lydia's ministrations to sustain his now highly pressured activities. Hayek's marriage had been tenuous and was now weakened by a renewal of his relationship with his first love. He would now endure a long separation from his beloved, a captive to closed borders in Hitler's Austria. Controversial and increasingly marginalized in his professional community, adrift in his personal relations, he was at the crossroads of a new life as the war began.

6

World War II: Destruction and Deliverance

In 1939, as the world tumbled once again into war, the forces conjured up by the failed settlement of the first war appeared as ideological phantasms in the minds of these three formative figures. Harold Laski saw the final collapse of the old order as a paroxysm of dialectics and pressed on toward the creation of a new socialist order. Friedrich Hayek's analysis focused not on the rivalry of fascism and socialism, but on the common impetus of both ideologies in precipitating the decline of individual freedom and with it the capacity to adapt and survive. Maynard Keynes set in motion the machinery for rationalizing economic and political forces so that in the postwar world they might be constrained and directed toward the progress of civilization.

The critical events for each of the three were somewhat different. For Keynes, there were the all-consuming tasks of finessing Britain's financing of the war and then preserving its position in the postwar world. He brought to these tasks a now fully formed system of political economy. Keynes became the consummate insider.

Having raised his red flag, Laski, the establishment-connected outsider, fought for revolution in the midst of war, just as the Bolsheviks had, but on his terms of "revolution by consent." The opportunity for a bold strike lay in the shifting plates of partisan politics that underlay Churchill's coalition and the pressing cause of working-class mobilization that both enabled the military response and unsettled the politics of the war effort.

Hayek, sidelined in the war mobilization for reasons of nationality and the political incorrectness of his views, found his front lines in the trenches of ideological warfare. For him, the essential struggle was not about rival nationalisms, or even the classes and the masses, but rather the assertion of individual freedom against rationalist schemes for the improvement of society. The forties were to be a time of political confrontation that would reset his life course and, with it, the ultimate course of the West.

6.1 – KEYNES: SAVING ENGLAND

For Maynard Keynes, World War II was the logical consequence of the failures of the Versailles settlement. The inability of Western leaders to deal with reparations and the depression in any more than a patchwork fashion led to the rise of fascism in Germany and Italy. The British political establishment suffered a body blow with the discrediting of appeasement following the Munich Agreement of 1938. Chamberlain's failure to prevent the outbreak of the war brought once again into full view the profound weakness at the heart of the British polity. His replacement by Churchill rehabilitated a fringe figure known for a hard line against England's enemies. However, Churchill's party was damaged by Chamberlain's fecklessness. Churchill was tied in coalition to a Labour Party that had taken over the leadership of mass opinion on domestic issues.[1] In a time of desperation, the conditions were at last favorable for the introduction of new ideas.

Keynes's response as the new war broke out was threefold: a salvation operation designed to preserve as much of Britain's position in the world as possible, the adaptation of war economy measures to domestic schemes that were to ensure greater security in the postwar period, and the creation of an institutional framework for international monetary stability that would avoid the mistakes of the Versailles settlement. He succeeded temporarily at the first, surprisingly well at the second, and for the longer term in the latter. In 1939, as the Panzer divisions were on the march across Europe, Keynes was back to doing what he did best: proposing governmentally sponsored remedies to a crisis in public finance—this time the financing of the war effort. He proposed that a compulsory savings scheme, along with a tax on capital accumulation, be implemented to supply the necessary funding. The savings accounts would pay interest, but would not be given back until after the war—and then released as an antidote to a postwar recession.[2]

Keynes's mastery of policy entrepreneurship was evidenced by the support he garnered for the scheme. William Beveridge had been in on its formation, and both Laski and Hayek became its public advocates. The progressivity of the scheme, with its disproportionate impact on the "haves," attracted the support of Laski who tried to advance the plan in Labour Party councils and among the trade union leadership.[3]

The fact that Keynes's plan made use of a Hayek proposal, a capital levy on postwar profits, gained him another ally.[4] Hayek foresaw his old nemesis, inflation, as the principal postwar problem and was willing to endorse so confiscatory and coercive a measure as a wealth tax to forestall it.[5] Keynes wrote to Hayek, "I am extremely glad that we should find ourselves in so much agreement on the practical issues."[6] Perhaps Hayek took some satisfaction that enforced savings was, in effect, the opposite of Keynes's usual recourse, namely government borrowing.[7]

Most of the plan found its way into the government's program. The Treasury needed a way to improve its political standing after being associated throughout the thirties with a parsimony that failed both as a depression remedy and as a response to the need for a military buildup.[8] Keynes was pleased at last to have had a real impact on a critical matter. The coalition's 1941 budget went beyond this proposal in its significance, however. Donald Moggridge comments: "It shifted the criteria for budgetary policy from the balance or lack of balance in the public accounts to the balance of the economy as a whole. . . . It was all rather crude, relying heavily on the judgmental skills of someone with Keynes's intuitive feel for orders of statistical magnitudes, but it was a beginning."[9] Macroeconomics had taken over from the microfocus of balancing the public accounts. Here was the initial triumph of *The General Theory*. What is more, it worked. Inflation was contained. Moggridge cites a cost-of-living index that rose only five points, from 127 to 132, between March 1941 and January 1945.

Such was his eminence that Keynes came back to the government in June 1940 for the duration as simply "Keynes." He had no specific portfolio, rather an understood mandate to roam the Treasury and beyond looking for solutions to the war's problems. His office was across from a counterpart of considerable eminence, Lord Catto—which led inevitably to Keynes being anointed "Lord Doggo." Keynes's office was adorned only by a self-portrait of Duncan Grant. Next door was the Chancellor of the Exchequer. Bloomsbury had once again made its way into the redoubt of the establishment.[10]

Skewering the incompetent in the wartime bureaucracy was his favorite sport, and now he had worthy quarry. He stirred many tempests among the bureaucrats, but took good advice in resituating his colleagues on a better course. His shots went wide as often as not, but he had learned a certain humility.[11] He was partnered with the very able Sir Richard Hopkins, his repentant adversary Lionel Robbins, and competent lieutenants for whom he had great respect.

Domestically, his life was divided between sleeping on a bunk in the basement of his Gordon Square home the better, hopefully, to survive the bombing, and trips down to Tilton for respites with Lydia and their Charleston friends. They witnessed the heroism of British pilots overhead as the channel coast became the front line of the war in 1940.

Keynes's writ at the Treasury Department ran to domestic affairs as well as wartime finance. When the government decided to solicit Beveridge's recommendations on a social insurance scheme, Beveridge and Keynes served on a small committee to work out the financing. Joined by a chastened Robbins, now at work in the Treasury's economic section, Keynes and Beveridge agreed on a range of modifications that muted Treasury opposition on grounds of fiscal prudence. The historic Beveridge Report appeared at the end of 1942. The Beveridge Report was destined to lay the basis for the British welfare state for the remainder of the century. Jose Harris, in her seminal study of Beveridge, summarizes the principles as "full employment, free health care, insurance rather than 'means tests,' and communal provision of social security 'from the cradle to the grave.'"[12] Notably missing from this list are the public ownership and control of the means of production, as advocated by Laski and the left wing of the Labour Party.

When polled, 86 percent of the public supported adoption of the scheme.[13] The cabinet was ambivalent; a tepid reception from the Conservative Party dimmed the prospects. The cabinet responded accordingly, agreeing with it "in principle," but putting off implementation until after the war.[14]

In fact, Beveridge was persuaded early in the war that a democratic form of socialism would be preferable to existing arrangements. However, he limited his advocacy to principles that could attract broad agreement. Beveridge had come to this middle way by successive approximation through a long, eventful career of experimentation in social policy informed by a close study of the social sciences. The report represented, as Harris observes, truly a political *via media*. Keynes pronounced it good and welcomed it with "wild enthusiasm."[15] He no doubt saw in it the practical realization of that which his new economics could be calibrated to finance.

By this time, the eminence of a peerage was bestowed, and he became Baron Keynes of Tilton on June 11, 1942. Now the scribble at the bottom of the Treasury memos was just "K." Feted by Churchill on the occasion and saluted by Lloyd George and even Margot Asquith, Keynes had entered the inner sanctum of Britain's elite.[16] Yet there still were limits to his freedom of action. He hoped to make his maiden speech to the Lords in support of the Beveridge plan. He would tout it as the least expensive of the popular proposals for ensuring minimum security, and it was easily affordable if British industries were to become even marginally less inefficient than they were during the depression.[17] He planned to close his speech with a peroration that invoked his perspective on the postwar world:

> It is not any fear of a failure of physical productivity to provide an adequate material standard of life that fills me with foreboding. The real problems of the future are first of all the maintenance of peace, of international co-operation and amity, and beyond that the profound moral and social problems of how to organise material abundance to yield up the fruits of a good life. These are the heroic tasks of the future. But there is nothing, My Lords, in what we are discussing today which need frighten a mouse.[18]

Treasury colleagues were, notwithstanding, frightened by the prospective costs and made known their displeasure at his intended remarks. They were not about to be reassured or, worse, dismissed. Keynes changed direction to avoid damaging his effectiveness on other fronts. The "other fronts" were mainly to do with overseas issues of finance, credit, and the structure of postwar economic arrangements among the powers, great and small. Keynes became the Treasury's "dominant force," carrying with him the added cachet of a directorship of the Bank of England.[19] He had seen the outwash of inflation and recession that followed the first war and was determined to insulate England, and as much of the world as possible, against these twin evils. The bombs falling around him did not deter his focus on the future.

Meanwhile matters moved ahead in domestic policy. Beveridge was again called on to address a critical issue, this time the matter of full employment in a postwar economy. Even Churchill had, in seeking broadened support for the war effort in the spring of 1943, endorsed "national compulsory insurance for all classes for all purposes from the cradle to the grave."[20] In his 1944 report titled *Full Employment in a Free Society*, Beveridge established the principle that social minimums, including the right to a job, should serve as the benchmark for public policy. As Richard Cockett points out, the report in fact endorsed "'a high and stable level of employment,' defined as unemployment less than 8.5 percent of the population."[21] If Keynesian measures were sufficient to secure that rather moderate goal, then so much the better. If not, Beveridge was prepared to endorse the stronger measures of the Labour Party militants.[22]

With the Beveridge reports as the new policy standard, Keynesian economics became the best hope for the preservation of capitalism and simultaneously for the amelioration of social ills without massive changes in British

society. However, as we shall see, the forces of polarization had been unleashed, on both the right and the left. Hayek's *Road to Serfdom* was published in the same year, and Laski, as Chair of the National Executive Committee (NEC) of the British Labour Party, would drive the party's platform to
the left as the postwar elections approached. Harris notes that Beveridge, for
his part, feared that if there were any delay in implementing his reports, "the
widespread popular disenchantment of the mid-war years might explode at
the end of the war into revolutionary turmoil and collapse."[23]

Robert Skidelsky illuminates the sense in which Keynes's views were less
than revolutionary. Keynes distinguished "public investment" from "government ownership and control." Keynes saw as long ago as the twenties that
the simple distinction between private and public was breaking down as a
matter of practice.[24] Corporations were publicly chartered, ownership
through stock was effectively separated from control by professional managers responsive to public pressures, and disposition of private capital was
interwoven with publicly observable financial controls. Keynes regarded the
blurring of the private–public distinction as an irreversible and generally
nonthreatening trend.

This benign interpretation of public–private relations explains Keynes's
seeming endorsement of Hayek's *Road to Serfdom*, with its evocation of the
good uses of the market, along with Keynes's simultaneous claim that more
planning is needed rather than less. He did not see these as opposed possibilities. Purely private capitalism was increasingly a myth, and government intervention was increasingly a way of life. At the same time, a society where
investments were shaped by public preferences, even by government decisions, need not be totalitarian. The strands of the web that link private and
public finance run in both directions. He proposed, albeit without success,
that the government's budget be divided into an "off-budget" fund for investments, which would bear the brunt of countercyclical maneuvering, and an
ordinary budget to deal with questions of "efficiency and equity" in government operations and provisions.

Yet Keynes's main efforts in 1944 were directed to the international situation. With the Normandy invasion in view, the great powers were forced to
look beyond the war. The question before them was whether institutions
could be put in place to stabilize the world economy such that the excesses of
the previous decades might not be repeated. The United States convened a
conference of forty-four nations at a resort in New Hampshire, Bretton
Woods. The conductor of this attempt at diplomatic orchestration was Maynard Keynes. It was his apotheosis, the more glorious for the direct contrast

with the bitter discord of Versailles, with its triumvirate of the merciless Clemenceau; the Presbyterian idealist Woodrow Wilson; and the political alchemist Lloyd George.[25] At the Bretton Woods conference, Keynes was the maestro without peer. In the words of a now awestruck Robbins, Keynes in full flight was

> one of the most remarkable men that have ever lived—the quick logic, the bird-like swoop of intuition, the vivid fancy, the wide vision, above all the incomparable sense of the fitness of words, all combine to make something several degrees beyond the limit of ordinary human achievement. . . . The Americans sat entranced as the God-like visitor sang and the golden light played round. When it was all over there was very little discussion. But so far as the Bank is concerned, I am clear that we are off to a flying start.[26]

The bank was the International Bank for Reconstruction and Development that together with its financial counterpart, the International Monetary Fund (IMF), would form the basis for the postwar resurrection of economies around the world. The key would be stabilized currencies with an internationally regulated system of reserves to provide the confidence on which world trade could build.

These institutions and the monetary agreements that underlay them brought together both sides of Keynes's political persona. Keynes the nationalist pursued a central role for the British pound sterling, the better to focus financial affairs in London. Keynes the theorist of political economy co-opted the international community into a set of institutions that would apply interventionist macroeconomics to the whole of the globe. The nationalist and the theorist came into conflict politically when Keynes overpromised British government leaders about the prospects for American recognition of the "moral debt" to Britain.[27] The Americans turned out to be more hardheaded than expected, and that was to complicate the negotiation of the foundations for the international institutions. Keynes would have to apply all of his persuasive arts on the Americans, his own government, and public opinion to get the requisite agreements and loans approved.

The intensive and detailed negotiations over a period of weeks "were dominated by verbal duels between Keynes and (the American Treasury's Harry Dexter) White—the rapier versus the blunderbuss."[28] White held the upper hand, but he was a man with an assertive style torn by the need to keep ahead of his masters in the U.S. Treasury, while acting on a personal commitment to forge a working partnership with the Soviet Union. White was at the time passing secret information to KGB agents. He was therefore in sympathy with

Keynes's social democratic design for the postwar partnership but at odds with his nationalist project of continuing the preeminent position of the pound in international commerce. In the end, the Americans held the upper hand and secured dominance for the dollar. However, Keynes achieved enough of what he wanted by way of institutional arrangements and currency convertibility that he could deliver a resounding defense of the agreements when he returned to the House of Lords.

Keynes was accompanied to America by Lydia, no stranger to stardom. Her dancing exercises disturbed the repose of their downstairs neighbor at the lodge, American chief delegate Henry Morgenthau. Keynes had just as surely become a star on the world stage. When it was over, Robbins reports, "the delegates rose as one man and cheered Keynes to the echo."[29]

Keynes had wanted to go one step further and establish an International Clearing Union as a mechanism for stabilizing exchange rates and capital flows. He settled for the establishment of the Bretton Woods Agreement that fixed currency rates. While the Bretton Woods regime would last for nearly thirty years, it would be attenuated as increasingly technical neoclassical solutions were applied in managing crises. Keynes's insights as to the subjective nature of international capital flows were left behind and, with that, the effectiveness of the regime declined.[30] Prior to the final collapse of the Bretton Woods Agreement in 1973, Western economies grew at an average rate of 4 percent.[31] For twenty years after the collapse, the economic growth of the developed world averaged one-third less, and the frequency of banking and credit crises steadily increased. The IMF remains a powerful force to this day. However, in the 1980s it became an agent of free market ideology rather than an institution involved in pragmatic rescue operations for economies in crisis.[32]

The achievement, whatever its ultimate fate, was more than an institutional victory. Keynes had completed a revolution in economics. Alfred Borneman, summarizing half a century of progress in economics, comments that by 1945, the Keynesian revolution had succeeded:

> The perfect rationality of the timeless competitive general equilibrium came to an end with imperfect competition and the recognition of uncertainty. Money became psychological liquidity for use in decision-making under uncertainty rather than simply the accounting reckoning unit.[33]

But the triumph went beyond economics to politics and beyond Britain to the world. The institutions Keynes had brought into being would manage the world toward stability, while substantive initiatives such as the Beveridge Report would guide Britain toward a secure and prosperous future. Keynes told the House of Lords that Bretton Woods would abet the "invisible hand" of Adam Smith, not replace it. Disavowing "totalitarian" approaches to economic management, as well as the "law of the jungle," Keynes suggested he had laid down the infrastructure for the middle way.[34] It was a claim that could hardly be contested, and it represented the apogee of his unique perspective on political economy. However, his calculations would have to contend with another force of rising significance: the socialist militancy of Harold Laski and a resurgent Labour Party.

6.2 – LASKI: WORLD WAR AND CLASS WAR

With the outbreak of war in 1939, Harold Laski brought together theory and practice in a manner that would have profound consequences for the postwar world. The tide of events, disastrous though they were, delivered him and his cause to a new height of respectability and public acceptance. The year 1940 was to bring the "Battle of Britain" and Churchill's mobilization of every ounce of commitment from the bewildered British populace. The political meaning was that the unions were incorporated into the government. The task of appealing to the working class by recognizing their interests became the theme of a propaganda campaign that pervaded the radio, the army's extensive education program, and the statements issuing from government leaders. World War II would be "the people's war."[35]

By the beginning of the 1940s, Laski's radicalism had taken a decisive turn to the left. His declaration of affinity for Marxism identified what he was for, and a lecture in the spring of 1940 at the London School of Economics (LSE) gave him the opportunity to disavow what had been left behind. Speaking on "The Decline of Liberalism," Laski declared that liberal idealism had been eclipsed by events in a manner as startling as the fall of the doctrine of the divine right of kings. He called for increasing the level of social control. "We must make of our society a co-operative and not a competitive adventure; it is now historically beyond discussion that the mere conflict of private interests can never produce a just Commonwealth."[36]

Elevated into the power structure of the Labour Party, he was the top choice of the constituency Labour organizations for membership on the National Executive Committee (NEC) throughout the war.[37] The NEC, along with the Parliamentary Labour Party (PLP) and the Trades Unions Congress (TUC), was the principal organ of British socialism. With a mass base, a platform for policy proposals, and influential colleagues, Laski was positioned to intervene in every important debate. Unlike his parliamentary and ministerial colleagues, however, he did not have to be accountable either to the electorate or to the other elements of the coalition government—only to the party faithful at the grassroots level. He used the position to define a course well to the left of that set by the coalition government.

Though persuaded by a Marxist analysis of the war's causes, Laski was decisively opposed to a Leninist strategy for converting it into a civil war on the model of Russia's revolution of 1917. In early 1941, he denounced the strategy of British Communists who called for a working-class mobilization to rise up against the Churchill government. The Communists proposed that a British worker's state, having overthrown imperialist capitalism, could then offer a "people's peace" that would ignite revolutions against Hitler and Mussolini backed by the power of the Soviet Union. "It is impossible not to conclude," he wrote in the *Nation*, "that either the British Communist Party is dwelling in cloud-cuckoo land or its purpose is to assist in the defeat of Great Britain."[38] Laski was every bit as intent on a socialist outcome from the war, but he formulated a strategy that rejected violence and drew instead on his ambitions for democracy. As for the Communists, they would learn in June 1941 with the German invasion of the Soviet Union, that rather than being the target of a revolution, the British government would now become the Soviet Union's essential ally in a fight to the death with Hitler.

A happier moment in June 1941 was provided by the birth of a grandson, Christopher, the first of four, to his daughter Diana and her husband Robin Mathewson. The grandparents were permitted to dote on Christopher, and they maintained generally good relations with his parents. There were strains in the relationship arising from Robin's Tory sympathies and aloof personality, and the young classicist was not as energetic about his teaching and scholarly responsibilities at St. Paul's School and Exeter as the senior Laski thought he should be. Diana remained close to her parents, though her decision to become active in the Anglican Church set her apart from family traditions.[39]

Unfortunately 1941 was also to hold a personal tragedy for the Laski family. Nathan Laski, his father, was struck and mortally injured by a motorist in October. At the age of seventy-eight, he was still vital. Harold often went home to his mother and family. He wrote to Felix Frankfurter of his father's courage in speaking out for the Jews in the face of much hostility over so many years. Prime Minister Churchill wrote to Harold of his warm recollections of the Laski household.[40] Never reconciled to the wealth and status of his family, Laski had slowly found his way back into the good graces of the patriarch he so rudely challenged.

The crisis of the war escalated the significance of Laski's analytic distinction between historical forces and the intentions of human actors. Shortly after the beginning of the hostilities, it fell to Laski to draft a document that would define the terms of the Labour Party's position on the war. *Is This an Imperialist War?* was premised on the analysis that "the war cannot be separated from the capitalist forces which produced it; it is an inherent function of their nature, not something willed apart from them by the deliberate designs of malevolent men."[41] Fascism's purpose was to crush socialism, and socialists must fight back and win the peace for "humanity." Laski's view directly opposed the pronouncement of the Fascist propaganda chief, Joseph Goebbels, that the Nazis intended to destroy the "principles of 1789." Kingsley Martin, Laski's ally and biographer, summarizes Goebbels' expressed intentions: "Liberty, Equality and Fraternity, the basic concepts of democracy, were to be submerged for a 'thousand years.'" For Laski and his comrades, socialism, the child of the Enlightenment, must rise up in resistance to the fascist counterrevolutionaries.[42]

Laski set out a statement of war aims that envisioned a "Cooperative World Commonwealth" that would prevent future wars. The foundation was to be built on democratic socialist states, and a "new and world-wide Declaration of the Rights of Man." The latter project would come to fruition at the initiative of UNESCO after the war. On the question of colonialism, there was a mandate of self-government and provision for "bold financial and economic planning" to restore shattered economies.[43] The pamphlet was seen as an effective response to the militant left—so much so that the U.S. government ordered twenty-five thousand copies for distribution in America.

Though urged to do so, Churchill was not interested in proposing a statement of war aims. Given the issues Laski was advancing, it would be politically divisive at a time of grave national emergency, and conservatives might lose out on critical issues. The Labour leadership dragged their feet in forcing the issue, which prompted Laski to write an open letter to the *Daily Herald* demanding that war aims be set out. The circumvention of his party's leadership led to a rebuke by the party's Emergency Committee and an acknowledgment by Laski that he had erred in publicly challenging Clement Attlee, Labour's party leader and principal government minister, on such a vital issue.[44]

Keynes took a step toward weighing into the war aims debate in January 1941 by drafting his own list that centered on economic regulation so as to ensure social security and drive down unemployment both domestically and, through the creation of an international currency, internationally. The internationalization of Keynesianism through the prior step of currency stabilization prefigured what Keynes would set out to do in the postwar world. His draft, however, was never published. The theme of ensuring social security found its way into the broad generalities of the Atlantic Charter that summer, and that was as close as the government would get to a statement of war aims.[45]

Laski felt the war personally, though he was unfit for service and not wanted in the government by the cautious ministers of the coalition cabinet. To escape the bombing, LSE was moved to Cambridge for the duration. Laski found himself situated in a small office above a chemist's shop across from the entry to Keynes's King's College. His office was adorned only by a picture of his wife. Frida was often away on her own public activities. She served on the Fulham Council, as a justice of the peace, and as an air-raid warden in Essex where they had their small retreat, the cottage in Little Bardfield not far from Cambridge. In addition to a heavy teaching load, Laski adjudicated industrial disputes around England, addressed education programs for soldiers and workers, engaged in Labour Party politics in London and elsewhere, and kept up a stream of writing in articles, books, letters, and pamphlets. Their London home was hit twice but never destroyed, a train he was riding on was strafed, and a hotel he was lodged in was bombed. Rarely in decent health, all of these pressures tested his stamina to the limits.[46]

Laski was driven onward by a vision of a socialist future arising out of the ashes of war. In his powerful imagination, the war was recast into a historic opportunity for the rising of the proletariat behind the banner of the Labour Party. As Michael Newman suggests, it was for him a "revolutionary war" and "the more 'total' the war became, the greater would be the extent of the necessary collaboration."[47] Just as the first war had mobilized the Russian peasantry and created the massed forces that could carry through the revolution, so the civilian and military mobilization of Britain could be seen to have great political potential.

Laski faced the crisis with the outlines of a grand plan. The centralization of political and economic control for war purposes would be seized on to begin the permanent transition to a socialist system at home. Internationally, the upwelling of democratic aspirations would undo the injustices of imperialism. The postwar Western democracies, once socialized and freed of imperialist ties, could then confront revolutionary communism on a basis of shared values and a superior commitment to human rights. What he proposed was nothing less than a "revolution by consent."[48]

Laski saw the war as a surrogate for a working-class revolution. Newman brings together the threads that bound Laski's psyche to his politics:

> For the first time since the 1920s his theory and his emotions were therefore integrated. This meant that there was no contradiction between his thought and his action, and he could devote his vast energy to the attempt to transform his vision into reality. . . . This meant that this political activity was driven by the most powerful forces of all: the belief that success would lead to a brave new world and failure would bring about Armageddon.[49]

Breathtaking in its sweep, Laski's vision prompted him to a frenetic round of advocacy and action. The adversary that seemed of most concern to Laski in early 1940 was not Hitler, nor even Stalin, but rather the timidity of British leadership. First, there had been the disaster of appeasement, and now that a revolutionary opportunity presented itself, the mild-mannered Attlee and his moderate colleagues led the Labour Party. He declaimed to Frankfurter, "There will obviously be big Govt. changes soon, but if Attlee and Co. knew their job, they could, even in this House, sweep the world." Instead, they "mangle every problem they touch. It makes me sick to death."[50] Though bland in demeanor, Attlee, in the memorable image of Paul Addison, "resembled the frog who sits motionless on a stone, occasionally snapping up an insect with its tongue."[51] Attlee was to prove more than a match for the colorful professor and polemicist.

The collapse of the Chamberlain government in May opened the way to shared power for Labour under Churchill's leadership. The Labour Party conference that summer became Laski's platform for rallying the party faithful to his vision. "We want to use the grim experience of the months that lie ahead for the radical transformation that is required. . . . Power is on our side, if we use that power." He called for the "intensification of social services, and not the lowering of standards."[52] The gauntlet was laid down, and Laski's supporters found inspiration in their tribune. His friend and colleague Martin shared those halcyon days and nights. He pictures Laski on the march:

> If the manual workers of Britain, already bitterly anti-Conservative as a result of experience in the 'thirties, became during the war instructed, conscious and resolute Socialists, then Socialism would succeed at the end of the war even if its arguments had never convinced the orthodox political and trade union leaders. Therefore he (Laski) spent his physical strength, which was never large, and nervous vitality, which was immense, in travelling night after night after a day's teaching at the School of Economics or a day of committees in London, to address local labour parties, factory meetings, miners' lodges, discussion groups

of soldiers, sailors and airmen; therefore he emphasised day in and night out with eloquent conviction that the first essential task was victory, but that victory must mean a victory not for the old order, but for the workday people, who demanded permanent peace abroad and social justice at home.[53]

However popular he was in working-class precincts, Laski's fervor met with a cool reception among Labour's Ministers in power. Laski used his NEC position in 1940 to table a request that the Labour Ministers in the new government enact "at least a number of those definitely socialist measures approved by the Bournemouth conference." Attlee shelved the request, and a rift opened between them that would widen as the battle over the "revolution by consent" intensified.[54]

Attlee argued, in reply to Laski's revolutionary scenario, that the course of action would divide the government just when unity was needed. The general observance of a "party truce" during the early years of the war worked to Attlee's advantage. Insofar as it was pressured on the social front, the government had a less radical course available: encouragement of the budgetary and policy initiatives emanating not from the Laskian left, but from the redoubtable Keynes and his allies in the Treasury who were advancing worker-friendly ideas for financing the war and planning for employment security in the future.[55]

As relentless on the inside of the establishment as on the hustings, Laski proceeded to lobby at the highest levels for a permanent transition to socialist prescriptions such as economic planning and the nationalization of industries. At the 1942 annual conference, he introduced a resolution committing the party to economic planning. He declaimed, "The age of competitive capitalism is over. A democracy means nothing less than a society of equals planning full production for community consumption."[56]

Laski's rising profile was visible across the Atlantic. He had already attracted the attention of American right-wingers who saw his influence on Roosevelt as an indicator of what was really afoot. On the floor of Congress, Representative Tinkham of Massachusetts read into the record an article equating the "Roosevelt Program" with the "Laski Program," namely the introduction of socialism in the United States. "Laski has for years not merely denounced Capitalism . . . (he) has preached the doctrine sustained by Lenin and all good Communists—which was incorporated in the President's message of January 6th—that the great, Messianic reform (by which) he is to free the people of the world" is at hand.[57] Felix Frankfurter, Supreme Court Justice and frequent correspondent with Laski, was identified as the key link in the "communistic cabal," along with Eleanor Roosevelt. When asked by a *Times* correspondent what he thought of the rumor that the New Deal was the invention of a Jewish professor, President Roosevelt named Laski as the suspect. He retorted that his program was about the salvation of capitalism, not its destruction.[58]

To accuse Laski of being a socialist plotter out to take over the West was indeed quite accurate. His activities during the war years took him to the centers of power where he pushed with all his might for rapid conversion to a socialist economy even before the war would be concluded. However, to call him a communist was to ignore his opposition to the Communist Party throughout the 1930s; his identification of Leninism as a deviation from Marxism; and his support for wartime measures to suppress communist publications.[59] And to characterize him as an *éminence grise* was to ignore his role as acerbic critic, privately and publicly, of the very leaders he was alleged to be manipulating. His differences with Attlee, and even Roosevelt, were stated openly in opinion articles and newspaper columns.

Of Laski's influence on the Labour Party vanguard, however, there is no question. With the German invasion of the Soviet Union, Laski drafted a Labour Party pamphlet intended to instruct the public on how to view the new alliance with the Russia of Stalin and the Bolsheviks. He began by declaiming that "the outbreak of the Russian Revolution was, for the masses of Britain, one of the most beneficent events in modern history." He proceeded to separate out the abuses of Leninism and Stalinism from the Marxist intent of the revolution. He suggested that the deviations into dictatorship were the result of Russia's insecurity in the face of capitalist hostility and the abortive invasion by Britain and the United States.[60]

Attlee, one of the commentators on the draft, succeeded in having the pamphlet rejected, observing that Laski had overlooked nationalist, as opposed to economic, explanations for Russia's behavior. "Nationalism is far from having been eliminated from the Russian soul." Attlee notes that communists were quite as hostile to democratic socialists as to capitalists, thus giving the lie to notions that the differences with the British Labour Party were merely the consequence of militancy in the face of insecurity. "Communist parties in fact played into the hands of reaction not so much by fighting the capitalist as by scaring away from any left movement the masses of ordinary people." Finally, Attlee undercut Laski's pretence of speaking for the masses: "Generally speaking, I regard the pamphlet as one written for the intelligentsia rather than for the rank and file of the Party. I should prefer something written in more simple and homely language."[61]

Laski was not daunted by the resistance of moderates. Since early 1941, he knew that Attlee and the other Labour Ministers were not going to act on his program. In a daring initiative, he bypassed his own party leadership and

went directly to Prime Minister Winston Churchill. Churchill had signaled a
willingness to consider any measure that would strengthen the nation's resistance to the overwhelming foe.[62] Just a few months earlier Churchill had
written Laski to acknowledge a warmhearted letter of support.

> I have been led to believe, as a result of many inquiries, that the very great mass
> of the people have for the time being put their faith in me to try to find a way
> out of the terrible plight into which we and the world have been led by the un-
> wisdom of politicians of all parties. If I did not feel the conviction, which your
> letter confirms, that this was so, I should find it impossible to bear the load
> which is fastened on my shoulders.[63]

Against the backdrop of German advances, Laski proposed his bold plan directly to the Prime Minister. He wrote in February that the rallying of the
masses at this decisive hour could only be accomplished by a commitment at
the highest level to a socialist postwar program. He sent along a secret memorandum with a list of measures including state control of key economic sectors and a direct attack on inequality. If Churchill would propose the measures
on behalf of the government, Laski promised to carry the fight in Labour's
Executive Committee. In exchange, Laski made the audacious suggestion that
Churchill continue in office after the war.[64] Militant and opportunistic simultaneously, Laski pressed his campaign fearlessly.

Churchill's letter in reply met Laski's hard charge with a fusillade of his
own:

> It is entirely beyond my share of life and strength to deal with all the issues
> which your letter raises. In my view, we ought to win the war first, and then in
> a free country the issues of Socialism and Free Enterprise can be fought out in
> a constitutional manner. I certainly should think it very undemocratic if anyone
> were to try to carry Socialism during a party truce without a Parliamentary ma-
> jority. I have always accounted you a friend rather than a follower. I think it
> would be a pity to break up the national unity in the war and that I believe is the
> opinion of the mass of the people.[65]

Adroitly changing the issue to the question of unity and democratic process,
Churchill absolved himself from concern with the social justice issues. His
sole concern was winning the war.

Churchill's rejection of a "revolution by consent" ignited Laski's rage. He
set upon Churchill in public, writing commentaries that tested the limits of ci-
vility. In the *New Statesman and Nation*, the *Tribune*, and the *New Republic*,
he assailed Churchill as a Whig, and aristocrat, an enemy of the working

Harold Laski. Reprinted by permission of Corbis.

class, and a reactionary interested only in preserving the status quo.[66] The attack was personal: "Having habit rather than philosophy as the basis of his ideas, he improvises conviction with a fury which makes him deaf to the give-and-take of discussion. . . . The actual sight of what the victims of aerial bombardment have suffered will arouse in him at once the impulse to action; but the unseen suffering of the under-privileged masses hardly registers itself upon his mind."[67]

These attacks led to back-channel communications between Churchill and the White House vetoing a visit to the United States by Laski. Despite the personal interest of Eleanor Roosevelt in the invitation, Churchill cabled Harry Hopkins, the President's close aide, that Laski was a "nuisance over here and will I doubt not talk extreme left wing stuff in the United States. Although I liked his father and have maintained friendly relations with the son he has attacked me continually and tried to force my hand both in home and war politics."[68]

That same summer Laski hounded the leadership of his own party with broadsides and speeches accusing Labour Ministers of giving way too easily to Conservative policies.[69] Attlee had become Deputy Prime Minister in a cabinet reshuffle that broadened Labour membership while weakening their hold over domestic policy. Attlee knew the attacks were meant for him. Laski was actively conspiring with Aneurin Bevan to make Bevan Attlee's replacement.[70]

Privately, Laski began to doubt the prospects for a peaceful change to socialism in Britain, writing in August 1942 to Beatrice Webb: "I find it hard to convince myself that there is any longer a chance here of a peaceful transition to socialism." In the same letter, he excused the atrocities of the Soviet regime:

> I am confident that the main defects are either the outcome of external fear or the grim growing pains which result from imposing the dynamic of a modern industrialised state on a backward and illiterate population. The price has been tremendous, the follies, even the crimes, immense. I still believe that, with victory, it will, fifty years from now, prove to have been worth while.[71]

Publicly in the *Daily Herald*, he saluted the twenty-fifth anniversary of the creation of the Soviet Union by picturing Russian and British socialists as comrades: "They will do everything necessary to make certain that swift and audacious attack which is the herald of victory to enable the two great movements to march together side by side."[72] The contrast between Laski's forgiving attitude toward Stalin and the remarkable hostility to Churchill is striking.

His break with Churchill seems to have snapped the last strands of his allegiance to Britain's establishment. Newman observes that Laski came into his own during the war and that

> his theory and practice were in harmony once again, and he was prepared to court unpopularity and personal hardship in the attempt to translate his vision into reality. The war had also eliminated the elitist strain which had often been evident in his attitudes in the past. He constantly expressed the fear that political leaders were unworthy of the masses . . . , and he devoted himself to the effort to ensure that they were not betrayed. During the Second World War he was therefore what he most wanted to be: "a soldier in the liberation army of humanity."[73]

The vision that guided him was apocalyptic. In a BBC discussion with the American journalist Edward R. Murrow, Laski set out his conception of postwar politics:

> Laski: My feeling is that we are midway between two extremes: the extreme of big business in America and the extreme of Russian communism, and that we might act as a bridge between the two—a mediator that would find common terms for the common adventure.
> Murrow: Or you might be between two millstones.
> Laski: Well, that's a grave danger. That's why I have insisted on an understanding before the war comes to a close.
> Murrow: What happens if we fail to reach that understanding?
> Laski: If we fail to reach that understanding we go straight into the conditions out of which there's another world war, and therefore our job is to see to it that we secure that understanding whatever the price that any private interests have to pay.[74]

Laski flung himself at those who opposed him, leaving behind the vestiges of moderation. Indefatigable despite the rigors of wartime travel and the uncertainty of his marginal health, he traveled the country speaking, writing, and participating in workers tribunals, all the while continuing his teaching at LSE.

Moving forward on all fronts in the struggle for a socialist democracy, Laski was hobbled by the reticence and timidity of many in his own movement. Even George Bernard Shaw who for decades had fired his pen at the heart of the capitalist establishment was, by 1941, writing to Webb: "The wisdom of the people is a myth. Democracy should secure them a means of ventilating their grievances and give them a choice of *qualified* rulers every four of five years. . . . The problem to be solved is the qualification. I can't solve it, nor can anyone else."[75]

Laski's grand plan institutionalizing a socialized economy now had been rebuffed by Churchill as well as by Attlee and the other Labour Ministers of the coalition government. Nevertheless, he pressed the fight in Labour's NEC. Socialists were at risk of being used, he claimed, to fight a war that would only solidify the preeminence of capitalism. Absent progress on socialist measures, the rank and file would end the war no better off, for all their sacrifices, than before. He even used the threat that failing Conservative acquiescence in these measures, Labour should consider breaking up the wartime coalition and going into opposition. This gave Attlee a strong card to play, namely the paramount need for unity in Britain's hour of mortal peril. Laski's radical program would require a general election that could not possibly be held with the war consuming every resource, and the developing alliance with the United States would be gravely disrupted. Attlee prevailed with the party's leadership, but just barely.[76]

Laski fought back as the Parliamentary Labour Party (PLP) pressed the government for implementation of the Beveridge Report that had been published on December 1, 1942. Laski's presumption that a plan to address working-class security would yield a huge dividend in public unity at a time of crisis turned out to be correct—but the plan was that of the ever-cautious Beveridge, suitably coached on economics by Keynes, not the nationalization scheme of the radical Laski.

Laski saw the report as a preliminary step to true socialism. He saluted Beveridge, with whom relations had nearly been broken over differences during his last years at LSE, for advancing principles that would save democracy.[77] In the preface to a new book, Laski appropriated Beveridge's initiative for the promotion of his own plan: "The whole burden of Sir William's remarkable analysis seems to me to reinforce the conclusion . . . that it is in the months between now and our victory that we have to take those vital decisions upon which depends our power to use it for great purposes. If we wait beyond the victory before we make our choice, we shall throw away one of the supreme opportunities of history."[78]

Beveridge's scheme did not impress Churchill or the parliamentary Conservatives. They resisted the rush to adoption, speaking only platitudes in support of its objectives. Labour challenged the cabinet on the issue in the House of Commons and got the largest opposition vote of the war.[79] While the Labour Ministers supported the government's response, only two Labour M.P.s could be found to vote for delay. As a result of the skirmish over the implementation of the Beveridge Report, Laski and his allies on the left now commanded the overwhelming support of the PLP.[80] This marked the beginning of the resumption of party contestation that had been suspended at the outbreak of hostilities.

The personal strain on Laski was becoming immense. There were the battles with and between his colleagues in the Labour leadership and the Conservatives. Within his family, the friction with his older brother, Neville, that existed since childhood was aggravated by Neville's disapproval of the engagement of Laski's niece to a Christian. Neville referred to his brother as a "phoney" in conversations with political colleagues and held him responsible for a diminution of his career prospects in the judiciary.[81] Together with the passing of his father and his mother's series of heart attacks, Laski's familial commitments were increasingly a source of grief and tension. Only the steadying reassurance of Frida and the delight over their grandson gave him private solace as he battled for his grand plan.

As he had when the government fumbled the response to the depression, Laski turned to the leader for whom he had the greatest hopes: President Franklin Delano Roosevelt. In an open letter published in the *New York Times* and the *New Statesman*, Laski put his plan to the President:

> Were you to say that a war for democracy and freedom must be directly concerned now with those problems of ownership and control in the economic sphere upon which a real and lasting victory depends, our propagandists in the United States would cease to promise their press conferences that there is no danger of Britain going Socialist after the war. You would reinforce the influence of that large body of opinion here which is ready for great experiment in the field of social and economic justice. Only freedom from want and fear deliberately organised now can make the foundations of democracy secure in the post-war world.[82]

Whether he seriously expected a response from the President is not known. However, the letter had begun with a blunt attack on named members of the Roosevelt administration for countenancing right-wing opposition groups in occupied countries and bringing in business leaders to help run the war. To preface a plea for endorsement with accusations of a sellout was hardly diplomatic.

The letter did draw angry notes from Roosevelt to Frankfurter and from Laski's friend, American Ambassador Winant, for whom Laski had written speeches. Laski wrote to Winant that he was "completely unrepentant" about it. "My regret is that I have no means of making what I said clear to the millions who hope for the four freedoms and will find they are slowly left to drift into a new feudalism."[83] Politesse gave way to political passion.

A few days after the letter appeared, Laski was attacked from another quarter. Lord Haw-Haw, the expatriate British citizen turned Nazi propagandist, devoted his whole broadcast to a vitriolic denunciation of the subversive professor and his Jewish plot to anesthetize the public against the rise of Bolshevism. Beset by the continuing revelations of the massacre of Jews, Laski was caught in a crosscut of loyalties because of Churchill's resolute resistance to Hitler. If Jews were to hope for survival in Europe, the Allies must unite on victory at all costs. Advancing his plan and defending his race were becoming conflicting goals.

The tensions drove Laski to the breaking point. In August 1943, Laski was weakened by a nervous breakdown. Little is known of any medical or psychological evaluation. Simple physical exhaustion was clearly a factor. His biographers, Isaac Kramnick and Barry Sheerman, list a host of pressures that cumulatively bore down on a chain-smoking man of uncertain health: his father's death, the revelations of Jewish extermination on the continent, and his own daughter's embrace of Christianity. They continue:

> The world was falling apart at the seams with evidence of nightmarish inhumanity, just as his own world seemed to self-destruct. The carefully woven contradiction that constructed his life as the consummate insider friend of the Great and the Good who also thundered from the outside at their power and privilege was unraveling. . . . Laski might have confronted the limits of his life's strategy, the ultimate impossibility of supping with the mighty and the miners, with both Mr. Wigglesworth of the Harvard Board of Overseers and the wives of the police strikers.[84]

Laski's inner circle of personal commitments was weakened by these pressures, just as the calamity of his larger Jewish community was being made known and the apostasy of his militant policy views was setting him apart from the notables of his time.

Laski thus confronted a crisis that went to the core of his identity. Newman points to the link between Laski's optimism about the prospect for a postwar turn toward socialism and his willingness to undertake a punishing and highly controversial course of action to bring it about. Laski's optimism encountered the foot-dragging by Attlee, the rejection of his plan by Churchill, and the consolidation of power by a moderate coalition government. Faced with the loss of his father, Frida's skepticism about the wisdom of some of his confrontational maneuvers, and strain of the frequent absences from home surroundings, Laski's personal reserves were badly depleted. Newman concludes that "it is probable that psychological factors were a *primary* cause" of the breakdown.[85]

Laski would not be deterred. He recovered after the breakdown and continued to engage at all levels in the fight to vindicate his hopes for Britain's future. He returned to the battle with Churchill, accusing him in October of "seeking to win the war, so far as possible, for the Britain of September 3, 1939." His aspersions were cast on Attlee as well: "Coalition Government is only possible, as Mr. Attlee is fond of saying, as a process of give and take. But Mr. Churchill interprets that process to mean that the Labour Party does the giving and the Tory Party the taking."[86]

In the fall, his new book, *Reflections on the Revolution of Our Time*, appeared to skeptical reviews by colleagues such as Karl Polanyi and George Orwell. Polanyi, whose epic analysis of economic history, *the Great Transformation*, would be published shortly, faulted Laski's "crudity" in advancing the simple thesis of capitalist collapse, the socialist revolution, and the abolition of the profit motive. Polanyi points to Soviet reliance on expansionist monetary policy and its belated recognition of the importance of commercial markets, but most of all to the importance of social values rather than simple economic panaceas as the key to a better future.[87] George Orwell professed support for Laski's objectives, but doubted that the consequences for freedom would be benign:

> Professor Laski knows pretty well what reforms he wants, and few thinking men will disagree with him: he wants centralised ownership, planned production, social equality and the "positive state." Much too readily, however—indeed with an almost Nineteenth Century optimism—he assumes that these things not only can but certainly will be combined with democracy and freedom of thought.[88]

Still tied to conventions of laissez-faire economics and moderation in advancing the claims of the working class, the Labour Party membership was confronted by Laski's militancy. As Chair of the 1944 annual conference, he got through an endorsement of nationalization over the objection of Attlee and other moderates. Recruiting allies, he got his Socialist League comrade, Aneurin Bevan, elected to the NEC.[89]

In the spring of 1944, he wrote again to Attlee complaining bitterly about the moderate course taken by him and other Labour Ministers. Attlee's long reply in a letter marked "private and confidential" is a plea for understanding and cooperation. Attlee cites the successful introduction and acceptance over the previous decade of key elements of socialist thinking: "the doctrines of abundance, of full employment, and of social security." What had been controversial at the beginning of the thirties was now widely accepted. Attlee sketched the road by which the next step could be taken: "The transfer to public ownership of certain major economic forces and the planned control in the public interest of many other economic activities." Two key conditions would have to be met: the preparation of public opinion and the mollification of socialism's critics in the international community.

The latter problem, the balancing act between serving Britain's desperate economic needs in the postwar world and advancing a socialist program that threatened world capitalism, clearly was the most vexing. Attlee saw Britain as situated between the USSR and the United States and in no position to deal with the Soviets without the full support of the Americans. The implication was clear. Britain would need to constrain its moves toward socialism in order to keep the United States as an ally.[90]

But Laski was intent on working the triangle of relationships between Britain, the United States, and the USSR from another salient. In a book review, he celebrated the USSR as the "one effective Socialist State in the modern world." Blaming the tensions between Britain and the USSR on the concerted attacks by all elements of the capitalist ruling class, Laski points to the wartime alliance as a time to recognize the value of the Soviet experiment. "The future of Anglo-Soviet relations seems to me to be bound up, if it is not to repeat the tragic history" of the World War I settlement.[91]

On the American side, Laski envisioned an alliance based on the progressive extension of the New Deal, together with advances toward socialism in Britain. His hopes were not altogether chimerical. He was accused in 1944 of having been the inspiration for Vice President Henry Wallace's speeches advocating a leftward course for America after the war. These positions cost Wallace the vice presidency, and Wallace's later remarks blaming the United States and the USSR equally for postwar tensions cost him his place in the Truman cabinet. Kramnick and Sheerman suggest that Wallace was "the closest parallel in American politics to Laski in Britain's."[92] Britain would become, in Laski's conception, the active force in showing Russia a better kind of socialism, and the United States a more thoroughgoing progressivism. Together, the three would forge a new world. This was the international extension of Laski's plan for Britain.

The reelection of Roosevelt in 1944 gave Laski fresh hope, and he wrote a warm letter of congratulation urging him onward in the struggle "to lay the foundations of peace and civilized living."[93] Roosevelt's gracious reply mentioned only the international side of the equation. At home, the forces opposed to Laski's vision were gathering their strength and received a huge boost from Laski's own colleague, Hayek. In 1944 Hayek's *Road to Serfdom* names Laski in a direct attack on economic planning. Laski's hitherto amiable relationship with his contrarian colleague was severed for good.[94]

6.3 – HAYEK: REJOINDER TO REVOLUTION

When the bombing of London precipitated the moving of LSE to Cambridge, Maynard Keynes arranged rooms for Hayek, and their personal relationship was restored. Keynes, his wife, and the Hayeks socialized on the weekends. Their conversations ranged over shared interests outside of economics. Hayek found Keynes, like the great Austrian economist Joseph Schumpeter, to have "a puckish itch *pour épater le bourgeois* (to shock the conventionally-minded) and a certain pretence to omniscience and a tendency to bluff which went far beyond their astounding knowledge."[95] Nevertheless they became "very friendly" according to Hayek.[96]

The fundamental political and economic views of the two combatants were never reconciled. Hayek's former ally, Lionel Robbins, had come over to Keynes's position on the role of government in the economy.[97] Robbins had admitted to regretting bitterly his earlier opposition to Keynes's pump-priming measures. This left Hayek, as an economic policy adviser, truly the odd man out.

The problem with Hayek's opposition to economic planning was it seemed to condemn postwar Britain to a replay of the twenties and thirties. Once again, there would be rising unemployment hopefully to cure high wages and presumably to reintroduce competitiveness to Britain's trade position. Having just fought the century's second war, the public was not in a mood for returning to the insecurities and deprivation of the status quo ante.

Beveridge's second great initiative, *Employment Policy*, a report issued in May 1944, pointed the direction away from Hayek's cherished principles of market primacy, though he stopped short of recommending the nationalization of basic industries. The fact that Churchill's government commissioned the Beveridge Report attests to the reality of Labour's power in the coalition, as well as to Churchill's awareness of the need to cultivate the support of the British masses. Hayek was unmoved by these political calculations.

Perhaps Hayek's animosity to Beveridge's conduct as Director of LSE influenced his reaction to the reports. In later years, he viewed Beveridge as merely "a marvelous expositor. He had the gift of making it lead to any bridge you gave him. . . . He knew no economics whatever."[98] At the time, he characterized the report on unemployment as pure Keynes. In a review,

Hayek sees that Beveridge "swallows the demand-deficiency theory lock, stock, and barrel."[99] Here was the policy form of what he had labeled in 1941 as Keynes's "economics of abundance" in which "no real scarcity exists." In Hayek's view, Keynes was inviting policy makers such as Beveridge to disregard prices as motivators, substituting instead a kind of directed consumption that would channel the flow of resources toward socially useful purposes.[100]

Enthusiasts of Keynes in the United States would take the blueprint Beveridge supplied and use it in 1943 to begin drafting a similar proposal, originally entitled the Full Employment Act. It was passed by the postwar Congress as, simply, the Employment Act of 1946. With that, the Council of Economic Advisers was put in place to guide the United States toward maximum employment.[101] The U.S. Congress did not, however, fund the public jobs that were part of the strategy until the late 1960s—and then only on a very limited basis. This more direct approach to full employment would not meet with broader approval until, paradoxically, the welfare "reforms" of the 1990s when job subsidization, at least in some states, was traded for an end to entitlements.

For Hayek, these early moves toward state guarantees of economic security were confirmation of his darkest fears. As disturbed by the rise of fascism as he was by socialism, Hayek saw them as false gods graven on two sides of the same coin—a view contrary to Laski's and Beveridge's popular analysis that fascism was the work of capitalists intent on defeating democratic socialism. Hayek saw both fascism and socialism as regimes intent on constructing social and economic outcomes through bureaucracies. These civil servants, politicians, and planners inevitably, and dangerously, undermine the economic efficiencies that are achieved through the market's utilization of dispersed knowledge. These distortions lead to ever-increasing inflation as governments make work for the unemployed and pay for it by printing money.[102]

Hayek also condemned both fascism and socialism as the logical result of the abdication of individual responsibility to government control. This was directly counter to the view taken by, among legions of others, Laski. In 1941 Laski had stated the prevailing view among intellectuals in the draft of a Labour Party pamphlet on Russia's entry into the war:

> It is not, I think, true to say that Bolshevism was the true parent of Fascism in all its forms. It is more accurate to insist that, as a consequence of the war of 1914, capitalist Democracy was struck a heavy blow from which it could only have recovered in an age of expanding welfare. That expansion did not come;

and the unrest to which disappointment and the frustrations of defeat had given birth made the price of Democracy seem excessive to those who felt that it was a threat to their privileges. The significance of Bolshevism was that it provided privilege everywhere with an excuse for counter-revolution.[103]

Moving from the economics of knowledge to moral philosophy, Hayek began to invoke cultural themes from the canon of Western civilization. Stephen Kresge notes the parlous wartime circumstances in which Hayek, with bombs falling around him, memorialized his fears:

> Frightening as the bombs were, perhaps even more alarming were the changes going on in the minds of economists and philosophers in the still-free world. . . . Outwardly, people seemed to be who they had been. Inside, they were captured by an alien spirit. The irony was that Hayek was treated as an alien while he, increasingly alone, preserved a devotion to that very liberty being fought for against the Axis powers.[104]

At this dark hour, Hayek published his polemical *Road to Serfdom* (1944). The book made his reputation as a political thinker of great consequence. By his own admission, the book also completed his fall from grace among professional economists. What his differences with Keynesianism precipitated, his diatribe on planning completed.[105]

The dedication of *The Road to Serfdom* to "the socialists in all parties" displays a hint of irony not present in the rest of the book. While the focus on the fallacies of economic planning is responsible for its fame, the intent of the book, according to its introduction, was to extricate the liberal tradition from the peril it was placed in by the combination of conservative statism and socialist political economy.

At the outset, Hayek argues that the rise of fascism has nothing to do with the German character and culture and everything to do with a doctrinal appeal to the masses. "It was the prevalence of socialist views and not 'Prussianism' that Germany had in common with Italy and Russia—and it was from the masses and not from the classes steeped in the Prussian tradition, and favored by it, that National Socialism arose."[106] The role of German industrialists in sponsoring the rise of fascist politicians is unmentioned. Then, deeper into the discussion, we find a curious turn in the argument:

> Few people will deny that the Germans on the whole are industrious and disciplined, thorough and energetic to the degree of ruthlessness, conscientious and single-minded in any tasks they undertake; that they possess a strong sense of order, duty, and strict obedience to authority; and that they often show great

readiness to make personal sacrifices and great courage in physical danger. All these make the German an efficient instrument in carrying out an assigned task, and they have accordingly been carefully nurtured in the old Prussian state and the new Prussian-dominated Reich.[107]

Contradictory as the apparent denial and then affirmation of Prussian stereo-typing appears to be, it is just possible to disentangle a thread of argument.[108] Hayek was at pains to avoid mimicking German anti-Semitic racism by es-chewing any endorsement of the reverse argument that character was some-how ingrained in a given nationality. But Hayek was fully aware of the power of cultural tradition, in this case Prussian conservatism. It was the alliance be-tween this conservative cultural tradition, with its emphasis on the over-weening role of the state, and the newer doctrinal appeal of socialism, eager to enlist the state in its quest for equality in the economic sphere, that formed the danger to liberalism. The latter, Hayek argues, has its Germanic exponents of great distinction, and the true struggle is between liberalism, with its valu-ation of individualism, on one side, and the collectivist impulses of traditional conservatives and socialists alike, on the other.

What Hayek wants to do is to separate out the influences of cultural tradi-tions and doctrines from national character in some deeper sense and to argue that doctrines can be confronted and changed and traditions modified and redirected. This element of humanism provided a common bond between Hayek and other continental and American intellectuals, many of whom were to be involved later in the Mt. Pelerin Society. Yet the argument is rather at odds with his later invocation of the spontaneous evolution of moral tradition as the basis for the progress of society. Prussianism may be deviant from some other perceived moral and cultural tradition, but why is one tradition to be valued and not another?

Hayek's point was to address what he saw as the peril of England that, he claimed, "finally took the headlong plunge and, in the short space of the in-glorious years 1931–1939, transformed its economic system beyond recogni-tion."[109] He includes America in the same generalization, making no distinc-tion between the activist New Deal and the considerably milder initiatives of the Conservative British government of the 1930s. The tepid response in En-gland that alienated Keynes from politics, and infuriated the socialist Laski, was, to Hayek, tantamount to a crisis in the future of the West.

The key point was whether centralized coercive power is to be used to im-plement planning or whether processes will be put in place that permit indi-viduals to most efficiently plan for themselves.[110] Even the comparatively modest measures of the 1930s Conservatives were perceived by Hayek to involve a dangerous slide toward centralized coercion. During the war, the rapid escalation of price and wage controls fleshed out the phantom that haunted his vision of the West in the postwar era.

While founded on deep distress about England's slide to collectivism, the book contains surprising acknowledgments of the fundamental role of government in providing for minimum sustenance and social insurance. He begins by distinguishing two kinds of security: "the security of minimum income and the security of the particular income a person is thought to deserve." This distinction, he believes, "largely coincides with the distinction between the security which can be provided for all outside of and supplementary to the market system and the security which can be provided only for some and only by controlling or abolishing the market." The former kind of security is acceptable according to Hayek:

> Where there was no threat to competition, as in the provision of basic minimums of income and welfare, or of services for which there can be no viable market, or no profit potential, there is a role for government action if the ends are socially worthy.[111]

In addition to such minimums, Hayek explicitly endorses social insurance:

> Where, as in the case of sickness and accident, neither the desire to avoid such calamities nor the efforts to overcome their consequences are as a rule weakened by the provision of assistance—where, in short, we deal with genuinely insurable risks—the case for the state's helping to organize a comprehensive system of social insurance is very strong. . . . There is no incompatibility in principle between the state's providing greater security in this way and the preservation of individual freedom.[112]

Hayek then aligns his endorsement of the market, as opposed to coercive government, with the cause of morality in human behavior. In an argument that would have substantial implications for his personal situation, he argues:

> Only where we ourselves are responsible for our own interests and are free to sacrifice them has our decision moral value. We are neither entitled to be unselfish at someone else's expense nor is there any merit in being unselfish if we have no choice.[113]

Morality relies entirely on the existence of individual choice. Unless we have the possibility of being immoral at someone else's expense, there can be no morality. Better there should be immorality than the foreclosure of choice, because without choice there could be no morality. Morality, in this view, depends for its existence on the possibility of its opposite.

By this same argument, there is no shared moral responsibility in a culture, society, or nation. Never mind the links of consent between the individual and a democratically accountable government. On Hayek's argument, what such a government does with its coercive power is indistinguishable from what a dictatorship does—both remove choice through coercion. Never mind either the ineluctably social character of human development; individual autonomy is taken as the fundamental desideratum.

Furthermore, he sees the decline of personal morality as the correlate of rising collectivism. "Almost all the traditions and institutions in which democratic moral genius has found its most characteristic expression, and which in turn have molded the national character and the whole moral climate of England and America, are those which the progress of collectivism and its inherently centralistic tendencies are progressively destroying."[114] "National character," excluded as a consideration in dealing with the Germans, is brought back in to the argument to bemoan the decline of morals in the West.

While the book is often taken as a blanket endorsement of laissez-faire, Hayek is at pains to note the essential contribution of the "the rule of law" to liberal society. By this he means laws that permit people to work out their own destiny, not those laws that either advantage particular people or permit individuals to use the coercive power of the state for their own interests.[115] This distinction leaves out an extensive list of conventional government activities well short of "centralized planning."[116] The maintenance of the distinction would very clearly call for a high degree of shared agreement and discipline on the part of the populace. Certainly, the ability of governments to address the grievances of those who had been victimized or discriminated against would be sharply curtailed. The power to privilege one group is the power to make restitution to another.

Remarkably, Beveridge is not mentioned in *Road to Serfdom*. Beveridge's proposals, for all their moderation in a climate of socialist and communist rhetoric, represented a much more elusive target than the images of commissars and coercion that Hayek would evoke. Beveridge reviewed Hayek's book and declared, that Hayek "is not I think a man who understands the British mentality. . . . I did not find his book the least convincing."[117] Keynes, for that matter, is not mentioned by name except for a passage in which Hayek quotes his rival as having a frightening analysis of German statism in 1915!

Laski was an easier target. He rates three direct references in the book, all suggesting that Laski's views are parallel in their endorsement of statist power, even in the face of democratic resistance, to those of fascists.[118] He cites Laski's references to the depreciation of liberty under conditions of economic privation and his endorsement of security provided by the state. Hayek declaims that "it is disquieting to find Professor Harold Laski employing the very same argument which has perhaps done more than any other to induce the German people to sacrifice their liberty."[119] Small wonder that, as Hayek later remarked, Laski had "got in his mind that *The Road to Serfdom* was written against him" and their social relationship was terminated.[120]

The book had not been out long when Hayek received a letter from a most significant reader, Maynard Keynes. Hayek, and his defenders, would often cite in later years the following passage: "You will not expect me to accept quite all the economic dicta in it. But morally and philosophically I find myself in agreement with virtually the whole of it; and not only in agreement with it, but in a deeply moved agreement."[121] Fulsome praise indeed, though such complimentary, sometimes flowery openings were typical of Keynes's critical interchanges with numerous interlocutors. Keynes's manners, at least in his letters, were impeccable. Criticism was nearly always preceded by a compliment, even flattery.

What Hayek does not quote is the remainder of the letter that is a catalog of dissents on every major point. Keynes wants Hayek to admit that the thesis of prospective abundance is not all wrong in view of the progress made against unemployment. Next, Keynes argues that "quite likely from the purely economic point of view it [planning] is efficient," contrary to Hayek's claim. Citing "technical advancement" through planning in existing communities, he points out that limited planning need not, in current circumstances, "require the superfluous sacrifice of liberties." That said, he comes to his "only serious criticism," that Hayek gives no "guidance whatever as to where to draw" the line between too much planning and not enough. He points to the "slippery path" nature of Hayek's argument. Keynes continues by suggesting that more, rather than less, planning is desirable. However, "the planning should take place in a community in which as many people as possible, both leaders and followers, wholly share your own moral position."[122]

Several ironies present themselves. Keynes, once perceived as an immoralist, now recognizes the moral foundation of political economy. Hayek seems to want to dispense with moral considerations by ingeniously defending a "spontaneous social process" in which "unintended consequences" absolve individuals from moral responsibility for collective problems. Hayek wants to replace the cultural content of morality with a *process* for allowing moral behavior to emerge. Keynes had seen enough of moral stupidity in India, World

War I, and the depression to make him skeptical of such an unreasoning faith
in spontaneity.

Keynes concludes his letter with one of his justly famous prophecies:

> What we need therefore, in my opinion, is not a change in our economic pro-
> grammes, which would only lead in practice to disillusion with the results of
> your philosophy; but perhaps even the contrary, namely, an enlargement of
> them. Your greatest danger ahead is the probable practical failure of the appli-
> cation of your philosophy in the United States.[123]

Keynes's prognosis is the more interesting now that Hayek has become the
leading spirit of the right in Britain, America, and much of the world.
Keynes's point was that a too strict application of laissez-faire might well
lead to the discrediting of capitalism entirely and, with that, the loss of its
virtues.

Skepticism similar in tone characterized the review of Hayek's book by
Joseph Schumpeter, fellow economist, Austrian, and sometime admirer of
capitalism—at least for its entrepreneurial drive. Schumpeter points to the
utopian quality of Hayek's premises that

> the author deals with ideas and principles as if they floated in the air. If he had
> gone into the historical conditions from which the ideas arose which he dislikes
> so much, he could not have helped discovering that they are the products of the
> social system which he does like. The principles of individual initiative and self-
> reliance are the principles of a very limited class. They mean nothing to the
> mass of people who—no matter for what reason—are not up to the standard
> they imply. It is this majority that the economic achievement and the liberal pol-
> icy of the capitalist age have invested with dominant power.[124]

Schumpeter picks up on what will increasingly trouble Hayek: the relationship between capitalism and democracy.

His old mentor, Ludwig von Mises wrote to praise his protégé's work
highly. He was not optimistic about how persuasive it would turn out, fearing
that the "Laski–Keynes ideology" had too firm a hold on England.[125] The evidence for von Mises' prophecy would follow in the climactic year of 1945.

The seeds of doctrinal divergence that had been sown in the twenties and thirties sprang to full life in the pressured years of the war. Lord Keynes, now the
unofficial master of Whitehall, could implement his *via media* with the tools
provided by the necessities of mobilization. Finance was foremost, and this

was his supreme accomplishment. He put in place measures that left England with less inflation than after World War I and with at least a chance of a return to prosperity with the assistance of a carefully cultivated ally, the United States. Less noticed at the time was his instrumental role in shaping the Beveridge plans to reflect some fiscal and political realities that gave them a far better chance of practical success.

Harold Laski's war of socialist liberation took place mainly on the home front, as he mounted a furious charge toward a revolutionary transformation of the British economy. Rejected by Labour and Conservative leaders alike, he took his case to the masses and built a popular movement that would overtake the government once the war had ended. Both Laski and Keynes paid a fearful price. Sustained by their wives, they teetered on the edge of physical collapse. Yet there was no loss of resolve, and the advent of peace found them still ready to fight on for their distinctive visions of Britain's future.

For Friedrich Hayek, the war brought a sharp diminution of his eminence as an economic theorist and an opening to a new identity as political theorist and polemicist. Isolated politically, withdrawn personally from his marriage, and engaged more and more with like-minded dissident intellectuals, he gathered his resources for a new initiative both professionally and personally. The publication of his most famous book and the impending disavowal of his marriage would set him on a new course of life.

7

The Postwar World: Denouement

The advent of peace brought to fruition key elements of the ambitious plans for Britain's future that Maynard Keynes and Harold Laski had each developed in the course of the war and the realization of the fears that had motivated Friedrich Hayek's life work. The Beveridge reports laid out a program of mild socialism, and this program became the focal point for differing responses from all three. However, for Keynes, the primary role was to take him to center stage as the wizard of international stature who could fashion the institutional framework of the postwar recovery. The Bretton Woods conference in 1944 laid the foundations of a new order in international political economy. The loan negotiations with the United States redefined Britain's relationship with its most powerful ally, even while it set the terms for the dissolution of the empire.

Laski's rise to the pantheon of Labour leaders placed him at the center of the climactic election effort in 1945. Even as he would battle to make the Labour Party's program more militant, he found his rendezvous with history in the amazing victory over Winston Churchill. His subsequent blunders in the penumbra of success would precipitate a fall from grace and the decline of his physical vitality.

Hayek had nailed to the door of the public forum his characterization of the drift toward a government-directed society as the road to serfdom. He was now embarked on a new course with fresh allies. His personal circumstances would change as well, interweaving strongly felt emotions with his quest for a new life across the Atlantic. All three men were to find their views adapted and repositioned for a new conflict: the Cold War.

7.1 – KEYNES: CREATING THE POSTWAR WORLD

Maynard Keynes's reformist economics may have come to center stage, but the politics of moderation were not aligned as the war ended. In the election of 1945, Lord Maynard Keynes could not vote by virtue of his new status; however, he made a small contribution to the Liberal Party, a vestige of his old loyalty.[1] William Beveridge stood as a Liberal candidate, hoping to enter Parliament to see through the implementation of his life's greatest work. However, the mood in England was by now polarized. Loyalists to Churchill, even among Liberals, defeated Beveridge who, in any case, lacked the common touch needed for constituency campaigning.[2] The Labour Party, with Laski as Chair of the National Executive Committee (NEC), won the overall election resoundingly.

Events overtook the process of postwar economic planning in successive thunderclaps. Franklin Roosevelt passed away in April 1945. Hitler died by his own hand on May 1. Germany surrendered. In the space of less than a month in the summer of 1945, the new Labour cabinet replaced the coalition government of Churchill. The atomic bombs were dropped, ending the war in Asia. Britain found itself catapulted into the postwar world with huge debts, immense damage, and a disintegrating empire. President Truman abruptly terminated the Lend-Lease program. There was also a threat to Europe from the Soviets, an experiment in socialism about to be launched, and the partnership of Churchill and Roosevelt gone.

The sudden rift with the United States was ominous for Britain's postwar prospects. The cancellation of Lend-Lease in the summer of 1945 was driven mainly by the U.S. quandary regarding the Soviet military threat. George Kennan, then on the embassy staff in Moscow, had argued for the termination of Lend-Lease after the Warsaw Uprising of 1944. The Soviet advance into Germany raised the clear prospect of aggression in Europe at the end of the war. Lend-Lease would have provided supplies to Russia that could make that possible.[3]

However, to cancel Lend-Lease to Russia only, and not to Britain and France, was to invite the collapse of the Western alliance at the critical moment when a framework for a postwar international order was being put in place. Truman's action on Lend-Lease, which he later regarded as his greatest mistake, was not intended to humiliate Britain. He had signed an order without reading it that bade Lend-Lease ships currently under way to turn around. He countermanded the order when he was advised of its adverse impact on U.S.–British relations.[4]

The initial favorable public reaction in the United States to the termination of Lend-Lease was increased by an American perception of the ingratitude of Britain as made evident by British hostility upon the program's termination. Public discussion of the plight of the British led to a reversion to remorse, however tepid, that left open a bit of negotiating room for the British. The British saw this only through their own eyes, not understanding the interplay with the question of postwar American–Soviet relations.[5]

The abrupt transition from war to peace led to the false hope in England that the United States would provide a financial bridge to peacetime economic stability. Keynes was the bearer of the bad news after soundings in the United States.[6] The American refusal to consider a grant to Britain was influenced by the same policy quandary, as there was similar pressure to provide a grant to Russia.[7] The American position was fiercely contested between isolationists in the Congress and internationalists in the administration. The net result was a stringent provision for credit to tide the British over until better days. Keynes had the task of selling both the Bretton Woods arrangements, which diminished Britain's primacy in financial markets, and the terms of a loan he feared were inadequate.[8]

Keynes took personal responsibility for nearly every detail of negotiation and persuasion involving Bretton Woods and the loan arrangements. Charged with rescuing Britain's grievously wounded trade relations, he was caught between the interest of British conservatives in maintaining a preference for trade from the Commonwealth and the socialist suspicion of propping up capitalism by collusion among Western powers.[9]

Keynes's campaign received support from an unexpected source. The British Ambassador, Lord Halifax, remarked in his dispatch at the time of the struggle for approval: "It is amusing to note that Professor Friedrich von Hayek, upon whom the economic tories in this country placed so much hope, founded upon the Professor's indubitably anti–New Deal views, has proved a most embarrassing ally to them since his passion for free trade makes him no less hostile to tariffs and monopolies."[10] While the measures of government involvement in the economy might be objectionable, they were preferable to the regime of tariffs and the return of economic nationalism that would likely result from a failure to approve of the scheme. Hayek was joined in this position by eminent figures from Wall Street who helped to secure the overwhelming approval of the agreement in the U.S. House of Representatives.[11]

Whatever Hayek did, or refrained from doing, that may have helped the loan negotiations, was more than balanced by the hostile reaction to pronouncements from Laski. The *New York Times* featured Laski's depiction of big business as "hard, relentless, and grasping." Why, asked a columnist, should the capitalist United States float billions of hard-earned dollars for the socialist experimentation of "panhandlers" such as Laski.[12] American senators and congressmen raised with Keynes questions about Laski's influence as he met with them over dinner to cultivate support for a loan.[13]

Just as Keynes's primacy in postwar political economy was most visible, his personal vitality was steadily undermined. Keynes's health had been marginal since 1937 when he had his first heart attack. The diagnosis involved bacterial endocarditis, a form of infection that would progressively weaken the heart. Though there was no cure in 1937, he was treated two years later with partial success by a doctor who used an experimental antibiotic. His wife, Lydia, took over his care and applied all the discipline and dedication that made her a great ballerina to the care of an increasingly invalided husband. To the wit that sustained their lively marriage, she added a regime of enforced care that doubtless made possible the nine-year extension of his life and prodigious energies.[14]

Now minor heart attacks were part of his travels, and he confided to Lionel Robbins that he was running out his string.[15] The government put the agreements through the House of Commons by a vote of 343 to 100, and it was left to Keynes to carry the debate on the loan agreements in the House of Lords. Skepticism about Keynes's "sellout" of British interests in the negotiations had been fanned by Lord Beaverbrook and the British media. With one hundred abstentions, the Lords approved the loans by a margin of 90 to 8, and the Bretton Woods Agreement was then ratified without a division. Keynes's advocacy likewise persuaded the British government to ratify the agreements for the International Monetary Fund (IMF) and the Bank for Reconstruction and Development in December of 1945. When the Soviets declined to ratify Bretton Woods, the thought that Russia more than Britain might be the Americans' best strategic partner in the postwar era was disproven.[16]

Altogether, it was a heroic victory for Keynes's grand plan, and one that had been "snatched from the jaws of defeat." Peter Clarke and Robert Skidelsky, who studied the record in great detail, agree that Keynes might have approached the negotiations in a stepwise fashion and perhaps avoided the possibility of a great humiliation. However, Keynes imperiously pressed on, perhaps conscious of the dwindling horizon of his own mortality. An additional factor may well have been a fear of the gathering storm over Britain's leftward direction. Laski's plan for Britain may have inadvertently provided an impetus for Keynes to forge ahead. That the agreement was "unworkable" according to Skidelsky may have been the consequence of this pressure. A postwar run on the dollar caused the suspension of convertibility to sterling

Maynard Keynes and Harry Dexter White at the Savannah Conference in March 1946. Courtesy of Milo Keynes.

within six weeks. The $3.5 billion loan, however, did enable Britain to begin its experiment with socialism. Another $2.6 billion in Marshall Plan aid likely saved the pound.[17]

In the spring of 1946, Keynes was called on again to go to the United States, this time to a conference in Savannah, Georgia, to work out the implementation of the Bank and the IMF. The negotiations were vexing owing to the assertion of American authority in a manner Keynes found to be predictable but poorly informed. This was his fifth trip to the United States in four years, each time for exhausting and highly consequential negotiations.

Keynes returned to England after Savannah, suffering at least two more minor heart attacks. At Easter time he finally received a respite from work and returned home to Tilton in the South Downs. Keynes, along with Lydia and his mother, visited their neighbors at the Charleston farmhouse, the scene of so many memorable gatherings of the Bloomsbury set. Leaving Lydia at Tilton, he made his way along the lane to Charleston for tea with old friends Vanessa and Clive Bell and the other great love of Keynes's life, Duncan Grant. Two days later, he set his sights once more on Firle Beacon, a long steep hill that separates Tilton and Charleston from the sea. Firle offered its peaceful vista, and the Keyneses ascended by car. Deciding to walk down, he and Lydia conversed animatedly. The next morning, Easter Sunday, April 21, 1946, he was taken down by a heart attack that ended his life within minutes. With Lydia at his side, he died at the age of sixty-three.[18]

That evening Vanessa Bell and Duncan Grant dined with a composed Lydia at Tilton.[19] Then the public tributes began. Services were held at Westminster Abbey, attended by his elderly parents and the principals of the British establishment led by Prime Minister Clement Attlee. Memorials took place within a few days at King's College Chapel and in Washington Cathedral across the Atlantic. Friedrich Hayek stated simply, "He was the one really great man I ever knew."[20]

Though his repose was to have been at King's College Chapel, his brother Geoffrey, having forgotten that instruction, returned him to his favorite retreat and scattered his ashes on Firle Beacon. Lydia's ashes would join his at the hand of Geoffrey's son, Richard, thirty-five years later in 1981. She lived to be eighty-nine, a record eclipsed by Grant, who died four years earlier at the age of ninety-three.

The man who had been born on the day Karl Marx died, himself died on a beautiful Easter Sunday in rural England. In between birth and death, John Maynard Keynes had committed his life to finding a secular morality to guide public policy, a morality intelligible to those who would but learn its meaning. He foreswore Marx and Christ in his quest, but remained a man of supreme faith. His last recorded thought was a comment to Lydia on a poem by Thomas Parnell: "And the meaning of it all is, don't worry, there is always divine justice."[21] He even, toward the very end, had a kind word for the Invisible Hand. In the maturity of his personality, he was neither fearful of admitting that the world had its own ways of surviving nor any the less convinced that the application of intelligence to policy and the design of institutions could improve the lot of humankind.

Keynes's wife, his parents, and a remarkable circle of friends and colleagues, had sustained him and enabled a rise to global eminence and a position of unparalleled influence over the postwar world. Here was a coherent identity firmly seated in durable personal commitments, an ever-wider community of disciples and advocates, and a competency that few dared to challenge.

Keynes had become a policy colossus astride the worlds of international and domestic affairs. In his persona, he represented the aspirations of a new generation intent on using intellect and humane sensibility as guides to a far better world than the prior generation had left them. His student and biographer, Roy Harrod, framed the deeper significance of his life and career for Britain's politics:

> Some credit must be given to the British democracy. Happy is the land where a wise man can wield power, simply because he is wise, although he has no support from any political group or from any financial or trade-union interest.[22]

Keynes the economist was, by most estimates, the dominant figure at least as early as 1948 when Paul Samuelson's *Economics: An Introductory Analysis* inaugurated the standardization of economics instruction on a version of the Keynesian model that was remarkably easy to grasp. What had been recognized at the practical level in the British government's budget of 1941 and the epochal Beveridge reports was now encased in axioms and memorialized as writ for a burgeoning profession of economists.[23]

Seymour Harris of Harvard saluted his achievement in 1947 with a volume of encomiums written by the leading economists of the age. It was dedicated to "those economists who, following the leadership of Keynes, are endeavoring to make of economics a useful tool for the diagnosis and treatment of economic disease."[24] The war, as a massive exercise in demand-side management, had swept away skepticism about Keynesian "pump-priming." With the notable exception of Hayek, the postwar institutionalization of regulated currencies at the international level affirmed Keynes's ascendancy.

Keynes's legacy of the managed economy dominated the politics of the fifties, sixties, and seventies through to the elections of Margaret Thatcher and Ronald Reagan. As Richard Nixon said on entering the White House, "we're all Keynesians now." As we will see, that legacy was then to be disputed by the resurgence of monetarist economics and by the popularization of

Hayek's notions of the primacy of the free market over government intrusion. First, however, the old order of capitalist political economy was to confront a fundamental challenge from democratic socialists now installed as the government of Great Britain.

7.2 – LASKI: VICTORY AND DEFEAT

By May of 1945, Laski arrived at a position of real power. He became Chair of the NEC of the Labour Party. The NEC stood at the apex of the constituency associations that formed the backbone of the party organization. Together with the Trades Unions Congress (TUC) and the Parliamentary Labour Party (PLP), they constituted a troika that determined Labour's course. As was to become clear very shortly, the roles of these respective groupings were neither well understood by the party and the public nor were they agreed on among the principal leaders.

A portrait of Harold Laski, the man, penned by a journalist at the time, suggests a strikingly odd figure among the union leaders and worker advocates of the period:

> Laski is of medium height, of slim figure. He gives the impression in his dark, well-cut clothes and white collar, with his exquisitely kept hands and well-barbered face, with his dark brown eyes behind their spectacles and his dark brown hair plastered down from its centre-parting, not of a Labour leader, but a schoolmaster—which, of course, he is.[25]

He was a schoolmaster bent on power and change. With the elections imminent, Laski was positioned to bring theory and practice together.

Despite all the dismissals by conservatives and the foot-dragging by Labour colleagues, the "revolution by consent" was now in prospect. He had reached the apogee of his power. The election would be, in Laski's mind, a referendum on a socialist future for Britain. What the revolution needed was a real leader, and Attlee, in his view and that of some of his colleagues, did not measure up. With the election only weeks away, he wrote Attlee suggesting he step down as leader and make way for a more dynamic figure. Attlee dismissed the suggestion: "Dear Laski, thank you for your letter, contents of which have been noted."[26]

Labour refused the Conservative request that the election be put off until Japan surrendered and left the government in late May 1945. Churchill formed a caretaker government and prepared for a July 5 election. Now he was the direct legatee of Conservative mismanagement in the thirties. As Clarke notes, "The 1930s were retrospectively viewed as a devil's decade, at home and abroad, with slump sliding through appeasement into war, and all presided over by Conservative politicians . . . Guilty Men! Never Again! This was the spirit of 1945."[27] Beginning from a position twenty points behind in the polls, Churchill cast about for a theme that would recapture the initiative from Labour and their popular program for social justice in postwar Britain.[28]

In early June, Churchill opened his campaign with a speech that would make Laski, the prominent intellectual and party leader, famous among the electorate at large. Distinguishing between the radicals on the NEC and the moderates in the PLP, Churchill decried the doctrinaire belief in socialism that would take Britain away from its cultural and political traditions. "Socialism is inseparably interwoven with totalitarianism and the object worship of the state. . . . Socialism is an attack on the right to breathe freely without having a harsh, clumsy, tyrannical hand clasped across the mouth and nostrils. . . . No socialist system can be established without a political police."[29] The consequence of nationalization would, he predicted, be a "Gestapo" state that would come into being to make up for the failures of planning and doctrinaire reform of the society. Churchill's speech caused a sensation in the press.[30]

Churchill, who had been constrained by the need for national unity in the war effort, had now taken off the gloves. No one could mistake the target of his blows: Harold Laski. Churchill's popularity throughout the war was attested to by polls that showed approval by more than three-quarters of the public up until May 1945.[31] But it was the prewar Churchill, the bad boy of British politics, who now came into view. David Cannadine charted the transformation of Churchill from 1940 to 1945:

> The aristocratic anachronism became the embodiment of the bulldog breed. The drinker, the gambler, the spendthrift became a national "character" . . . the belligerent class warrior, the man once likened to Mussolini, became the champion of freedom and liberty. The reactionary authoritarian became the saviour of his country. The ungentlemanly cad became the greatest Englishman of his time.[32]

This speech marked the return of the "belligerent class warrior" and the "reactionary authoritarian." To declare that democratic socialism was alien when it was the ideology of his partners in the wartime coalition struck the public as preposterous. Even the *Times* and the *Economist* cried foul.[33] A little over two weeks after the Gestapo speech, Churchill named "Professor Laski" as an intervenor among the counselors of moderation such as Attlee with whom he had worked to win the war.

The attentive public thought they knew where Churchill's lines had come from: Friedrich Hayek. Richard Cockett reports that Churchill had been apprised of Hayek's *Road to Serfdom* by Ralph Assheton, the Conservative Party Chairman. Assheton had adopted Hayek's message, and previewed the lines in the Gestapo speech, several months earlier claiming in a political speech that "when the state owns everything, the State is the only master and every man must work for the State or starve. In such a condition of affairs, we should indeed be slaves." Churchill, who read the speech and noted some comments on it, wrote to Assheton that he "thought it very good."[34]

As Isaac Kramnick and Barry Sheerman observe:

> Churchill's decision to campaign against socialist planning by equating it with a Gestapo state created the bizarre phenomenon of a general election being fought on one level between the rival doctrines of two LSE professors. . . . Not that Labour was above pandering to nationalism either. In his radio reply . . . , Attlee drew out carefully for criticism Churchill's use of the equally foreign "second-hand version of the academic views of an Austrian professor Friedrich August von Hayek."[35]

Though not named in the Gestapo speech, Laski's notoriety was reinforced two weeks later by the claim that he had given a speech advocating violent revolution. The story was prompted by a letter to the editor of one of Lord Beaverbrook's papers, and the allegation was given a wide airing in the *Daily Express*. Beaverbrook, who would later be accused of having himself masterminded the Gestapo speech, was a strident defender of his hero, Churchill.[36]

Laski took immediate offense at the accusation, protesting that his whole career had been about securing peaceful change. Laski announced that he had in fact been libeled and sued the newspapers. The suit would not be tried until after the election, but the issue could no longer be discussed in the papers.[37] Meanwhile, the Labour Party rushed out a statement denying the advocacy of violence as a party position. Churchill seized the issue and continued to use the term "violence" in association with Labour, characterizing even the mild-mannered Attlee as having given a "violent speech" in disavowing NEC control of government policy.

As NEC Chair, Laski campaigned tirelessly to defeat Churchill.[38] He injected himself directly into the campaign in mid-June with the published assertion that Attlee, invited by Churchill to participate in the Potsdam conference on the postwar settlement, would be not be bound by any undertakings that had not been previously discussed by the NEC and the PLP. Attlee should attend as an observer only since Labour was no longer part of the National

Government coalition. The professor was putting his conception of party control of government policy to the test. Laski was immediately identified in Beaverbrook's *Daily Express* as the unaccountable czar of an NEC cabal that would undermine democracy in the event of a Labour victory.[39]

There followed a press war with Churchill tearing into Laski's claims of preeminence for the "Socialist National Executive Committee." "Churchill Forces Laski Show-Down" headlined the *Daily Express.* Attlee responded with an outright rejection of Laski's position. While there would be consultations with the NEC, the Labour M.P.s and their Ministers would have full authority to decide on positions to be taken.[40]

Churchill reprised the dictatorship theme in his last speech before the vote and tied it to Laski's attempt to place the NEC in charge of government policy.[41] In truth, Churchill was trying to have it both ways. The Conservative Party platform had vaguely supported key elements of the Beveridge reforms. Churchill was making an issue of the further extension of those reforms into a planned economy and picking out Laski as an icon for the extremist interpretation of socialism.

The right-wing assault had some effect: Churchill closed the gap in the polls to 6 percent by election day.[42] A last-minute survey by the *Daily Express* indicated that 54 percent of the voters expected a Conservative victory, up four points over mid-June when the Laski charges were aired.[43]

The day after British troops marched into Berlin, England went to the polls. On Thursday, July 5, the *Daily Express* headlined Churchill's boast, "We Are Winning." "I feel it in my bones you will send me back with a great majority," he declared. Even the *Manchester Guardian* concluded that Labour's chances were remote.

The surveys and the press notwithstanding, Labour trounced the Conservatives. Labour's majority of two hundred seats more than reversed the Conservative coalition's advantage in the prior government. Labour received 47.8 percent of the vote, the Conservatives a shade less than 40 percent, and the Liberals only held twelve seats. It was a huge victory for Laski, the very visible NEC Chair, and for Herbert Morrison, the leftist Campaign Chair and Laski ally, as well as for party leader Attlee. In the new Parliament, 67 of the 393 Labour M.P.s were Laski's former students.[44]

At the moment of electoral victory, Laski tried to overthrow Attlee by a breathtaking maneuver that would have placed Herbert Morrison at the head of the new government. The "cockney of genius," as Laski called him, Morrison had come to prominence as the leader of the London County Council where "municipal socialism" had succeeded in establishing a model for public control over utilities through the use of public corporations.[45] Morrison had challenged Attlee for the leadership once before in 1935. Morrison served as Home Secretary in the war cabinet, and he was the colleague Churchill was "least sorry to have lost" when Labour left the coalition.[46]

The drama played out as the election results were announced at Labour headquarters. Throughout the campaign, the public understood that Attlee would be Prime Minister if Labour won. He had, after all, served as Deputy Prime Minister from 1942 to 1945. When Attlee received the summons to the palace by King George on Churchill's concession, Laski and Morrison told the gathering of party leaders that there should be a "time out" for two days while the PLP acted on a provision in the party rules for selecting a new leader at the opening of each Parliament. Morrison was willing to run. If successful, the maneuver would have switched Prime Ministers *after* the election.

Attlee would have none of it. Departing from the headquarters, he got into his car with his wife at the wheel, went to the palace, and accepted the commission from the King. The next day he assembled the PLP and received their unanimous endorsement. At the moment of triumph, Laski had risked his credibility as a party leader, and lost dramatically.[47] Once again, Laski was trying to democratize government by increasing the accountability of the leaders to the party's representatives.

Elated nevertheless, Laski celebrated his personal role in the victory with a newspaper article, "Why I Didn't Make a Good Red Herring." Taking off from a David Low cartoon of Churchill offering the electorate a saddled red herring to ride off into "Britain's Glorious Future," Laski reassured the electorate that they "need not lie awake o'nights dreaming of the terrible things the Socialist Gestapo is planning."[48] While taking pains to salute Churchill as a great wartime leader, Laski pinned the "red scare" strategy on Beaverbrook. He saw the election as the fulfillment of his own plan for a revolution by consent. Hailing the victory as equivalent, for the working class, to the middle-class accession to power in the 1932 election, Laski declaimed:

> 1945 is the beginning of the end of capitalist privilege. I hope and think that we shall, at long last, have our own "New Deal," and that it will be a new deal built upon those socialist principles which alone can drive the spectres of poverty and fear from men's lives. I hope and think that it will mean the end of our curious zeal for semi-Fascist monarchs and obsolete social systems abroad. Certainly, it will mean the end of those invisible governments of bankers and Press lords who regarded themselves as the masters, not merely of the ordinary people, but even of those who had been chosen by ordinary people to rule.[49]

What followed was the enactment of most of the Beveridge Report, even though Beveridge himself lost the seat he had won in a by-election as a Liberal candidate the previous fall. The government put through the creation of the National Health Service, the Town and Country Planning Act, the takeover of the Bank of England, and a limited nationalization of rail, coal, and, by 1951, the nationalization of iron and steel. Ironically, as Noel Annan points out: "Every item in the Labour legislation had been proposed before 1945 by men who were not socialists. Even nationalization was an extension of the model of a public corporation."[50] Churchill had previously advocated for the nationalization of railways, and many other elements of Labour's program had precedents in nonsocialist initiatives and legislation.[51]

Attlee, ever the moderate, proceeded to launch Britain on a distinctive course of socialism joined to British conceptions of rights and liberties. Annan recalls the mood: "It was a vote for fair shares against grandiloquence in foreign policy, for reconstruction, a planned economy, technocracy and also (for voting is always self-contradictory) for greater personal freedom and less respect for authority."[52]

Attlee read the mood better than the doctrinaire Laski. The Labour Party had succeeded in part by attracting the moderates and by resisting the radicalism of the communist left. The Conservative Party, for all its claim to Churchill's brilliant leadership of the war effort, was discredited domestically by its timidity over the Beveridge Report. That and the impressive victories of the Red Army, the product of a nationalized economy, built up the credibility of Attlee's approach.[53]

Laski may have seen Labour's program as the prelude to the abolition of capitalism, but it was possible for many citizens to see it merely as an extension of wartime lessons in planning and the rationalization of provision for basic needs. Peter Clarke argues that the nationalization of what were already oligopolies was not a radical step. "In all of these examples, a strong pragmatic case existed, in line with classical principles of free competition, for eliminating private monopoly by taking essential utilities into public ownership."[54]

The wartime regime of rationing and price controls had created a public mentality that accepted the rationalization of the economy through government action. The socialization measures, in effect, phased in as the wartime controls phased out. As Paul Addison tells the story in *The Road to 1945* and in *After the War*, a communitarian sentiment arising from the memory of prewar inequities and fortified by wartime sacrifice and victory, along with a wry tolerance for the trade-offs between efficiency and egalitarian distribution, prepared the way for the transition to moderate socialism. The ambition of reordering the economy through detailed workforce planning gave way fairly soon to a reliance on Keynesian financial techniques to secure employment. Addison concludes that the change was due less to Marx than to "two great Whitehall mandarins, Beveridge and Keynes. Beveridge was the founding father of the welfare state, and

Keynes of the managed economy."[55] Laski, not content with half measures, pushed for a more explicit embrace of socialist nostrums.

Convinced of his destiny as the oracle of the Labour masses, Harold Laski came to grief not long after the election by alienating the moderates who held actual power. He was disappointed in his expectation of being named Ambassador to the United States.[56] For all his successes in pushing the Labour Party to the left on domestic policy, Laski was caught in a riptide on foreign affairs. Rather than following Laski's scenario for socialist solidarity with left-wing comrades in Greece, India, and the empire, the prevailing view was quickly established that democracy in its attenuated British and American form was the best that could be achieved. Resolute resistance to totalitarianism and the ideologies, including Marxism, that tended in that direction was seen to be essential to future stability. The cabinet decided on nonintervention in Franco's Spain and against supporting the anticommunist forces in Greece.[57] Furthermore, the extension of democracy and self-determination to the colonies posed enormous political risks for the Labour government.

Never really having had full power before, the Labour Party was organized to gain power rather than to exercise it. The Professor of Political Science was working out in practice what he had advocated in theory: that government could be made responsive to the interests of ordinary citizens. He saw the Labour Party as the vehicle for their views and the NEC as a legitimate formulator of policy that the government ministers, as agents of the party, were bound to acknowledge. He himself undertook to be the mouthpiece, largely without consulting anyone as to what he should be permitted to say.[58] He looked forward to the socialization of nearly all the economy, including land.[59]

Attlee, burdened now with the all too real responsibilities of domestic transformation and foreign stabilization, was exasperated by Laski's speeches, letters, and articles all advocating a more leftward course different than the one taken by the elected government. On August 20, he wrote that Laski was "embarrassing" the government and was taken to be speaking for it by a public not familiar with the fine distinction between the NEC and the cabinet. The government's "task is quite sufficiently difficult without the embarrassment of irresponsible statements of the kind which you are making. . . . I can assure you there is widespread resentment in the Party at your activities and a period of silence on your part would be welcome."[60]

Attlee's stinging rebuke prompted the members of the cabinet to move to take over the NEC through the placement of ministers in key positions on the council. Laski tried to interest the Fabian Society, the legatee of Sidney and Beatrice Webb's socialist advocacy, to take up the constitutional problem of the relationship between the Labour cabinet and the NEC. They did not respond, nor did Laski's allies among the cabinet ministers. He proposed that the party constitution be changed so that ministers would not be seated as members of the NEC, and the motion failed 10 to 7.[61] This issue would return again in the sixties and seventies in the ministries of Harold Wilson and James Callaghan.

The broken relationship with the cabinet deeply affected Laski. He knew that his influence had been used in some of the right places when the government moved toward independence for India, a cause of long-standing interest. He also approved entirely of the implementation of the Beveridge Report and did not interfere in the struggle over the degree of nationalization.[62] Laski's disaffection focused on three areas: the timidity of the leadership, the acquiescence to Cold War rivalries at the expense of backing international socialism, and the constitutional issue of the relation of the party followers to their leaders.

On all these issues, he was outmaneuvered by Attlee and his colleagues. Attlee would be forever put down by Churchill's famous quip: a modest little man with a great deal to be modest about. From the left, Attlee was peppered by the rancorous Laski. Yet throughout the war, the socialist transformation of domestic politics, and the arrival of a tenuous peace during the onset of the Cold War, Attlee stayed the course of moderation and preserved the initiative, at least until 1951, against the forces of reaction on the right and radical socialism on the left. Laski went from being a leader of opinion to the foil of an able politician in need of support from the center of British society.

Projecting himself onto the American scene, Laski traveled to the United States for the first time since 1939. His arrangements were held up by the British government, fearful of his impact on the delicate matter of the loan negotiations. His appearance at a December 1945 conference on the atomic bomb let him bring together economic and international peace themes. Socialism and planning were the road to peace, he proclaimed, and capitalism and markets the path to war. In an atomic age, the world could not afford the risk. As Kramnick and Sheerman summarize his point, "turning Hayek on his head, Laski described the American economy as 'the direct road to serfdom.'"[63] Howls of protest from two leaders of the American right, Congressman J. Parnell Thomas and Senator Homer Capehart, did threaten the approval of the loan until cooler heads prevailed.

Forging ahead on a wide front, Laski responded enthusiastically to a call to participate in drafting a preface to the United Nations Universal Declaration of Human Rights. His proposal laid out a far-seeing program of full political, economic, and social rights for men and notably for women. Equality was its guiding principle, and the justification of differentiation among persons was only authorized with the approval of those affected and in the name of over-all improvement of the prospects of the community.[64] Still, he was skeptical that the UN document would be more than window dressing without a com-mitment to the practical steps to make such rights real. Michael Newman notes that "this was an accurate prediction of international arguments over human rights for the next forty years, although it is debatable whether this made the Declaration worthless."[65]

Hayek was more than skeptical of the Universal Declaration of Human Rights. Years later he recorded his incredulity at Laski's contribution to the rationale that accompanied the declaration. He notes that the authors intended that the declara-tion be founded on common ground between a Marxist conception of equality and the liberal tradition of "inherent individual rights." Hayek notes that by in-cluding rights to economic benefits, Laski and his coauthors introduced a cate-gory that would require claims on the productive activities of citizens, rather than simply the tolerance of differences of expression or belief. Hayek punctuates with exclamation points his note about Laski's approach to broadening rights so as to indicate his disbelief that anyone would contemplate such an effort.[66]

George Orwell, who had covered the 1945 election as a journalist, saw it as a mandate for serious reform but not for Laski's revolution. Orwell, who had come by skepticism the hard way in the bitterness of fighting the repub-lican cause in Spain, trusted neither the gradualists who would act too slowly to meet public discontent nor the intellectuals "in whom the acceptance of power politics has killed first the moral sense, and then the sense of reality." Too little change and Labour became indistinguishable from the Conserva-tives; too much and a dictatorship would result. Orwell saw the need for a balance of "restraint and boldness."[67]

The balance Orwell spoke of was tested almost daily as Labour brought through an unprecedented number of bills. By the beginning of 1946, they were twenty points ahead in the polls and poised to make dramatic changes. Yet Ben Pimlott reports there was no diminution of support for the monarchy. Forty thousand turned out for Princess Elizabeth's twentieth birthday cele-bration, a far larger crowd than ever seen in the thirties.[68] In a climate of Con-servative remonstration on the right and Communist agitation on the left, Laski positioned himself as the leftist outrider who was attempting to be the conscience of the party.

The main front for Laski was now international affairs. He wanted to put over a "revolution by consent" on the world stage by uniting the strands of socialist advances in Europe, Britain, and, with the New Deal, the United States. Just as Keynes used Bretton Woods to assemble the institutional means for his interventionist reforms, Laski aimed at a partnership among socialist comrades that would defuse the Cold War and set the West on a course of socialist amelioration. It would also provide cover to protect and foster the socialist advances in Britain.[69]

To accomplish this yet grander scheme, he needed to reclaim whatever was salvageable from the Russian revolution. He asserted in the spring of 1946 that Russia had a better title to being called a "democratic *society*" than Britain, while Britain did indeed have a "democratic *government*" and Russia did not. Parsing the distinction permitted him to point to the preeminence of public demands being met in Russia where:

> No special privilege attaches either to birth or to wealth, to race or to creed. There is a wider and more profound attempt to satisfy maximum demand than in this country. Opportunity—for example in education—is not restricted by class position. Vested interests cannot frustrate, as they here frustrate, scientific experiment or the full use of technological discovery.[70]

Then, in terms as bold as his avowal of Russian social democracy was disingenuous, Laski denounced the Russian regime for its reliance on secret police and the suppression of dissent. In Britain, by contrast, the capitalists were seen to be privileged and too often successful in using the appearances of democracy to legitimize their advantages. Yet democratic government is real enough in Britain, he argued, and there is a genuine commitment to electoral democracy and basic rights. The lesson was clear, Britain must learn to imitate the classlessness of the "democratic society" of Russia, while offering its own example of democratic governance as a replacement for Russian dictatorship.

While Laski may have harbored illusions about what was being attempted in Russia, he was clear eyed about the Communist Party. On behalf of the NEC, he drafted a pamphlet to explain why the Communist Party should not be permitted to affiliate with the Labour Party. Citing a history of duplicity and conspiracy, he placed the communists outside the democratic traditions of the Labour Party and its constituent unions. Yet he clung to the idea of Britain as uniquely positioned to lead the world to socialism: "The British Labour Party does not propose to follow either the communist road to dependence upon Moscow or the road of dependence upon Washington." Instead, the Labour Party must hold the torch for a better way:

> It would be foolish indeed if, in the hour when democratic citizens of every country look to the Labour Party for inspiration and leadership, it should substitute for its own philosophy an outlook which is built upon distrust of the common people and denial of their right to experiment with the institutions of freedom.[71]

Treading a fine line clearly visible only to him, Laski wished to use the Soviets as an example of socialist reform, while disavowing the methods by which these had been achieved. Skepticism about the Communist Party was evident from the Labour Party's rejection of their application for affiliation by a vote of better than 5 to 1 at its 1946 conference.

Laski used his valedictory as outgoing NEC Chair to argue for an internationalist socialism. "Try friendship" with Russia was his plea to the party faithful. As a grand gesture of good faith, atomic secrets should be shared with Russia.[72] Laski wanted to rest Britain's foreign policy on an alliance of socialists across national boundaries, rather than on the conventional considerations of national commercial and military self-interest. Greece as a putative ally of the West was less important than Greece as the new site for socialist revolution. Spain as an anti-Communist bulwark was less important than ending Spain's resistance to the rising tide of European socialism.

Laski's speech was warmly applauded, but not so warmly as Ernest Bevin, who received an "overwhelming endorsement" of a more cautious foreign policy. Resolutions attacking "monopoly capitalism" and promoting Laski's views on Spain and Palestine were either defeated or withdrawn. Laski was succeeded as NEC Chair by Philip Noel-Baker whose address to the convention was a defense of Labour's conduct of the Ministry of Foreign Affairs.[73]

That summer, Laski participated in a Labour Party delegation to Russia. At Laski's insistence, they met with Joseph Stalin. The delegation's official account of their meeting reveals what an interesting analysis Stalin had to offer. Recognizing that Britain had an educated working class and a democratic tradition, he saluted their path to socialism through nationalization and parliamentary legislation. However, for Russia, with its revolutionary background, its vast masses of illiterate peasants, and the combined forces of international capitalism arrayed against it, a militant approach was the only one possible. He feared that Britain would take too long and suffer a fatal reaction, whereas the Soviet method offered a faster transformation, albeit at the price of violence.[74]

Stalin's willingness to at least acknowledge the British approach did not extend to his agents. The organs of his state were busy denouncing moderate professors of the Laski stripe. Taking the Leninist line that nothing other than apologies for the bourgeoisie could be expected from them, Laski's writings in particular were dismissed as "improbable nonsense."[75]

Laski returned home and was to face an ordeal of his own making. He was harshly rebuked through the sort of process he defended as an expression of democratic rights. Laski's libel suit against Beaverbrook's newspapers came to trial in November 1946, a year after the election. A letter to the editor citing Laski's violent rhetoric in an election speech had prompted the action. The letter was followed by articles in the local papers as well as the national press, all part of the Beaverbrook chain. "Revolution by consent" had been the theme of Laski's writings for at least twenty-five years.[76] Consequently, Laski had good reason to take umbrage at the charge of advocating violence. The charge was a politically motivated accusation fired off in the heat of the election campaign.

The exchange had occurred at the end of a speech when Laski was asked why he had not served in World War I and why he had advocated violence in speeches during the second war. Laski dismissed the first question, citing his medical rejection for service. Then, according to the interlocutor, Laski stated, "as for violence, if Labour could not obtain what it needed by general consent, we shall have to use violence even if it means revolution." Laski claimed that he had been misquoted; the words he recalled were that "great changes were so urgent in this country that if they were not made by consent they would be made by violence." He saw himself as offering a caution to the electorate, rather than advocacy.[77] On this scholar's distinction, the case rested.

The incident had all the earmarks of a classic provocation. By mid-June 1945, just after the Gestapo speech, the Conservatives were warming to the violence theme as a way to attack Labour. The questioner, Wentworth Day, was a party activist who was primed in advance and consulted note cards. The first question was clearly designed to raise the temperature, and the second asked Laski to prove a negative—that he had not advocated violence. The journalist's shorthand notes from the event did not include the fateful phrase; it was added by the editor, a Conservative Party official, and the quoted words were written by Day himself. The letter to the editor, supposedly the work of a concerned citizen, was in fact composed by a Beaverbrook journalist. The sensational press account was written in consequence of the provocative letter.[78]

Laski was confident of victory, citing a plethora of writings on the theme of revolution by consent. Furthermore, his antagonist, the waggish Day had written a book speaking of Laski as the "garrulous little petrel of Socialist politics . . . evidently a man with a disturbed mind. He appeared on a sort of French Revolution cart fitted with a microphone instead of a guillotine. He was dressed in a tight-fitting hip-slinky overcoat of the sort that dance-band leaders wear." Day defended his account as "descriptive" rather than "disparaging."[79]

Still, Laski had reason to be wary of libel proceedings, having tried vainly as a juror two decades earlier to render an unpopular verdict in a politically sensitive case.[80] Furthermore, he was up against a formidable barrister, Sir Patrick Hastings, whom he had once praised in a letter to Frida as the most brilliant advocate he had ever heard.[81] Hastings was familiar with Labour and its politics, having been a Labour Minister in the twenties before switching sides to the Conservative Party.

In the trial, Hastings used every device of innuendo and insinuation. Hastings dwelt on the foreign nature of Laski's creed, the dilettantishness of his politics, the rejection of British institutions made explicit in his more radical commentaries, and the lurking danger of revolution in a fragile postwar world. The indignant barrister whipsawed the verbose professor with rhetorical questions for which yes or no answers were demanded.

The presiding judge was Lord Chief Justice Goddard, an establishment fixture appointed by Attlee to ensure conservative opinion about Labour after the election. Justice Goddard gave Hastings free rein. Hastings handed Laski's head to him on a plate. One exchange is a classic worth quoting at length. Hastings questions Laski:

Q.: Have you consistently preached this doctrine, that the time is ripe for revolution?

Laski: The time is ripe for great changes.

Q.: Listen to my question, you are a Professor of so many things.

Laski: Of one thing only.

Q.: Have you for years past preached the doctrine that the time is ripe for revolution?

Laski: Revolution in the sense of a great transformation always.

Q.: You have written many books in which the word revolution is contained, and you define it in your books. Have you preached the doctrine that this revolution may be brought about in one of two ways, either by consent—you call it a revolution by consent—or else a revolution by violence?

Laski: That is so.

Q.: And by a revolution by consent do you mean this—because the enemy are always the capitalists, are they not?

Laski: Broadly.

Q.: Do you mean, that the enemy, if there is to be a consent, must in the very nature of things consent to their own elimination—that is to say, they have to consent to go?

Laski: They have to consent to great changes.

Q.: Did you hear my question? If you do not hear any question, please say so, and if you do not understand it, please tell me. I have in front of me, and I have read, some twenty, thirty or forty different publications of yours, so I know something about them. I want you to answer this question if you will: Have you stated that what you mean by a revolution by consent is that the capitalists must consent to their total erosion; that is your word; I thought it might have meant "elimination" but you say "erosion"?

Laski: No, I do not mean by what I have said the elimination of the capitalists.

Q.: What do you mean by your word "erosion"?

Laski: "Erosion" means rubbing away.

Q.: Rubbing away do you say?

Laski: Rubbing away.

Q.: How do you consent to rub yourself away?

Laski: By fading out of the picture in which you have been previously the most prominent part.

Q.: By disappearing?

Laski: Yes.

Q.: Consent to their own disappearance?

Laski: To their loss of power.

Q.: And have you pointed out that that is unlikely if not impossible?

Laski: No, not impossible; I have said that it is historically unlikely.

Q.: Let us just look and see what you did say.[82]

Here, Hastings had a rich choice of quotations to select from. Laski, after all, had written in 1935 in *The State in Theory and Practice* that

My case has been that, whenever the class-relations of a given society make it impossible to distribute the results of the productive process, men whose expectations of material benefit are continuously disappointed will seek to change those class-relations; and I have suggested that, unless the possessing class voluntarily abdicates—the rarest event in history—the resultant position involves a social revolution. I have not suggested that the revolution will necessarily be successful; I have suggested only that such an attempt is inescapable.[83]

As for the idea of a revolution by consent, Annan later remarked, "Seldom has illogicality in the writings of a political scientist met with such dire punishment."[84]

Laski lost. The jury was led by the judge to construe the law so as to moot the issue of whether the newspaper quotation at issue was precise or merely a fair and accurate representation of views Laski might have expressed. The justice exonerated Laski of any sort of treasonous intent, but gave the jury considerable leeway in deciding whether libel had been committed by his accusers.

Ralf Dahrendorf, in his history of LSE, muses on the "difference between the lecture room and the market place . . . a strict Marxian analysis suggesting the inevitability of violent revolution may be historicist and mistaken, but it must be allowed in an academic context. . . . A similar set of statements before an audience of voters, let alone potential revolutionaries, can be incitement and certainly reflects on the democratic credentials of the speaker."[85] Still, there was a fair amount of hypocrisy in the Conservative indignation. One of their own rising stars, Quintin Hogg, had warned the House of Commons in 1943 that "if you do not give the people social reform, they are going to give you social revolution."[86]

Deeply wounded by the verdict, Laski concluded he had been on trial, rather than Beaverbrook, and the jury was made to believe that Laski held dangerous views.[87] Seemingly undaunted, Laski continued speaking and writing on Labour causes. However, he offered his resignation to LSE and the NEC. Both were refused. His wife and daughter knew what the verdict had done. He collapsed in tears upon coming home after the verdict, and his daughter thought it "broke his heart." The costs imposed were met by more than five thousand contributions from the rank and file, as well as notables such as Albert Einstein, Edward R. Murrow, and Henry Wallace.[88] Several months later, a rueful Laski acknowledged to his friend Felix Frankfurter that it was all he could do to keep up appearances in the face of such total humiliation.[89]

The libel case went to the core of his self-concept as a man of moderation, nonviolence, and reason. He had lost to a jury of his peers, albeit a special jury selected from among property-holding citizens—citizens who also happened to share an evident loyalty to the British traditions of law and governance that Laski had so often criticized. What the jury saw and heard was rhetoric that threatened the basis of their own identities as the oak of British culture. Frida thought the debacle shortened his life, and the respiratory illnesses that plagued him became more frequent.[90]

In the bottom of his despair, there was still the foundation in the love shared by Harold and Frida. He wrote to her late that climactic year:

> I wish to tell you all you have meant to me in these hard months since the election. . . . I do want you to know how good you have been and how deep

is my sense of love and devotion to you. . . . I shall always be your lover and all my life is in your dear hands. I kiss you a thousand times and send you my heart full of love.[91]

As the Labour government moved forward with its program, the transformation of domestic policy proceeded on two levels: the establishment of a welfare state and the nationalization of the basic means of production. Both galvanized tremendous public support, and both ran into problems generated in large part by Britain's position in the postwar international economy. A nation close to bankruptcy, deeply in debt, and with a fading empire was hardly the most fortuitous place to launch a massive new program of social insurance from the cradle to the grave.

As for nationalization, the initial moves were to take over the fuel and power, railways and road transport, the Bank of England, and, later, iron and steel. As the ever-trenchant C. Northcote Parkinson observed, "in point of fact the industries first nationalised were not merely ripe but rotten."[92] Damaged by war, deprived of the latest technology, and bound into relations of trade that could not be sustained, these industries needed massive infusions of capital and innovative yet experienced leadership to adapt to the postwar world. Socialism meant a transformation of the internal culture, as well as the most fundamental managerial relations, of these industries. Struggling through such changes in the midst of postwar shortages and the combined forces of the capitalist world arrayed against them, it is small wonder that nationalization became associated with inefficiency and the prolongation of wartime rationing.

Recognizing the increasing unpopularity of the rationing and regulation that crept into every corner of postwar British life, the Labour government began backing away from the further extensions of its program. Fee-paying medicine was retained alongside the National Health Service, much to Laski's disgust. Labour Minister Harold Wilson held a "bonfire of regulations" on Guy Fawkes Day in 1948 to celebrate the elimination of sixty economic regulations. The planning ministries began to look toward Keynesian methods of indirect control rather than direct planning of the sort that orthodox socialists, such as Laski, advocated. Viewed from a doctrinal perch removed from the day-to-day complexities, these were all measures that led away from equity and justice.[93]

The maintenance of rationing through the forties placed the British population on an even footing during the time of socialist reform. However, the fits and starts in the birth of socialism must have weighed Laski down as he yearned for bolder moves. In any event, Prime Minister Clement Attlee dominated the pace of domestic reform, and the firmly anti-Communist (and anti-Zionist) Ernest Bevin commanded the foreign policy line. In their hands, Britain's road to socialism would veer away from a more leftward course and never stray so far as to alienate the Americans. American leadership of the postwar coalition of capitalist democracies would be supported, rather than resisted, by socialist Britain.

On the international front, the reverses to Laski's hopes were beginning to accumulate. In the summer of 1946, he headed a London meeting of the newly formed Socialist International, a move to supplant the Comintern of the past. Weakened by defections of Germans and Italians, the hope of a permanent footing for Laski's international movement proved illusory.[94] The Marshall Plan provided welcome relief to Europe, but with the rejection by the Soviet Union, relief came at the price of a bipolar world.

In America, the Truman forces consolidated their hold over the Democratic Party. The left found itself diminished by the sidelining of progressives such as former Vice President Henry Wallace, the communist infiltration of labor unions, and the fecklessness of socialists with their interminable factional warfare.[95] Laski saw the Truman Plan of 1947 as an endorsement of reactionary regimes standing in the way of socialist advance. His example was Truman's support for Turkey's resistance to Soviet expansion. Laski predicted that the subordination of socialist advances in the Mediterranean to Cold War imperatives would mean that "the peoples of the Middle East are to be pinned down in vassalage to obsolete regimes until there arises a power strong enough to rescue them from the dependence America will be driven to force upon them."[96] The prophecy may yet rank with Keynes's on how "vengeance will not limp."

Laski's hopes for socialism had been sustained during the dark hours in the thirties by America's New Deal, but now he despaired in writing to Frankfurter:

> All that American policy does is to give an even deeper impression of deliberate *enkreisung*, of making ideological conflict where there need be none, of a self-righteousness which is almost as infantile as the propaganda of Moscow. . . . I do not believe that F.D.R. would have looked on America's role as the U.S. Government now does. The initiative for peace is being lost, and, as I see it, needlessly lost; and not all Russia's mistakes justify the decision of Marshall to go down a road at the end of which lies war.[97]

Yet Laski could not entirely let go of his faith in America, and he kept on seeking an enlightened leader for those aspirations. Perhaps his most paradoxical maneuver was his endorsement of the idea that General Eisenhower should run for President as a Democrat in 1948.[98] Laski was not alone in his confusion about the General's politics, which were not to be publicly revealed until his Republican candidacy in the following Presidential election. Perhaps the gesture was the analog of his overture to Churchill during the war.

The objective of displacing Truman, whom Laski saw as the betrayer of Roosevelt and a "pipsqueak" compared to Ike, led him to consider the Eisenhower possibility. He thought that the general's stature would give him the power to make fresh moves to break down the walls of the Cold War. This had become the key problem, even more than the direction of domestic policy, as evidenced by Laski's failure to support Wallace in 1948. He thought that Wallace, Roosevelt's most progressive acolyte on domestic policy, was too pro-Soviet. Wallace would encourage the Stalinists and sabotage an effective resolution of East–West differences.[99]

With the publication in 1948 of his massive 750-page commentary on U.S. politics, *American Democracy*, Laski displayed all that he had learned in the preceding thirty years as a transatlantic participant observer. It is the work of a would-be Tocqueville comes to socialism. By turns verbose and trenchant, he toured the landscape of American culture, institutions, classes, and practices. Bemused by the variegation of American society, fascinated by the commitment to democracy, and repelled by the passion for property, Laski puzzled over the future of American politics.

Reviewing the failure of New Deal structural changes under the pressures of war mobilization, Laski saw that the war had returned the commanding heights of the economy to the capitalists whose hold had merely been weakened in the thirties. In the war effort, rather than the government taking over industries, industrial leaders were invited into government to use its powers to speed up production. The cooperation of Roosevelt's capitalist antagonists cost his reforms their energy and momentum. New Deal experimentation was subsumed in the drive for efficiency. Furthermore, with Roosevelt, America was led by a "physician" who wanted to cure its ills by rooting out evil practices, rather than a visionary who could plumb "the essential logic of their inherent nature."[100]

With Truman, "the relationship between the major political parties had practically swung back to what it was before 1933."[101] American liberals, the best that the country had to offer with socialists and communists reduced to "small sects," were hobbled by their ambivalence about the imperatives of power:

> All this is to say, I think, that liberals viewed Americanism less as a concept of power than as a concept of ethics. . . . They retained the illusion of a security

for the American which could be enjoyed by all other peoples if they would only exercise the virtues of reason and goodwill. And there was an inner conviction, inevitably strengthened by their sense of overwhelming power, that it was their mission to lead the world to righteousness.[102]

The final puzzle of the American is the "constant tendency . . . to shrink, whether internally or externally, from collective action on the ground that because collective action must involve coercion, it destroys that power of self-regeneration in man without which no reform is every fully achieved."[103] Americans he sees as dreamers; naïve about power, though faithful to an ideal; and doubtless Christian in inspiration, yet lacking the staying power for transformative change of the kind Laski so desperately desired.

Laski ended *American Democracy* with words that portray his own mental state under the pressure of postwar events. Pleading for a joining of progressive forces in Europe and the United States, he forecast,

> Without that understanding and that preparation the future is dark indeed. Injustice within each national society, and a sense of general insecurity brooding over the chaos of international relationships, might well confront our civilization with that sense of disaster which goes too deep for recovery to be possible. That would be an infinitely tragic fate for mankind at a moment when the possibilities before us are so great of a conscious mastery over the alien forces of Nature.[104]

For Laski the Cold War was a global replay of the run-up to the World War II, with capitalists struggling against the forces of social change. The moves toward democratization in the West did not, in Laski's view, change the nature of the more fundamental economic conflict.

Laski's hopes were imperiled in another realm. On the centennial of its publication, Laski wrote a preface to a commemorative edition of *The Communist Manifesto*. Striving to rescue the meaning of Marxism from its practice by the Soviets, he adduced evidence that Marx would have disapproved of the single-party dictatorship so evident in Russia. Marx and Engels designated the communists as "the vanguard of the ruling class . . . not its masters." Their job is to lead in the abolition of capitalism, but also to enlist all those forces, and political parties, friendly to the cause.[105]

The relationship of coercion to rights and democracy was being illustrated in stark and terrible terms on the ground. The division of Central Europe along Cold War lines was speeding up. A communist coup in Prague in February 1948 overthrew Europe's best hope for a nonrevolutionary socialist transition. Laski was demoralized.[106] A year earlier, Laski had celebrated the

Czech example of a working parliamentary democracy on the road to socialism, only to see the Russians conspire to undermine it and force Laski's
friend, Prime Minister Jan Masaryk, to a tragic demise. Weakened by the
sense of impending failure for his lifelong dreams, Laski's students at LSE
witnessed the change in their beloved professor's mood. The ebullience was
gone; cynicism had set in.[107]

In almost wistful terms, Laski found the words to praise the memory of the
erstwhile Fabians who had set Britain on its distinctive path to socialism. In
a BBC broadcast, he cited the historic initiative of the Webbs, George
Bernard Shaw, and their colleagues. With the mildly indulgent tone of one
who is convinced he is made of sterner stuff, he concluded his salute to the
early Fabians:

> They did not cry for the moon; they did not even confuse the public mind with
> some transcendental world-outlook. They did a cleansing and creative job by
> persuasion and intelligence in a sober and practical way. They deserved well of
> the nation they served.[108]

George Orwell assayed the degree of Laski's sternness in a letter to Sir
Richard Rees commenting on whether Laski could be counted as a "fellow
traveler."

> I don't think Laski is a fellow traveler, much as he has aided them by his boost-
> ing of Russia. *In this country* he loathes the CP, because they menace his job. I
> suppose he imagines they are different elsewhere. I also think he is too inte-
> grally a part of the LP, and too fond of being in an official position, to go over
> to the enemy if, for instance we were at war with the USSR. The thing one can't
> imagine Laski doing is breaking the law.[109]

Orwell's searing experience in the Spanish Civil War and his devotion to
the British side in the war on fascism prompted him to keep a list of such
"crypto-communists" that he shared with friends, including one who worked
for the Foreign Office. Laski's name appears on the list, but apparently Orwell later had second thoughts. In fact, Orwell signed a public letter along
with Laski urging that those government employees accused of being Communists or Fascists be accorded open hearings with full legal rights.[110]

One last visit to the United States exposed Laski to the rising tide of anti-
communism that was reaching into universities across the country. On arrival,
he was asked to register as a "foreign agent" and declined without consequence. Addresses at UCLA and even at the University of Washington which
had stood by him ten years earlier were cancelled by administrators fearful

that his presence would escalate the legislatures' attention to the political beliefs of faculty members. He left America with a sad feeling that its promise
as a bastion of freedom had been badly undercut.[111]

While there, Laski lectured on the theme of the role of trade unions. His remarks were prophetic of the problems Britain would encounter in attempting
to marry the power of large unions to the formal role of governing a state-led
economy. Laski identified the strictures labor leaders would have to place on
themselves. Increasing productivity would be "the only permanent way to advance the standard of life." Calibrating pay demands would be critical "since
an uncontrolled inflation usually is paid for by working-class suffering." The
focus should be on union leadership familiar with the "management and financial sides of industry" who could "play their full part in moving from the
era of scarcity to the era of abundance."[112]

The strain of his feverish pace on mind and body began to tell. Increasingly
troubled by persistent bronchitis and chain-smoking as he always had, Laski
came back to England in poor health. He planned to return to the United
States for a lecture tour, in the course of which he was to have debated
Friedrich Hayek. However, his doctor would not let him go.[113]

Laski's career as a leader of the Labour Party was now over. He had resigned from the NEC after thirteen years over the issue of the failure to recognize Palestine. Albert Einstein nominated him for the Presidency of the
newly formed Brandeis University, but he declined. His influence on American politics continued through his students, among them, Michael Straight,
son of the founder of *The New Republic* and now its editor.[114] Straight would
later confess to having been a willing accomplice of spies for the Soviet
Union, Guy Burgess, Donald Maclean, and Kim Philby.

With an election scheduled for February 1950, Laski nevertheless went on the
hustings at times barely able to manage a whisper of his former eloquence. Forgiving old antagonisms, he wrote Attlee of the Prime Minister's "dignity, . . .
simple directness, and . . . clear expression of faith" in addressing the nation. He
concluded, "What a grand thing it is for you to lead the Party to victory with dignity and without showmanship."[115] One detects a note of self-reproach from a
man whose style of expression had cost him allies among his old comrades.

Laski had become seriously ill with a bronchial infection during the
Christmas season of 1948. The weakness of Laski's lungs had been of constant concern. Now, two years later in 1950, his doctor detected signs of
pleurisy. Laski consulted a private specialist who suspected there had been a
dormant lung infection ever since 1948. The infection apparently had become
active. The very night of the consultation, Laski awoke in distress and was

taken to the hospital with a collapsed lung. He did not survive another day. An abscess had burst. Harold Laski died on March 24, 1950, with Frida and Diana next to him. He was fifty-six years old.

Frida wrote words of Heinrich Heine on her husband's coffin: "A soldier in the liberation war of humanity."[116] Messages of love and respect arrived from around the world. At a funeral gathering four days later, Prime Minister Attlee and eight cabinet ministers joined family, colleagues, students, friends, and party loyalists in a ceremony without speeches. After silent meditation, Chopin's funeral march was heard.[117] The tribune was laid to rest.

What the left lost in Laski, it never regained. Britain had a number of contenders, but none of these bridged the worlds of professor, polemicist, and politician of the left so persuasively and with such a powerful effect on elites and masses as well. In Britain, the intellectual fragmentation and decline of the left may be dated from the passing of Laski.[118] The split between moderate and doctrinaire socialists weakened the Labour Party in the 1950 election, contributed to its defeat in 1951, and bedeviled the party through the second half of the century.

In America, the long night of McCarthyism descended on the left. When Felix Frankfurter tried to raise money in memory of his friend Laski, one correspondent wrote that people were "scared to have a book by Keynes or Laski lying on their table." Ed Murrow would be questioned by Senator Joeseph McCarthy himself about his friendship with Professor Laski.[119] After McCarthy's demise, Michael Harrington came to perform a somewhat similar role to Laski in inspiring John F. Kennedy's New Frontier and Lyndon Johnson's Great Society. Harrington, however, pointed to the problem that Laski did not foresee and which rendered his militant socialist views obsolete:

During the post-World War II period, the relative decline in the number of blue-collar workers and the growth of higher education and a salariat with college degrees, changed the class structure and politics of every Western country. There came to be two Lefts: one based in the class proletariat, the other the product of the "new class" of the postindustrial economy. That the non-proletarians often spoke in the name of the "real" working class and against the attitudes of the actual workers should surprise no one. But on issues like the war in Vietnam, feminism, and the environment, the new strata were the proponents—even if sometimes dilettantish and irritating proponents—of critically important new values.[120]

Paradoxically, the educated scion of an upper-middle-class family, having rebelled and joined the side of the proletariat, could not have addressed these concerns because his solution, the empowerment of the state in economic matters, ran counter to the concerns and temper of the new class.

Yet Laski did have an enduring impact. The leftist critique of liberalism was powerfully influenced by a student of Laski's, C. B. Macpherson. In 1962, Macpherson adapted ideas he heard from Laski and wrote a reinterpretation of classical liberalism from a socialist perspective, *The Political Theory of Possessive Individualism* (Oxford, 1962). The identification of liberal "possessive individualism" as the problem, rather than the solution, to the question of social improvement undercut Laski's own version of pluralism. A generation of young radicals would take aim at pluralism, as advertised by yet another auditor of Laski's, Robert Dahl, as a cover for "elitism" and the suppression of the interests of minorities and the working class. In this skewed form, Laski's idea lived on to shape the counterculture of the sixties and seventies.

We will return to the question of Laski's influence and effect on the course of twentieth-century political history in the final analytical section of the book. For now, I will complete the triptych of figures that shaped the forties and so much else in subsequent decades, by recalling the decade as experienced by Friedrich Hayek.

7.3 – HAYEK: DEPARTURE AND RENEWAL

The war was grinding toward an end in the spring of 1945. Friedrich Hayek's *Road to Serfdom* had made him a *bête noir* among intellectuals. Nearly all of the "thinking people" were on the side of the Labour Party as it gathered its forces for the 1945 election. The political impact of the work was substantial in both England and the United States. The Book-of-the-Month Club selected *The Road to Serfdom* for its list; *Reader's Digest* published an edited version and the Scripps-Howard newspapers printed a summary. The National Association of Manufacturers recommended the book to its members, and it became a best-seller in several urban markets. In a dispatch most likely drafted by Isaiah Berlin, the British Ambassador to the United States reported in March 1945 that

> Wall Street looks on Hayek as the richest goldmine yet discovered and are peddling his views everywhere. . . . Professor Hayek should not be surprised if he is invited to address the Daughters of the American Revolution to provide them with the latest weapons against such sinister social incendiaries as Lord Keynes and the British Treasury.[121]

Though intended to rally classical liberals, Hayek had been surprised that the message of *The Road to Serfdom* was taken up in 1945 by the Conservative Party.[122] His thesis was attractive as an attack on socialist planning and as a celebration of traditional English moral virtues. The Conservative Party offered to republish the book out of its own rationed supply of paper.[123] Winston Churchill had, as we have seen, used Hayek's arguments in the election campaign.[124] Clement Attlee, who had also been sent a copy, attributed the remarks about the Gestapo to Hayek's influence on Churchill, and identified Hayek as a supplier of ideas to Britain's Conservative Party.

Hayek denied having any connection with the Conservative Party.[125] However, he wrote an article a few days later for *The Sunday Chronicle* specifically to respond to Attlee's remark. He reprised the themes that he and Churchill had stressed:

> Private ownership of the means of production is nearly as important for the millions who do not own much property as for the thousands who do, because dispersed ownership of property is the essential and indispensable condition of individual freedom. This old truth, deeply embedded in the British political tradition, has been confirmed hundredfold by recent experience. Yet it is against this very foundation of individual liberty that all socialist theory and practice is directed. Socialism to-day has therefore become the greatest threat to the freedom of the individual.[126]

As Richard Cockett observes, "Churchill had put Hayek's thesis at the centre of the election debate, and Attlee, backed by his own Party Chairman Harold Laski, was quite content to fight Churchill on the ground laid out by Hayek."[127]

While *The Road to Serfdom* had its polemical uses, Hayek told listeners in a 1945 radio broadcast in the United States that it was an attack, not on government per se, nor even on socialism necessarily, but on centralized planning. Hayek makes the rather disingenuous comment that

> It is not really an attack upon socialists; it is rather an attempt to persuade socialists, to whom I have dedicated my book. My main thesis is that they are mistaken in the methods for getting what they want to achieve. There are two alternative methods of ordering social affairs—competition and government direction. I am opposed to government direction, but I want to make competition work . . . the method of relying upon competition, which, if it is to be made effective, requires a good deal of government activity directed toward making it effective and toward supplementing it where it cannot be made effective.[128]

In the 1945 radio broadcast, he did not disavow the line of argument Churchill had taken with the Gestapo comment. Asked directly by one panelist whether it was not possible that a democratic process could control planning, he replied:

> If you use central planning in the sense in which I use it—government direction of production—I am quite convinced that it cannot be effectively controlled by the democratic process. It requires a degree of agreement among the people which we can never expect in a free society. It requires methods by which people are meant to agree; otherwise you will never get your democratic checks.[129]

Hayek was increasingly distrustful of government's ability to resist the expansion of such activities as minimum provision.[130] The analytical hinge of his argument turned on a critique of contemporary government as an instrument of progress and moral improvement. His polemics set him apart most emphatically from many of his intellectual colleagues; however, it endeared him to conservatives, especially in England and the United States.

In the spring of 1945, Hayek visited the United States for a lecture tour. There were men with powerful connections who understood the need for pro-market advocacy and they would make Hayek's visit to the United States an event of major significance for twentieth-century politics. He gave an address at the Economic Club of Detroit that was to have great consequences for his personal situation and for the future course of the ideological competition that would follow World War II. The business leaders were warned that "I do believe we are at the parting of the ways for western civilization and that the danger is the greater because we may choose the wrong way, not by deliberation and concerted decision, but because we seem to be blundering into it."[131]

Having stated the theme of *The Road to Serfdom*, he went on to admit that it had become his purpose to rescue people from the "middle of the middle, a very serious disease" that was confusing their understanding of the emerging crisis. He had not been thinking of the American situation when he wrote *The Road to Serfdom*. Rather he had seen a pattern in what happened in Europe in the thirties that he feared was to be repeated in England. But now he found "somewhat to my surprise that the conclusions I have drawn seem to have a great deal more direct application to America than I ever expected and anticipated."

Warming to his theme, Hayek pointedly distanced himself from those who argued against all forms of government activity, insisting that his "real task" was to come up with a "set of principles which enables us to distinguish between what form of government activity is good, is necessary, and where government intervention in economic affairs is of a dangerous nature."[132] He was forecasting his next major project that would not appear for fifteen years, *The Constitution of Liberty*.

His message, delivered in the heartland of American capitalism, found an especially attentive listener. Loren Miller, the head of an organization in Detroit dedicated to civic education along capitalist lines, immediately wrote to Hayek suggesting that he get in touch with a foundation executive named Harold Luhnow.[133] Luhnow directed a well-financed foundation established by William Volker, a merchandising magnate in Kansas City. They met, and Luhnow proposed to Hayek that he write a book favoring free enterprise in the American context. Hayek responded with a three-year, $25,000-per-annum proposal. The project would involve producing the desired book, with himself in an advisory position, and the financing of an international Acton-Tocqueville Society to engage German intellectuals in postwar discussions about the future of freedom.[134]

A similar set of remarks generated a similar response on the East Coast. On the same day Hayek received a telegram from Claude Robinson, President of the Opinion Research Corporation in Princeton, New Jersey. Robinson suggested that he could obtain the necessary support to bring Hayek to Princeton on a faculty appointment for a year or longer.[135] Hayek responded that his work demanded he stay in England. "The decisive struggle of ideas will have to be fought in Europe," and given his obligations to help LSE get reestablished in London, "I cannot abandon a post where during the next two years every man will count."[136] Robinson acknowledged Hayek's hesitation, but left open the offer for a future appointment.[137]

Meanwhile, arrangements with the Volker Foundation moved forward. He began making contacts to find a suitable author for the proposed book. Hayek continued to press for the creation of the Acton-Tocqueville Society, but was rebuffed by Luhnow who wrote that such groups are difficult to control once established. Luhnow had talked with the Chancellor of the University of Chicago, Robert Hutchins, about the book project and urged Hayek to contact him about giving a seminar there on a foundation-financed visit to the United States.[138] Luhnow specified that the book was to involve "a complete plan for a workable society of free enterprise." He sent along a copy of *How We Live*, a popularized depiction of the American way of life, as an example of how the book should be written.[139]

Summer brought the climactic election of 1945. Attlee's victory in July could be seen as a rejection of all that Hayek stood for. Hayek was now surrounded by a polity that was headed in the opposite direction from his deeply held convictions.

With the end of the war in Europe, Hayek traveled to Vienna where he was reunited once again with his first love, Helene Warhanek, amid the draconian circumstances of the postwar four-power occupation. The experience of their reunion moved him deeply.[140] Hayek and Frau Warhanek decided to seek divorces. Her husband, Herr Warhanek, agreed; however, he died of a heart attack two days before the divorce was completed.[141] Hayek apparently waited to request a divorce from his wife. Other matters needed to be settled first.

Hayek was now a man with a mission, or rather two missions. The confluence of these missions, financed by conservative interests in the United States, would launch him on a new career as a political philosopher and a new marriage to the love of his life. Behind him was the career as an economic theorist of capital and credit, and before him was the political task of making "the building of a free society once more an intellectual adventure, a deed of courage."[142] To accomplish this, he set out deliberately to recruit not just academics but a wider range of business magnates and professionals in various fields who could spread the excitement of his utopian project. His plan was diametrically opposed to Laski's scheme for the socialization of Britain that with the 1945 election seemed at last to be on its way to realization. The United States, with its vast resources—and its liberal divorce laws—beckoned.

As the new year of 1946 dawned, Hayek's correspondent at Princeton, Claude Robinson, wrote back to tell him of reading Herman Finer's rejoinder to Hayek titled *The Road to Reaction*. Robinson compared it to "a transcript of the *Daily Worker*" and inquired whether its author might be a "buddy of Laski's."[143] Hayek dismissed Finer's work as the product of personal resentment and exonerated Laski from any culpability.[144]

Funded by the Volker Foundation, Hayek traveled to the United States in the spring of 1946 in search of an author and a host institution for the book project. He visited three universities, Princeton, Chicago, and Stanford. Contacts included Leonard Read of the newly founded Foundation for Economic Education, an organization Hayek and Ludwig von Mises had joined.[145] Read's strategy for defeating socialism was to move beyond denunciation to "upholding its opposite . . . expertly, proudly, attractively, persuasively."[146] He solicited corporate sponsorship actively. Hayek was soon to be fitted into those plans.

After their meeting, Luhnow wrote to suggest that when *The Road to Serfdom* is reprinted, Loren Miller, or his wife, be invited to rewrite passages to "improve its readability and understandability."[147] Miller wrote to urge that Hayek focus the new book on the connection between "a free economy and freedom of men." He wanted Hayek to emphasize the positive impact of "a free economy on human values," the better to counteract leftist appeals to such values.[148] Hayek responded by indicating a willingness to receive suggestions, but with no promises as to his compliance.[149]

Hayek recommended that Aaron Director be brought from Washington to the University of Chicago where he could benefit from the assistance of his colleagues, Henry Simons and Milton Friedman, in conducting the study and writing the book. Funding by the Volker Foundation, including five years of salary for Aaron Director at the University of Chicago Law School, was to make this possible. Hayek drafted the necessary memorandum to finalize the agreement between the Foundation and the University.[150] The funds were duly transferred in a letter to the Dean of the Law School.[151]

Hayek was determined to go ahead with the Acton-Tocqueville Society idea, and in the winter of 1946, asked for Volker Foundation funding of travel costs for a list of participants from America. Luhnow was dismayed at some names on the list. He proposed a screening committee "where we have no doubts whatsoever," and that they be given the responsibility for determining who would be funded. Hayek could then invite others who would pay their own way.[152] Correspondence followed with negotiations over who would be funded and who Luhnow wanted added to the list.[153] Hayek took most of the list, but demurred at including the representative from du Pont de Nemours, Jasper Crane, on the grounds that he and his colleagues wished to include only scholars and writers and "to avoid any impression that the conference has been instigated by any business interests."[154]

The conference was held in the spring of 1947 in a village near Montreux. It was decided that the Society was now to be named the Mt. Pelerin Society, a "closed society" devoted to studying the "threats to liberty" that were evident in the postwar West.[155] The Society included several like-minded colleagues from LSE, as well as luminaries among European and American intellectuals. Lionel Robbins played a central role in drafting the Society's Statement of Aims.[156] Russell Kirk, an early participant, saw the society's antistatism as a tonic for believers in the classical liberal approach to the market as well as for institutional traditionalists such as himself. A diminished state would be less of a threat to religious institutions and private associations.[157] As events in the latter half of the century would demonstrate, the marriage between free-marketers and moral traditionalists would not be so easily consummated. This "fusionist" movement would be the locus of tensions that would deeply affect the evolution of rightist movements in British and American politics.

Hayek wrote to invite Luhnow to become a member of the Mt. Pelerin Society and to request assistance for another visit to the United States.[158] Hayek's cultivation of financing in the United States was running into difficulty on another front, however. Aaron Director wrote a blistering letter to Leonard Read reproaching him for characterizing his colleague Henry Simons's work as "advocacy of collectivistic ideas." Director was "astounded" by such an allegation and concluded that "if free enterprise is to mean opposition to governmental measures indispensable to free enterprise, then the cause of free enterprise is dead."[159] Hayek sent his copy of the letter to Luhnow urging him to read Simons's book and to regard it as "in the spirit" of the way Director would conduct his study.[160]

In the summer of 1947, Hayek corresponded with his old friend, Jacob Viner, seeking his intervention in approaching the Princeton Institute for Advanced Study about an academic appointment. Viner promised to look into it, though he refused an invitation to join the Mt. Pelerin Society, disdaining activity for "political purposes."[161] Hayek's prospects for coming to the United States were thus clouded at the outset by the political turn in his work and reputation.

The pressure of his personal situation was increasing. He later wrote that Hella agreed to a divorce in the spring of 1948. He then went in search of a position that would support both his family and his new wife in an appropriate manner.[162] He wrote Claude Robinson at Princeton to say "the period for which I felt to be morally committed to stay on here seems now to be approaching its end and that my personal circumstances might now make it possible for me seriously to consider a sufficiently attractive position in the states such as you urged me to contemplate three years ago."[163]

Luhnow, along with Robinson, had meanwhile been at work on the project of securing a university appointment for Hayek with the salary to be paid by the Volker Foundation. The first result was a disappointing letter to Luhnow from Princeton's Institute for Advanced Study. The Director, Robert Oppenheimer, reported that it was contrary to their practice to accept "funds as specifically allocated by the donors as would be implied by your offer."[164] The principle was fundamental to academic freedom. University professorships should not be controlled by outside interests who wished to borrow academic credibility for the advocacy of their positions.

Hayek then sent Luhnow an anguished letter revealing aspects of his personal dilemma. He told the story of his long devotion to Frau Warhanek and the crisis that the war had created for them. The chance of remaining close enough to continue his visits to her was given as the reason for his reluctance to accept the first teaching offer from America. They now wished to begin a new life in America, but financial pressures would mean the necessity of a salary of $15,000 on a permanent appointment basis. He forgave Luhnow in advance if, in view of these personal matters, the Volker Foundation's assistance would come to an end.[165] He received a gentle nonjudgmental response.[166]

Hayek, with this assurance, wrote immediately to Viner declaring his desire for a Research Professorship at Princeton, independent of the Institute for Advanced Study, and mentioning that Volker funds would pay his salary. "I should now feel no hesitation to accept a position at an academic institution out of means provided by his fund."[167] Viner replied that, though they might like to have him come, the authorities found the arrangements "impossible to accept." Viner suggested that "any of the respectable institutions" would have the same objection and that some sort of independent status as "guest professor" paid by the Foundation might be less controversial.[168]

The negative response from Princeton left Hayek "depressed." Next on his list were Yale and Columbia. Neither bore fruit. The Economics Department at Chicago, according to Milton Friedman, was apprised of the possibility of Volker funding for a Hayek appointment and declined on principle.[169] However, encouraging signals from another Chicago source soon raised his hopes of going to America. Aaron Director, Friedman's brother-in-law, had been approached by Loren Miller about the possibility of a funded professorship. Director advised Hayek that an appointment to the faculty of the Committee on Social Thought, chaired by Professor John U. Nef, might meet with the support of Hutchins, the dynamic young Chancellor of the University of Chicago.[170] Hayek wrote back that he would be delighted at the prospect.[171] Matters moved along. Nef wrote that Hayek's appointment was approved by his colleagues.[172]

Chancellor Hutchins, prompted by Nef, lost no time in visiting Kansas City to work out the arrangements in person with Luhnow. Luhnow's condition was that Hayek be able to spend the "major portion of his time" on research.[173] Ensured that Volker would pay his salary for ten years, Hutchins wrote to confirm the arrangement.[174] In making possible Hayek's appointment with the deliberate assistance of a conservative foundation, Hutchins was true to the University's origins, if not to accepted practice among great institutions. Founded in 1892 by the Rockefeller family, the University was destined to play a major role in reorienting the social sciences and the legal profession to a pro-capitalist frame of reference.

Hayek's quest for release from England, and from his wife, was now at the point of success. The possibility of a new academic home and of at last marrying his great love provided Hayek with new hope. Hayek was to be given a permanent appointment to the faculty and "the amount of teaching is entirely at your own discretion."[175] He proposed to come the next autumn and begin an ambitious program of research into such topics as "the place of mind in the universe of nature," and into "more recent 'Keynesian' developments and on what I like to call the logic of choice or the economic calculus."[176] Luhnow was pleased at the completion of the arrangements but hoped that Hayek would give the slow-moving project of the book his "first attention."[177]

However, Hayek's situation at home had now become a full-blown crisis. On hearing of his appointment at Chicago, Hayek claimed, Hella reversed her earlier decision and rejected the idea of a divorce. She informed him in the fall of 1948, according to Hayek, that she had taken legal advice and would resist the divorce and had been ensured that he could not get a divorce without her cooperation.[178] She refused henceforth to discuss the matter further. Threatening a personal breakdown that would force him back to the home, she averred that she would take action to annul a divorce if he got one elsewhere. Hayek saw this as a final rupture—one that might make it impossible for him to accept the Chicago position and, with it, the prospect of financial security for her and for him.[179]

As Christmas of 1948 approached, he wrote a long letter to Hella pleading with her once more to understand his reasons for wanting to accept the Chicago position. His plea continued with the proposal that the family not come with him and that the divorce be concluded. The children would not want to move. Besides, after thirty years, he could not go on without Helene Warhanek. He was determined to leave home and commence divorce proceedings. He begged for her cooperation, saying he was on the verge of a breakdown and sketched the disastrous consequences of a contested divorce. He pointed out that she could not fight an American divorce in any event. Hayek was upset that she had written to John Nef to discourage his prospects at the University of Chicago. He wrote to her a day before his final resignation from LSE only so that she would not hear it elsewhere. He left her the choice of telling the children, indicating he would write to them at school if necessary.[180]

Hella would not cooperate. Hayek's hopes were shattered.[181] Faced with the collapse of his plan, he wrote to Nef explaining his situation and reporting that it would not now be possible to accept the offer. Nef responded sympathetically that Hayek's letter had made him "not less, but more anxious to have you as a part of our enterprise here." The offer was left open pending a change in Hayek's situation.[182] Hayek then wrote in near despair to Luhnow telling of the need to postpone his Chicago appointment in view of his personal difficulties.[183] He now faced the prospect of either a contested divorce in England, which would take two years or more, or some kind of more expeditious arrangement in the United States. Hayek now committed himself to go ahead without Hella's assent.[184]

Hayek continued to work away at improving the terms of his offer to Chicago so as to cover the expenses he anticipated in connection with the divorce. One possibility was a one-quarter appointment at Chicago that would serve the dual purpose of firming up the permanent arrangement should he be able to take it and of getting him to the United States where a less onerous divorce procedure might be available.[185]

A temporary one-quarter appointment as professor of social and moral science was offered from the first of the new year in Chicago. Two days after Christmas in 1949, he parted from his family in Hampstead Garden Suburb.[186] Hayek assured Nef privately that the one-quarter appointment was the preliminary to a longer term commitment.[187] Chancellor Hutchins wrote to welcome Hayek by giving a small stag dinner with a guest list of industrial notables.[188] Publicity about his appointment was withheld in view of Hayek's delicate personal circumstances. An understanding between Nef and Hutchins was reached by which Hayek could be added to the budget on his arrival.[189]

Hayek arrived in Chicago and soon found that letters from Hella speaking of resuming family relations complicated his prospect even further. His colleague Lionel Robbins had learned of the true reason for Hayek's "leave" from LSE and the parlous state of his relations with Hella. He wrote that a divorce might well be best, but he was concerned about an inadequate provision for Hella and the children. In a postscript, he reported that Hella had told the children he is not coming back.[190] Thus commences a long, acrimonious, and emotional correspondence between Hayek and his former patron at LSE.

Determined to go ahead, Hayek made arrangements to obtain an immigrant visa to the United States. Hayek, with the advice of attorneys, had found a venue where he could complete the divorce without his wife's participation. Rejecting Reno, Nevada, among other possibilities, he settled on Arkansas since that state's laws were far more permissive than England's. He assured Luhnow that his visit to Arkansas would be temporary and that he would return to Chicago in the fall.[191]

Hayek approached the Chair of the Economics and Business Department at the University of Arkansas and arranged for a spring term appointment at the University of Arkansas in Little Rock. He took up his post on March 20, 1950, for a term ending four months later. On this basis, he would attest to permanent residence in Arkansas for legal purposes.[192] These maneuvers would permit him to complete the divorce in circumstances in which Hella could not contest it.[193] The distance would make it difficult, if not impossible, for his wife, who was in poor health, to assert her rights in person at the proceeding. Arkansas law allowed an immediate remarriage to another party. All that done, he could take up his new life at the University of Chicago.[194]

With this plan in place, Hella was confronted with a fait accompli in advance of any concrete assurance of a provision for her welfare. Robbins was outraged. He reproached Hayek for leaving Hella in difficult circumstances with only Hayek's word that she would not wind up destitute.[195] Hayek was now in a position to pressure his wife for a settlement. He assured Robbins of his intent to provide for Hella and set about suggesting terms with the understanding that if she somehow prevented his appointment at Chicago, the terms would necessarily be less than she was accustomed to receiving.[196]

Robbins reported that Hella was now persuaded to have the lawyers commence discussions.[197] On that basis, Hayek filed for divorce in Arkansas. On July 13, 1950, the divorce was decreed in view of the "indignities to the person of the plaintiff" rendered by the defendant. The settlement provided for a net payment of $1,500 per year, with an allowance for each of the two children of $280 per year each. The house and some insurance policies were signed over to her. There was no mention of book royalties in the decree.[198]

There followed a bitter row over the provision for his family. Hayek's salary at LSE had been £2,040 ($43,452 in current dollars plus a retirement benefit).[199] At Chicago he was to receive $15,000 or ($106,500 in current dollars). Robbins was aghast that Hayek, who would be earning a handsome salary, plus royalties on his books, would be leaving his wife and children with a disposable annual income of only £750 ($2,100 or $14,910 currently).[200] Hayek protested that the cost of the divorce would take nearly all of his annual income for the first year and that Hella would have their home in Hampstead Garden Suburb.[201] Whether supplementary arrangements were made in consequence of this correspondence is not known.

The divorce left Hella and their two children, Christine, just twenty-one, and Laurence, nearly sixteen, with the aftermath of a scandalous divorce.[202] The divorce offended his LSE colleagues, some of whom, including Robbins, had been his neighbors in Hampstead Gardens. Robbins refused to participate further in the Mt. Pelerin Society, writing to its director that Hayek's treatment of Hella had been so shabby that he wished to have nothing more to do with him.[203] Their friendship would not be resumed for more than a decade. Hella Hayek, unreconciled to the divorce, died ten years later of a heart attack at the age of fifty-eight.[204]

In August 1950 Friedrich and Helene were married in Austria. Hayek's new wife had no financial resources. He was forced from this point forward, as he commented to his private secretary Charlotte Cubitt, "to do everything for money," though he claimed that he never did anything he would not have done otherwise.[205] Hayek and his new wife, Helene, set sail for America on the SS *Britannic* on October 1950. That they traveled First Class suggests that travel funds at least were not in short supply.[206]

A political apostate and intellectual dissident, he was now, in England at least, a social outcast.[207] With the bitterness of the divorce behind him, Hayek turned toward building on his contacts in the United States. The Volker Foundation underwrote five fellowships to supply Hayek with a cadre of students of his choosing. The Mt. Pelerin Society had met for the second and third times in 1949 and 1950. The next project was to rectify the "frequent distortions and misrepresentations of the effect of a free economy on the position of the working classes."[208]

The Mt. Pelerin session resulted in a volume underwritten by the Volker Foundation, *Capitalism and the Historians*, published in 1954.[209] Hayek here asserts that "the actual history of the connection between capitalism and the rise of the proletariat is almost the opposite of that which . . . theories of the expropriation of the masses suggest." The truth was that capitalism made possible the extension of the possibility of survival to those who otherwise would have lacked the means of sustenance. It was a historical first for one class, though "certainly not from charitable motives," to use its wealth to enable the survival of another.[210]

Another of Hayek's Volker-financed projects was a study of the "political tendencies of intellectual journalism" to be completed by his graduate student, Shirley Letwin, and her husband. They were to prepare a card index "indicating the political tendencies of the material" that they were to analyze.[211] In the climate of McCarthyism that was sweeping the United States, and especially its universities, the purposes of this project remain murky.

The price of his turn toward politics was the decline of his reputation as an economist. Hayek recalls commenting at the time of Keynes's death that "now Keynes was dead, I was probably the best known economist living. But ten days later it was probably no longer true. At the very moment, Keynes became a great figure, and I was gradually forgotten as an economist."[212] Looking back many years later, he remarked, "In the middle 1940s—I suppose I sound very conceited—I think I was known as one of the two main disputing economists: there was Keynes and there was I. Now, Keynes died and became a saint; and I discredited myself by publishing *The Road to Serfdom*, which completely changed the situation."[213]

The polemics of *The Road to Serfdom* had led his colleagues to decide that Hayek had defected to the world of politics. His collegial relations were disrupted as well by his divorce and remarriage. However, Hayek's even greater fame as a political theorist lay ahead of him.

For Friedrich Hayek, the forties were the time of a substantial shift in the components of his own sense of identity. An economist, he would now become a political philosopher. A married man inclined to celebrate the virtues of traditional morality, he would now divorce and remarry amid bitterness and controversy. An independent, even dissident, voice within his university, he would become the client of a conservative foundation devoted to changing the ideological cast of Western civilization.

These changes in his competencies, communities, and commitments have about them a single constant: a deepening animosity toward government as practiced in industrial democracies. Behind the forces generating the war, he saw a single vice, socialism, where others saw divergent movements of left and right. In his personal life, it was the constraint of individual choice in the restrictive English divorce law that led him to step outside its bounds. Among his colleagues, now nearly all gone over to Maynard Keynes, economics had become a tool for "constructivist" governmental tampering with the spontaneous forces of the economy. In the decade to come, Hayek would consolidate an alternate sense of identity as an exponent of individual freedom of choice and as a profound critic of mass democracy. On these foundations, he would construct a rationale for the primacy of the market of far-reaching significance for the politics of our time.

Maynard Keynes and Harold Laski came prematurely to the end of their lives exhausted by their heroic efforts to secure a future for Britain and the West that would reflect their intense beliefs. Each had advanced a plan, and each had experienced historic successes. For Keynes, the victories were institutionalized in economic arrangements, international organizations, and university courses that would carry his influence far into the future.

For Laski, the victory of 1945 was the beginning of a personal defeat as he propelled his own fall from grace and influence. He died honored and beloved, but having lost his hold on the public imagination. By overreaching, he contributed to the withdrawal from the most ambitious of socialist goals. Striving to preempt the Cold War, he knew that his efforts had failed by the time of his death.

It remains now to complete the narrative of these three lives by examining the remarkable revival of Hayek's career and fortunes and the lingering effect of Keynes and Laski, as the second half of the twentieth century commences.

8

The Second Half Century: From Ideas to Ideologies

In the latter half of the twentieth century, the epic of the Cold War would unfold as the confrontation of capitalism and communism reached a frenzy of military and economic competition. The foundational strength of the Western nations lay in their effort to mitigate class struggle by amelioration. The broad popular support of the Western cause abetted a dynamic economy in overwhelming the exertions of the communist world.

Yet the strains in the political system of the West would produce a reaction against government, the instrument of mitigation. The compromises that underlay Western political economies would be tested by a rival dispensation: a doctrinaire commitment to the market with its disproportionate rewards to capital. The reformulation of ideological positions around institutional issues and away from explicit class struggles created the context for contemporary politics. The question became whether the market was preferred over government, rather than whether the rich were advantaged thereby.

Maynard Keynes and Harold Laski were now gone, but the agendas they did so much to advance were fully in play. Keynesianism was the rising force from the fifties through the seventies and beyond; socialists remained contenders but rarely victors. As the century advanced toward its end, Friedrich Hayek would rise at last to prominence as the inspiration for a political revolution in Britain and the United States that rippled around the globe.

8.1 – KEYNES: THE FALL AND RISE OF THE CENTER

In Britain, Keynesianism became the property of moderates in both the Labour and Conservative Parties. The outlying forces of militant unionism on the left and individualist entrepreneurealism on the right found themselves contesting on terrain defined by Maynard Keynes's "middle way."

The underpinnings of the Keynesian revolution in policy making and of the socialized welfare state bequeathed by Laski and his colleagues were severely shaken as Britain's empire disintegrated and its trade position became less and less competitive. In 1972, a coal strike prompted large concessions on wages from the Conservative government, and unemployment reached one million. Conservatives could not manage the unions any better than Labour had. The average number of workdays lost to strikes in basic industries rose to five times what it had been a decade before.[1] Paradoxically, the Keynesian notion of governmental regulation of the economy led the public to blame the government for whatever went wrong in the economy whether the troubles arose from bad decisions by corporate or union leaders or for whatever other reason. The same pattern held in spades with Laski's prescription for nationalization.

By 1973, the British trade deficit was over £1 billion. The Bretton Woods system of fixed exchange rates collapsed, and the British pound was left to float downward. Within a year, the pound lost 30 percent of its value against the deutsche mark.[2] Britain was caught in the oil-shocks that triggered the worldwide recession of the early seventies. Labour returned to power in 1974; however, by 1976 the Labour Prime Minister told his annual conference that public spending could no longer be seen as a cure for recession—a moment some identified as the end of Keynesianism.[3]

Oddly, a reprieve, such as it was, came because a committed socialist Tony Benn had, as Labour Minister of Energy, insisted on hanging on to the government's share of the ownership of the domestic oil industry. By 1977, oil produced a surplus in the balance of payments. But even the gush of North Sea oil could not reverse the unemployment crisis. Persistently over 5 percent, double what it had been in the fifties and sixties, unemployment disillusioned the working class, and unemployment compensation drained the public coffers, even while taxes reached further and further into discretionary income.[4] As militance rose, Britain lost four times as many days to strikes as France, and sixty times as many as Germany in 1977. The Labour Party was tarred as incapable of governing. By 1979, cabinet papers were being sent to the Trades Unions Congress (TUC) headquarters for approval and Prime

Minister James Callaghan admitted privately that the government had become subservient to the unions.[5] Lord Annan's verdict was:

> In pursuing what they believed to be their interests, the trade unions split the Labour Party in the seventies. They also destroyed social democracy for a decade and the political assumptions of my generation.[6]

Keynes had never addressed the problem of union dominance; that could not have been foreseen given the weakness of British unions after the General Strike of 1926, the depression, and the union truce of the war years. He had, of course, labored most of his career with the problem of "sticky wages." But that was a different matter than dealing with a power that could raise wages by government fiat in the teeth of inflation and unemployment.

On many levels of public opinion in the United States, there was an increasing disenchantment with the corruption of the political process through tax breaks, subsidies, and provisions for the "undeserving." These policies and the compromising character of political leadership in a mass democracy led to a feeling that government had lost its moral legitimacy. For the disgruntled and disaffected, Hayek supplied a critique of social justice claims and a defense of common law morality, which legitimized a retreat from government regulation and welfare provision while relieving capitalist consciences—along with, perhaps, his own.[7] The slow deterioration of socialist hopes provided the backdrop to a gathering crisis as Britain made its way between the two ideological colossi of the Cold War.

8.2 – LASKI: THE LEGACY OF CLASS POWER

Harold Laski's legacy was the legitimation for nearly fifty years of extensions of government power into the fields of industrial relations, health provision, comprehensive schemes to ensure the welfare, and regulation and nationalization of major sectors of the economy.[8] Most of these initiatives might well have been taken without Harold Laski, but his role as advocate was vital in shaping public opinion, and no one can be sure that, absent Laski, the welfare state would have achieved such a high degree of development. Aneurin Bevan attributed the 1945 victory to Laski's work in political education.[9]

What Laski offered to Britain was a particular kind of identity carrying with it a set of ideas that addressed the major concerns of interwar life. His message was, as he liked to summarize it, "No cake for anyone 'til there's bread for everyone." Rebellious against his family traditions, he was also a class rebel whose speeches to trade union members opened with an apology for being born rich.[10] He demonstrated a genius for political communication at both the elite and the mass levels. In his persona of the intellectual as workers' advocate and in his pluralist prescription, there was the assurance that democratic socialism could be achieved through the instruments of mass politics.

There is an essential symmetry between the style and tone of Laski's personal rebellion and the restrained form taken by English working-class militancy. Laski's revolt against his upbringing was at once intense and yet moderated by strong bonds to his family and political culture. Similarly, the English working class, at a time when many of their continental brethren were being taken into camp by communist revolutionaries, marched to a different drummer. The congruence is as striking as it is fateful for English politics of this period. A. J. P. Taylor points to Laski's critical role in "remaking English social democracy and giving it its present form," concluding that "if today (1953) in this country, there is still no communist movement of any size, if all socialists can still be at home in the Labour Party, we owe it more to Harold Laski than to any other single man."[11] The revolution prompted by Marx and Engels using examples from British working-class life failed to catch hold in capitalism's core. Spared communism, England was likely spared fascism as well.

While few would cite his work today, Laski was a prophet of the prospects of the left in the postwar world. His progressive colleague and biographer, Kingsley Martin, wrote not long after Laski's death that

> Though he welcomed and brilliantly defended the achievements of Mr. Attlee's Government, he could never persuade himself that they would be permanent unless they were based on a real transference of power. He proved right; the redistribution of income, which was the main result of Labour policy, and the Welfare State, which depended on this redistribution, were soon to be menaced by the world struggle, rearmament, the shortage of raw materials, the inflation of world prices, and the international monetary crisis which it provoked.[12]

The left could see the failure of the international "revolution by consent" as the cause of the reversal of the domestic revolution. It took many years for these forces to play out, and there will never be consensus as to whether an international socialist movement could have sustained the drive to egalitarianism without suppressing critical freedoms that would make equality meaningful and morally desirable. Still, new concepts of social justice were firmly planted in the consciousness of mass electorates.

After his passing, Laski's chair at the London School of Economics (LSE) went to a conservative—or, as Michael Oakeshott described himself, a skeptic. In his 1951 inaugural lecture, Oakeshott saluted Laski and praised him for his human qualities, but then he offered a distinctly different view of politics. Bemused by the uncertainty of our understanding of the social universe, Oakeshott used the metaphor of a voyage on a "boundless and bottomless sea" to capture his view of politics, and the timidity and hesitance with which policy should be approached.[13] Diminutive, as was Laski, and brilliant too, Oakeshott had nearly the opposite take on British political thought.[14] Devoted to Hume and Burke, he was regarded as an ally by Friedrich Hayek.

Also in 1951, the Conservatives narrowly recaptured power in England. Labour actually polled more votes than the Tories, but the near collapse of the Liberals gave to Churchill's party a majority of seventeen. However, the ideological die, once cast, was left on the table. Churchill, now seventy-seven, grumbled about what Attlee had done, but his ministers kept to the course Labour had charted.[15] A key election issue was that the Conservatives promised to build more council houses than Labour, a promise kept by the Minister of Housing, Harold Macmillan, when he reached the goal of three hundred thousand new houses by 1953.[16] A more serious rejoinder to 1945 would await the rise a quarter of a century later of a politician named Margaret Thatcher who had read a theorist named Friedrich Hayek.

8.3 – HAYEK: REDEEMING CAPITALISM

In 1950 Friedrich Hayek took up his Volker-financed position as professor of social and moral science at the University of Chicago and remained there until 1962. This brought him into close contact with Milton Friedman and the developing "Chicago School" of free market economists. Critical of Friedmanesque exaggerations of the rationality of the marketplace, Hayek nevertheless fit well with the pro-capitalist bent of his colleagues.[17]

While Hayek had left England behind him, the seed of an encounter three years before his departure took root in a manner that would vastly amplify the political significance of his work. In 1947, Antony Fisher, an enthusiastic reader of the *Reader's Digest* condensed version of *Serfdom*, found his way to LSE where, across from the office of Laski, he found his hero, Hayek. Hayek encouraged the young war veteran to crusade for his beliefs not by running for office, but by founding a scholarly organization that could advance ideas of freedom in the way that the Fabian Society had sponsored socialism. Nearly a decade later, Fisher, now a wealthy chicken farmer, fulfilled his dream and formed the Institute of Economic Affairs (IEA) specifically to counter the legacy of Laski and the Fabian Society.[18]

The IEA was destined to play a major role in advancing Hayek's free market ideas and encouraging the development of a worldwide network of privately funded ideologically conservative think tanks.[19] The first director, appointed in 1957, was Ralph Harris, an economist trained at Cambridge by a member of the Mt. Pelerin Society. Along with Arthur Seldon, another conservative of working-class origins, Harris created over the next quarter of a century a heterodox center for the exploration of an alternative to conventional policies.[20] A generation of conservative politicians, among them Margaret Thatcher, have acknowledged the critical role of these institutions in shaping their views and making conservatism politically acceptable.[21]

Moving from his role as critic to his own prescription for politics, Hayek wrote *The Constitution of Liberty*, published in 1960. Here he elaborated functions of government that embraced a fair amount of what reform liberal, if not socialist, governments do: provide a safety net for the poor and insurance for health care, accidents, and old age, along with disaster assistance and policies for the prevention of monopolies, environmental pollution, and the depletion of resources.[22] His rationale was that government should do what markets cannot do, though this was the minor premise of his assumption that the main purpose of the constitution is to limit democracies from transgressing the boundaries requisite to the maintenance of the market.

Progressive taxation and the remediation of inequalities of opportunity were beyond the pale. Hayek took pains to say that he was not opposed to moves toward "social equality," and that where such moves could be made without undermining "equal law," they might be desirable. However, "economic inequality is not one of the evils which justify our resorting to discriminatory coercion or privilege as a remedy."[23] Indeed economic inequality seems to be a condition for material progress.[24] A "constitution of liberty" designed to secure individual freedoms from claims of social justice was his alternative to the postwar welfare state.

The attraction for his followers was in his polemical reduction of the state to an agency of coercion and his parallel claim that morality attaches only to free individual choice—in the use of capital, among other areas. "Coercion occurs when one man's actions are made to serve another man's will, not for his own but for the other's purpose. . . . Coercion implies both the threat of inflicting harm and the intention thereby to bring about certain conduct." Coercion, Hayek says, "is bad because it prevents a person from using his mental powers to the full and consequently from making the greatest contribution that he is capable of to the community."[25]

Thus freedom is praised, not quite for its own sake, but because it liberates knowledge, and this redounds to the benefit of the community. In this sense,

Hayek is not an anarchist. He is, in a curious way, a communitarian who believes that individual freedom will lead to voluntary collusion for the common good.[26] No evidence is offered, however, for his central assertion that knowledge will be maximally deployed only if every individual is given the greatest latitude for choice. It was sufficient, for the political purposes of his argument, to point to the weakness of the opposite argument *in extremis*—that something so complex as an economy could be centrally planned by officials having the power to coerce.

While libertarians embraced Hayek's ideas, his strictures about the "rule of law" are profound and systematic.[27] However, he means by this the fundamental sort of laws that protect property and individual freedom. He reserves particular contempt for "positivist law," which he identifies as "a movement led by a group of socialist lawyers and political scientists gathered around the late Harold Laski."[28] The positivists, impressed by the blatant favoritism of the law toward those with property and by the use of discretion to reinforce class privileges, looked to an innovative and progressive use of legislation to undo privilege and assert equality on a broader front. This meant that the courts themselves would have to become willing participants in the adjudication of such legislation.

While he was at it in *The Constitution of Liberty*, Hayek took the opportunity yet again to attack Keynes. Noting that Keynes was accurate in his diagnosis that wages in the thirties were too high, he assailed the prescription of increasing the money supply by deficit fiscal policy. In that circumstance, "each separate union, in its attempt to overtake the value of money, will never cease to insist on further increases in money wages and that the aggregate effort of the unions will thus bring about progressive inflation."[29] This appears to have been historically prescient in view of what was to happen in Britain particularly.

There are two historical problems with this analysis, however. First, while the unions were strong enough to prevent wholesale wage decreases in the mid-1930s, they were certainly not powerful enough to seek substantial improvements in their wages in Keynes's time. Had they been, Keynes might well have taken a different view. Deficit fiscal policy was a means to an end for Keynes, not an end in itself. Second, as to the situation in 1960, the other sources of inflationary pressure, the defense budgets and oligopolistic pricing practices by corporations, are not factored into Hayek's thinking. He continued to maintain that worldwide inflation was simply "the economic consequences of Lord Keynes" for many years, though by 1975, he recanted his deflationary policy advice of the 1930s.[30]

Reviews of *The Constitution of Liberty* were decidedly mixed. Even his colleagues and friends were skeptical. Lionel Robbins, who had written Hayek upon reading the book and wishing him well, found much of value in it, but demurred at Hayek's penchant for predicting calamity: "I cannot suppress the conviction that Professor Hayek is somewhat too apt to extrapolate his apprehensions of evil and to assume that deviations from his norm lead cumulatively to disaster." In particular, Robbins thought it fair to attribute some of the social and economic progress of the previous four decades to government intervention and improved social services of the kind Hayek denounced.[31]

Jacob Viner, who had abetted Hayek's efforts to find a position at Princeton, found that Hayek had a way of "reaching substantially unconditional conclusions and in avoiding what is, in social thought, the generally unavoidable and troublesome necessity of coping with major conflicts between values."[32] Such observations must have troubled him, for he had hoped that the book would be the century's equivalent of Adam Smith's *Wealth of Nations*.[33]

A substantial part of the great effort behind the writing was no doubt made possible by the turn in his domestic circumstances. Hayek's second marriage afforded him the intellectual companionship of a wife who took an interest in his work. Lena Hayek attended his seminars on occasion, did major work on the German translation of *The Constitution of Liberty*, and was acknowledged as a cogent critic in the preface to his *The Sensory Order*. Alan Ebenstein observes that "Helene Hayek was a beautiful woman, though possessed of a difficult personality."[34] The anxiety over his divorce was never fully resolved, though his new marriage provided him with a measure of personal security sufficient to support a new and highly successful phase of his career as academician and political theorist.

The publication of *The Constitution of Liberty* was followed by a bad turn for Hayek personally. He endured a winter of depression in 1960–1961 that he attributed to a misdiagnosis of a medical condition. It is also the case that Helen Hayek, his first wife, died in that year. Hayek broke down in tears on hearing the news. A happier event was the marriage of his son, Laurence, in 1961. The wedding became the occasion for reconciliation with his old friend, Robbins.[35]

On reaching the age of sixty-two, and with a troubled winter behind him, Hayek wrote to his sponsor at the Volker Foundation and presented the choices, as he saw them, for the remainder of his academic career. With Chicago's retirement age of sixty-five looming in just three years, he was anxious about the provision for his pension that he found to be quite inadequate for himself and insufficient to provide for his wife should he die.[36] The possibility of staying on for several years beyond retirement might be an option, given the continuation of outside support. Another possibility would be a return to Europe where a lifetime salary provision might be possible.[37]

On the promise of a lifetime salary, he decided to leave Chicago in 1962 for the University of Freiburg where he remained until his second retirement in 1967. He accepted an invitation from the University of Salzburg in 1969 and moved there only to be disappointed by the lack of serious Ph.D. students. Increasingly unhappy, he stayed until 1977 and returned thereafter to Freiburg, which was to be his residence for the final fifteen years of his life.

Hayek left behind him American organizations he had participated in and that would proselytize on his behalf: the Intercollegiate Society of Individualists for college students, the Foundation for Economic Education aimed at high school and college economics curricula, the American Enterprise Institute, the Cato Foundation, and the Heritage Foundation.[38] These believers, together with his internationally esteemed colleagues in the Mt. Pelerin Society, magnified Hayek's impact on political ideas throughout the West.

Apart from intellectuals, Hayek's work was being read in the early sixties by citizens who were dissatisfied with the leftward drift of American society under the presidencies of John Kennedy and Lyndon Johnson. A businessman named Barry Goldwater had read Hayek prior to becoming a U.S. Senator.[39] By 1964, Goldwater's crusade for a libertarian conservative alternative to establishment Republican politics resulted in his nomination to take on the formidable Lyndon Johnson for the presidency. Goldwater's overwhelming defeat for a time discredited these ideas; however, a small band of activists acquired experience and motivation that would prove durable in the sixteen-year struggle to install a conservative president. The campaign provided a launching platform for a movie actor turned conservative orator named Ronald Reagan. He was asked to give a partisan speech to raise money for Goldwater. Reagan invoked patriotic themes of liberty and free markets and drew on his college economics major as well as his experience in the Screen Actors Guild. The television address raised significant money for Goldwater and for the prospect of a national candidacy for Reagan.

Across the Atlantic, Hayek seemed increasingly marginalized by the turn in Britain from an indirect form of Keynesian demand management to a more directive stance, with growth targets and negotiated pay settlements. The critique of these settlements and the consensus approach behind them provided the text for a rising star, junior Minister Margaret Thatcher, as she stepped forward to claim a leadership role in the Conservative Party Conference of 1968.[40]

Meanwhile, just as Hayek seemed about to fade from the political stage, the IEA picked up Hayek's ideas on freedom and the market, and selected out Hayek's emphasis on reducing the "monopoly power" of unions. This and the monetarist gospel of Milton Friedman formed the heart of a political program. While Hayek had reservations about Friedman's rationalist approach, they were both advocates of the market. In advancing these themes through conferences and seminars, the IEA brought Hayek once again to the attention of a wide audience.[41] Another institute, the Center for Policy Studies, founded by Margaret Thatcher and Keith Joseph in 1974, amplified the Hayekian message.[42]

Hayek's early economic works were recognized in the award of a Nobel Prize in Economics in 1974, an award shared with a figure of comparable stature on the left, Gunnar Myrdahl. Both were saluted for "their penetrating analysis of the interdependence of economic, social and institutional phenomena."[43] Though he treasured the honor, Hayek was diffident about the existence of such an award, explaining in his toast to the King and Queen of Sweden that he would not have advised the creation of an award in economics. His co-awardee, Myrdahl, threatened to take things one step further by introducing a motion in the Swedish Academy of Sciences to eliminate the award because "economics was 'soft,' . . . just a bunch of political opinions."[44] Despite the demurrals, the Nobel Prize elevated Hayek's stature greatly, and he was seen once again as an economist of note as well as a political theorist.

By 1975, Thatcher had become a devotee of Hayek's *Constitution of Liberty*. She produced a copy in a direct confrontation with moderates in the Conservative Party's Research Center, proclaiming, "This is what we be-

Friedrich Hayek receiving the Nobel Prize in Economics from King Carl Gustaf of Sweden in 1974. Reprinted by permission of AP/World Wide Photos.

lieve."[45] She acknowledged that she had not "fully grasped the implications of Hayek's little masterpiece" when she read *The Road to Serfdom*. However, under the tutelage of Joseph, she "really came to grips with the ideas he put forward." She particularly resonated to "the rule of law" in the way that Hayek conceived of it. She was reminded of her training in the works of the great English jurist, A. V. Dicey.[46] Faced, as she was, with insurgent movements of workers and radicals, she could use the language of legal supremacy to take the repressive sting out of her militancy against the unions.

What Thatcher added to those ideas was an intuitive politician's gift for recognizing how Hayek's nostrums could be detached from the patronage of wealthy corporate benefactors and made sensible to the broad mass of the British public. The visible break with the "wets" in her own party and the elevation of grammar school—trained advisers steeped in the new doctrine—set up the stage play that made her a novelty and a hit with the British public. She found the script in a shrewd assessment of Hayek's appeal:

> Perhaps because (Hayek) did not come from a British Conservative background and did not in fact ever consider himself a Conservative at all, Hayek had none of the inhibitions which characterized the agonized social conscience of the English upper classes when it came to speaking bluntly about such things.[47]

Hayek's views may have been broadcast courtesy of those who had the most to gain, but they had a plain populism about them that engaged a new stratum of activists in the hurly-burly of political combat.

Newly selected as leader of the Opposition in 1975, Thatcher was introduced to Hayek in person that year at IEA headquarters at Lord North Street in London. Their relationship became warmly personal, though, as we shall see, there were to be disagreements on political initiatives. Thatcher's most famous comment on public philosophy was: "There is no such thing as society. There are only individual men and women and there are families." The first part, at least, sounds as if it is straight from Hayek's essay on social justice. The quote however appeared in *Women's Own* magazine, which says more about Thatcher's feel for public opinion.[48] Tony Blair would get around to denying the premise in the 2001 election with the statement that borrows on the "wet" tradition of British conservatism by allying a concern for community to patriotism:

> We admire individuality, but we are not exclusively individualists. Emphatically we believe that there is such a thing as society with all the rights and responsibilities that go with membership of a community of people. These are the values that make people proud to be British. And I believe a forward-looking modern patriotism can be built on them.[49]

The Labour Party in 1975, however, was beleaguered as its leadership sought a way out of the inflation, stagnation, and rising debt that was dragging down the British economy. In 1976, Callaghan turned on the fundamentals of what had become "Keynesianism" to argue for a break with the doctrines of the past. As Richard Cockett notes, Callaghan's remarks were a "rather eerie recapitulation of Hubert Henderson's memorandum criticizing Keynes's initial proposals for demand-management present to the Economic Advisory Council in 1930." The International Monetary Fund (IMF), Keynes's creation, placed requirements on Britain to show restraint in monetary expansion, reflecting now the ideas of Hayek's colleague and friend Milton Friedman who was to receive the 1976 Nobel Prize in Economics.[50]

Hayek's stature had become that of a world-class interpreter of political and economic trends. He visited Chile in 1977, met with General Pinochet, and endorsed the economic "reforms" under way as the regime suppressed the democratically elected socialist government, rounded up and executed dissidents, and reversed the nationalization and social reform policies of Salvador Allende. Roundly criticized in the press for lending his prestige to an authoritarian regime, Hayek was unrepentant.[51] In a lecture the next year, he left no doubt about what he conceived to be the moral status of "unlimited democracy."

> With regard to the fundamental immorality of all egalitarianism I will here point only to the fact that all our morals rest on the different esteem in which we hold people according to the manner in which they conduct themselves. While equality before the law—the treatment of all by government according to the same rules—appears to me to be an essential condition of individual freedom, that different treatment which is necessary in order to place people who are individually very different into the same material position seems to me not only incompatible with personal freedom, but highly immoral. But this is the kind of immorality towards which unlimited democracy is moving.[52]

Hayek had, by the end of the seventies, identified "unlimited democracy" as the principal danger. "The omnipotent and omnicompetent single democratic assembly, in which a majority capable of governing can maintain itself only by trying to remove all sources of discontent of any supporter of that majority, is thereby driven to take control of all spheres of life." During Labour's rule, Britain was being driven down the slippery slope by its own parliamentary system. The powerful unions, with their hold upon the policies of the Labour Party, were his main case in point.[53]

The argument ties morality, economic standing, and freedom together with syllogistic precision and turns these values toward an attack on unlimited democracy. The argument does not address the issue of whether political executions, as in Chile, of the practitioners of democracy can be justified.

On May 3, 1979, a political revolution took place in Britain. In the election contest, Thatcher had used Hayek's views to pick up where Churchill left off in the attack on the British welfare state.[54] Suited by background and temperament to the views of a "nation of shopkeepers," Thatcher (née Roberts) was the daughter of a grocer and Rotarian who had sent a congratulatory letter to the editor when Laski's newspaper libel suit had failed.[55] She was also the wife of a man made wealthy by a family business.[56]

Hayek saluted her victory with a telegram, saying that her victory was the best present he could have received on the occasion of his eightieth birthday. She replied warmly in a personal letter that she was "very touched" and that she was "very proud to have learned so much from you over the last several years." The Prime Minister intended that "some of those ideas will be put into practice by my Government in the next few months. As one of your keenest supporters, I am determined that we should succeed."[57] With Thatcher in office, Hayek's work became politically fashionable. Thatcher was known to prize his *Constitution of Liberty*.[58] Richard Cockett reports that *The Road to Serfdom* and Popper's *The Open Society* were named as the two most influential books by those involved in the Thatcherite revolution of the 1980s.[59]

Hayek began writing to his protégé urging rapid action to restrain monetary growth, limit debt, and legislate a referendum on whether "special privileges" in the law for trade unions should be removed.[60] She responded patiently that his drastic monetary and fiscal programs "would have caused too much social and economic disruption in the short run." On unions, she promised that legislation limiting their powers would be forthcoming.[61] After another letter on trade unions, Hayek received a response from Secretary of State for Employment Norman Tebbit, who was to introduce restrictive labor legislation for the government, that "a step so radical as that which you propose would I fear be so controversial that it would be frustrated in this overconservative nation."[62]

Voices of dissent within the Conservative Party were led by Sir Ian Gilmour, a minister in the Thatcher government. Gilmour attacked on the basis that "economic liberalism, à la Professor Hayek, because of its starkness and its failure to create a sense of community, is not a safeguard of political freedom, but a threat to it."[63] The "Wets" of the traditional wing of the Conservative Party fought a running battle over the course of the decade with the powerful Prime Minister who gave her name to a new era in British politics.

With the publication of the third volume of *Law, Legislation, and Liberty* in 1979, Hayek's political testament was fully formulated. His antipathy to modern democratic governance had taken him to the point of declaring that the public monopoly on the supply of money must be broken. He advanced a radical, and quickly dismissed, proposal for the privatization of currency.[64] He thought that "competing monies" might provide a discipline of currency that governments *would* not, and under democratic pressures *could* not provide. The way to stamp out Keynesianism was finally to dismantle the institutional means of regulating economic activity.

In case any recalcitrant Keynesians were tempted otherwise, the imagery of the economy as a system where equilibrium could be restored by adept policies was undercut by Hayek's new image: "In order to explain the economic aspects of large social systems, we have to account for the course of a flowing stream, constantly adapting itself as a whole to changes in circumstances of which each participant can know only a small faction, and not for a hypothetical state of equilibrium determined by a set of ascertainable data."[65]

Washed out to sea, from Hayek's perspective, were any vestiges of Keynes's carefully constructed probabilism as a rationale for action. As for a "third way" between capitalism and socialism, the concept was rubbish for it involved the compromise of "irreconcilable principles": a "functioning market" and "central direction."[66] While logic divided government from the market, spontaneity ruled in the "sensory order."

A divorced man and an advocate of spontaneity might seem to be an odd counselor to the Pope; however, Hayek had at least a brief chance of becoming one when he and other Nobel laureates had a private audience at Christmastime in 1980. Asked to describe the problems that are most urgent for contemporary society, Hayek chose the scientistic and constructivist assault on morals. He wrote a statement in advance for the Pope's consideration:

> To tell our fellows that science and technology are not omnipotent, that we owe what we have achieved to submitting to those moral restraints on our desires which were never designed as a means to serve the satisfaction of our own pleasures, but which made possible the formation of an order of human actions more extended than any human mind can fully comprehend, seems to me the most urgent moral duty now placed upon scientists on whom opinion has placed special distinction.[67]

The curious elision of any mention of the role of institutions, such as government or the church, in encouraging the observance of moral behavior must have seemed striking to the pontiff. That the source of the advice had rather conspicuously broken with "moral restraints" on his desires in the instance of his divorce might have made the advice stranger still.

Returning to a more draconian scene of institutional power, Hayek traveled to Chile in 1981. Charlotte Cubitt reports that "he took time off from his official commitments to see for himself whether people were cheerful and content. It was the sight of many sturdy and healthy children that convinced him that they were."[68] He and Mrs. Thatcher dined together at a small party arranged by the banker W. H. Salomon in 1982, and she delighted him by suggesting that he was the guest of honor, not her.[69] Moved to write to Thatcher about the progress made under the Pinochet regime, he received an unexpected rebuke from the hand of the Prime Minister:

> The progression from Allende's Socialism to the free enterprise capitalist economy of the 1980s is a striking example of economic reform from which we can learn many lessons. However, I am sure you will agree that, in Britain with our democratic institutions and the need for a high degree of consent, some of the measures adopted in Chile are quite unacceptable. Our reform must be in line with our traditions and our Constitution. At times the process may seem painfully slow. But I am certain we shall achieve our reforms in our own way and in our own time. Then they will endure.[70]

The rebuke seems to have marked the end of his role as an unofficial adviser.

On the other side of the Atlantic, Reagan credited Hayek by name as an influence in shaping his victories over entrenched versions of liberalism in the Republican Party as well as the Democratic Party.[71] Reagan, who read von Mises and Hayek, was credited by his closest adviser with having acted directly on their insights.[72] Twenty members of the Mt. Pelerin Society were to be among the seventy-four economists employed on Reagan administration task forces.[73] His zealous Budget Director, David Stockman, had imbibed Hayek as scripture and wrote the lessons into a dramatic proposal to slash and consolidate domestic spending programs.[74] Stockman was later to become disillusioned when a rapid expansion of military spending undermined, in his view, all that might have been proven by a full test of Hayek's theory.[75]

In Britain, Margaret Thatcher proceeded to sacrifice employment to deflation and succeeded in reducing inflation from 18 percent in 1980 to 4.5 percent in 1983; meanwhile employment rose to 3.3 million, though it fell to just under 3 million in time for the election that year. An upturn in economic growth to a rate of 4 percent promised better things to come. The Falklands War gave her a palpable military victory that buoyed her sinking popularity. The victory was adroitly converted into a symbol for her battles on the economic front.[76] A resounding victory in 1983 assured the "Iron Lady" of the power to rule over the disputatious factions in her own party, as well as a

Friedrich Hayek being received by President Reagan in 1983. Courtesy of the Ronald Reagan Library.

country that was seeming to turn its back on fifty years of experimentation with socialist ideas.[77]

Hayek was now to be celebrated. He was presented with a large check by Reverend Sun Myung Moon at their U.S. Plenary Conference in 1983.[78] In 1984, the Prime Minister at least partially redeemed an earlier slight when she proposed Hayek be appointed a Member of the Order of the Companions of Honour. He had once hoped for a Baronetcy; however, the news of the lesser honor cheered him greatly, and he was most pleased and impressed with the Queen when she chatted with him at the ceremony.[79] Ralf Dahrendorf, former director of LSE and its centennial historian, observed that the honor was a way of saluting a figure who had to be set aside for political reasons.[80]

Hayek did not let up on his campaign against the unions. He wrote to the *Times* in 1984 decrying union wage practices and proposing that "those who suffer from this monopoly would form a libertarian anti-labour union" to confront the union bosses and Labour politicians in the interest of open shops.[81] By the mid-eighties, Prime Minister Thatcher had her confrontation with the miners union. In a strike reminiscent of 1926, they went out only to be put down forcefully.[82] The class compact Keynes and the Liberals had endeavored so long to preserve lay broken. The days of union dominance of British politics were clearly at an end. Rising unemployment cut their membership and Labour Minister Norman Tebbitt's legislation weakened the internal hold of trade union suzerains.[83]

The analogous development in the United States was the air traffic controllers strike. The controllers were both federal employees and well organized in a union, so the strike was a high-visibility challenge to the new administration. President Reagan addressed the challenge by simply firing them all, supplying replacements from the military, and speeding up training procedures. For this and a variety of reasons, union membership in the United States entered a slide that saw its strength cut in half by the nineties. Reagan saluted Hayek on his eighty-seventh birthday by recalling his contribution to the cause of freedom:

> More than forty years ago, you warned the Western world against "The Road to Serfdom." We are all indebted to you for this advice and I think it is clear that your wise counsel is being heeded.[84]

Meanwhile, Antony Fisher, the founder of the IEA, was busy through his Atlas Foundation advising similar groups that were springing up in numerous countries. Involving more than seventy institutions around the world, their direct sponsorship contributed to the global spread of Hayek's ideas and the preparation of a corps of committed believers who stood ready to staff the regimes that would implement free market nostrums.[85] In the United States, William Simon, former Secretary of the Treasury under President Richard Nixon, put out the call for a massive corporate subsidy to "non-egalitarian scholars and writers," including Hayek, who could carry the message in books subsidized by conservative foundations.[86] The template of the Volker Foundation's success in importing Hayek to confront the left was available for extension across a wide range of intellectual and political activities.

In Britain, Thatcher's sway was not complete, however. A resilient civil service dedicated to salvaging social provision for those in need managed to preserve a strong position in budgetary politics. Members of her own cabinet abetted these moves on occasion. Thatcher did not fully address the question of social services until the next election in 1987. By then the accumulating unpopularity of her initial measures weakened the force of her position. Inflation reappeared by 1990 at levels higher than 1979, along with a dangerously negative trade balance and interest rates of 14 percent. Defense became an obsession with the Prime Minister, and the cost was ruinous to basic government services. Homeless people in the streets, a row over the European Community, and an aggressive effort to implement a poll tax — all wore down her power.

For all her political adroitness, the issue that was to ultimately undo her ministry, the poll tax, was a case of pure Hayekian theory without regard to custom and political common sense. The poll tax is a uniform levy on all citizens regardless of income. It meets Hayek's criteria for justice in taxation, or, rather, avoids his stricture against redistributive progressive taxation in line with some conception of social justice.[87] In the political firestorm occasioned by the poll tax debate, Thatcher resigned the leadership, having lost her bid for a first-round endorsement by the Conservative Party.[88]

Thatcher's chosen successor, John Major, was up from poverty, not given to indulging in doctrine, barely prepared, and soon overwhelmed. The Labour Party finally began to adapt to the new winds, and their 1990 platform endorsed the market economy, jettisoned the memory of Laski, and opened the way to Tony Blair's stunning victory seven years later.

After struggling through declining health, with numerous misgivings and considerable assistance in the writing from his secretary, Cubitt, and his putative biographer, William Bartley, Hayek published his final book, *The Fatal Conceit* (1988).[89] It is an interesting distillation of his political views, even if the reader cannot always be sure that the words are Hayek's. He comes to this Manichaean statement of his essential position:

> The main point of my argument is, then, that the conflict between, on the one hand, advocates of the spontaneous extended human order created by a competitive market, and on the other hand those who demand a deliberate arrangement of human interaction by central authority based on collective command over available resources is due to a factual error by the latter about how knowledge of these resources is and can be generated and utilized.[90]

The slippery slope reasoning of *The Road to Serfdom* is augmented in *The Fatal Conceit* by the either/or bifurcation of reality with one path leading upward and onward and the other to degradation and ruin. That markets may themselves empower actors who succeed by position rather than superior knowledge or that governments might make use of democratic techniques to aggregate individual knowledge escapes consideration.

In 1989, with the fall of the Berlin Wall, Hayek and his followers saw the ultimate vindication of his critique of socialism. In 1991, President George Bush had awarded Hayek the Presidential Medal of Freedom, the highest U.S. civilian decoration. The award recognized that "your work has contributed so signally to the rebirth of freedom in central and eastern Europe and to the revival of ideas of economic liberty throughout the world."[91] His health would not permit him to travel, so his son, Laurence, received the award for him.

His advancing years weakened his health, and episodes of fainting signaled the approaching end. He and his wife continued to live in an apartment with little outside assistance until near the end. Friedrich Hayek died in Freiburg im Breisgau near the Swiss border on March 23, 1992. It is fitting that he should have breathed his last in a country recently reunited after the downfall of the communist regime he so detested and in a city named for freedom.

He had reason to believe that his warnings about collectivism had been heeded. Hayek was widely read by Eastern European dissidents and his ideas had a powerful presence in postcommunist politics.[92] Margaret Thatcher projected onto the struggles against Soviet domination her own sense that Hayek's ideas spoke to the aspirations of ordinary people. She records in her memoirs a moving experience of having been valorized in a sermon at the Church of the Holy Cross in Warsaw in 1993 as one whose voice had given hope to the Polish people in their struggle against communism. She recalled that "all the general propositions favouring freedom I had either imbibed at my father's knee or acquired by candle-end reading of Burke and Hayek were suddenly embodied in the worshippers and their children and illuminated by their smiles."[93]

Meanwhile the successors to Thatcher and Reagan tried to keep the fusionist coalition of traditionalists and free market libertarians together, but internal factionalism between social conservatives and economic libertarians weakened their successors and, by the nineties, created an opening for a centrist opposition.[94]

The more moderate elements of Hayek's political views were lost in the enthusiasm with which the antisocialist Keynesian critic was greeted by vanquished traditional conservatives, as well as by disaffected leftists who were gravitating toward a libertarian position.[95] The political necessity for the revival of the right was that conservative traditionalists form an alliance with advocates of free markets and individual liberty. For those in the "fusionist movement," Hayek was embraced as both a free market advocate and the defender of moral traditions. Hayek links the two as inseparable:

> To understand our civilization one must appreciate that the extended order resulted not from human design or intention but spontaneously: it arose from unintentionally conforming to certain traditional and largely *moral* practices, many of which men tend to dislike, whose significance they usually fail to understand, whose validity they cannot prove, and which have nonetheless fairly rapidly spread by means of an evolutionary selection—the comparative increase of population and wealth—of those groups that happened to follow them.[96]

The moralism is especially interesting in view of his divorce. It is a morality that does not takes its justification from theology or ethics or from any notion of responsibility for others. Rather, Hayek's morality rests on a test, "the comparative increase of population and wealth," that appears to be nothing more than materialism allied with a kind of secular relativism.[97] The assault of the marketplace on all traditions, morality included, is never confronted.

In the second half of the twentieth century, an ever more appreciative and well-financed movement of rightist intellectuals, politicians, and corporate leaders provided the wherewithal to translate Hayek's pro-market theories into action.[98] His principal supporters also knowingly financed his private behavior—in the name of saving Western civilization from the perils of socialism. Hayek rebuilt his identity on a new community and a new marital commitment. The transition in his competency from economic theorist to political philosopher attracted sponsors among conservatives that permitted him to resituate his professional activities at a higher level of visibility.

By the end of the twentieth century, all three, Maynard Keynes, Harold Laski, and Friedrich Hayek had seen their ideas become the dominant view for a formative period of time. They shared the characteristics of great courage and insight built on strong identities that survived great challenges. It is now time to consider how the particular content of those identities shaped the genesis of the ideas they put forward and of the ideologies that claimed them as authorities.

9

Developmental Turning Points and the Formation of Ideologies

The narratives of these three lives provide rich material for further analysis. In this final part of the book, I propose to step out of the role of narrator and into the role of analyst. The purpose is to explore and illustrate the ties between the maturation of these individuals and the formation of their ideas about political economy. Thereby perhaps we can gain a working perspective on the links between identity formation and ideology that will illuminate aspects of contemporary politics.

In probing the development of identity, we have considered the three critical markers of identity formation and change: the kinds of *competencies* or skills each came to have; the *communities* they were a part of; and the interpersonal ties and *commitments* that defined their private lives. Changes in these three areas provide observable developmental turning points by which people come to be who they are. These turning points are also where ideas are decontested to become ideologies. I have termed this approach *identity relations analysis*. We will now see what these three cases reveal when approached in this way.

Whence came Maynard Keynes's faith in the power of intellect to regulate a troublesome world? What was it that undermined his willingness to trust conventional views of the role of government and markets in shaping political economy? What propelled Harold Laski's opposition to his class and to the prevailing views of governance and the economy? How did he arrive at his distinctive mix of radicalism and activism? Why did Friedrich Hayek turn on government when he at first aspired to a position in one of its ministries? What led him to become the tribune of the capitalists?

In seeking answers to these questions, we have looked at each figure in a developmental perspective. We have seen how each identity was shaped in confronting the challenges of developing competence, participating in communities, and working out personal commitments. The next step, to be taken in this chapter, is to match these developmental turning points with the emergence of the ideas that shaped each person's political views. In chapter 10, we will draw the lessons from the common elements in these patterns. The analysis concludes in chapter 11 by drawing some lessons about the relations between identity formation and ideology that may shed light on our contemporary political situation.[1]

As Isaiah Berlin suggests, "One of the deepest human desires is to find a unitary pattern in which the whole world of experience, past, present, and future, actual, possible, and unfulfilled, is symmetrically ordered."[2] It is this desire that promotes the conversion of ideas into ideologies, and the desire is most powerful when the fundamentals of identity are jeopardized or challenged by transitions in one's communities, competencies, and personal commitments.

Erik Erikson's landmark study using a similar methodology is his *Young Man Luther* (New York: Norton, 1958). Here we see Luther's dramatic turn from a personal commitment to his father's vocational plan to a new life as a monk, his apostasy from the Holy Father and his church, and the formation of new commitments, a singular competency, and a community of protesters. In my approach, as distinct from Erikson's, I focus on a *broader* array of social factors influencing identity and rely *less* on the psychiatric interpretation of stages of development prior to young adulthood. The purpose is to see what level of explanation can be reached without going beyond biographical information about behavior, as opposed to psychiatric evidence about internal states of mind.[3] *Identity relations analysis* is an alternative to more speculative psychological and psychoanalytic approaches.[4] The emphasis is on *observable* aspects of character and behavior.

What is similar to Erikson's strategy is the linking of identity formation and cultural and political change. In reflecting later on his view of psychohistory, Erikson suggests:

> To put it in terms of what must be studied concertedly: in every . . . historical period there are types of individuals who ("properly" brought up) can combine the dominant techniques with their identity development, and *become* what they *do* . . . they can settle on that *cultural consolidation* which secures them what joint verification and what transitory salvation lies in doing things together and doing them right—a rightness proven by the bountiful response of "nature,"

whether in the form of the prey bagged, the food harvested, the goods produced, the money made, or the technological problems solved.[5]

Or, one might add, the ideological problems solved or perhaps created.[6]

The method of this study may not only be of interest to scholars, but perhaps it will also be of interest to readers in search of a perspective on politics, on the claims of politicians for the truth of their creeds, and on the ways that personal agency can most effectively be deployed in improving the human condition.

In this chapter, the patterns linking identity development to the formation of ideas will be set out. As unique as each of these persons' individual histories may be, there are developmental patterns that reveal the origins of their ideas. These patterns predisposed each to perfect an ideological approach to contemporary events that captured mass sentiments at critical historical moments.

9.1 – KEYNES: MENTALITY AND SENTIMENTALITY

Maynard Keynes's own persona expressed the desperation of a culture in crisis. He lived in a nation that underwent shattering despair and a perilous regeneration in the course of a fascinating life. He shared England's profound desire for a better, more certain path to security. It became his mission to create the assurance that intellectual mastery of economic forces was indeed possible.[7] Living, as he did in the earlier half of his life, outside the norms of conventional society and within a community of dissidents, he was poised to press the search for a more promising "general theory" that embraced a larger moral and practical universe than "little England" allowed.

Anna Carabelli offers the view that Keynes broke open the discipline of economics by recognizing that the economy could not be isolated, as the modelers would have it, from the intangibles and uncertainties of the cosmos. She notes that economics was of a class of systems with special properties:

> These are the systems to which a *general* theory applies. They are the non-isolable systems, which are genuinely *complex* or *open*, and in which the non-independent variables are connected to each other in an organic interdependence.[8]

Keynes's competency as a theorist and practitioner of a probabilistic approach was fitted perfectly to this task. In a larger social sense, a culture living prior to the first war in a cocoon of imperial preeminence and Victorian certitude was now to be thrust by an awful war into a frenzy of uncertainty that ate away at all the old verities. English life was no longer "isolable," and they became a nation in need of a guide to the probabilities of a threateningly unstable cosmos. Their military supremacy was shaken, their self-confidence undermined, and their economy was in a bad way. The traditional ruling class, the verities of British culture, the models of rectitude, and a standard made of gold—none of these could guide England's ship amid dangerous riptides in human affairs.

Into this malaise came the peculiar personage of Maynard Keynes. Gifted above his contemporaries, steeped in cultural patrimony, yet separated by homosexual commitment and cultural community from prevailing orthodoxies, Keynes could marshal his forces on the edge of society. Roy Harrod's word picture conveys the interplay of community and identity:

> Maynard's sparkling spirits and his impishness made their contribution. He might go forth into the grave world of high finance and politics; but he came back full of stories of how ludicrously and comically people were behaving, often parodying them, and exaggerating shamelessly. And the others too [of the Bloomsbury set], plying their daily affairs, returned to the fold full of absurd anecdotes.[9]

In many ways a loner, Keynes had, in the community that sustained his identity, a bastion where his own self-confidence was constantly reinforced.

What was Keynes's identity? Robert Skidelsky points to the perception by Keynes's colleagues that he was "not of a piece." Skidelsky observes:

> Keynes's "character" was a set of stratagems, a matter of checks and balances which allowed his life's work to unfold. His sense of duty triumphed in the end because the world needed to be saved from its folly.[10]

I am inclined to think the many colors and shapes in the portrait of Keynes did comprise a picture in focus, but perhaps not in the way that a painter would have it. Keynes was a man in motion. As Skidelsky hints in the use of the term "stratagems" and suggests when he shows his responses to the world's need, Keynes engaged the dynamics of identity relations at full tilt. The coherence of his identity may not have been evident at a moment *in* time, but it becomes clearer as Keynes moves *through* time.

There was the private Keynes, the man of personal commitments that were tangled as to objects and bifurcated by his own sexual ambivalence as well as by the mores and customs of his age. From his earliest days (and nights), Keynes was negotiating between a private preserve of high motivation and intense feeling, and a public world filled with drama, beckoning with expectations and challenges. The successive communities he drew around him at Eton, with the Cambridge Apostles, and in Bloomsbury provided the preserves from whence he could sally forth to encounter a world that was never quite trustful of his genius.

Skidelsky again senses the connection: "The manipulation of economies by governments was but an extension of the management of external relations that Keynes had long practiced to protect his private life. The projects conjured up by his nimble mind fitted a world no longer solidly rooted in Victorian certainties."[11] Released from a cultural patrimony by both predilection and historical trends, Keynes in a conceptual sense went to sea, as Englishmen do, and navigated his ship through half a century of dangerous passages. But the voyage was not a defensive act so much as a matter of exploration eagerly embraced and vigorously pursued. He knew where he wanted to go, which was to use economics for the improvement of life. Keynesian economics was the last great initiative of the British Empire. Like the Victorian evangelism that preceded it and similar to the democratic socialism that was its rival, the crusade required a stout heart and a resolute head.

What Keynes charted was, as Skidelsky suggests, not so much a "third way" as a "new way." But the forces of ingrained ideologies have taken its elements and they have "entered as new ingredients into established habits of thought, where they have lodged."[12] What Hayek started with his dedication to "the socialists of all parties" has been completed by latter-day ideologues who lump Keynes in with the socialists and lose thereby the cogency and institutional subtlety of his views. The same affliction is visited on Hayek when he is taken to be the foe of all government, a charge he and his biographer, Alan Ebenstein, strenuously object to. Fortunately, perhaps, the practice of mixed systems of governance and economics rarely tends toward either extreme.

Some may see Keynes as less a crusader than a personality who discovered early that the best defense is a good offense. Michael Holroyd viewed Keynes from the wry perspective of his biographical subject Lytton Strachey:

> He went through life as if he had to fill an eternal vacuum within himself, and appeared scarcely capable of relaxing. Above all, he was stimulated not chiefly through his emotions, but by problems which acted directly upon his brain. With all his great charm, his view of things remained cold and almost mechanical.[13]

Yet Strachey found his great paramour so "oddly and unexpectedly emotional." [14]

I suspect here again that there is a search for consistency that is misdirected. It was Keynes's great strength as an identifiable human being to sail on through storms that would have wrecked nearly all of us. It is this courage that carries the message of who he was, rather than the compositive wholeness of his personality at any given time. One does not have to concede that in the words of Robert Skidelsky, "The main cleavage running through his life is precisely between the worlds of Bloomsbury and Whitehall."[15] My thesis would be that one enabled the other.

John Maynard Keynes lived, after all, in one of the most disjointed half centuries of human history. World War I tore up his cultural patrimony, just as the depression undermined the foundations of an economic empire. In the midst of an even greater calamity, World War II, it was Keynes who could be called on to try to put the world back together. His singularly personal approach, without benefit of ministerial authority, was a final testament to his brilliance as well as to the architecture of his identity.

What Keynes illustrates so profoundly is the curious relationship between the particular and universal elements of identity. The narrative of his life reveals then interplay between the very special world of Eton and British society more generally, of Cambridge University and the cosmology of Victorian England, of the Apostles and conventional social relations, and of Bloomsbury and, successively, of the Treasury, Europe, and the rest of the world. Perhaps, for illustrative purposes, one episode seems the most promising: the connection between the Apostles and the creation of a new morality.

In the cultural surroundings of the young Keynes, Christianity provided the dominant universality. For a homosexual prodigy in turn-of-the-century Cambridge, another form of universality would have to be found.[16] From the redoubt of the Apostles, Keynes and his friends could invent their own universality: G. E. Moore's aestheticism, with a method of probability to give it a connection to reality. That new universality was kept in play by a similarly particular community: Bloomsbury. From such redoubts, Keynes would expand these "states of mind" to comprise a worldview, one that was deliberately more secular, and rather more worldly, than Christianity. Much of that worldview—tied to the emerging discipline of economics—would come to be shared by the world itself.

Skidelsky cites the crucial significance of Keynes's youthful work, at a time when his identity was in its formative stage, in joining epistemology and political theory:

> Probability might be the "guide of life"; but the guide had to make his way through the fog of uncertainty. Keynes's decision to connect "ought" to "probability" was a decisive event in his intellectual formation. It limited his respect for tradition and "rules of thumb," while immunizing him from the appeal of revolutionary socialism.[17]

We have seen the curious, yet durable, relations between the various communities of Keynes's life. There was the shifting, yet solid grounding of his intimate commitments. The ever-broadening reach of his competence pushed Keynes to the edge, but not over the edge, of his culture's concerns and sensibilities. There he could make new meanings, illuminate old mysteries, and strike a confident pose in a time of radical uncertainty.

Out of this remarkable life, one can see where the strength comes from both to confront change and to change oneself. Keynes's move in later life to a more mature perspective on the varieties of knowledge and motivation was the precondition to his versatility in orchestrating the framework for postwar political economy. In the first war, he could only resign from the treaty delegation and express outrage at the play of motivation in the settlement process. In the aftermath of the second war, a wiser Keynes finessed the powerful Americans to maintain at least a minimal role for Britain in the postwar world. He also brought together the international framework for durable institutions that would far outlive him.

9.2 – LASKI: REBELLION WRIT LARGE

Harold Laski was the outsider's insider more often than the reverse. What impelled him was a personal rebellion. The particular style of historical brinkmanship that led Laski repeatedly to suggest that revolutionary violence would be the alternative to change of the sort he recommended has about it a deep-seated psychological determination to take on the world. His confrontational approach is reminiscent of the rude shock he administered to his parents and family over the question of his marriage and his unorthodox political views. His friend, Kingsley Martin, observed that "psychologically, he was always fighting his father."[18]

It is not hard to see the classic pattern of a rebellious second son who carries throughout his life a sense of estrangement from his familial home. He wrote to Oliver Wendell Holmes in 1928 that on visiting Manchester the principal discussions were about the price of cotton and the comparative merits of the Rolls and the Daimler. "The main feeling which arises in me is that of the poor relation who ought to crouch in a corner. . . . I feel woebegone and count the hours until I return."[19]

Laski died without having returned to the faith of his family. While he had pronounced himself a Zionist, out of political conviction, he explicitly withheld assent to the Jewish faith. Isaac Kramnick and Barry Sheerman observed that "Laski never, in fact, returned to his Manchester 'home.' As his parents never fully embraced Zionism, he could not accept their traditional Judaism."[20]

His life experience broadened the base from which he could mount his assault. The many communities that influenced his identity included his Manchester origins, an Oxford education, American and Canadian universities, his Jewish roots, as well as his early Liberal affiliation, the conversion to Labour, and his lifelong affinity for elite counsels. As Rodney Barker of the London School of Economics (LSE) recalls, "people always used to say that his accent was a mixture of Manchester, Oxford, and New England."[21] The variety of communities was consonant with an initially pluralist approach to politics.

Yet there was always an element of restraint in Laski's politics and of regard for the underlying values of British culture. The rebellion was about a better Britain, not about the rejection of his native society. John Strachey, a close collaborator in the creation of the Left Book Club in the thirties, wrote that

> The deepest layer of his mind undoubtedly rested upon the main nineteenth century, Manchester, radical, rationalist, Benthamite tradition. But he had extrapolated that tradition further and further to the Left . . . until it touched, overlapped, and both collided and intermingled with Marxism. The result could not be consistency.[22]

Laski found in his own community of Manchester a native form of radicalism that illuminated his struggle for justice. It was to this community that he resorted when he bolted from the commitment to his family. Striving for a competency that would legitimize his apostasy, he encountered Frida and her protest movements devoted to eugenics and feminism. He turned from science to politics. Then came antiwar and pro-labor agitation, pluralist theorizing, and political radicalism increasingly expressed in word and deed.

The tension Strachey points to between English radical liberalism and Marxism was expressive of the political crisis of the thirties. Laski's private struggle, fueled by his familial revolt, captured the stress felt by those who were disillusioned by World War I, confused by the depression, and alarmed at the return of war in 1939. The search for a political resolution of these episodes was the essence of Laski's life. Strachey continues, "Laski performed an immense service for us by making these contradictions conscious and articulate; he gave us therefore at least one prerequisite for solving them."[23]

The two pluralist axioms that Laski held on to, according to socialist scholar Ralph Miliband of LSE, were that citizens do not owe exclusive loyalty to the state and that they should expect the state to accept and even abet their relationships in civil society.[24] For Laski the state is never more than a means to the end of liberation of the individual person. In the heat of revolutionary combat and postrevolutionary consolidation, most other radicals lost sight of that view.

Yet Michael Newman points to the lasting meaning of the effort to marry pluralism and the active state. He recalls that

> four considerations pushed him toward "state-centrism": first, the belief that it was a moral imperative to transform capitalism so that liberty might become meaningful for all; secondly, that the use of state power was necessary if socio-economic change was to be effected; thirdly, that a reforming party needed a doctrine, a programme and determination if it was to prevail over the privileged classes; and finally, that only radical changes could safeguard democracy and prevent violence or dictatorship.[25]

Newman sees these considerations as relevant still. The suborning of state provisions for social welfare, in an era characterized by the surging power of globalizing corporations, makes Newman's argument all the more persuasive.

Harold Laski could not bring the threads of his protest together into a seamless garment. Seeking to remedy in action what he could not quite resolve in theory, he turned to practical politics on the grand scale in the attempt at "revolution by consent" during the second war. Perhaps, in his libel trial, the collision between the dominant theme of his writings, which was "revolution by consent," and the minor theme of impending violence is what made the loss of the suit so personally devastating.[26] Here Laski was forced to confront the public perception that his views were dangerous, possibly ill motivated, and, worst of all, foolish. His inability to accept the measured terms of Labour's policy initiatives after the war and his carping at the party leadership gave force to the views of skeptics and prepared the ground for his dismissal from public favor.

9.3 – HAYEK: DECONTESTING THE MARKET

Friedrich Hayek was to come into his own as an influential intellectual in a time of economic uncertainty coupled with the resolution of an ideological struggle that had consumed the postwar world. For many reasons, the culprit in the uncertainties of the time turned out to be government. As disillusioned by government regulation as Laski was by capitalist exploitation, Hayek became the intellectual tribune of the antistatist reaction in the latter third of the twentieth century. As David Miller observes, "To the Thatcherites and the Reaganites of the 1970's and 1980's, he was what Marx had been to the socialists of the 1880's and 1890's."[27]

Hayek supplied the counterargument for those who claimed that "social justice" required that there be a welfare state. How could it be that, in the name of equality, individuals would be treated differently by the state? That would surely be the result of any attempt at redistribution. Besides, if morality is an attribute only of individual voluntary acts, not of collective or coerced actions, then government actions are amoral at best.[28]

His distrust of government and the determination to constrain it to basic constitutional functions must be seen against the background of his early disillusionment with imperial Austria, his observations on economic and political collapse in the interwar period, his exclusion from government counsels in the second war, the apostasy from socialist politics, and his personal struggle with England's policies on divorce. Hayek had in mind his own utopia: a world of principled individuals acting on their own knowledge independently of coercion and control. Perhaps, oddly in view of his personal circumstances, he saw himself as such a person.

The thesis of this book is that connections between identity development and ideological formation are to be found in episodes in which the elements of identity undergo challenges and changes, and the resolution involves decontesting complex concepts as a way of clarifying meaning for oneself and for others. For Hayek, the key decontestation involves the concept of liberty. As Michael Freeden emphasizes, Hayek chooses a specific meaning of liberty, a condition "in which a man is not subject to coercion by the arbitrary will of another or others."[29] Hayek leaves aside other possible meanings of this complicated concept such as having real substantive alternatives to choose from, or the possibility of reasoning about the connection between means and ends. A life experience of an irrational war, an ill-founded marriage, and a doctrinal disaffection with the dominant socialism of his time must have constantly reinforced the feeling of being subjected to forms of coercion that seemed arbitrary for not fitting with Hayek's own intellectual perspective and personal desires.

The fall of his native Austria must have seemed to Hayek to prefigure the "fall" after the war of England, his adopted community. Years later, the antipathy to his homeland was a source of tension between him and his second wife, who defended her country against Hayek's incessant denigration of the politics and culture of the Austrian people. The complicity of hundreds of thousands of Austrians in Hitler's rise to power was a principal theme in these disputes, but the beginning of the disillusionment was in Hayek's experiences in World War I.[30] What the follies of the prewar regime had brought on Austria would be repeated, he feared, on the enticement of intellectuals such as Laski who failed to understand the limits of socialism.

His revolt against the modern democratic state was the political counterpart of a philosophical rejection of rationalism. *The Road to Serfdom* was, in his mind, the practical half of a two-volume study on the errors that had visited on the Western world by philosophical rationalism. He never completed the other half, though the theme appears repeatedly in his later works.[31] Reason, it appeared to him, had become the friend of the socialists and planners. To be sure, reason can be of assistance to the individual in making choices. However, government bureaucracies, no matter how logical their organization and decision-making criteria, displace forms of spontaneous interaction that would otherwise produce a superior result because of the mobilization of individual knowledge. This view is rarely supported by so much as an illustration; rather, it is derived from axioms about individual choice and knowledge.

He also could see the constructivist urge behind efforts to legislate morality. For purposes as consistent with his philosophical position as with his personal circumstances, Hayek needed an opening in the moral system for change over time—for spontaneous evolution. Morality must be a work in progress. As a philosophical matter, an evolutionary perspective created the context of choice and experimentation whereby morality is enabled and survival chances are improved.

More particularly, the episode of Hayek's divorce perhaps provides a motivation for Hayek's advocacy in *The Constitution of Liberty* (1960) of "truly voluntary" relations between husband and wife with no mention of a role for governmental protection of aggrieved parties. He defends this as a deduction from his general position on individual freedom and governmental coercion.

> In some degree all close relationships . . . provide opportunities for coercion . . . a morose husband, a nagging wife, or a hysterical mother may make life intolerable unless their every mood is obeyed. But here society can do little to protect the individual beyond making such associations with others truly voluntary. Any attempt to regulate these intimate associations further would clearly involve such far-reaching restrictions on choice and conduct as to produce every greater coercion: if people are to be free to choose their associates and intimates, the coercion that arises from voluntary association cannot be the concern of government.[32]

The argument is a paraphrase of the "slippery slope" thesis of *The Road to Serfdom*. Hayek makes no acknowledgment here of the emotional or economic dependency of a nonworking spouse, or of children, on a provider in a traditional marriage. Nor is there any mention of the role of the state in adjudicating the dissolution of contracts of marriage voluntarily entered into.[33]

He never seems to confront the difference between a marital commitment, itself the product of a choice underwritten by a vow of constancy, and the sort of choice one makes in a marketplace. The former, in his case, entailed the rearing of children, again, one presumes, a matter of choice. The government protection of the institution of marriage, while coercive in some sense, comes not at the behest of rival claimants on someone's productive activity, but rather as a way of protecting those to whom commitments have been freely made from the consequences of the abandonment of those promises. That such protections are found in all civilized societies suggests that they may have some standing in Hayek's catalog of practices conducive to the survival of the species.

Hayek may have felt that England's divorce laws were unconscionably restrictive since they only permitted divorces on the grounds of adultery or desertion—and made it extremely difficult for there to be a divorce without the participation of both parties.[34] The selection of Arkansas was based not only on their less restrictive regulations but also on his wife's diminished, if not precluded, ability to participate. By Arkansas rules, he would then be free to remarry immediately. As his friend and neighbor Lionel Robbins pointed out, he in effect coerced his wife into the divorce and made a minimal provision for her in the settlement. Hayek's justification for the fait accompli was her refusal to accede to his wishes; however, her refusal was based on Hayek's own earlier commitment in their marriage vows. It would seem that the burden of morality lay on his shoulders and that any defense of such behavior on the grounds of libertarian principle is here revealed to belie Hayek's reverence for moral traditions.

Indeed, Hayek saw a symmetry of assumptions between Christianity and economics. In a lecture in 1945, he proposed that "the real question, therefore, is not whether man is, or ought to be, guided by selfish motives but whether we can allow him to be guided in his actions by those immediate consequences which he can know and care for or whether he ought to be made to do what seems appropriate to somebody else who is supposed to possess a fuller comprehension of the significance of these actions to society as a whole."[35] However, this view is inconsistent with the value he places on moral tradition, as when he endorses the view that "freedom has never worked without deeply ingrained moral beliefs and that coercion can be reduced to a minimum only where individuals can be expected as a rule to conform voluntarily to certain principles."[36] Who knows best? Society, as expressed in its traditions, or the individual?[37]

In fact, Hayek came to acknowledge that capitalism depends on a religiously based moral tradition. He told W. W. Bartley III in the mid-eighties that "capitalism presumes that apart from our rational insight we possess a traditional endowment of morals, which has been tested by evolution but not designed by our intelligence. . . . It so happens that these traditions, essentially a religious tradition, and I am as much an agnostic as Mises was, but I must admit that the two decisive traditions which make it possible for us to build up an order which extends our vision cannot be the result of our intellectual insight but must be the result of a moral tradition."[38]

In his personal life, the constraints of one of society's oldest moral codes, the protection of marriage, formed an intolerable burden. While Hayek's private behavior may not be seen by some as pertinent to the evaluation of Hayek's work, the fact that he justifies such a course of action in his *Constitution of Liberty* (1960) and that his argument provides a rationale for the weakening of social protections for the institution of marriage makes, I believe, the case for this discussion compelling. Hayek himself later admitted to Charlotte Cubitt, his private secretary, that "divorcing a partner against their will was wrong, but that he had done it, and so he had been wrong."[39] In an interview in 1978, Hayek was queried about the moral aspects of his decision by Arman Alchian, an economist at UCLA working on an oral history project. The exchange is revealing:

Q.: I want to ask you one question which is impertinent. . . . I detect a strong respect for moral standards and their importance in society. Now, all of us . . . in our lifetime have faced problems where we have said, "Here is a moral standard, and I want to break it." . . . You must have had some. . . . Would you be willing . . . to maybe indicate what some of them were? And what went through your mind at the time, if that happened, and what your response would be now to someone in the same situation?

Hayek: There's only one thing— . . . I know I've done wrong in enforcing divorce. Well, it's a curious story. I married on the rebound when the girl I loved, a cousin, married somebody else. She is now my present wife. But for twenty-five years I was married to the girl whom I married on the rebound, who was a very good wife to me, but I wasn't happy in that marriage. She refused to give me a divorce, and finally I enforced it. I'm sure that was wrong, and yet I have done it. It was just an inner need to do it. When asked as an immediate follow-up question whether he would do it again, Hayek responded—though only with agitation, discomfort, hesitation, and consideration: "I would probably do it again."[40]

His private reflections about the contradiction between his public philosophy and his personal behavior are, however, not the issue. The question here is whether Hayek's struggle over the divorce influenced the development, or even motivated the intensity, of his increasingly antistatist attitudes. The evidence is here made available for the reader to judge.

Whether what remains of Hayek's theory, given his skepticism about reason may be called liberalism, is a serious question.[41] Rationality was classical liberalism's trump card. John Locke and others played it against the theocratic orthodoxies of divine right prescription. What Hayek does is to replace the supposedly benign effects of rationality with the presumed evolutionary benefits of spontaneous orders as a way of justifying his particular kind of liberty. Whether his antirationalism and amoralism undercuts the foundations of civilization, including the framework of law within which property relations exist, will continue to be hotly debated.

Viewed biographically, *The Constitution of Liberty* (1960) represented a sober reconsideration of the role of the state as the consort of the market. There are traces of moderation in his views. He, for example, denies the simple equation of taxation and coercion that his more ideological followers never tire of repeating. Both taxes and compulsory national service "are at least predictable and are enforced irrespective of how the individual would otherwise employ his energies; this deprives them largely of the evil nature of coercion."[42] Yet the state he does authorize is sharply limited by modern standards.

In the course of advocating a minimalist state, Hayek feels compelled to erect barriers between popular pressures and the legislative power so that the state's functions will not expand. As an example, he argues for a bizarre system of elections to the legislature where only forty-five-year-olds would be entitled to run and to vote, and the victors would be elected to life terms. Hayek would limit both the range and content of inputs to the political system as a way of controlling its outputs. Paradoxically, given his epistemological views, barriers such as these would make the democratic process less efficient as an information-gathering and compromise-seeking process.

In later years, Hayek seemed to recant his support of the measures of minimum provision and social insurance that had saved his *Road to Serfdom* from reactionism. In a biographical interview, he commented:

Many of the contemporary socialist parties have at least ostensibly given up (socialization of the means of production) and turned to a redistribution/fair-taxation idea—welfare—which is not directly applicable. I don't believe it alters the fundamental objection, because I believe this indirect control of the economic world ultimately leads to the same result, with a very much slower process.[43]

The concomitant development in his thought was an ever-greater invocation of the superiority of "spontaneous" processes of societal adjustment and adaptation. By the end, there is a near mystical faith that spontaneity has its own wisdom, and it is superior to the insights afforded by reason. The notion of an "intertemporal equilibrium" that would reveal some true state of public desires to produce and consume was the economic version of this faith.[44]

The idea that society's moral evolution would be the counterpart of a long-term adaptation to the requirements of survival is a further illustration of his faith. He could imagine a world freed of collective purpose where individual choices would somehow conduce to the most productive result no matter what intention lay behind them and no matter how the moral content of these choices might be judged. Yet, especially in his later works, he emphasizes the need for the constraints of tradition in shaping the moral order that makes a market society possible.[45]

The irony is that Hayek himself was an intensely rational, purposive person who dedicated his life to creating a political movement to support his theories. His works can be read, for the most part, as sequences of reasoned rhetoric derived from fundamental axioms and principles. He seems never to have suffered any uncertainty about the rightness of his views, and he accepted financial assistance from quarters that his colleagues in the academic world would find distasteful. His biographer, Alan Ebenstein, portrays him accurately as "a convinced intellectual elitist."[46] While Keynes's elitism led him toward the valorization of a specific kind of analytical approach, if not of a proprietary class of thinkers, Hayek paradoxically becomes the defender of everyman's judgment. It was the latter point that Margaret Thatcher and Ronald Reagan would turn to very effective political uses.

It is possible then to see in this life story a portrait of a person driven to seek vindication for both personal and professional apostasies. The dubious causes he aided and the ideological allies he cultivated were symptoms of a deep dedication to a mission that was both personal and social: the justification of free choice despite palpably negative consequences in one case for his family, in the other for the least advantaged members of society. At the same time, as apostates will, he constructed a fortified position to defend the rightness of his dicta and ridiculed those whose judgments differed from his. What appear to be troublesome paradoxes and contradictions in his thought at least become more understandable when his personal struggles are made evident.

As Peter Clarke points out, the serviceability of a set of ideas for social or psychological purposes is analytically separate from the question of their basis in logic and reason. What *identity relations analysis* does is to demonstrate the mechanics of that serviceability, and thereby to cast some light on how logic and reason are filtered in the conversion of ideas to ideology. It is not the purpose here to discredit the notion that ideas "have their own force, rules and congruence."[47] Rather, I am trying to show how complex political ideas are, in the phrase of Freeden, *decontested* into simplified ideologies.[48] The analysis demonstrates that these decontestations are explicable as the corollary of turning points in the formation of identity.

So much for the explanation of individual cases. Are there any generalizations that may be drawn from the three cases taken together—generalizations that will point the way to a better understanding of politics in our own time? For that, we must turn in the next chapter to look, not at what each theorist favored, but at what they opposed.

10

The Oppositional Bind of Ideology

If ideology is to be understood in a manner that permits us to control its worst effects, the observation that developmental turning points yield the stuff of ideological commitment does not yet tell us all we need to know. For that, we need to gain perspective on the workings of ideology more broadly.

Ideologies are customarily presented as *affirmative* beliefs in values, institutions, and policies. While all ideologies contain critiques of society, the burden of analysis for the student of ideology most often rests on determining the validity of suggestions for the improvement of the human condition. In these three cases, the ideological residue of their work amounts to the celebration of democratic socialist government for Laski, of the market in the instance of Hayek, and of a progressive intellectualism with Keynes. While the followers of Laski and Hayek, in effect, ideologized institutions, Keynes's project was to establish the credibility of a method for analyzing problems of public policy. In this, he sets up a counterreaction. The elites who practice this method of analysis are seen from the left to be purveyors of middle-class values and from the libertarian right as self-interested partisans.[1]

A careful consideration of the views of each theorist would moderate and refine these stereotypes. However, those nuances are lost in the heat of political battle. A few minutes listening to the gross characterizations of "the government," "the market," and "the elites" that comprise contemporary political discussion in the popular media would illustrate the point.

What is striking, however, is that each characterization derives its impact from the presumed faults of the alternative. The disciples of Hayek assume the faults of government flow from a basic defect in the way information is used; Laski's followers have no doubt that capitalism is exploitative by the nature of the profit motive; and for contemporary Keynesians, the alternative to an intellectual elite is seen to be rule by a dogmatic and superstitious mass. For these reasons, I will now attend to what it was that each of the three was *against*.

We are seeking clues to the dynamics of ideology. The thesis is that we will find them on the *oppositional* side, rather than the affirmative side, of their work. In this loss of acuity about the institutional and cultural targets of criticism, we have what I term *the oppositional bind of ideology*. Deriving from developmental crises of great consequence, we need not be surprised to find that such forceful opposition constitutes the blind side of ideology. Powered by emotion rather than intellect, opposition of this sort leads to blinkered judgment.

James Glass, in his memorable study, *Life Unworthy of Life: Racial Phobia and Mass Murder in Hitler's Germany*, examines this phenomenon *in extremis*. Speaking of the practice of "dumping unwanted or despised self-objects into an other invested with properties of abjection," he goes on to point out the danger:

> The politically frightening development appears when this narcissistic self becomes defensive, frightened, anxious, and projects out of itself a destructive urge (in the form of ideology) it cannot contain. . . . Fear, hate, and conflict frame not only individual identity but also group and national identity.[2]

In milder form, something of the same phenomenon is at work in these life stories.

Whether the opposition emerges from psychoanalytic sources, as Glass suggests, or from life experiences, as this study hypothesizes, the result is similar in form if not in intensity. Life experiences at least can be analyzed, as we shall see that Keynes did, and one's course can be altered. Internal psychoanalytic configurations are far harder to confront and to change. For these reasons, the present chapter avoids the determinist bent of more classically psychoanalytic approaches. The point, however, is that opposition seems to have a visceral drive behind it that is highly consequential for ideological development. The disruption of one or more of the pillars of identity can be an observable explanation for this drive to oppose.

The approach taken here also includes the possibility that identities can rest on affirmations as much as on negations. It is not only "fear, hate and conflict" that frame identity, but also the achievement of competence, the experience of community, and the meaningfulness of personal commitments. All three of these people were extraordinarily strong. Clearly, however they got there, each of the three assembled a three-legged stool upon which they could not only sit, but stand and address the world. Still, what it was they had to say seems to have been scripted at crucial moments of opposition to the practices, people, and conditions they found around them. This was the voice their followers heard most clearly.

In this chapter, I will depart from the usual chronological rotation and deal with Laski, followed by Hayek, and then Keynes. The first two illustrate the *oppositional bind* in simplest terms. With Keynes, the picture is more complicated—and the lesson more redeeming.

10.1 – LASKI: MISUNDERSTANDING THE ECONOMY

In Harold Laski's rebellion against capitalism, we search in vain for any particular understanding of the workings of an economy. Laski never really confronts the question of the ways that scarcity can be overcome and competing preferences resolved. Lionel Robbins, his student before becoming a colleague at the London School of Economic (LSE), noted this early impression of his teacher: "Talked to Laski about Socialism today. Most disappointing. I am convinced he knows little or nothing about Economics. . . . There is a curiously unsatisfactory ring about his phraseology—so synthetic and so superlative. It seems to indicate behind his amazingly acute analytical apparatus an almost juvenile personality—a lack of emotional balance that is nearly painful."[3]

What Laski would not understand, he was given to denouncing. "No social type in the modern world is more completely the slave of habit without philosophy than the average business man," he wrote in 1930.[4] In place of explanations of the forces at work in the economy, we find stereotypes such as the following published near the end of Laski's life:

> So many business leaders in the United States are, on the one hand, afraid of all new thinking lest it breed a challenge, and, on the other, have an outlook for which it is difficult to find any other word than totalitarian; by which I mean that they seek either directly or through the agents whom they control to allow no important aspect of social life to be beyond the range of their power. . . .
>
> The philosophy of the business man emerges in its historical setting as simply and naturally as the philosophy of the slave-owner in the ancient world or the feudal lord who must rarely have doubted that by enabling him to maintain or even increase his well-being, his tenants were adding to their own.[5]

While Laski has no trouble producing examples to buttress these claims, and they are pleasing to the ears of capitalism's critics, there is no real attempt in his work to provide an alternative to the competitive model of interest satisfaction other than through consultation and, with it, the hoped for resolution of rival claims on a reasonable basis. There is a naiveté about the task of coordinating production to meet scarcity that is unrelieved by any effort to address the concrete realities of supply and demand.[6]

Had Laski been less in need of self-certainty about the rightness of his rebellious course as a young person, he might have turned his powerful intellect more carefully on the nature of the economic system that produced the inequalities he confronted. He would not have indulged in such generalizations about capitalism as "it implies a distribution of property at no point referable to moral principle. It means waste and corruption and inefficiency."[7]

Ralf Dahrendorf avers that "there is a sense in which Laski did not want to know any economics. Economics is the science of more or less, but Laski was interested in all or nothing . . . economic choices are never absolute alternatives." The drama of rebellion does not play well with these cautious phrasings. Laski's "extravagant language" increasingly became, Dahrendorf speculates, a way of making up for the lack of a durable achievement of the kind Beveridge and Keynes could point to.[8]

The enthusiasm of Laski's denunciation of capitalism led him to find reasons to overlook obvious faults in the logic of his political philosophy. As early as 1924, William Y. Elliott pointed out that Laski's detachment of the concept of sovereignty from the rule of law through the state, in order to vest sovereignty in the will of the community expressed in such groups as labor unions, was merely evasive. "To challenge it (sovereignty) in the name of one set of interests (trade unions) is the same fault that Mr. Laski has condemned as its abuse by another ('capitalism')."[9]

More systematically, Laski had the bad habit of substituting, as Michael Newman remarks, moral arguments for economic arguments.[10] Virtue arises in a realm of motives where scarcity is not an issue. Economics belongs to the sphere of effort and substance that are often in short supply. Even in a material world where good motives have ample scope, there is no assurance that they will out. Adam Smith, whose foundational work is really *The Theory of Moral Sentiments*, not *The Wealth of Nations*, had a no less austere vision of virtue; however, Smith designed institutions so that both the virtuous and the vicious would likely be able to eat.

Laski's conceptual attachment to notions of liberty weakened steadily as he embraced the state ever more closely in his quest to confront capitalism. By

1939, he was ready to admit that "only after the equal society has been attained can the process of pluralism come into view." The achievement of equality required the takeover of the capitalist state by the Labour Party.[11] George Orwell could fault him for refusing to own up that the loss of liberty was inevitable with the rising power of the state and that the Soviet example demonstrated that a victorious revolution did not lead to a relaxation of central control.[12]

Laski abandoned pluralism for a Marxist apology for state power in view of his recognition after the 1931 election that capitalists do indeed control the state. The state must therefore be taken over rather than modified.[13] With the success of that strategy in 1945, Britain began its experiment with nationalization. Laski's belief in state-run nationalization lasted until nearly the end. However, in a posthumously published book *The Dilemma of Our Times*, he recognizes that ownership, whether by the state or the corporation, can lead to a loss of initiative and energy at the worker level. He harks back to his earlier ideas of industrial democracy as a possible solution.[14] Only at the very end did Laski return to the problems of liberty within industrial society, and then only to suggest a reprise of pluralism. One can sense the incipient maturation of his views and even of his underlying sense of identity. Yet he never did confront the main issues of scarcity and productivity.[15]

The experiment set in motion in 1945 foundered with the rise of powerful unions and the economic disasters of the 1970s and 1980s. The end came with divisions among the left and the insurgency that brought Margaret Thatcher to power. In effect, Laski got both of his wishes—trade union rule and strong state sovereignty. The result was paradoxical. To be sure, Thatcher weakened unions considerably and advanced the primacy of the market in economic matters. However, she had no doubts about the sovereignty of the state in other areas such as foreign policy and internal governance. She used state power to combat socialist innovations on nearly all fronts. While she effectively undermined nationalization, she did not undo the basic structure of William Beveridge's welfare state or the primacy of the state itself.

The near disappearance of Laski's intellectual prominence can be attributed to several factors. In his role as a popular tribune, many of his ideas became nearly conventional at least among educated elites of the left. A host of his students became academicians, politicians, and active citizens in countries around the world. His works may have been cited with rapidly decreasing frequency, but the memory of his care and concern for the least advantaged in society remained with his followers. Intellectual fashions then changed with the advent of behaviorism in the social sciences making his legalist and historical style of writing passé. Politically, class conflict was submerged by the rising tide of middle-class culture. Not least, the unresolved contradictions of his work—not to mention his personality—gave his critics many targets.[16]

Laski was ultimately faithful to the impulse that propelled him from Manchester, namely a passion for the welfare of the working class. He enjoyed their company at least as much as the company of the powerful whose attention he craved. But he could not push beyond the question of power realignment that first animated the utopian-minded child of a powerful father. He failed to get at the operational issues of how productive effort would be elicited and made efficient.[17] For all his virtues as a person and teacher, the failure of Laski to address the hard questions of economics was endemic to the socialist left in the twentieth century.

The aversion of socialists to serious economic analysis left the field open to Keynes, who would inspire a generation of moderates within the Labour Party to step away from class analysis and nationalization. However, the cumulative effect of Britain's loss of empire, the costs of the second war as well as the Cold War, the expense of greatly expanded public services, and the increasing militancy of unions all conspired to render difficult progress along socialist lines. In the union-induced wage inflation and regulatory gridlock of the seventies, moderate opinion veered toward Friedrich Hayek and the economists of the right.

Had Laski examined the processes of entrepreneurship and wealth creation as carefully as he searched out rationales for reconciling the institutions of government with the political aspirations of the working class, he might have assembled a lasting contribution to political and economic theory. As it is, his intellectual legacy has nearly disappeared. The failures of the British left in dealing with the dynamics of economics prefigured eighteen years of conservative rule beginning in 1979 followed by the remaking of Labour's program.

10.2 – HAYEK: GOVERNANCE DIMINISHED

With Friedrich Hayek, the later work reveals a purified hostility to rational attempts at policy making. Edward Crane, a leader among libertarian intellectuals and President of the Cato Institute, concluded that Hayek's final views in "The Fatal Conceit" were so extreme that "reason turns out to be the *bête noir* of his thesis, though he offers an occasional disclaimer," and that "there is, regrettably, a reactionary undercurrent to Mr. Hayek's final work."[18] Hayek's consultations with the Pinochet government in Chile, even over the objections of Margaret Thatcher, illustrate the extent of his disavowal of modern democratic governance. He told an interviewer that authoritarianism was not to be confused with totalitarianism, and that Chile's economic recovery was nothing short of miraculous.[19] His visits to South Africa in 1963 and 1978 and his criticism of outside attempts to pressure the apartheid regime provide a further illustration. While he told a South African journalist that government-enforced discrimination in the administration of law could not be justified, he also believed that private racial discrimination was defensible.[20] The acceptance of an award from the Reverend Sun Myung Moon is yet another indicator.

Hayek had good reasons in the late seventies to see Britain as victimized by powerful unions, but it is indicative of the determinist cast of his thought that he confused a passing phase with an inevitable trend. The facts are that subsidies appear and disappear, levels of social expenditure have gone up as well as down, and powerful groups both win and lose. His determinist thinking interfered with his judgment as an economist. He argued with Keynes in the 1940s that unless exchange rates were pegged to a basket of commodities that would enforce stable price levels, the result would be price gyrations that would undermine world trade. Keynes won the argument with the establishment of the Bretton Woods Agreement, and trade flourished while prices were largely stable. His frequent postwar predictions of another major depression consequent on inflationary government policies were simply wrong.[21]

The benightedness of Hayek's views about the workings of politics and government are the analog of Laski's economic illiteracy. His famous assertion that planning puts a strain on information gathering permits him to dismiss, rather than to analyze, what governments in fact do. Those whom I interviewed agreed that he was remarkably unrealistic about how modern mass democracies actually work. Ralph (Lord) Harris, Founding President of the Institute of Economic Affairs, remembered Hayek's suggestion that the National Health Service be abolished, to which Thatcher responded that it would cost her the Prime Ministership.[22] Ralf Dahrendorf, former Director of LSE and author of its centennial history, recalled an incident where Hayek upbraided Thatcher for socialist tendencies in her willingness to retain some aspects of government activism. Dahrendorf noted that Hayek was given a high honor and "shelved" by the conservative government.[23] The persistent exaggeration of his thesis illustrates the drivenness of his personality. Looking at Hayek's near final words on the subject of government:

> The more one learns about economic history, the more misleading then seems the belief that the achievement of a highly organized state constituted the culmination of the early development of civilization. . . . Governments have more

often hindered than initiated the development of long-distance trade. . . . It would seem as if, over and over again, powerful governments so badly damaged spontaneous improvement that the process of cultural evolution was brought to an early demise.[24]

Precious little here would explain why societies with highly developed political systems have generated cultural, and indeed economic, enterprises of great sophistication and scope, while those that lack developed governments have remained at subsistence levels. As John Kenneth Galbraith points out, the best counterexample to Hayek's views is Austria itself, now one of the wealthiest countries in the world. The very techniques Keynes recommends were responsible for an enviable record of postwar economic recovery.

The intensity of Hayek's condemnation of government planning appears to lead to exaggerated counterclaims for the market:

> The market is the only known method of providing information enabling individuals to judge comparative advantages of different uses of resources of which they have immediate knowledge and through whose use, whether they so intend or not, they serve the needs of distant unknown individuals. This dispersed knowledge is *essentially* dispersed and cannot possibly be gathered together and conveyed to an authority charged with the task of deliberately creating order.[25]

This view places in jeopardy all exercises of planning whether by governments or by corporations. Hayek's perspective elides any consideration of the role of expert analysis and shared intelligence in estimating parameters, assessing experience, and forecasting future developments. These forms of activity are the stuff of corporate planning as well as government regulation.[26]

While Hayek distinguishes government activity from private enterprise by the government's access to the means of coercion and the pervasiveness of its power, the distinction would be puzzling to those fired by a corporation without recourse, as well as to those familiar with the means of political or juridical response to unpopular or unconstitutional exercises of governmental power.[27] The procedures by which democracies aggregate and articulate people's desires and aspirations are derided when they are not dismissed. The fact that public power is accountable through constitutions and elections while private power is far less restrained as a form of coercion is downplayed or ignored.[28]

As Michael Oakeshott, whom Hayek thought of as an ally, wrote of Hayek's approach to politics: "The main significance of Hayek's *Road to Serfdom*—(is) not the cogency of his doctrine, but the fact that it is a doctrine. A plan to resist all planning may be better than its opposite, but it belongs to the same style of politics."[29] What Hayek understood about the state was in-delibly shaped by a series of disillusioning experiences wherein governments appeared to be the culprits.

Hayek's undergraduate law degree oriented him to the Germanic concep-tion of the state and did little to prepare him for the realities of modern mass democracies. Hayek was heir to a Kantian tradition in which the role of the state was very clear: it was to be the "Rechtsstaat" (or limited constitutional state). He famously claimed that

> Liberalism is therefore the same as the demand for the rule of law in the classi-cal sense of the term according to which the coercive functions of government are strictly limited to the enforcement of uniform rules of law, meaning uniform rules of just conduct towards one's fellows.[30]

As Andrew Gamble points out, Hayek learned as a young man that the state was supposed to be "a government of universal laws which prescribed strict limits for government intervention in civil society."[31] He came to see the gov-ernments of his time, whether fascist, socialist, or even modern democracies, as *both* defilers of their true purpose and underminers of the economic sys-tem. There is a strong theme of betrayal in Hayek's work.

The irony of Hayek's turn toward political philosophy after 1944 is that he came to believe in law as a phenomenon somehow separable from the world of bargaining and compromise by which politics proceed. The kind of law Hayek favors is, to be sure, not spontaneous in its origins; rather, it partakes of ideals such as justice and freedom from coercion. Richard Bellamy ob-serves that conflicts between, for example, differing kinds of liberties such as association and privacy are not part of the discussion:

> If no non-normative objective ideal of liberty exists, then claims to uphold the greatest possible freedom within the framework of the rule of law will depend either on some substantive account of essential human interests, the hall-mark of a positive account of liberty and most constructivist theories, or on differing subjective understandings of the relative importance of various liberties which are themselves likely to collide.[32]

It is crucial to Hayek's enterprise that there be some neutral realm of ob-jective law wherein the appropriate boundaries of government and the market are cast in stone. Where that is so, Alan Ebenstein's summary of his position is accurate: "Liberty is the supremacy of law."[33] What is missing in this ac-count are the activities of life that lie between the spontaneous and the tran-scendent. Law has other uses than those approved of by Hayek: laws settle conflicts between values, deal with the consequences of actions for others including dependents, incorporate choices among conflicting priorities for public resources, encode moral understandings, and express myriad judgments about the tasks of common living in civilized communities. Some laws involved huge orders of coercion, but there is, in a constitutional democracy, always recourse through the courts and the political process.

The very basis for his argument against the state, his famous insight about dispersed knowledge and its utilization in the market, depends on a dubious use of the term "knowledge." By failing to distinguish between knowledge, opinion, feeling, intuition, prejudice, and the many other shades and kinds of mental activity, Hayek dignifies all human musings with an encomium that privileges individual mental activity.[34] He avoids facing up to the corrupting influence of self-preferment, instinct, will, and malice on knowledge.

What is meant by the term "knowledge" is something different than other kinds of musings. At the least, knowledge has about it the legitimacy of some kind of validation. Evidence, logic, or the sanction of authority of some kind will be key elements that distinguish knowledge from random musings. Knowledge thus has a social dimension. The system of logic, the standards of evidence, and the practices of authority are all artifacts of society. They exist precisely to separate mental constructions that are self-serving fantasies from those that have validity in some larger sense. The individual learns to do this separating in the rough school of experience where formal instruction pales. Societies learn this by experimentation, controversy, and deliberation. Both the market *and* democracy institutionalize this process. What democracy does that the market does not do is to add the possibility of equity of participation in a context of rights. Democracy provides forms of collective deliberation where consequences can be examined, lessons can be drawn, and a common course of action can be decided.

As I have argued elsewhere:

> *The purpose of democracy is to mobilize knowledge while limiting the effects of self-preferment.* The double test of an argument in a properly deliberative democracy is whether it makes sense or not and whether it is socially useful or merely self-serving. Because democracies might well simply aggregate the self-preferring decisions of a majority at the expense of minorities, we have constitutions that are designed to place boundaries upon such preferences, even while establishing processes that include the open pursuit and free expression of knowledge. Yet, to say that knowledge is dispersed and particularistic does not mean that it cannot be communicated, shared, and validated by communities. It is the *control* of knowledge at the community level that contains the seeds of

tyranny, not the nurturing and aggregation of shared experience in a democratic society.[35]

To establish individual knowledge as the epistemological "gold standard," as Hayek does, and to vest the institutionalization of this standard in the market, is to advantage mental activity most often arising from the impulse to self-preferment. It is also to accord the power of deciding contested issues to those with the most resources while removing moral accountability for their actions. By adding that collective outcomes are "unintended," Hayek removes the possibility, as well as the means, of learning lessons through shared deliberation.[36] "Knowledge" is thus reduced to power—the power of the purse.

The irony of wrapping this maneuver in the language of freedom is that Hayek's system simply authorizes the suborning of the less advantaged by their economic masters. The market contains few, if any, of the protections against the corruption of knowledge by self-preferment that due process and basic rights provide in constitutional democracies. Here is where Hayek departs from one of his mentors, Adam Smith. Smith sees the struggle of the marketplace *not* as the competition between shrewd assessors of self-interest so much as an arena of rivalry among contestants for admiration and respect.[37] There is little virtue to be found in this rivalry. Indeed most people, says Smith, seek respect by material means and fall into the trap of avarice.

Neither can one expect in the rivalry of the market any sort of epistemological purity. Smith, in fact, suggests that one of the roles of the state should be to wean the people from the "superstitions" and "enthusiasms" that will likely consume them in the mentally impoverished world of commerce. Public promotion of the arts and sciences is commendable for this reason.

What remains of value in Hayek's argument about the mobilization of knowledge through the engagement of individuals with their "local knowledge" in the process of decision making is hardly controversial. Laski, in 1921, pointed to the same problem:

> Liberty, it is argued, is derived from the existence of avenues of creative activity for the mass of citizens. It is obvious that the hierarchical structure of our present order does not offer such opportunities save to a small group of men. In the result we lose a vast welter of experience while we balk at the disposition of many whose faculties are capable of far greater use than that to which they are normally devoted.[38]

For Laski, the small groups of people who do the deciding were the lackies of the capitalists; for Hayek, they are the socialist planners. However, Laski goes on to make a connection that Hayek evades: "Liberty, in short, is incompatible with the present system of property; for its result is a concentration of power which makes the political personality of the average citizen ineffective for any serious purpose."[39] The market does not solve the problem of engaging the knowledge of the average citizen, it just hands decisive power to a self-preferring set of corporate masters. Democracies, at least, retain the principle of participation on the equal basis of the vote. In doing so, democracies hold out the prospect of confronting arbitrary uses of economic power.

Hayek ignores the "due process" that governs governmental power in a democratic society. What he authorizes is the arbitrariness of power based on the dramatically unequal levels of individual control of wealth and property. When the latter comes to dominate the former, the effect, as Laski rightly observed, is a suppression of true liberty and creativity. Where Laski failed to address the economic side of this equation, Hayek failed to clarify its political dimensions.

Keynes's epistemological position appears, by contrast with Hayek's, to be more realistic. In his work on probability, Keynes recognizes that the essential issue is the reliability of a basis for action. That according to Keynes is not a question of whether knowledge is dispersed or aggregated, but whether the analysis is sensible. His work on probability specifies the logic of the sensible. Hayek may be right that our knowledge is an inchoate assembly of insights derived from various faculties, and Keynes (especially after 1939) would not disagree.[40] However, the point is what sort of *analysis* is performed on these insights? There is no warrant for believing that individual analysts will necessarily do better than experts. And there is a strong warrant for subjecting *any* analysis to a process of mutual deliberation and contestation.

Hayek's peculiar pessimism about the capacity for knowledge and action was expressed in his *Constitution of Liberty*: "Human reason can neither predict nor deliberately shape its own future. Its advances consist in finding out where it has been wrong."[41] To say this is to absolve all those who benefit from injustice of the burden of responsibility. To contest it, as Keynes and Laski did, is to at least struggle against uncertainty. To develop a measured logic for acting in these circumstances, as Keynes did, is to enhance democracy. In 1923, he said with respect to the gold standard that

> we must free ourselves from the deep distrust which exists against allowing the regulation of the standard of value to be the subject of *deliberate decision*. We can no longer afford to leave it in the category of which the distinguishing characteristics are possessed in different degrees by the weather, the birth rate, and the Constitution—matters which are settled by natural causes, or are the result-

ant of the separate action of many individuals acting independently, or require a revolution to change them.[42]

Hayek visits on politics a utopian design derived from his vision of the market and what is required for its sustenance.[43] His utopian view ignores the actual history of the creation of Western market economies. John Gray makes a telling point when he recalls that the "free market" was itself a creation of the state, and a temporary interlude in nineteenth-century England—for good reason.

> By the First World War, it had been re-regulated. A host of uncoordinated legislative interventions, arising not as parts of any grand design but in response to particular problems such as safety in factories, made the workings of the market less hostile to social ends. Constructed by deliberate statecraft, the free market withered away spontaneously.[44]

The denigration of political institutions, and the blanket endorsement of the market, that has followed on the contemporary rise of the right ignores the interdependence of the state and the market.[45] The ideologized version is just now playing out as an incapacity to address in any intentional fashion major problems of inequality, drugs, domestic abuse, the environment, and care of the young and the marginalized. Perhaps George Orwell's perspective provides a more balanced view. In his review of *The Road to Serfdom*, Orwell gave respect to Hayek's insight while pinpointing his political insensitivity:

> In the negative part of Professor Hayek's thesis there is a great deal of truth. It cannot be said too often . . . that collectivism is not inherently democratic, but, on the contrary, gives to a tyrannical minority such powers as the Spanish Inquisitors never dreamed of. Professor Hayek is also probably right in saying that in this country the intellectuals are more totalitarian-minded than the common people. *But he does not see, or will not admit, that a return to "free" competition means for the great mass of the people a tyranny probably worse, because more irresponsible, than that of the State.* The trouble with competitions is that somebody wins them."[46] [italics added]

Indeed, Hayek's antipathy to state planning *predated* his 1937 formulation of the epistemological argument about economic knowledge. In his inaugural address at LSE in 1931, he took pains to denounce the folly of centralized planning. In fact, political processes generate information too—through elections, hearings, interest group representation, surveys, research on a multitude of fronts, and the accumulation of experience. There is no prima facie case for rejecting this information-gathering capacity. Hayek's opposition to Keynes's views very likely contributed to his inability to see the distinction between Keynesianism and socialism. Hayek could not see the distinction between government regulation and government central planning because he was unwilling to consider the shades and nuances of governing in a modern mass democracy.

Just as he was blinded to key distinctions in the area of politics, so also was his moral theory an argument from design. In a 1945 essay, Hayek endorses English individualism as opposed to Cartesian individualism of the rationalist variety. He claims, "The anti-rationalistic approach, which regards man not as a highly rational and intelligent but as a very irrational and fallible being, whose individual errors are corrected only in the course of a social process, and which aims at making the best of a very imperfect material, is probably the most characteristic feature of English individualism."[47] In this approved view, Hayek admits to egregious human imperfection. When juxtaposed to his moral argument, however, the results are curious. While virtue is claimed for freedom of choice, there is simultaneously the admission that choice will be exercised by "irrational and fallible" human beings. The saving grace of this arrangement is that the right sort of social process will provide the means of correcting bad choices, so to make less fallible, and presumably more rational, the behavior of humankind.

Yet Hayek is not able to see that the learning experience of democratic politics could have such a redemptive effect. It is only the market, he theorizes, with its sphere of choice screened from consequences that cannot be known in advance, that offers such a possibility. However, the market, by this logic, offers irrationality and flawed judgment with the maximum of leeway as compared with the state. It lets us see what people *want*, and Hayek argues that we cannot know what people *need* or *deserve*. Yet the processes of democratic engagement and the devices of limitation and accountability of power require the kind of interindividual deliberation and judgment that permit considerations of *need* and even *desert* to become clear to individuals and to communities—conditions that do not apply in the pure form of the market.

Indeed Hayek wishes to limit the state by confining its actions to what these fallible and irrational beings can comprehend. "The essential point is not that there should be some kind of guiding principle behind the actions of the government but that government should be confined to making the individuals observe principles which they know and can take into account in their decisions."[48] Yet Hayek's own scheme for the role of government in setting up a market economy relies on a set of rationally articulated distinctions about what government may and may not do. Where he perceives that these distinctions have been overstepped, he is willing to endorse forceful means to rectify the balance. So great is his certainty on these matters that he was willing to lend his credibility to the Pinochet regime in Chile, the South African government prior to Mandela's release, and the authoritarian Reverend Moon. The finely tuned arguments Hayek deployed in defense of spontaneous institutions were of a far higher quality than the analysis he brought to the politics and regimes of his own time.

10.3 – KEYNES: OF RATIONALITY AND POLICY MAKING

With Maynard Keynes, the *oppositional bind* results from a dismissal of forms of knowledge outside his conception of rationality. Stupidity was his target. Stupidity was defined so as to include all utterances not conforming to Keynesian probabilistic rationalism. The illustrations of the point are copious and interesting, as are the changes in his perspective that emerge later in his career.

Stereotypical characterizations of the less enlightened abound in his writings. As Donald Moggridge, a principal editor of the collected works and author of *Maynard Keynes: An Economist's Biography,* notes, Keynes was specific about seeing his own conception of economics as "sensible."[49] He relegated other views of economics to the form of ignorance known as "self-interest." His essential objections were to raw materialism, avarice, usury, and the "insatiable" demand for positional goods such as status commodities.[50]

Keynes was a consummate denouncer of bad policies. On the refusal of the conservatives to increase expenditures to counter the depression, Keynes declaimed:

> Every person in the country of super asinine propensities, everyone who hates social progress and loves deflation, feels that his hour has come, and triumphantly announces how, by refraining from every form of economic activity we can become prosperous again.[51]

When it came to assessing the work of colleagues in the profession, a telling example would be his review of Hayek's book *Prices and Production:*

> The book seems to me to be one of the most frightful muddles I have ever read, with scarcely a sound proposition in it. . . . It is an extraordinary example of how, starting with a mistake, a remorseless logician can end up in Bedlam.[52]

Even this was toned down slightly from the original draft, in which Keynes declaimed that, in Hayek's book, there was "scarcely a proposition in it (after Lecture I) *which is not untrue*."[53]

As for ideologies and ideologues, Keynes's denunciations of right and left were evenhanded. He wrote to George Bernard Shaw:

> I can see that they [Marx and Engels] invented a certain method of carrying on and a vile manner of writing, both of which their successors have maintained with fidelity. But if you tell me that they discovered a clue to the economic riddle, still I am beaten—I can discover nothing but out-of-date controversialising.[54]

Marxism was, for Keynes, "the final *reductio ad absurdum* of Benthamism . . . [an] economic bogus-faith."[55] Additional manifestations of ignorance, in his view, included nationalism and class war. These were forms of "madness" that afflicted leaders as well as the masses.[56] The influence of these forces must be countered by the intervention of rational elites.

According to Keynes, laissez-faire and free competition were "hypotheses" of declining relevance to the way the world works and, therefore, were clearly not sensible models for policy making. Only with properly managed capitalism might it be possible to fulfill basic needs. Once secure, mass publics would be released from the pressure of constant striving sufficiently to permit a return to "sane wisdom."[57]

Assaying the qualities of leaders as well as masses was a specialty. The crisis over the gold standard in the early thirties was played out with the same rituals of resistance as the matter of reparations. In a letter to a friend, he complained, "Why do we always have to go through these dilatory and disastrous stages before facing up to anything?"[58] And in public, he puzzled about "the sort of deep reasons, difficult to express adequately, which genuinely divide us."[59]

In the field of social policy, labeled plainly in his writings as "sex and drugs," he thought prevailing public views were "medieval." New policies should be built on what "civilized" opinion and the practices of "educated and uneducated" folk in their private lives reveal. There is little room here for a positive valuation for any notion of natural law or of divinely inspired morality. And there certainly is no particular regard for precedent or tradition in the Burkean sense.

Keynes did not, however, engage in phobic characterizations of nationalities. At Versailles, he freely denounced the proposals of the Allies as well as the Germans.[60] His identity did not rely on ethnicity, though he implicitly believed that more sensible people could be found in Britain than anywhere else. Class was perhaps another matter. As Skidelsky remarks, "Aristocrats were always absurd; the proletariat was always 'boorish.' The good things in life always sprang from the middle-class."[61]

On the whole, he took an ecumenical view of stupidity. No one is immune, but neither is anyone condemned beyond the possibility of reprieve. He could be as acerbic face-to-face as in print. As a young Treasury Department official at Versailles, he courteously informed Lloyd George that the Prime Minister's disquisition on the problems of France was "rubbish."[62] Yet Keynes specialized in offering reprieves. But, for all his truculence when criticized, he also accepted them. Keynes was often seen to acknowledge a point and change tack accordingly — a trait that eluded Hayek and that caused him great consternation when Hayek needed to fix the moving target in his sights.

That said, in Keynes's case, there was a progression to a more mature perspective on his early enthusiasm for rational motivations. Keynes's emerging wisdom is expressed in a startling memoir given as an informal address to his Bloomsbury colleagues in 1938. Subsequently published as *My Early Beliefs,* this remarkable tract contains his musings about the views of his Cambridge circle:

> this pseudo-rational view of human nature led to a thinness, a superficiality, not only of judgment, but also of feeling. . . . The attribution of rationality to human nature, instead of enriching it, now seems to me to have impoverished it. It ignored certain powerful and valuable springs of feeling. Some of the spontaneous, irrational outbursts of human nature can have a sort of value from which our schematism was cut off. And in addition to the values arising out of spontaneous, volcanic, and even wicked impulses, there are many objects of valuable contemplation and communion beyond those we knew of — those concerned with the order and pattern of life amongst communities and the emotions which they can inspire.[63]

Peter Clarke cautions us against reading too much into this disavowal. The link between methodology and morals can indeed be found in his early work, and there were personal and historical reasons in 1938 for a recent heart-attack victim being somewhat skeptical of the human condition.[64]

Keynes did remain a rationalist. However, his maturation as a progressive intellectual consisted in realizing that there is no necessary linkage between individual rationality and social good.[65] As he argued in supporting the public spending of the New Deal, "a course of behavior which might make a single individual poor can make a nation wealthy."[66] As a philosopher, he concluded that a wider array of evidence had to be subjected to his probabilistic analysis than just the data of the statistician and the premises of the logician.

Keynes came to the realization that beneficial social action could only be attained by applying logic to the *"order and pattern of life amongst communities* [italics added]." This provides the basis for intervention in individual behavior by institutions that make intentional and deliberative judgments on behalf of the community. Keynes's *My Early Beliefs* represents, not a rejection of probabilistic act utilitarianism, but a maturation of its premises. Keynes reaches out to incorporate a broader range of evidence into the calculation, namely "expectations," "psychological forces," or even, in a more famous Keynesian phrase, "animal spirits."[67] The *patterns* manifest in these motivations are the stuff from which intelligent assessments can be made. It remains for progressives to link these patterns to public policy thus forming a basis for action.

The methodology of his progressivism is illustrated in *The General Theory* when Keynes summarizes his discussion of the marginal efficiency of capital:

> We should not conclude from this that everything depends on waves of irrational psychology. On the contrary, the state of long-term expectations is often steady, and, even when it is not, the other factors exert their compensating effects. We are merely reminding ourselves that human decisions affecting the future, whether personal or political or economic, cannot depend on strict mathematical expectation, since the basis for making such calculations does not exist; and that it is our innate urge to activity which makes the wheels go round, our rational selves choosing between the alternatives as best we are able, calculating where we can, but often falling back for our motive on whim or sentiment or chance.[68]

Skidelsky suggests that "economics was, largely still is, built up from the logic of choice under conditions of scarcity. Keynes's vision, which one can trace back to his youth, has to do with the logic of choice, not under scarcity, but under uncertainty."[69] Keynes did not have much visceral experience with scarcity, but a person raised in an intellectual and emotional hothouse had always to cast a wary eye on his surroundings peopled, as it was, with creatures of divergent impulses and unfathomable motives.

While scarcity is ubiquitous, uncertainty was the great issue between the wars and after. It remained for those who had the will, the intelligence, and the self-confidence to take action for the common good. Keynes came to the realization that "civilization was a thin and precarious crust erected by the personality and the will of a very few, and only maintained by rules and conventions skillfully put across and guilefully preserved." The skill and the guile were in his hands more than any other person of his age. Keynes was a near-obsessive observer of other people's hands—his own he often kept concealed within especially tailored sleeves.[70] His hands, in the presence of uncertainty, were, from long practice, steadier than most others.

As is readily apparent from any reading of his work or on perusing any memoir of his personality, Keynes was a brilliant put-down artist. Bruised egos were often left in his wake. However, a more balanced assessment offered by Skidelsky notes that "he could demolish any argument, including good ones, and pulverise people into accepting bad ones of his own. However, he had the redeeming quality of self-correction. Many noticed his habit of expounding opposite ideas with equal confidence."[71] Hayek, among others, found this confusing. Yet it is clear that he respected a good argument in the end and was well aware that ego must ultimately yield to evidence.

For Hayek to have dismissed Keynes's *General Theory* as a brief for a political view based on the intractability of unions with respect to wage reduction was a case of the pot calling the kettle black. Hayek was just as intent on finding a rationale for his visceral convictions about the evils of contemporary government and the virtues of the market. The difference with Keynes was that his political convictions played tennis with his theoretical concerns, and his game improved steadily. Clarke points out how, in 1929–1930, Keynes scrambled to find ways to justify an activist response to the crash in time to assist Lloyd George and the Liberals in the election. He came up with a crude version of the famous "multiplier" which, after the election, led him into a reevaluation of his theory. Clarke comments,

> It was only when he reached this point that he saw a consistent rationale in his past writings which he had rarely glimpsed at the time. He recognized a coherent economic justification for policy initiatives which he had supported through a mixture of political prejudice and sheer intuition.[72]

Keynes confronted the meaning of his policy views for his theory, worked out the basic concepts as early as 1932, and was led to a vastly more fruitful formulation of his views in *The General Theory*.[73] What Hayek denounced as an unprincipled shifting of position was, in fact, a process of learning and discovery. Hayek, by contrast, seems not to have learned very much at all.

A character as complex as Keynes of course attracts analysts with a variety of perspectives. Authors who would take a more psychoanalytic approach to Keynes, such as Charles Hession and Piero Mini, attribute the reach of his remarkable personality to androgeny, in the case of Hession, and to a protean "nervous system" in Mini's analysis.[74] Mini offers a compelling image:

> Some reality consists totally of a hard core of physical actions and reactions which we interpret through narrow reason, logic and mathematical relations. . . . But another type of reality is the social world, where "forces" are not atoms and molecules but avarice, lust, anger, vengeance, self-abnegation, blood, culture, customs, love ambition, courage . . . and the amazing interactions of these imponderables. Our cultural and philosophic predisposition is either to ignore them or to treat them by the method of physics. Classical economics, for instance treated "greed" by the method of Euclid and created a beautiful if imaginary world, the general equilibrium model. But the broad-minded sensitive person will try to go beyond mere mathematics, and his insights will be at war with those of "materialist" thinkers.[75]

Mini suggests that guilt, as much as anything, was the driving force behind the generation of so much nervous energy.[76]

The methodology of the present work does not reach to these levels of explanation. The emphasis has been on observable behavior as a clue, no more, to psychology rather than on the direct analysis of the psyche. For our purposes, the descriptions by Hession and Mini of the breadth of Keynes's personal repertoire fill out the thesis that here was a true case of identity "achievement." Whether that achievement was powered by an internal state of mind (or nerves) is, and must be, speculative. The evidence appears to this writer to lead to the conclusion that Keynes's identity formation involved a particular synthesis of soma, psyche, *and* society, rather than any one of those forces acting determinatively. If that was true, what can be learned by all of us less extraordinary personalities is that at least part of our fate is within the reach of cognition and reshaping. And part of that reshaping involves shared action with those around us.

To be sure, Paul Sweezy's avowedly Marxist critique of Keynes holds a measure of truth. He emphasizes "Keynes's habit of treating the state as a *deus ex machina* to be invoked whenever his human actors, behaving according to the rules of the capitalist game, get themselves into a dilemma from which there is apparently no escape. Naturally, this Olympian interventionist resolves everything in a manner satisfactory to the author and presumably to the audience."[77] However, Keynes had no illusions about the need for the right temperament and wise judgment. He was willing to face that need rather than to rely on the determinations of class struggle and the "forces of history"—or of the "free" market. He trusted democratically accountable decision makers more than he trusted party commissars—or bankers.

There is nothing unwitting in Keynes. He was, above all, a theorist of human agency. He was also a democrat, though not a populist, in that he felt that leadership should be judged by results apparent to the citizenry. There is respect only for the willingness to be reasonable and act on sensible values. The wisdom that is to characterize the interventionist is available to all who will study the situation, and so are the benchmarks by which performance can be measured, for example, the unemployment rate.

Keynes's version of economics inspired a generation of policy-minded analysts whose influence pervades every corner of contemporary society. He also coined a common parlance for assessing the effectiveness of policies and of leaders—the language of economic "health" to confront the very real pathology of the times.[78] Seymour Harris dedicated his influential 1947 collection of essays, *The New Economics*, to "those economists who, following the leadership of Lord Keynes, are endeavoring to make of economics a useful tool for the diagnosis and treatment of economic *disease* (emphasis added)."[79]

Unlike Laski or Hayek, Keynes had the direct experience of *both* the market through his speculations and business operations *and* the government through his brief, but highly instructive, tenure in the India Office and his later government service in the Treasury, in the armistice negotiations, and in numerous encounters with economic policy making.[80] He saw plenty of stupidity in both realms, but he also saw the possibility of redemption.

Keynes could see, unlike Hayek, that the distinction between public and private was increasingly an artifice that concealed as much as it revealed about the flow of pressures and accountability that shaped major economic investments, monetary policy, and fiscal decisions. The distinction he made in the twenties between "public investments" and "government expenditures" has come back into play at the beginning of a new century to revive the role of democratic governance in shaping the West's economic and social fortunes. Both former President Clinton and Prime Minister Tony Blair advanced this usage in articulating the meaning of the "Third Way."

Keynes's faith in the partnership of governance and business is, of course, famously based in his comment that "dangerous acts can be safely done in a community which thinks and feels rightly." The same community shapes both public and private activities through myriad customs, institutions, and values. Skidelsky replies that "no one who lived through the 1970s (in England) can fail to see a great pathos in Keynes's so English response to Hayek's warning."[81]

Anyone who has experienced bureaucratic excess—or a heartless act of exploitation by a capitalist—might join in skepticism. But Hayek's solution is largely to disable government, and with it collective decision-making processes, in favor of "spontaneous" individual decision making—just as Laski would remove from individuals the possibility of exploiting others. And Hayek came, in the end, to accept that a community of values, even of religious values, was necessary to yield a good result from "spontaneous" behavior. For Keynes, the solution is, simply, prudence informed by imagination and analysis. The excesses of the seventies and the more egregious forms of exploitation do, over time, get remedied in democracies. It is only when polities cannot respond to great social crises that governments slip into tyrannies with mass support.

For Keynes, the institutions were not the problem so much as the analytic failures of the diagnosticians who made the decisions. He never really questioned the legitimacy of the institutions themselves. To understand John Stuart Mill's famous witticism, he tried to play Socrates to the pigs in both the market and the government. His faith in the policy makers capable of applying his kind of analysis could improve life remained whole.

The famous rejoinder of Keynes to Hayek on the publication of *The Road to Serfdom* was that there need not be a slippery slope to serfdom if right-minded people are in command of policy making. This statement is often greeted with mild derision by market advocates who point to examples where such people have manifestly not been in control. However, the point of the passage goes further. Keynes makes the kind of political judgment that Hayek, and his acolytes, are insensitive to. He forecasts that an unvarnished laissez-faire would lead to manifest inequities and cyclical depressions. These consequences would so antagonize a democratic electorate that they would turn to a much more authoritarian regime that would undermine democracy and free markets as well.[82] Ironically, Hayek would deliver us to serfdom faster than Keynes. The trip down the slippery slope was precipitated by the avoidable failure of democratic governance rather than by the ineluctable rise of coercive power. He no doubt based this prophecy on the collapse of democracy that he witnessed in the thirties. In Keynes's world, there are balancing political and economic forces and a critical role for human agency in mediating the stresses between them.

Hayek's world lacks any such "equilibrium" between the market and the government. He evinces no faith in either the political processes or the political leadership that would mitigate inflation and other abuses of the relationship. Laski's cosmology is oddly apolitical in the same way. He did not quite believe what he preached: that a democratized polity could control the excesses of capitalism without expropriation. This led him to temporize about the excesses of socialism evident for all to see in the Soviet experience and its extensions throughout eastern Europe.

The oppositional bind of ideology appears in all three cases. Keynes alone seems to have overcome the most debilitating aspects of his early prejudice against what he so freely labeled as stupidity. There was a progressive moderation in Keynes's understanding of admissible evidence about the order and pattern of life. However, for Hayek and Laski there is only a trajectory that leads to ever-stronger antipathies and to ever-greater claims for and upon the institutions at the heart of their ideologies.[83] Perhaps the maturation of Keynes's complex personality explains this result, while for Laski and Hayek, events, both public and private, continued to reinforce the original impetus of their identities.

11

Ideology, Identity, and Contemporary Politics

As we began this inquiry, we noted the ideological shift in the twentieth century from partisanship of the government, to regulated relations between government and market, and, finally, to the market as the solution to our society's problems. This has left us in the twenty-first century with the legacy that the central institutions of our society, the government and the economy, have become, in contemporary politics, objects of ideology. The ideologized versions of these institutions ascribe uniform and predictable qualities to what are in fact complex and intertwined entities. The reality of governments and economies is that they vary enormously in the range and moral content of their activities. Governments can deliver us to or from wars, help the poor or the undeserving, and save or ruin the environment. Likewise, markets can lead us to waste and profligacy, to productivity, and to cycles of prosperity and depression.

Yet the ideologized version of these institutions ascribes uniform and predictable qualities to governments and markets—qualities that create reassurances and threats that bring forth public support and opposition. Rather than being perceived as entities that contain processes and practices of a diverse and complicated nature, these institutions are seen to resemble the gods of Greek mythology—actors imbued with motivation, an inner nature, and designs on our individual well-being. These politicized responses undermine the ability of citizens to understand how these institutions work and what new possibilities may be found within them.

One side of the ideological standoff in American politics was neatly captured with the declaration that "the market is rational; the government is dumb." With that, Representative Dick Armey, former Majority Leader of the U.S. House of Representatives and a Friedrich Hayek devotee, summed up the "conservative" credo. The statement recalled propositions on the other side such as capitalism is wasteful and irrational; only good government can save us from its ravages. These opposite positions form the brackets on media discussions, political campaigns, and editorializing across the Western democracies as the twenty-first century begins.

How did we come to this pass in our politics? Now that we are in the new millennium, it may be worth understanding where this last century has taken us. We need to find the threads that tie the story together so we can draw out the meaning of it for contemporary political economy. Perhaps if we understand the story well enough, we can find our way to better politics at the dawn of a new age.

11.1 – LASKI: THE RISE AND FALL OF CLASS CONSCIOUSNESS

On Harold Laski's passing, Oxford Historian Max Beloff, who had termed the preceding decades as "The Age of Laski," wrote that such an age was now over. The consummation of Laski's synergy with his times was the election of 1945. Socialism, the doctrine of intellectuals more than workers, was married to electoral politics to produce a tangible result. The victory "represented precisely that social and ideological amalgam of which Laski had long been the leading intellectual exponent."[1] Navigating between the Marxism–Leninism of the ideologues, and the practical-mindedness of the trade union politicians, Laski brought a palatable set of ideas to political action. His fulsome feeling for the working class, a root commitment to English liberal values, and an affinity for British institutions and their leaders made such navigation possible.

Paradoxically, while Laski's own reputation may have declined, a moderated version of the program he did so much to advance became the standard of British politics for fifty years. The Conservatives quickly learned the message of their stunning defeat in 1945, and under the crafty guidance of R. A. Butler, Harold Macmillan, and other leaders, remodeled their ideology to at least approach the problem of the "two Britains." Butler recognized that the British electorate would never permit Conservatives to form a government until they had earned a bit of credibility on the question of economic and social disparities.[2]

The Thatcherite rebellion against the excesses of monopoly unionism and deficit spending brought about huge changes in policy, but little change in the underlying policy views of the British electorate. As Ivor Crewe and Donald Searing point out, Margaret Thatcher rose to power for reasons other than the appeal of her ideology. She won the party leadership in 1975 because of anti-Heath sentiment. Thatcher won the general election in 1979 because "she benefited from Labour's collapse during the 'winter of discontent'; and in both 1983 and 1987 she was re-elected to office because the anti-Conservative vote was divided between two opposition parties [which were themselves internally divided]."[3] Thatcher's years in power did not change the underlying structure of public opinion according to surveys on key issues of economic and political power. To the extent that she "worshipped at the shrine of Hayek," her prayers for the conversion of the electorate were unfulfilled.

On the left, the steady disavowal of socialist doctrines by a succession of Labour leaders culminating in Tony Blair has repositioned Labour toward the center of the spectrum. Labour returned to power in 1997 not by reclaiming the majority of voters but by turning the tables on the Conservatives. Labour usurped the Liberal program and even elements of the Conservative agenda to the point where Labour could get the requisite 45 percent of the vote. A similar vote share had propelled Thatcher to power in a three-way split. Socialists, liberal democrats, and moderates voted for Blair. The Conservatives, the Liberals, and the nationalist parties split the rest.

As contemporary political leaders struggle toward a definition of the "Third Way," disparities of wealth and income are increasing sharply. After a decade of Third Way politics, the developed nations seem ever further from meeting Laski's standard: "No cake for anyone 'til there's bread for everyone." The Third Way has opened more opportunities for those at the bottom, albeit in exchange for a weakening of safety net provisions. Yet the Third Way, far from restraining the cake-eating proclivities of the rich, has positively encouraged them as evidenced by the rising inequalities in income and wealth.[4] In this respect, the Third Way has accepted Hayek's view of the legitimacy of capitalist accumulation and private investment, while retaining some vestiges of the welfare state.

If Laski were born into the same comfortable circumstances today, he might well, for personal reasons, have made the same journey of rebellion and apostasy from his class. Absent the dramatic evidence of the evils of class available from World War I and the depression, it is unlikely that nearly so many would follow him. It is not the existence of inequality that validates widespread rebellion, but the demonstrated dangers of the selfishness and intransigence of the rich in the conduct of affairs, foreign and domestic. The net result of these variations in institutional power is, however, that government has been discredited and the market has been legitimized.

Other agendas—feminism, racial justice, the environment, and terrorism—have apparently taken over from the old politics of democratic socialism. Understandable and essential as these movements are, what is no longer in place is a broad-scale strategy for uniting the dispossessed, disadvantaged, and marginalized elements of society. The fact remains that government is the only instrument with the power to confront corporate dominance and to serve as the means of peaceably advancing democracy and social equity. But the question remains, how can government act most effectively? For lessons on this, we turn one last time to Maynard Keynes.

11.2 – KEYNES: PROBABILITIES AND PROGRESS

In the cacophony of the twenties and thirties, Keynes was only one of several powerful voices contending for public attention. His influence initially arose out of his prophecies about the consequences of the settlement of World War I for Europe and the West and the disputes over responses to the depression. The full measure of his power came into being only with the second war when he became the lawgiver for new institutions and policy directions. As Peter Clarke observes, there was a congruence between the Keynesian institutional prescription and the historical situation of Britain after World War II. In the "Keynesian period of triumphalism," Clarke suggests

> not only was there a commitment by government to maintain a high and stable level of employment; the redistribution of income to the working class received the sanction of economic theory as well as of social justice; and the enhanced position of the trade unions was applauded as working in the same direction. This was a social democratic vision for which the authority of Keynes could be claimed.[5]

Thereafter, Keynes belonged to the world. His ideas were taken up in different countries for different reasons.[6] However, all Western governments in the postwar era were in need of insulation from the shocks of boom and bust and a rationale for meeting the bursting demands for housing, transportation, education, health and other services. Among the ideas on offer, Keynesianism threatened no establishments, incited no revolutions, and risked no irreversible consequences.[7] Because of his moderation, he became the best hope for progressivism and the alternative to stagnation or revolt.

Internationally, Keynesianism morphed into a rationale for a kind of economic developmentalism, centered on the government direction of economic assistance, that reached into protected corners of the world and enabled technocrats to see themselves as bearers of a recipe for prosperity that would displace local fare and substitute new chefs.[8] These technocrats set aside existing institutions and ways of doing business in their enthusiasm for scientized Keynesianism. They prefigured, though with more constructive results, the destabilizing role to be played in the former Iron Curtain countries at the end of the century by advocates of the free market with the works of Hayek in their briefcases.

The remanufacture of Keynesianism into a "system" of its own has been well documented by those who have analyzed the influence of textbook writers such as Paul Samuelson. Just as with Engels's recasting of Marxism into a precise-sounding science of history, the creative core of Keynesian, and Marxian, thought has often been lost to view.[9] Keynes's penchant for estimating quantitative parameters of the economy gave the impression of a system, as did his talent for evoking devices such as "the multiplier." But Keynes was "not the first of the modern statisticians, but the last of the magicians of number," in Robert Skidelsky's memorable phrase.[10] The numbers connote science, but the arts and crafts of analysis and interpretation are what characterized Keynes's best work.

The favorable reception of Keynes's regulative approach to political economy requires a public with sufficient hope to think that the mediation of fortune is possible and, yet, with a degree of skepticism as to how far down the list of misfortunes mediation can reach. The despair of the thirties and the wartime, and postwar, dramas of conflict and reconstruction undermined these assumptions. Socialism, by contrast, offered a more vigorous approach: a radical restructuring of the forces and institutions that shaped the fate of societies and individuals. As we have seen, Britain arrived at Keynesian domestic policies in the forties not by acclamation, but in retreat from the further reaches of the socialist revolution. In the fifties through the seventies, when the public could hope that intelligence and moderate forms of intervention would improve their lives, Keynes's way fit the public mood.

For all his creative originality, Keynes carried with him to the end a reverence for classical approaches to economics and to culture more generally. David Felix cites Keynes's last remarks on his legacy as an economist to demonstrate that Keynes valued Adam Smith's feel for the interactions of the marketplace and even for the pressures that moved the economy toward an optimal equilibrium.[11] Keynes clearly saw his own work as not displacing classical analysis, but as adding at the margin a set of insights about when, why, and how intervention could supplement the strength of those forces.

The problem with Keynes's particular form of universalism is that it was not based on any real understanding of how the average person gets by. Felicific states of mind can be hard to come by in the daily struggle with life's realities. As Elizabeth and Harry Johnson confirm, Keynes "had no sort of imagination for what life might be like for the working class, although he was very concerned with making their life richer and safer and extending to them the delights of leisure and culture enjoyed by his own kind of people."[12] As for the common touch, Quentin Bell remembers from 1938 "a tremendous beano for the Fifth of November" at which Keynes's tenants were treated on the occasion of Guy Fawkes Day to a "no doubt highly intelligent speech" by their squire that left them cold, disapproving not so much of the speech as of the waste of money on such a celebration.[13] The masses, sensing they were not full citizens in the cosmology of their betters, may be excused for becoming antielitist.

Still, while Keynes is often accused of elitism, he did not think that intelligence was the preserve of the establishment. He saw stupidity as a vice as evenly distributed as original sin. He also saw, in the words of an Indian admirer, Anand Chandavarkar, that "the key to development lies in the creation of a society based on mass competence rather than on elitism."[14] He believed that his perspective on economics, values, aesthetics, and life itself was available to all who would consider the world thoughtfully. While he remained skeptical of the "vast mass of more or less illiterate voters," it was not because they were innately inferior to their betters, but because they were neither required nor enabled to acquire the techniques of economic analysis.[15] While mass democracy might therefore be suspect, Keynes's elitism was, as he saw it, a matter of practicality rather than of class-based conviction. The end object was the broad improvement of all sectors of society rather than the privileging of aristocrats or of capitalists.

The point of significance for contemporary politics that emerges with respect to Keynes is that although his views may have matured, there remains a legacy of disjunction between elite affinities for secular rationalism, on the one hand, and the religious and ethical mores of society, on the other. The failure of Keynes's progressive heirs to effectively address these concerns for morality and developmental nurturance disables their efforts to respond to the challenges of a pervasive media culture that erodes faith and undermines critical processes of human development. Public disillusionment with institutions and decision makers is consonant with sagging rates of mass participation in politics, as well as with the mobilization of moralist movements among the most disaffected.

11.3 – HAYEK: WITHDRAWAL AND REGENERATION

Ironically, Friedrich Hayek, the doyen of the capitalists, made the masses feel included. A woman named Margaret Thatcher who said, "My 'Bloomsbury' was Grantham—Methodism, the grocer's shop, Rotary and all the serious, sober virtues cultivated and esteemed in that environment," could bring the message home.[16] On the other side of the water, an actor who played Everyman, and did not always get the girl, could make Hayek's lines plain and popular.

By the 1980s, the public had reason to fear that regulation and moderation were insufficient as approaches to the economy and social problems. The perception that public spending, domestic and military, was out of control and that economic well-being was seriously threatened by inflation, along with the allied threats of rising crime and social decay, led to a turn toward populism. It was the appropriation of populism by the peddlers of pro-market ideology that redirected the ire of populists away from corporations and greedy capitalists toward maligning government and intellectual elitism.

Hayek had learned to loathe government as a young man witnessing the collapse of the Austrian monarchy. It did not seem to occur to him that there was little similarity between that undemocratic, decadent, and defeated regime and the modern mass democracies of the late twentieth century. The outlines of his thought, if not its genesis, were now consistent with the public mood. The resolute tone of his denunciations of government meddling harmonized with the *vox populi*.

Friedrich Hayek's paradoxical views captured the public imagination: paradoxical because, with one hand, he offers a swingeing criticism of existing governmental practices and, with the other, a utopian faith in the restorative powers of spontaneous forces set to work within a "constitution of liberty." The economic boom of the nineties was powered as much, one suspects, by the productivity increases afforded by computer technology and the advent of the Internet, itself a government project, as by any changes in taxation, the policy-making process, or social provision. However, on the rising tide, the mood of the public shifted against elites and the government they operated toward a kind of cultural populism that was consistent with Hayek's views. Now that the spontaneous forces of the market have generated another bursted bubble in the stock exchanges of the world, public sentiment may turn again.

Still, the weakness of Hayek's approach was its linear projection of potentialities into certainties. No matter that Hayek denied that he was a determinist, it was the determinist style that gave the ideological thrust to his arguments. Hayek achieved something profound by making a wide swath of opinion sensitive to the knowledge-mobilizing function of the market. Yet the hoped for benefits of this understanding may be undone by the market's ideologues with their promises of ever-greater social benefit concomitant on the reduction of government services.

Changes made to intricate arrangements of power solely on the assumption that the market is better than government (or vice versa) are likely to run the ship aground precisely because they are motivated by desire rather than practical navigation. It is time to step back from the examination of these three cases to see what the broader lessons are for an improved political economy.

11.4 – IDENTITY, THE GOVERNMENT, AND THE MARKET

We have arrived at the twenty-first century in a rather strange condition. Ideological controversy has moved from the extremes of left and right into a center that satisfies few partisans and bores or disillusions most citizens. In Western democracies, voter participation trends downward. Meanwhile, outbreaks of terrorism against the effects of globalization rattle the foundations of the system.

The irony is that the very institutions that brought decades of peace and rising prosperity, the government *and* the market, are coming to be discredited. Government wants "your money" so it can force you to do otherwise than what you would choose—and do that wastefully. The market sets off waves of growth and speculation, while chewing on people's security, threatening their environment, and concentrating wealth. Images of globalization run by powerful elites stimulate radical responses.

Yet most would agree on a moment's reflection that governments are capable of good deeds and are, in any case, absolutely essential to civilized living. Similarly, command economies, or corrupted political economies, that squash free enterprise and destroy the marketplace are the enemies of liberty. Why would anyone think that government is bad (or good) and that the market is good (or bad), when the evidence is there for all to see that both can be either good or bad and that political morality does not inhere in institutions, it arises out of the actions of citizens, producers, and consumers?

The successive targeting of capitalists in the marketplace, of politicians in government, and of elites in all spheres, as the perpetrators of plots against public well-being, is perhaps inevitable. We have seen how Hayek, Keynes, and Laski came to be icons of these struggles. All three illuminated our understanding of complex societies even while they engendered reactions that complicated the tasks of dealing with the realities of politics and economics. It is unfair to hold Hayek, Keynes, and Laski responsible for the distortion of their views.[17] However, as we have argued here, the distortion builds on the exaggeration of tendencies found within their work. Not all of what follows from such decontestations are bad, and it is certainly not entirely avoidable. Ideologies illuminate new possibilities and activate mass participation. As Michael Freeden concludes in his seminal study of ideologies and political theory, "Ideologies may be power structures that manipulate human action, but they are also *ideational systems that enable us to choose to become what we want to become* [italics added]."[18] The point of the tale told here is to encourage more reflective and deliberative choices about identities and ideologies.

While the oppositional bind may not be a universal feature of ideological behavior, it is surely one of the main types of linkage that we may expect to find. The identity-driven desire to confront some presumed obstacle to one's own, or society's, improved condition has its dangerous side. The danger is precisely in the failure of analysis that characterized these cases.

Albert Hirschman notes another such epistemologically dangerous pattern of linkage when he discusses the *rhetorics of intransigence* whereby both reactionaries and progressives tie their affirmative cases to arguments from inevitability.[19] The politically convenient feature of such arguments is that they cannot be proved absent knowledge of the future. Our discussion of the tie between identity and ideology suggests that this turn to the inevitable is the resort of those whose need for advocacy has outrun the means of verification available to bolster their case. Laski's forecast of violence as the inevitable alternative to socialism fits here, as does Hayek's vision of the direct path to serfdom.

The danger of arguments impelled by the need to oppose or by the resort to the inevitable is particularly great when their focus is on institutions of the complexity and versatility of governments and markets.[20] Institutions do not act in a unilinear fashion as Hayek and Laski were prone to argue, nor are elites entirely predictable as the critics of Keynes would assume. Institutions and elites are themselves capable of learning-behavior. As the American sociologist John Campbell demonstrates, institutions make their way by a process of interpretation, interaction, and "bricolage" or the deliberate adjustment and combination of prior institutional forms to address new problems.[21]

The evolutionary changes of the market in its cultural and political context are a prime illustration. Monetarist economics are increasingly seen as a partial, and partisan, approach that needs, at the least, to be supplemented by attention to fiscal and budgetary strategies for maintaining economic equilibrium and addressing the distributive aspects of the economy.[22] Keynes's mature progressivism supplies electorates and their leaders with a way of approaching this dynamic.[23] When ideologues, whether right, left, or even center, overlook these adaptive modalities, we have the recipe for the excesses that are so evident in twentieth-century political and economic history.[24]

Ideology was the great killer of the twentieth century, and its mutations as milder creeds within the mantle of modern democracies make ideology no less dangerous. The left is dangerous no less than the right. If the mentality that makes democracy possible requires a certain degree of intelligent judgment, then it is easy for antielitists to mobilize populist resentment that such qualities are associated with the classes rather than the masses. But a skeptic need only point out that rational judgment is not the property of a class—indeed Keynes's illustrations on this point are copious. To dismiss intelligence as a way of undermining class rule is about as sensible as wrecking machines to overthrow capitalism. Both intelligence and machines are crucial to the good society.

The translation of developmental challenges arising from changing commitments, communities, and competencies into ideological positions becomes most threatening when political leaders simplify creeds into slogans. Congressman Dick Armey's bromide that "the market is rational, the government is dumb!" is a case in point. Such Hayekian ideologizing of institutions has the utility for politicians of distracting attention from the substance of policies that advantage the rich at the expense of the marginalized, but the even graver loss is to the meaning of democratic discourse.

Deliberate community decision making is not optional if contemporary societies are to address their most critical policy problems. The full potential of social learning will be needed if this is to be done effectively. Democratic institutions make possible the kind of conceptual shaping and refinement that undermine ideological approaches and mediate between contending identities. The kind of intelligence possessed by Maynard Keynes, at least in the eyes of his devoted biographer, Roy Harrod, is crucial to this task:

> The power of apprehending simultaneously in his mind widely disparate theories and facts, the fine judgment of relevance and intense realism—these are his greatest qualities. To them we must add his faculty for developing a chain of rigid logical reasoning, once he had assured himself that he had achieved relevant premises and was not merely spinning fine theories in the void.[25]

While no polity can rely on a class of mandarins for decisions, the best of political *processes* can bring this kind of judgment to the surface so that electorates and their representatives can choose between sensible alternatives.

11.5 – POLITICS AND DEVELOPMENTAL FREEDOM

The political malaise that besets the West at the beginning of the twenty-first century is the product of a particular configuration of ideologically based arguments. The development of an analysis of democracy based on the pluralism of interest group politics, in part attributable to the early Laski, led directly to a conservative critique by Hayek and others that merely pointed to the self-serving tendencies of such groups and their agents. If democracy was pluralist, it was government by "special interests."

The erstwhile protestations of Keynesians that they were regulating for the public good were drowned out by an appeal to the atavism of disposing of "my money" rather than giving it up in taxes for the public good. By playing off the appeal of individual self-interest against the organized interests of elites, conservatives could recapture some legitimacy as friends of the downtrodden. Government came to be seen, through the lens provided by Hayek, as just another special interest. Reagan and Thatcher and their successors were the immediate political beneficiaries. Capitalists, freed thereby of government regulation, were the financial winners on an unprecedented scale as the distribution of income was skewed in their favor.

A return to a more moderate and historically grounded conception of democracy is required if we are to escape from this ideological box.[26] The fact is that *markets* cannot exist without the framework of law and mediation provided by governments. *Governments* exist to moderate and compromise interests—especially interests that arise in the course of market-based activity. A market that is unregulated provides no recourse against the basest of human motivations except the fragmented and uncertain processes of the pricing mechanism. Life itself can be bought and sold.

Constitutional democratic governments are quite distinct from "interest groups" precisely because they *do* have constitutions built on concepts of equal rights, public sovereignty, free expression, and limited power—and the backing of a sufficient number of believers to make the system operate. Only institutions so constituted can enable the exercise of intelligent judgment in the making of public policy, and they are bounded by protections against the abuse of such power. There is recourse against bad judgment or corruption through the electoral process, the assertion of rights through the courts, and the forms of resistance protected by civil liberties. The market enables no such potential for constructive public policy and contains no built-in limits against the motivations that are brought into play by its processes. Government and the market need each other, one for mediation and direction, the other to encourage productivity and efficiency.

The vital mission of a democratic society is the provision of institutions, practices, and developmental choices that meet the shared need for identity. Identity formation is well served by fostering the best ways of rewarding competence, sustaining commitments, and eliciting the strengths of communities. Yet these purposes cannot be achieved without protections against the fraudulent assertions of competence, the exploitation of commitments, and the discriminatory behavior of communities.[27] Neither the market, nor the government, nor elites can alone perform these complex tasks.

The maintenance of a free democratic society requires that citizens understand the need for a complex interweaving of institutions, processes, and constitutional safeguards so that the excesses of any one institution may be limited, while its virtues are brought to the service of society. The citizen stands at the base of civilization, and the institutions of political economy are the means, not the ends, in the struggle for human development.

Notes

Preface

1. For a preliminary survey of the project, see Kenneth Hoover, "Ideologizing Institutions: Hayek, Keynes, Laski and the Creation of 20th C. Politics," *The Journal of Political Ideologies* 4, no. 1 (February 1999): 87–116.

Chapter 1

1. Erik Erikson, *Young Man Luther: A Study in Psychoanalysis and History* (New York: Norton, 1958).

2. John Maynard Keynes, *The Collected Writings of John Maynard Keynes,* vol. 7 of *The General Theory of Employment, Interest and Money* (London: Macmillan/Cambridge University Press for the Royal Economic Society, 1936), 383.

3. Cf. Friedrich A. Hayek, "The Trend of Economic Thinking," *Economica* 13, no. 2 (1933): 129–31. John Patrick Diggins, *The Rise and Fall of the American Left* (New York: Norton, 1992), 30.

4. Unsurprisingly, given his political views, Friedman neglected to mention Laski, terming the period prior to Keynes as the "age of Adam Smith."

5. Kenneth Minogue, "The Escape from Serfdom," *The London Review of Books,* January 14, 2000, 11.

6. Michael Freeden, *Ideologies and Political Theory* (Oxford: Oxford University Press, 1996), 76. Cf. William Brice Gallie, "Essentially Contested Concepts," *Proceedings of the Aristotelian Society* 56 (1955–1956): 167–98; William Connolly, *The Terms of Political Discourse* (Lexington, Mass.: Concord Press, 1974).

7. Freeden, *Ideologies,* 76–77.

8. I have formulated this approach to *identity relations analysis* in my book, Kenneth Hoover, with James Marcia and Kristen Parris, *The Power of Identity: Politics in*

a New Key (Chatham, N.J.: Chatham House Publishing, 1997), and will apply it here. In that book, I used the term *integrity* for *community* as a way of incorporating Erikson's particular terminology into the analysis. However, Erikson's usage was meant to convey that which makes us whole or *integral* to our social surroundings. In common parlance, *community* communicates more clearly. Similarly, I used the term *mutuality* where here I refer to *commitment*. The latter term conveys a sense of the stronger bonds that are at the base of identity formation. I am grateful to Donald Emmerson for suggesting these terms. For the most recent account of the analysis, see "What Should Democracies Do about Identity?" in *The Future of Identity: Centennial Reflections on the Legacy of Erik Erikson* (forthcoming).

9. For a summary of the research supporting this finding, see James Marcia, "Ego Identity: Research Review," from James Marcia, "The Status of the Statuses: Research Review," in *Ego Identity: A Handbook for Research,* ed. J. E. Marcia et al. (New York: Springer Verlag, 1993), chap. 2. Reprinted in Hoover et al., *Power of Identity,* 85–109.

10. Cf. Hoover et al., *Power of Identity;* Michael Freeden, *Ideologies and Political Theory* (Oxford: Oxford University Press, 1996), 76.

11. Erik H. Erikson, *Identity: Youth and Crisis* (New York, Norton, 1968), 189.

Chapter 2

1. John Raybould, comp., *Hayek: A Commemorative Album* (London: Adam Smith Institute, 1998), 3–5.

2. Michael Holroyd, *Lytton Strachey: A Biography* (London: Penguin, 1971), 241.

3. Robert J. Skidelsky, *John Maynard Keynes: A Biography,* vol. 1, *Hopes Betrayed 1883–1920* (New York: Viking Penguin, 1983), 22–24.

4. Donald E. Moggridge, *Maynard Keynes: An Economist's Biography* (London: Routledge, 1992), 16.

5. Moggridge, *An Economist's Biography,* 18–19.

6. Elizabeth S. Johnson and Harry G. Johnson, *The Shadow of Keynes: Understanding Keynes, Cambridge, and Keynesian Economics* (Chicago: University of Chicago Press, 1978), 4–5.

7. Florence Keynes, *Gathering Up the Threads: A Study in Family Biography* (Cambridge: Heffer and Sons, 1950), 82, 89.

8. David Felix, *Biography of an Idea: John Maynard Keynes and the General Theory* (New Brunswick, N.J.: Transaction, 1995), 5–6.

9. Roy Forbes Harrod, Sir, *The Life of John Maynard Keynes* (New York: Harcourt Brace, 1951), 192.

10. Moggridge, *Economist's Biography,* 21–23.

11. Felix, *Biography of an Idea,* 6; Skidelsky, *Keynes,* vol. 1, 22–24.

12. Johnson and Johnson, *The Shadow,* 15; Robert J. Skidelsky, *John Maynard Keynes: A Biography,* vol. 2, *The Economist as Saviour 1920–1937* (London: Allen Lane/Penguin, 1992), xvi.

13. Skidelsky, *Keynes,* vol. 1, 75.

14. Skidelsky, *Keynes,* vol. 1, 67.

15. Keynes, *Gathering Up the Threads,* 64.

16. Skidelsky, *Keynes,* vol. 1, 1–2.

17. On British idealism, see Melvin Richter, *The Politics of Conscience: T. H. Green and His Age* (Cambridge, Mass.: Harvard University Press, 1964). Cf. Skidelsky, *Keynes,* vol. 1, 28–31, on the two posttheological traditions at Cambridge: utilitarianism and intuitionism, the poles of Keynes's practical and moral perspectives.

18. John Maynard Keynes, *Essays in Biography, New Edition with Three Additional Essays by Geoffrey Keynes* (New York: Horizon Books, 1951), 326. Cf. Richter, *Conscience,* 39.

19. Skidelsky, *Keynes,* vol. 1, 30.

20. Keynes, *Gathering Up the Threads,* 73–74.

21. Skidelsky, *Keynes,* vol. 1, 82.

22. Holroyd, *Strachey,* 241.

23. Moggridge, *An Economist's Biography,* 53, 66.

24. Noel Annan, *Our Age: The Generation That Made Post-War Britain* (London: Fontana, 1990), 73.

25. Felix, *Biography of an Idea,* 8–9; Michael Holroyd, *Lytton Strachey: The New Biography* (New York: Noonday, 1994), 91.

26. John Maynard Keynes, "My Early Beliefs," in *Two Memoirs* (1938; reprint, New York: Augustus M. Kelly, 1949), 81.

27. Holroyd, *Strachey,* 208–10.

28. Keynes, "Beliefs," 83.

29. Keynes, "Beliefs," 92.

30. Keynes, "Beliefs," 82.

31. Felix, *Biography of an Idea,* 26.

32. Skidelsky, *Keynes,* vol. 1, 241, 431; Skidelsky, *Keynes,* vol. 2, 222–24.

33. In Massie, *Dreadnought,* 649.

34. Keynes, "My Early Beliefs," 88. Cf. Skidelsky, *Keynes,* vol. 1, 137, on the practice of this style by G. E. Moore.

35. Keynes, "Beliefs," 84.

36. Keynes, "Beliefs," 97–98.

37. Rod O'Donnell, "Keynes on Aesthetics," in *New Perspectives on Keynes,* ed. Allin F. Cottrell and Michael S. Lawlor (Durham, N.C.: Duke University Press, 1995), 93–121.

38. Skidelsky, *Keynes,* vol. 1, 142–43.

39. Skidelsky, *Keynes,* vol. 1, 140–41.

40. This much he likely owes to the great conservative traditionalist Edmund Burke, the subject of his only written treatment of politics—an undergraduate essay on Burke that runs nearly a hundred pages. See Skidelsky, *Keynes,* vol. 1, 154.

41. Skidelsky, *Keynes,* vol. 1, 49–50; Moggridge, *An Economist's Biography,* 94.

42. Skidelsky, *Keynes,* vol. 1, 166.

43. Holroyd, *Strachey,* 242.

44. Anand Chandavarkar, *Keynes and India: A Study in Economics and Biography* (Basingstoke, U.K.: Macmillan, 1989), 3–4.

45. Skidelsky, *Keynes,* vol. 1, 206–7.

46. Letter to Lytton Strachey in Chandavarkar, *Keynes and India,* 19.

47. Letter to Swithinbank in Moggridge, *An Economist's Biography,* 179–80.

48. John Maynard Keynes, EJ, 6, 2, File: 1, Galleys of Economic Journal Review of Ludwig von Mises, Theorie Des Geldes und der Umlaufsmittel (Munich: Duncker and Humblot, 1912) and Friedrich Bendixen, Geld und Kapital (Leipzig: Duncker and Humblot, 1912), and Keynes Collection, Modern Archive Centre at King's College, Cambridge.

49. Harrod, *Life of John Maynard Keynes,* 131.

50. Keynes, *Gathering Up the Threads,* 81.

51. In Moggridge, *An Economist's Biography,* 219.

52. Harrod, *The Life of John Maynard Keynes,* 171.

53. Felix, *Biography of an Idea,* 14–15.

54. Moggridge, *An Economist's Biography,* 245–46.

55. Allan Janik and Stephen Toulmin, *Wittgenstein's Vienna* (New York: Simon & Schuster, 1973), 209–10; Skidelsky, *Keynes,* vol. 1, 250.

56. Richard Shone, with essays by James Beechey and Richard Morphet, *The Art of Bloomsbury: Roger Fry, Vanessa Bell and Duncan Grant* (Princeton, N.J.: Princeton University Press, 1999), 14.

57. Skidelsky, *Keynes,* vol. 1, 247.

58. Shone, *Art of Bloomsbury,* 19.

59. Skidelsky, *Keynes,* vol. 2, 294.

60. George Feaver, "More Guru Than Sage: Review of Harold Laski: A Political Biography," *Times Literary Supplement* 1996, no. 4708 (June 25, 1993): 28.

61. Massie, *Dreadnought,* 19.

62. Quentin Bell, "Recollections and Reflections on Maynard Keynes," in *Keynes and the Bloomsbury Group/The Fourth Keynes Seminar Held at the University of Kent at Canterbury, 1978,* ed. Derek Crabtree and A. P. Thirlwall (London: Macmillan, 1980), 71.

63. Kingsley Martin, *Harold Laski: A Biographical Memoir* (London: Victor Gollancz, 1953), 49.

64. Moggridge, *An Economist's Biography,* 838–39.

65. Homosexual acts between consenting adults would not be legalized in Britain until 1967. Peter Clarke, *Hope and Glory: Britain 1900–1990* (London: Allen Lane/Penguin, 1996), 308.

66. Clarke, *Hope and Glory,* 324.

67. Michael Newman, *Harold Laski: A Political Biography* (Basingstoke, U.K.: Macmillan, 1993), 6.

68. Newman, *Laski,* 5.

69. Isaac Kramnick and Barry Sheerman, *Harold Laski: A Life on the Left* (London: The Penguin Group, 1993), 19.

70. Newman, *Laski,* 6–24.

71. Kramnick and Sheerman, *Laski,* 23–25.

72. Newman, *Laski,* 15.

73. Kramnick and Sheerman, *Laski,* 54–58.

74. Kramnick and Sheerman, *Laski,* 19–20.

75. Frida Laski, University of Hull Library, October 1956, File: A/T 51, interview with Frida Laski by John Saville, Kingston-upon-Hull.

76. Kramnick and Sheerman, *Laski,* 32–33.

77. Harold Laski, University of Hull, DLA, 36, Laski: Frida Laski 01/09/10, Kingston-upon-Hull.

78. Newman, *Laski,* 7–9, 13.

79. Laski, interview with Frida Laski.

80. Martin, *Harold Laski,* 17.

81. Frida Laski, interview by Seville.

82. Harold Laski, University of Hull, DLA, 36, Laski: Frida Laski 13/10/11, Kingston-upon-Hull.

83. Kramnick and Sheerman, *Laski,* 52–53; Newman, *Laski,* 8–9.

84. Newman, *Laski,* 16–17.

85. Kramnick and Sheerman, *Laski,* 50–51, 58–60.

86. Frida Laski, interview by Seville.

87. Newman, *Laski,* 16.

88. H. W. Nevinson cited in Martin, *Harold Laski,* 20.

89. Kramnick and Sheerman, *Laski,* 74–75.

90. Harold Laski, DLA, File: 36, Letter to Professor Murray 17/07/17, University of Hull Library, Hull.

91. Newman, *Laski,* 29–30.

92. Kramnick and Sheerman, *Laski,* 79.

93. Martin, *Harold Laski,* 27.

94. Kramnick and Sheerman, *Laski,* 85–88.

95. Martin, *Harold Laski,* 21.

96. Friedrich Hayek, "Hayek on Hayek," in *The Collected Works of F. A. Hayek,* ed. Stephen Kresge and Leif Wenar, vol. supplement, *Hayek on Hayek: An Autobiographical Dialogue* (London: Routledge, 1994), 39–40.

97. Gitta Sereny, "Sage of the Free-Thinking World, The Times Profile: Friedrich August von Hayek," *Times* (London), May 9, 1985. Quoted in Raybould, *Hayek,* 5.

98. In Richard Cockett, *Thinking the Unthinkable,* rev. ed. (London: Fontana, 1995), 24–25.

99. Hayek, "Hayek on Hayek," 41.

100. Alan Ebenstein, *Friedrich Hayek: A Biography* (London: Palgrave, 2001), 13.

101. Hayek, "Hayek on Hayek," from an interview in the Oral History Program, Robert Chitester, President, Public Broadcasting of Northern Pennsylvania (London: Routledge, 1994), 43.

102. Hayek, "Hayek on Hayek," 47.

103. In a tribute to Ludwig von Mises, 1956, in Raybould, *Hayek,* 1.

Chapter 3

1. Donald E. Moggridge, *Maynard Keynes: An Economist's Biography* (London: Routledge, 1992), 254–58.

2. Robert J. Skidelsky, *John Maynard Keynes: A Biography,* vol. 1, *Hopes Betrayed 1883–1920* (New York: Viking Penguin, 1983), 253, 295–319; Moggridge, *An Economist's Biography,* 254–58.

3. Noel Annan, *Our Age: The Generation That Made Post-War Britain* (London: Fontana, 1990), 77.

4. Quentin Bell, "Recollections and Reflections on Maynard Keynes," in *Keynes and the Bloomsbury Group/The Fourth Keynes Seminar Held at the University of Kent at Canterbury, 1978,* ed. Derek Crabtree and A. P. Thirlwall (London: Macmillan, 1980), 71.

5. Skidelsky, *Keynes,* vol. 1, 302–27.

6. David Felix, *Biography of an Idea: John Maynard Keynes and the General Theory* (New Brunswick, N.J.: Transaction, 1995), 16–17.

7. Moggridge, *An Economist's Biography,* 269.

8. Skidelsky, *Keynes,* vol. 1, 335–36.

9. Felix, *Biography of an Idea,* 16–17.

10. John Maynard Keynes, *The Economic Consequences of the Peace,* ed. Donald Moggridge (London: Macmillan/Cambridge University Press for the Royal Economic Society), vol. 2 (London: Macmillan/Cambridge University Press, 1919), xx.

11. Skidelsky, *Keynes,* vol. 1, 353.

12. Skidelsky, *Keynes,* vol. 1, 399.

13. Keynes, *Economic Consequences of Peace,* 170.

14. Felix, *Biography of an Idea,* 41.

15. Keynes, *Economic Consequences of Peace,* 2.

16. Keynes, *Economic Consequences of Peace,* 6.

17. Keynes, *Economic Consequences of Peace,* 13.

18. Keynes, *Economic Consequences of Peace,* 148–49.

19. Keynes, *Economic Consequences of Peace,* 160.

20. Kingsley Martin, *Harold Laski: A Biographical Memoir* (London: Victor Gollancz, 1953), 223–25; Isaac Kramnick and Barry Sheerman, *Harold Laski: A Life on the Left* (London: The Penguin Group, 1993), 114.

21. Kramnick and Sheerman, *Laski,* 89.

22. Alan Ryan, *John Dewey and the High Tide of American Liberalism* (New York: Norton, 1995), 190.

23. Harold Laski, *Studies in the Problem of Sovereignty* (London: Oxford University Press, 1917), 25.

24. Laski, *Sovereignty,* 25.

25. William Y. Elliott, "The Pragmatic Politics of Mr. Laski," *The American Political Science Review* 18, no. 2 (May 1924): 251–75.

26. Michael Newman, *Harold Laski: A Political Biography* (Basingstoke, U.K: Macmillan, 1993), 44.

27. Elliott, "The Pragmatic Politics of Mr. Laski," 258.

28. Harold Laski, *Lecture: Introduction to Contemporary Politics*, ed. Francis G. Wilson (Seattle: University of Washington Bookstore, 1939), 68.

29. Kramnick and Sheerman, *Laski*, 197.

30. Ayn Rand, *The Fountainhead* (New York: Penguin, 1943), 231.

31. Rand, *The Fountainhead*, 269, 365–66.

32. Rand, *The Fountainhead,* 376.

33. Kramnick and Sheerman, *Laski,* 128–29, 138–39. Cf. Jose Harris, *William Beveridge: A Biography,* rev. ed. (Oxford: Oxford University Press, 1997), 284–88.

34. Kramnick and Sheerman, *Laski*, 128–29; Newman, *Laski,* 44.

35. Felix Frankfurter, DGA, December 10, 1918, File: 21, Telegram from Department of Labor, University of Hull, Hull, U.K.

36. Laski, *Contemporary Politics*, 68.

37. Hannah Pitkin, *Fortune Is a Woman, with a New Afterword* (Chicago: University of Chicago Press, 1999), 290.

38. Harold Laski, "The Problem of Administrative Areas: An Essay in Reconstruction," *Smith College Studies in History* 4, no. 1 (October 1918): 5.

39. Newman, *Laski*, 224.

40. Laski, "Adminstrative Areas," 43–44.

41. Cf. Rainer Eisfeld, "The Emergence and Meaning of Socialist Pluralism," *International Political Science Review* 17, no. 3 (1996): 267–79; Martin, *A Biographical Memoir,* 71–72.

42. Cecile Laborde, "Pluralism, Syndicalism and Corporatism: Leon Duguit and the Crisis of the State (1900–1925)," *History of European Ideas* 22, no. 3 (1996): 241.

43. Harold Laski, *Authority in the Modern State* (New Haven, Conn.: Yale University Press, 1919).

44. Kramnick and Sheerman, *Laski,* 126–27. Dedicated to Holmes, the book was read by the eminent jurist as he prepared his dissent in the Abrams sedition case that was to become his most famous defense of freedom of conscience.

45. Mark DeWolfe Howe, ed., *Holmes-Laski Letters: The Correspondence of Mr. Justice Holmes and Harold J. Laski,* vol. 1, *1916–1925* and vol. 2, *1926–1935* (Cambridge, Mass.: Harvard University Press, 1953).

46. Kramnick and Sheerman, *Laski,* 195–98.

47. Friedrich Hayek, "Hayek on Hayek," in *The Collected Works of F. A. Hayek,* ed. Stephen Kresge and Leif Wenar, vol. supplement, *Hayek on Hayek: An Autobiographical Dialogue,* from an interview in the Oral History Program, Jack High, Department of Economics, UCLA (London: Routledge, 1994), 48.

48. Charlotte Cubitt, *Hayek: An Affectionate Memoir,* Unpublished MSS of Draft of Memoir (Colchester, England, 1999), 42.

49. Hayek, "Hayek on Hayek," 48.

50. Friedrich Hayek, "The Economics of the 1920's as Seen from Vienna," in *The Collected Works of F. A. Hayek,* ed. Peter Klein, vol. 4, *The Fortunes of Liberalism* (Chicago: University of Chicago Press, 1963), 20.

51. Stephen Kresge, introduction to *Hayek on Hayek,* by Friedrich Hayek, ed. Stephen Kresge and Leif Wenar (Chicago: University of Chicago Press, 1994), 2.

52. Hayek, "Hayek on Hayek," 53.

53. Hayek, "Hayek on Hayek," 153–54.

54. Hayek, "Hayek on Hayek," 49.

55. Bertell Ollman, *Alienation: Marx's Conception of Man in Capitalist Society,* 2nd ed. (New York: Cambridge University Press, 1976).

56. Kenneth R. Hoover, *Ideology and Political Life,* 3rd ed. (Houston: Thompson/ Wadsworth, 2001), 85–110.

57. Philip Rieff, *Freud: The Mind of the Moralist,* rev. ed. (New York: Harper and Row, 1961).

Chapter 4

1. Ralf Dahrendorf, *LSE: A History of the London School of Economics and Political Science 1895–1995* (Oxford: Oxford University Press, 1995), 138.

2. Donald E. Moggridge, *Maynard Keynes: An Economist's Biography* (London: Routledge, 1992), 58–59.

3. Robert J. Skidelsky, *John Maynard Keynes: A Biography,* vol. 2, *The Economist as Saviour 1920–1937* (London: Allen Lane/Penguin, 1992), 58; Mark Blaug, "Recent Biographies of Keynes," *Journal of Economic Literature* 32, no. 3 (September 1994): 1, 204.

4. Robert J. Skidelsky, *John Maynard Keynes: A Biography,* vol. 1, *Hopes Betrayed 1883–1920* (New York: Viking Penguin, 1983), 151.

5. Skidelsky, *Keynes,* vol. 1, 153.

6. John Maynard Keynes, *The Collected Writings of John Maynard Keynes,* ed. R. B. Braithwaite, vol. 8, *A Treatise on Probability* (London: Macmillan/Cambridge University Press for the Royal Economic Society, 1921), 342.

7. Keynes, *Probability,* 356.

8. David Felix, *Biography of an Idea: John Maynard Keynes and the General Theory* (New Brunswick, N.J.: Transaction, 1995), 33–34.

9. Skidelsky, *Keynes,* vol. 2, 60.

10. Skidelsky, *Keynes,* vol. 1, 241; Peter Clarke, *The Keynesian Revolution in the Making, 1924–1936* (New York: Oxford University Press, 1988); Skidelsky, *Keynes,* vol. 2, 222–23.

11. Skidelsky, *Keynes,* vol. 2, xxii–xxiii, 170.

12. Moggridge, *Economist's Biography,* 553–54.

13. Skidelsky, *Keynes,* vol. 2, 118.

14. Skidelsky, *Keynes,* vol. 2, 102–6.

15. Kingsley Martin, *Harold Laski: A Biographical Memoir* (London: Victor Gollancz, 1953), 56–57.

16. John Maynard Keynes, *The End of Laissez-Faire* (London: Leonard and Virginia Woolf, Hogarth Press, 1927 [1926], 39–40.

17. Keynes, *End of Laissez-Faire*, 47–48.

18. Cf. Skidelsky, *Keynes,* vol. 2, 225–29.

19. Skidelsky, *Keynes,* vol. 2, 594–95.

20. From a debate at a Liberal Summer Camp in 1927—quoted in Skidelsky, *Keynes,* vol. 2, 233.

21. Felix, *Biography of an Idea*, 53.

22. John Maynard Keynes, "Am I a Liberal?" in *Essays in Persuasion,* ed. John Maynard Keynes (New York: Norton, 1925), 223–324.

23. Keynes, "Am I a Liberal?" 327.

24. John Maynard Keynes, "Liberalism and Labour," in *Essays in Persuasion*, ed. John Maynard Keynes (New York: Norton, 1926), 343.

25. In Moggridge, *Economist's Biography,* 452–54.

26. For a contemporary analysis of Tony Blair's record in his first term that uses this distinction, see Raymond Plant, "Blair and Ideology," in *The Blair Effect,* ed. Anthony Seldon (London: Little, Brown, 2001), 555–70.

27. In Skidelsky, *Keynes,* vol. 2, 202.

28. See Skidelsky's summary of the debate in Skidelsky, *Keynes,* vol. 2, 223–28. Cf. Moggridge, *Economist's Biography*, 454.

29. Skidelsky, *Keynes,* vol. 2, 192.

30. Clarke, *Keynesian Revolution*, 31–39; Skidelsky, *Keynes,* vol. 2, 19.

31. John Maynard Keynes, *The Collected Writings of John Maynard Keynes,* ed. Donald Moggridge, vol. 19, *Population, Protection, and Unemployment* (London: Macmillan/Cambridge University Press for the Royal Economic Society, 1981), 160.

32. John Maynard Keynes, "Persuasion," in *The Collected Writings of John Maynard Keynes,* ed. Elizabeth Johnson and Donald Moggridge, vol. 9, *Essays in Persuasion* (London: Macmillan/Cambridge University Press for the Royal Economic Society, 1972), 164–74.

33. Cf. Anand Chandavarkar, *Keynes and India: A Study in Economics and Biography* (Basingstoke, U.K.: Macmillan, 1989), 8–9, 189; Felix, *Biography of an Idea,* 61–65; Moggridge, *Economist's Biography,* 429; Skidelsky, *Keynes,* vol. 2, 200; Mary Furner and Barry Supple, "Ideas, Institutions, and the State in the U.S. and Britain: An Introduction," in *The State and Economic Knowledge,* ed. Mary Furner and Barry Supple (Cambridge: Wilson Center and Cambridge University Press, 1996), 22.

34. Robert Skidelsky, "The Labour Party and Keynes," in *Interests and Obsessions,* ed. Robert Skidelsky (London: Macmillan, 1993), 113.

35. Keynes was, in fact, party to discussions in the Treasury about alchemy and even an investor in one scheme. See Moggridge, *Economist's Biography,* 492. Further signs of his irreverence were his interest in Freud's theories about money and anality and the psychological pathology of an attachment to gold. Skidelsky, *Keynes,* vol. 2, 334.

36. Cf. Peter Clarke, *Hope and Glory: Britain 1900–1990* (London: Allen Lane/Penguin, 1996), 130–33; Susan Wolcott, "Keynes v. Churchill: Revaluation and British Unemployment in the 1920s," *Journal of Economic History* 53, no. 3 (1993): 601–29.

37. In addition to Niemeyer, they were Sir Richard Hopkins, F. W. Leith-Ross, and P. J. Grigg. See Peter Clarke, "The Treasury's Analytical Model of the British Economy Between the Wars," in *The State and Economic Knowledge,* ed. Mary Furner and Barry Supple (Cambridge: Wilson Center and Cambridge University Press, 1996), 173–76. Cf. P. J. Grigg, *Prejudice and Judgment* (London: Jonathan Cape, 1948), 182–83.

38. Robert J. Skidelsky, *John Maynard Keynes: A Biography,* vol. 3, *Fighting for Britain 1937–1946* (London: Macmillan, 2000), 138.

39. Niemeyer in 1925, in his version, went further to state the silent assumption of decreased expenditure and the remission of taxes. See Clarke, *Keynesian Revolution,* 31.

40. Peter Clarke, *A Question of Leadership: Gladstone to Thatcher* (London: Hamish Hamilton, 1991), 156–57.

41. John Maynard Keynes, "The Economic Consequences of Mr. Churchill," in *Essays in Persuasion,* ed. John Maynard Keynes (New York: Norton, 1925), 270.

42. Clarke, "Analytical Model," 177.

43. Felix, *Biography of an Idea,* 62–63; Clarke, *Keynesian Revolution,* 166–67.

44. Skidelsky, *Keynes,* vol. 1, 284. See Peter Clarke, *Liberals and Social Democrats* (New York: Cambridge University Press, 1978), 3.

45. Skidelsky, *Keynes,* vol. 1, 251, 284.

46. Skidelsky, *Keynes,* vol. 1, 329, 348.

47. Skidelsky, *Keynes,* vol. 2, 94, 98, 101, 210–11.

48. Quentin Bell, *Bloomsbury Recalled* (New York: Columbia University, 1995), 79.

49. Skidelsky, *Keynes,* vol. 2, 101.

50. Skidelsky, *Keynes,* vol. 2, 144.

51. Skidelsky, *Keynes,* vol. 2, 173.

52. Noel Annan, *Our Age: The Generation That Made Post-War Britain* (London: Fontana, 1990), 237; Skidelsky, *Keynes,* vol. 2, xvii.

53. Cited in Clarke, *Keynesian Revolution,* 67.

54. John Maynard Keynes, *Keynes,* L, 24, 8 June, 1929, File: 46, Prolegomena to a New Socialism, Modern Archives, King's College, Cambridge University.

55. Jose Harris, *William Beveridge: A Biography,* rev. ed. (Oxford: Oxford University Press, 1997), 341.

56. Clarke, *Keynesian Revolution,* 80.

57. Skidelsky, *Keynes,* vol. 2, 292–93.

58. Michael Newman, *Harold Laski: A Political Biography* (Basingstoke, U.K.: Macmillan, 1993), 65–66.

59. There is some speculation that Laski's softening attitude toward authority and the state amounted to the resolution of an Oedipus complex through reconciliation with his father. See Isaac Kramnick and Barry Sheerman, *Harold Laski: A Life on the Left* (London: The Penguin Group, 1993), 107.

60. Cited in Robert Massie, *Dreadnought: Britain, Germany, and the Coming of the Great War* (New York: Random House, 1991), 898.

61. Massie, *Dreadnought,* 889–99.

62. Annan, *Our Age,* 90–93.

63. Harold Laski, *The Foundations of Sovereignty and Other Essays* (New Haven, Conn.: Yale University Press, 1921), vi.

64. Kramnick and Sheerman, *Laski,* 175; Lionel (Lord) Robbins, *Autobiography of an Economist* (London: Macmillan, 1971), 80.

65. Laski, *Foundations*, vii.

66. Laski, *Foundations*, ix. It is an argument a student of Laski's, Professor C. B. Macpherson of Toronto University, would make into the foundation of an attack on liberal democracy, C. B. Macpherson, *The Real World of Democracy* (Oxford: Oxford University Press, 1965). Macpherson's writings would inspire a generation of scholar/activists from the sixties onward to revive the nostrums of the left.

67. Newman, *Laski*, 101–03.

68. Beatrice Webb, *The Diary of Beatrice Webb: The Power to Alter Things, 1905–1924*, ed. Norman and Jeanne MacKenzie, vol. 3 (Cambridge, Mass.: Harvard University Press, 1984), 399.

69. Webb, *The Diary of Beatrice Webb,* vol. 3, 392.

70. Kramnick and Sheerman, *Laski*, 170–71; Martin, *Harold Laski,* 56–57.

71. Martin, *Harold Laski,* 75.

72. Kramnick and Sheerman, *Laski,* 243.

73. Laski in a letter to Felix Frankfurter, quoted in Martin, *Harold Laski,* 67.

74. Peter Lamb, "Laski's Ideological Metamorphosis," *Journal of Political Ideologies* 4, no. 2 (June 1999): 245.

75. Clarke, *Hope and Glory,* 141.

76. Robbins, *Autobiography,* 82.

77. Robert Blake in an *Evening Standard* review of the Holmes-Laski correspondence cited in Kramnick and Sheerman, *Laski*, 203. His biographers are somewhat divided, with Kramnick and Sheerman quite persuaded of his congenital fibbing and Newman inclined to document the veracity of his claims.

78. Kramnick and Sheerman, *Laski,* 206.

79. Newman, *Laski,* 168–69.

80. Laski, *Foundations,* vii–viii.

81. Michael Newman, "Harold Laski Today," *Political Quarterly* 67, no. 3 (July–September 1996): 229–38. See Cecile Laborde, "Pluralism, Syndicalism and Corporatism: Leon Duguit and the Crisis of the State (1900–1925)," *History of European Ideas* 22, no. 3 (1996): 227–44, on Laski's democratization of the legacy of Leon Duguit, a principal source for his conceptualization of pluralism; Rainer Eisfeld, "The Emergence and Meaning of Socialist Pluralism," *International Political Science Review* 17, no. 3 (1996): 267–79, on other sources for Laski's pluralism and on Laski's place among other pluralist theorists; and Alan Ryan, *John Dewey and the High Tide of American Liberalism* (New York: Norton, 1995), 190, on Laski's impact on Dewey.

82. Harold Laski, *A Grammar of Politics* (London: Allen and Unwin, 1925), 432.

83. Cf. Lamb, "Laski's Ideological Metamorphosis," 244.

84. Newman, *Laski,* 83.

85. Michael Freeden, *Ideologies and Political Theory* (Oxford: Oxford University Press, 1996), 306–7.

86. Newman, *Laski,* 81.

87. Newman, *Laski,* 134.

88. Kramnick and Sheerman, *Laski,* 267, 269.

89. Friedrich Hayek, "Hayek on Hayek," in *The Collected Works of F. A. Hayek,* ed. Stephen Kresge and Leif Wenar, vol. supplement, *Hayek on Hayek: An Autobiographical Dialogue*, Oral History Program, James Buchanan, Center for the Study of Public Choice, Virginia Polytechnic University (London: Routledge, 1994), 57.

90. Friedrich A. Hayek, "The Trend of Economic Thinking," *Economica* 13, no. 2 (1933): 123.

91. Kari Polanyi-Levitt and Marguerite Mendel, "The Orgins of Market Fetishism (a Critique of Friedrich Hayek's Economic Theory)," *Monthly Review* 41, no. 2 (June 1989): 11–33.

92. Alan Ebenstein, *Friedrich Hayek: A Biography* (London: Palgrave, 2001), 37.

93. Stephen Kresge, introduction to *Hayek on Hayek: An Autobiographical Dialogue,* ed. Stephen Kresge and Leif Wenar (Chicago: University of Chicago Press, 1994), 4–5. Cf. Walter Block who quotes Hayek as referring to "the shock therapy by which, more than fifty years ago, the late Ludwig von Mises converted me to a consistent free market position" in Walter Block, WBlock@MAIL.UCA.EDU, "Minogue in the TLS," in *Hayek List Serv,* 1/23/00 (January 22, 2000); and Greg Ransom on myths about the relationship between von Mises and Hayek, "The Significance of Myth and Misunderstanding in Social Science Narrative: Opening Access to Hayek's Copernican Revolution in Economics" (paper presented at the History of Economics Society and Southern Economics Association, June 28–July 2, 1996; November 23–25, 1996 University of British Columbia; Washington, D.C., 1996), www.hayekcenter.org/friedrichhayek/hayekmyth.htm [accessed March 6, 2003].

94. Friedrich Hayek, "Hayek on Hayek," in *The Collected Works of F. A. Hayek,* ed. Stephen Kresge and Leif Wenar, vol. supplement, *Hayek on Hayek: An Autobiographical Dialogue* (London: Routledge, 1994), 70.

95. Bruce Caldwell, introduction to *The Collected Works of F. A. Hayek,* ed. Bruce Caldwell, vol. 10, *Socialism and War: Essays, Documents, Reviews* (Chicago: University of Chicago Press, 1997), 7–9.

96. Friedrich Hayek, "The Economics of the 1920's as Seen from Vienna," in *The Collected Works of F. A. Hayek,* ed. Peter Klein, vol. 4, *The Fortunes of Liberalism* (Chicago: University of Chicago Press, 1963), 35.

97. In Hayek, "Hayek on Hayek," 154.

98. Hayek, "Hayek on Hayek," 7.

99. Massie, *Dreadnought,* 872–82.

100. Massie, *Dreadnought,* 883.

101. Kresge, introduction, 7.

102. Erik Erikson, *Life History and the Historical Moment* (New York: Norton, 1975), 114.

103. Bruce Caldwell, introduction to *The Collected Works of F. A. Hayek,* ed. Bruce Caldwell, vol. 9, *Contra Keynes and Cambridge* (Chicago: University of Chicago Press, 1995), 12.

104. Hayek, "The Economics of the 1920's," 36.

105. Hayek, http://www.mises.org/misesbib/m78bnint.asp.

106. Hayek, "The Economics of the 1920's," 26.

107. Thomas Babbington Macaulay, "Southey's Colloquies on Society," in *Critical and Historical Essays* (London: Longman, Brown, Green, and Longmans, 1843), 217–69. Cf. Hayek, "The Economics of the 1920's," 28, n. 34.

108. Hayek, "The Economics of the 1920's," 29.

109. Charlotte Cubitt, interview by author, Colchester, U.K., August 8, 1997. Cf. Ebenstein, *Hayek,* 94.

110. Hayek, "Hayek on Hayek," 6.

111. Evan Bukey, *Hitler's Austria: Popular Sentiment in the Nazi Era, 1938–1945* (Chapel Hill: University of North Carolina Press, 2000), 16.

112. Friedrich Hayek, "The Economics of the 1930's as Seen from London," in *The Collected Works of F. A. Hayek,* ed. Bruce Caldwell, vol. 9, *Contra Keynes and Cambridge* (Chicago: University of Chicago Press, 1963), 59.

113. Cf. Hayek, "The Economics of the 1930's," 58–59; Hayek, "Hayek on Hayek," 88–89. Hayek goes on to comment "This sounds much more like Laski than like Keynes."

114. Caldwell, *Contra,* 16.

115. Hayek points out that Darwin derived his image of natural selection as an evolutionary process from contemporary views of "social evolution," not the other way around. Cultural inheritance, rather than genetic transmission, becomes the vehicle for the latter. Friedrich Hayek, *The Constitution of Liberty* (Chicago: University of Chicago Press, 1960), 59.

116. Hayek, "The Economics of the 1920's," 27.

117. Hayek, "Hayek on Hayek," 98.

Chapter 5

1. Cf. John Maynard Keynes, "My Early Beliefs," in *Two Memoirs* (1938; reprint, New York: Augustus M. Kelly, 1949), 38–39; Robert J. Skidelsky, *John Maynard Keynes: A Biography,* vol. 2, *The Economist as Saviour 1920–1937* (London: Allen Lane/Penguin, 1992), 130.

2. Cf. Robert J. Skidelsky, *John Maynard Keynes: A Biography,* vol. 1, *Hopes Betrayed 1883–1920* (New York: Viking Penguin, 1983), 386; Skidelsky, *Keynes,* vol. 2, 91; Donald E. Moggridge, *Maynard Keynes: An Economist's Biography* (London: Routledge, 1992), 325.

3. Harold Laski, *Studies in Law and Politics* (New Haven, Conn.: Yale University Press, 1932), 188–91.

4. In Robert Skidelsky, "The Labour Party and Keynes," in *Interests and Obsessions,* ed. Robert Skidelsky (London: Macmillan, 1993), 107.

5. Skidelsky, *Keynes,* vol. 2, 378–79.

6. Skidelsky, *Keynes,* vol. 2, 281–82.

7. Friedrich Hayek, "Reflections on the Pure Theory of Money of Mr. J. M. Keynes," in *The Collected Works of F. A. Hayek,* ed. Bruce Caldwell, vol. 9, *Contra Keynes and Cambridge* (Chicago: University of Chicago Press, 1995). Originally Published as F. A. Hayek, "Reflections on the Pure Theory of Money," *Economica* 11, no. 33 (August 1931) 270–295. (Chicago: University of Chicago Press, 1931), 145.

8. John Maynard Keynes, "The Pure Theory of Money: A Reply to Dr. Hayek," in *The Collected Works of F. A. Hayek,* vol. 9. Originally published as J. M. Keynes, "The Pure Theory of Money. A Reply to Dr. Hayek," *Economica* 11, no. 34 (November 1931), 387–97. (Chicago: University of Chicago Press, 1931), 153.

9. Skidelsky, *Keynes,* vol. 2, 331–32.

10. John Maynard Keynes, *A Treatise on Money,* ed. Donald Moggridge, *The Collected Writings of John Maynard Keynes,* vol. 6 (1930; reprint, Macmillan/Cambridge University Press for the Royal Economic Society © 1989, 1971), 132.

11. Skidelsky, *Keynes,* vol. 2, 236.

12. Adam Smith, *The Theory of Moral Sentiments,* in *The Glasgow Edition of the Works and Correspondence of Adam Smith,* ed. R. L. Meek, D. D. Raphael, and P. G. Stein (Indianapolis, Ind.: Liberty Fund, 1984), 86.

13. Smith, *Moral Sentiments,* 86.

14. Maynard Keynes, "Economic Possibilities for Our Grandchildren," in *Essays in Persuasion, The Collected Writings of John Maynard Keynes,* vol. 9, ed. Elizabeth Johnson and Donald Moggridge (Cambridge: Cambridge University Press, 1930), 329.

15. Peter Clarke, *The Keynesian Revolution in the Making, 1924–1936* (New York: Oxford University Press, 1988), 74.

16. John Maynard Keynes, Author, *The Collected Writings of John Maynard Keynes,* ed. Donald Moggridge, vol. 20, *Activities 1929–1931: Rethinking Employment and Unemployment Policies* (London: Macmillan/Cambridge University Press for the Royal Economic Society, 1981), 597.

17. Moggridge, *Economist's Biography,* 506–7, 526.

18. Clarke, *Keynesian Revolution,* 86–87.

19. Moggridge, *Economist's Biography,* 492; Skidelsky, *Keynes,* vol. 2, 368–77.

20. Clarke, *Keynesian Revolution,* 137, 156, 161, 176; Lionel (Lord) Robbins, *Autobiography of an Economist* (London: Macmillan, 1971), 151.

21. Clarke, *Keynesian Revolution,* 184, 197; David Felix, *Biography of an Idea: John Maynard Keynes and the General Theory* (New Brunswick, N.J.: Transaction, 1995), 108–9.

22. Clarke, *Keynesian Revolution,* 205–6; Felix, *Biography of an Idea,* 95.

23. Clarke, *Keynesian Revolution,* 295; Felix, *Biography of an Idea,* 100.

24. Robbins, *Autobiography,* 153–54.

25. The debate over how much good Keynes's approach would have done is of epic proportions. An assessment based on the data of the time may be found in W. R. Garside and T. J. Hatton, "Keynesian Policy and British Unemployment in the

1930s," *Economic History Review* 38, no. 1 (1985): 83–88, excerpted in *John Maynard Keynes (1883–1946),* ed. Mark Blaug (Cambridge, U.K.: Elgar, 1991), 400–405. Cf. Peter Clarke, *Hope and Glory: Britain 1900–1990* (London: Allen Lane/Penguin, 1996), 147–50.

26. Skidelsky, *Keynes,* vol. 2, 437.

27. Skidelsky, *Keynes,* vol. 2, 470.

28. John Maynard Keynes, "Mr. Roosevelt's Experiments," *Times* (London), January 2, 1934, 11.

29. Jose Harris, *William Beveridge: A Biography,* rev. ed. (Oxford: Oxford University Press, 1997), 316–17.

30. Robert J. Skidelsky, *John Maynard Keynes: A Biography,* vol. 3, *Fighting for Britain 1937–1946* (London: Macmillan, 2000), 92.

31. Alec Cairncross, "Keynes the Man," *The Economist* 339, no. 7,962 (1996): 75–77.

32. Skidelsky, *Keynes,* vol. 2, 504–5.

33. Felix, *Biography of an Idea,* 227–29.

34. Letter from John Maynard Keynes to Felix Frankfurter, May, 30, 1934, quoted in Skidelsky, *Keynes,* vol. 2, 506.

35. Don Patinkin, "On the Chronology of the General Theory," *The Economic Journal* 103 (May 1993): 647–61.

36. Clarke, *Keynesian Revolution,* 19.

37. John Maynard Keynes, *The Collected Writings of John Maynard Keynes,* vol. 7, *The General Theory of Employment, Interest and Money* (London: Macmillan/Cambridge University Press for the Royal Economic Society, 1936), 33.

38. Keynes, *The General Theory,* 254, 372–73.

39. Moggridge, *Economist's Biography,* 558.

40. Keynes, *The General Theory,* 145.

41. Felix, *Biography of an Idea,* 110.

42. Mark Blaug, *John Maynard Keynes: Life, Ideas, Legacy* (London: Macmillan, 1990), 22–23, 26–27.

43. Keynes, *The General Theory,* 269.

44. Clarke, *Hope and Glory,* 179.

45. Isaac Kramnick and Barry Sheerman, *Harold Laski: A Life on the Left* (London: The Penguin Group, 1993), 350.

46. Paul Addison, *The Road to 1945,* rev. ed. (London: Pimlico, 1994), 26.

47. Felix, *Biography of an Idea,* 210–11.

48. Richard Cockett, *Thinking the Unthinkable,* rev. ed. (London: Fontana, 1995), 54–55.

49. Kramnick and Sheerman, *Laski,* 107; Michael Newman, *Harold Laski: A Political Biography* (Basingstoke, U.K.: Macmillan, 1993), 54–55.

50. Kramnick and Sheerman, *Laski,* 291.

51. LSE economist John Hicks thought that the second quarter of the twentieth century belonged to Adolf Hitler, while the third should be assigned to Keynes. Hayek is reported to have commented, "I do not feel that the harm that Keynes did is really

so great as to justify *that* description." In Andrew Gamble, *Hayek: The Iron Cage of Liberty* (Boulder, Colo.: Westview Press, 1996), 156.

52. Norman Birnbaum, "The Elusive Synthesis: Review of Harold Laski: A Life on the Left, by Isaac Kramnick and Barry Sheerman," *Nation,* June 13, 1995, 835.

53. Harold Laski, "Can Business Be Civilized," in *The Dangers of Obedience and Other Essays* (New York: Harper and Brothers, 1930), 217.

54. Laski, "Can Business Be Civilized," 237.

55. Laski, "Can Business Be Civilized," 271.

56. Jean-Jacques Rousseau, "Du Contrat Social," trans. Gerard Hopkins, in *Social Contract,* ed. Ernest Barker (1762; reprint, Oxford: Oxford University Press, 1960), 291.

57. Laski, "Can Business Be Civilized," 291.

58. Harold Laski, *Authority in the Modern State* (New Haven, Conn.: Yale University Press, 1919), 78.

59. Kramnick and Sheerman, *Laski,* 184.

60. Laski, "Can Business Be Civilized," 286.

61. Kingsley Martin, *Harold Laski: A Biographical Memoir* (London: Victor Gollancz, 1953), 80–83.

62. Clarke, *Hope and Glory,* 159.

63. Martin, *Harold Laski,* 70.

64. Skidelsky, *Keynes,* vol. 2, 400–401.

65. Peter Lamb, "Laski's Ideological Metamorphosis," *Journal of Political Ideologies* 4, no. 2 (June 1999): 248.

66. Martin, *Harold Laski,* 88.

67. David Cannadine, *Aspects of Aristocracy: Grandeur and Decline in Modern Britain* (London: Penguin, 1994), 159.

68. Kramnick and Sheerman, *Laski,* 245.

69. Cannadine, *Aristocracy,* 158–59.

70. Harold Laski, *Lecture: Introduction to Contemporary Politics,* ed. Francis G. Wilson (Seattle: University of Washington Bookstore, 1939), 69.

71. Laski, *Contemporary Politics,* 70.

72. Laski, *Studies in Law and Politics,* 68.

73. Rodney Barker, "Socialism," in *The Blackwell Encyclopaedia of Political Thought,* ed. David Miller (London: Blackwell, 1987), 485–89.

74. Laski, "Can Business Be Civilized," 236–37.

75. Harold Laski, *The Limitations of the Expert,* Fabian Tract No. 235 (London: The Fabian Society, 1931).

76. Martin, *Harold Laski,* 85; Newman, *Laski,* 147–62.

77. Addison, *Road,* 140.

78. Kramnick and Sheerman, *Laski,* 311–12, 344–45. Cf. Noel Annan, *Our Age: The Generation That Made Post-War Britain* (London: Fontana, 1990), 238–39.

79. Martin, *Harold Laski,* 98–99; Elizabeth Durbin, *New Jerusalems: The Labour Party and the Economics of Democratic Socialism* (London: Routledge and Kegan Paul, 1985), 120.

80. Cited in Kramnick and Sheerman, *Laski,* 312.

81. Kramnick and Sheerman, *Laski,* 310–11.

82. Maynard Keynes, April 20, 1932, File: 13, Keynes-Laski. Unpublished writings of J. M. Keynes copyright © 2003 by the Provost and Scholars of King's College, Cambridge.

83. Newman, *Laski,* 162–64.

84. Martin, *Harold Laski,* 93–94.

85. Kramnick and Sheerman, *Laski,* 328–31; cf. Ralf Dahrendorf, *LSE: A History of the London School of Economics and Political Science 1895–1995* (Oxford: Oxford University Press, 1995), 279–83; E. Graham-Little, "Prof. Laski's Lecture," *Daily Telegraph,* July 14, 1936.

86. Harold Laski, Keynes, A, 34, File: 133, Laski: Keynes 22/7/36, Modern Archive, King's College, Cambridge University.

87. Laski, "No" from Maynard Keynes and Harold Laski, "Can America Spend Its Way to Recovery?" *Redbook,* December 1934, 76.

88. Newman, *Laski,* 150–51.

89. Harold Laski, *The Danger of Being a Gentleman, and Other Essays* (New York: Viking Press, 1940), 17, 20.

90. Laski, *The Danger of Being a Gentleman,* 29–31.

91. Harold Laski, *The State in Theory and Practice* (New York: Viking Press, 1935), 165.

92. The passage appears on pages 314–15 in *Essays in Persuasion* as reprinted by Norton Publishers, New York, 1963.

93. Cf. Laski, *The State,* 164–65; Kramnick and Sheerman, *Laski,* 360–61.

94. Cited in Kramnick and Sheerman, *Laski,* 322–23.

95. Dahrendorf, *LSE,* 197; cf. Harris, *William Beveridge,* 321.

96. Robbins, *Autobiography,* 141.

97. The story was told to the author by Norman Birnbaum, who was present at Sir Alexander Carr-Saunders retirement dinner in 1957.

98. Harold Laski, *The American Presidency, an Interpretation* (New York: Harper and Brothers, 1940); Newman, *Laski,* 176, 181–82.

99. Kramnick and Sheerman, *Laski,* 195, 397.

100. Clarke, *Hope and Glory,* 198; Newman, *Laski,* 206.

101. Newman, *Laski,* 199, 284–87.

102. Stéphane Courtois et al., *The Black Book of Communism: Crimes, Terror, Repression,* trans. Jonathan Murphy and Mark Kramer, ed. Consulting Editor Mark Kramer (Cambridge, Mass.: Harvard University Press, 1999), 291–97.

103. Addison, *Road,* 51.

104. Kramnick and Sheerman, *Laski,* 361; Harold Laski, "Why I Am a Marxist," *Nation,* Jan. 14, 1939.

105. Alan Ebenstein, *Friedrich Hayek: A Biography* (London: Palgrave, 2001), 56.

106. One Senator Orndorff wrote the governor that he was "running a temperature" over reports of Laski's speeches and recommended that measures of censorship be put in place such as had recently been undertaken at the Bellingham Normal

School, where the president had been fired for leftist sympathies. The school was the predecessor to this author's current institution, Western Washington University. W. R. Orndorff and M. G. Lowman, 46, Laski, April 17, 1939, Orndorff: Martin, Palo Alto, Calif., Hoover Institution Archives.

107. In Kramnick and Sheerman, *Laski*, 406.

108. Bruce Caldwell, introduction to *The Collected Works of F. A. Hayek,* ed. Bruce Caldwell, vol. 9, *Contra Keynes and Cambridge* (Chicago: University of Chicago Press, 1995), 16.

109. Friedrich Hayek, "Hayek on Hayek," in *The Collected Works of F. A. Hayek,* ed. Stephen Kresge and Leif Wenar, vol. supplement, *Hayek on Hayek: An Autobiographical Dialogue,* W. W. Bartley III Audiotape Archive, 1984–1988 (London: Routledge, 1994), 76–77.

110. Friedrich Hayek, "Hayek on Hayek," in *The Collected Works of F. A. Hayek,* ed. Stephen Kresge and Leif Wenar, vol. supplement, *Hayek on Hayek: An Autobiographical Dialogue* (London: Routledge, 1994), 77.

111. Ebenstein, *Hayek,* 53.

112. Robbins, *Autobiography,* 127–28.

113. Ebenstein, *Hayek,* 60.

114. Hayek, "Hayek on Hayek," 78.

115. Harris, *William Beveridge,* 80.

116. Charlotte Cubitt, *Hayek: An Affectionate Memoir*. Unpublished MSS of Draft of Memoir, rev. ed. (Colchester, England, 2000), sec. 1, p. 4.

117. Dahrendorf, *LSE,* 188; Cockett, *Thinking,* 29–31.

118. Dahrendorf, *LSE,* 223–24.

119. Quoted in Harris, *William Beveridge,* 289.

120. Harold Laski, *On the Study of Politics: An Inaugural Lecture,* delivered on October 22, 1926 (London: Humphrey Milford/Oxford University Press, 1926), 16.

121. In Cockett, *Thinking,* 29.

122. In Cockett, *Thinking,* 31.

123. John Kenneth Galbraith, *A Life in Our Times: Memoirs* (New York: Ballantine Books, 1981), 78.

124. Harris, *William Beveridge,* 281.

125. Dahrendorf, *LSE,* 223–24.

126. Hayek, "Bartley Audiotape Archive," 82.

127. Cockett, *Thinking,* 24–25.

128. Hayek, "Reflections," 121.

129. Caldwell, *Contra,* 28–31.

130. In Caldwell, *Contra,* 27.

131. See the account and the excerpts from the reviews in Caldwell, *Contra,* 25–31. Cf. Dahrendorf, *LSE,* 217.

132. Hayek, "Reflections," 122.

133. Keynes, "Reply to Dr. Hayek," 149.

134. Dahrendorf, *LSE,* 220.

135. Friedrich Hayek, "The Economics of the 1920's as Seen from Vienna," in *The Collected Works of F. A. Hayek,* ed. Peter Klein, vol. 4, *The Fortunes of Liberalism* (Chicago: University of Chicago Press, 1963), 37.

136. Keynes, "Reply to Dr. Hayek," 154.

137. Skidelsky, *Keynes,* vol. 2, 458–59.

138. Hayek, "Hayek on Hayek," 88.

139. Cockett, *Thinking*, 41; Moggridge, *Economist's Biography,* 544–45.

140. Dahrendorf, *LSE,* 211; Clarke, *Keynesian Revolution,* 284–85.

141. Cockett, *Thinking,* 34.

142. Friedrich A. Hayek, "The Trend of Economic Thinking," *Economica* 13, no. 2 (1933): 133.

143. Dahrendorf, *LSE,* 215–16.

144. Cockett, *Thinking,* 54–55.

145. Dahrendorf, *LSE,* 291.

146. Friedrich Hayek, "The Economics of the 1930's as Seen from London," in *The Collected Works of F. A. Hayek,* ed. Bruce Caldwell, vol. 9, *Contra Keynes and Cambridge* (Chicago: University of Chicago Press, 1963), 60.

147. In Dahrendorf, *LSE,* 219–20.

148. Hayek, "The Economics of the 1930's," 60.

149. Clarke, *Keynesian Revolution,* 238.

150. Clarke, *Keynesian Revolution,* 282, 310.

151. Cf. John B. Davis, "Keynes's Critiques of Moore: Philosophical Foundations of Keynes's Economics," *Cambridge Journal of Economics* 15 (1991): 61–77; Gladys Foster, "The Compatibility of Keynes's Ideas with Institutionalist Philosophy," *Journal of Economic Issues* 25, no. 2 (1991): 561–69.

152. Hayek, "The Trend," 129.

153. Friedrich Hayek, "Economics and Knowledge," *Economica* 4 (February 1937): 33–54.

154. Hayek, "Hayek on Hayek," 79–80; Hayek, "The Economics of the 1930's," 62–63.

155. Caldwell, *Contra,* 36.

156. Charlotte Cubitt, *Hayek: An Affectionate Memoir.* Unpublished MSS of Draft of Memoir (Colchester, England, 1999), 10.

157. Evan Bukey, *Hitler's Austria: Popular Sentiment in the Nazi Era, 1938–1945* (Chapel Hill: University of North Carolina Press, 2000), 1–39; Kenneth Hoover et al., *Ideology and Political Life,* 3rd ed. (New York: Harcourt, 2001), 135–46.

158. Cockett, *Thinking*, 9–10.

159. Cockett, *Thinking*, 54–55.

160. Dahrendorf, *LSE,* 220.

161. Caldwell, *Contra* 36.

162. Hayek, "The Economics of the 1930's," 62–63. This was a theme he adapted from von Mises who had published a famous attack on socialism in 1922 and had carried through as an Austrian opponent of fascism—a position that contributed to von

Mises' departure from Austria for Switzerland in 1934. Later, in the 1940s, Ludwig von Mises came to the United States and played an important role in the revival of classical liberalism among American economists and intellectuals. Cockett, *Thinking,* 23–24.

163. Hayek, "Hayek on Hayek," 102.

164. Caldwell, *Contra,* 42–43. Cf. Hayek, "Hayek on Hayek," 11–12.

165. Friedrich Hayek, *The Pure Theory of Capital* (London: Routledge and Kegan Paul, 1941), 374.

166. Gamble, *Hayek,* 22–23.

167. Hayek, *The Pure Theory of Capital,* 294–322.

168. Bruce Caldwell, introduction to *The Collected Works of F. A. Hayek,* ed. Bruce Caldwell, vol. 10, *Socialism and War: Essays, Documents, Reviews* (Chicago: University of Chicago Press, 1997), 29–30.

Chapter 6

1. Peter Clarke, *The Keynesian Revolution in the Making, 1924–1936* (New York: Oxford University Press, 1988), 321–22; Peter Clarke, *A Question of Leadership: Gladstone to Thatcher* (London: Hamish Hamilton, 1991), 168.

2. Donald E. Moggridge, *Maynard Keynes: An Economist's Biography* (London: Routledge, 1992), 631–32.

3. Michael Newman, *Harold Laski: A Political Biography* (Basingstoke, U.K.: Macmillan, 1993), 253.

4. Moggridge, *Economist's Biography,* 632–33.

5. Friedrich Hayek, "Hayek on Hayek," in *The Collected Works of F. A. Hayek,* ed. Stephen Kresge and Leif Wenar, vol. supplement, *Hayek on Hayek: An Autobiographical Dialogue* (London: Routledge, 1994), 91.

6. Maynard Keynes, Keynes: Hayek 6/3/40, Palo Alto, Calif., Hoover Institution Archives. Unpublished writings of J. M. Keynes copyright © 2003 by the Provost and Scholars of King's College, Cambridge.

7. Stephen Kresge, introduction to *Hayek on Hayek: An Autobiographical Dialogue,* ed. Stephen Kresge and Leif Wenar (Chicago: University of Chicago Press, 1994), 12–13.

8. Peter Clarke, *Hope and Glory: Britain 1900–1990* (London: Allen Lane/Penguin, 1996), 210.

9. Moggridge, *Economist's Biography,* 647.

10. Robert J. Skidelsky, *John Maynard Keynes: A Biography,* vol. 3, *Fighting for Britain 1937–1946* (London: Macmillan, 2000), 141.

11. Moggridge, *Economist's Biography,* 638–39.

12. Harris, *William Beveridge,* 40.

13. Paul Addison, *The Road to 1945,* rev. ed. (London: Pimlico, 1994), 217.

14. Moggridge, *Economist's Biography,* 708–9; Jose Harris, *William Beveridge: A Biography,* rev. ed. (Oxford: Oxford University Press, 1997), 399.

15. In Harris, *William Beveridge,* 399, 314, 414.

16. Skidelsky, *Keynes,* vol. 3, 264.

17. Moggridge, *Economist's Biography,* 308–9; John Maynard Keynes, "Draft for the House of Lords on 24 February 1943," in *The Collected Writings of John Maynard Keynes,* ed. Donald Moggridge, vol. 27, *Activities 1940–1946. Shaping the Post-War World: Employment and Commodities* (Cambridge: Macmillan/Cambridge University Press for the Royal Economic Society © 1980, 1943), 259.

18. Keynes, "Draft for the House of Lords on 24 February 1943," 261.

19. Moggridge, *Economist's Biography,* 643, 662–63.

20. Quoted in Addison, *Road,* 227.

21. Richard Cockett, *Thinking the Unthinkable,* rev. ed. (London: Fontana, 1995), 65.

22. Harris, *William Beveridge,* 441–43.

23. Harris, *William Beveridge,* 444.

24. Skidelsky, *Keynes,* vol. 3, 274.

25. Moggridge, *Economist's Biography,* 746.

26. In Moggridge, *Economist's Biography,* 740.

27. Skidelsky, *Keynes,* vol. 3, 386–92.

28. Skidelsky, *Keynes,* vol. 3, 310.

29. Lionel (Lord) Robbins, *Autobiography of an Economist* (London: Macmillan, 1971), 199–200.

30. Jacqueline Best, "Hollowing Out Keynesian Norms: How the Search for a Technical Fix Undermined the Bretton Woods Regime" (paper presented at the American Political Science Association, Boston, August 30, 2002).

31. Cf. comments by Robert Skidelsky and Milton Friedman in Mark Blaug, *John Maynard Keynes: Life, Ideas, Legacy* (London: Macmillan, 1990), 53–54, 85 and Peter Clarke in Clarke, *Keynesian Revolution,* 229.

32. Cf. John Cassidy, "The New World Disorder," *New Yorker*, October 26 and November 2 1998, 197–207; Joseph Stiglitz, *Globalization and Its Discontents* (New York: Norton, 2002).

33. Alfred Borneman, "Fifty Years of Ideology: A Selective Survey of Academic Economics in the U.S. 1930 to 1980," *Journal of Economic Studies* 8, no. 1 (1981): 23.

34. Moggridge, *Economist's Biography,* 824.

35. Addison, *Road,* 17.

36. In Cockett, *Thinking,* 50.

37. Isaac Kramnick and Barry Sheerman, *Harold Laski: A Life on the Left* (London: The Penguin Group, 1993), 434.

38. Harold Laski, "British Communists Help Hitler," *Daily Herald,* February 15, 1941.

39. Kramnick and Sheerman, *Laski,* 423.

40. Kramnick and Sheerman, *Laski,* 424.

41. Harold Laski, *Is This an Imperialist War?* Pamphlet (London: Labour Party, 1940), 13.

42. In Kingsley Martin, *Harold Laski: A Biographical Memoir* (London: Victor Gollancz, 1953), 193.

43. Laski, *Is This an Imperialist War?*

44. Newman, *Laski*, 206, 212.

45. Addison, *Road*, 168.

46. Kramnick and Sheerman, *Laski*, 421–22.

47. Newman, *Laski*, 208.

48. Martin, *Harold Laski*, 127.

49. Newman, *Laski*, 210–11.

50. In Martin, *Harold Laski*, 140–41.

51. Addison, *Road,* 113.

52. In Martin, *Harold Laski,* 142.

53. Martin, *Harold Laski,* 151–52.

54. Stephen Brooke, *Labour's War: The Labour Party during the Second World War* (Oxford: Clarendon Press, 1992), 92–93.

55. Addison, *Road,* 182.

56. In Martin, *Harold Laski,* 162–63.

57. The article was by Amos Pinchot. Quoted in Martin, *Harold Laski,* 196.

58. Kramnick and Sheerman, *Laski,* 453.

59. Newman, *Laski*, 292–93; Harold Laski, "Our Liberties a Fortress," *The Listener,* June 19, 1941.

60. Harold Laski, Modern Politics Collection, Dep. 4, 165-66, December 19, 1941, File: Ms. Attlee, Draft of Great Britain, Russia, and the Labour Party Circulated to N.E.C. Press, Publicity, and Campaign Sub-Committee, Bodleian Library, Oxford University.

61. Clement Attlee, Modern Politics Collection, Dep. 4, 165–66, File: Ms. Attlee, Attlee: Chamberlain 27/12/41, Bodleian Library, Oxford University.

62. Clarke, *Hope and Glory*, 207–8.

63. Winston Churchill, University of Hull, DLA, 18, Churchill: Laski 2/3/42, Kingston-upon-Hull.

64. Newman, *Laski*, 215–16.

65. In Newman, *Laski*, 231–32.

66. Kramnick and Sheerman, *Laski,* 436–37.

67. Harold Laski, "The Problem of Mr. Churchill," *New Statesman and Nation*, May 2, 1942.

68. In Newman, *Laski,* 242. Cf. August 13, 1942. PREM 4 26/3, PRO.

69. Brooke, *Labour's War,* 96–97.

70. Newman, *Laski*, 239–40.

71. Harold Laski, British Library of Economic and Political Sciences, vol. 5, 223, Laski: Webb 7/7/42, London School of Economics.

72. Harold Laski, "U.S.S.R. is Twenty-five Tomorrow," *Daily Herald*, November 6, 1942.

73. Newman, *Laski*, 256–57.

74. Harold Laski et al., "After the Armistice," *The Listener,* August 13, 1942.

75. George Bernard Shaw, British Library of Economic and Political Sciences, Passfield, II 4 m, File: 12v, Shaw: Webb 17/2/41, London.

76. Newman, *Laski*, 215–16, 233–35.

77. Harris, *William Beveridge*, 421.

78. Harold Laski, *Reflections on the Revolution of Our Time* (New York: Viking Press, 1943), vii.

79. Cockett, *Thinking*, 61–62.

80. Kramnick and Sheerman, *Laski*, 446.

81. Kramnick and Sheerman, *Laski*, 423–25.

82. Laski, Manchester Public Library, Laski, SC, April10, 1943, File: 920, Laski: Roosevelt, Manchester, England.

83. Kramnick and Sheerman, *Laski*, 451–52.

84. Kramnick and Sheerman, *Laski*, 465, 459–60.

85. Newman, *Laski*, 246–47.

86. Laski, "Coalitions and the Constitution," *New Statesman and Nation*, October 23, 1943.

87. Polanyi, "Mr. Laski's Thesis," *Manchester Guardian*, October 8, 1943.

88. Laski, "Revolt in the Urban Desert," *The Observer*, October 10, 1943.

89. Newman, *Laski*, 250–51.

90. Attlee, University of Hull Library, Laski, 13, File: DLA, Attlee: Laski 1/5/44, Kingston-upon-Hull.

91. Laski, "A Friendship That Can Change the World," *Reynolds News*, February 27, 1944.

92. Kramnick and Sheerman, *Laski*, 511.

93. In Martin, *Harold Laski*, 166–67.

94. Hayek, "Hayek on Hayek," 85.

95. Hayek, "The Economics of the 1920's as Seen from Vienna," in *The Collected Works of F. A. Hayek*, ed. Peter Klein, vol. 4, *The Fortunes of Liberalism* (Chicago: University of Chicago Press, 1963), 33–34.

96. Hayek, "Hayek on Hayek," 91.

97. Robbins, *Autobiography*, 188.

98. Hayek, "Hayek on Hayek," in *The Collected Works of F. A. Hayek*, ed. Stephen Kresge and Leif Wenar, vol. supplement, *Hayek on Hayek: An Autobiographical Dialogue*, Oral History Program, Axel Leijonhufvud, Department of Economics, UCLA (London: Routledge, 1994), 86.

99. Hayek, "Review of Sir William Beveridge's *Full Employment in a Free Society: A Report*," *Fortune* (Chicago) (1945): 234, *The Collected Works of F. A. Hayek*, ed. Bruce Caldwell (Chicago: University of Chicago Press).

100. The phrase "economics of abundance" was in the air. Laski had declared that the purpose of the war was to secure the Four Freedoms that, in turn, required that the postwar world "be one in which the principle of abundance replaces the principle of scarcity as the foundation of economic life." Harold Laski, "Great Britain, Russia and the Labour Party," in Modern Politics Collection, Dep. 4, 165-66 (note 60 in this section).

101. Felix, *Biography of an Idea: John Maynard Keynes and the General Theory* (New Brunswick, N.J.: Transaction, 1995), 230.

102. Friedrich Hayek, *The Constitution of Liberty* (Chicago: University of Chicago Press, 1960), 280.

103. Laski, "Great Britain, Russia and the Labour Party." Draft of pamphlet.

104. Hayek, "Hayek on Hayek," 16.

105. Hayek, "Hayek on Hayek," 106–7.

106. Hayek, *The Road to Serfdom,* introduction by Milton Friedman, Fiftieth Anniversary Edition (Chicago: University of Chicago Press, 1944), 11–12.

107. Hayek, *Serfdom,* 163.

108. Hayek had originally intended to discuss Russia and Germany as parallel cases of the slide to totalitarianism but deleted most of the references to Russia after the German invasion made the communist regime an ally of the West. Cf. Ebenstein, *Friedrich Hayek: A Biography* (London: Palgrave, 2001), 141.

109. Hayek, *Serfdom,* 15.

110. Hayek, *Serfdom,* 162.

111. Hayek, *Serfdom,* 132–33.

112. Hayek, *Serfdom,* 134.

113. Hayek, *Serfdom,* 231.

114. Hayek, *Serfdom,* 235.

115. Hayek, *Serfdom,* 92–93.

116. Gregory Christainsen, " What Keynes Really Said to Hayek about Planning," *Challenge* 36, no. 4 (1993): 51.

117. In Harris, *William Beveridge,* 442.

118. In *Serfdom,* 70–71, 146, 219–20: cf. xxiv.

119. Hayek, *Serfdom,* 146.

120. Hayek, "Hayek on Hayek," in *The Collected Works of F. A. Hayek,* ed. Stephen Kresge and Leif Wenar, vol. supplement, *Hayek on Hayek: An Autobiographical Dialogue,* W. W. Bartley III Audiotape Archive, 1984–1988 (London: Routledge, 1994), 85.

121. Maynard Keynes, *J. M. Keynes: F. Hayek 28/6/44, The Collected Writings of John Maynard Keynes*, ed. Donald Moggridge, vol. 27, *Activities 1940–1946, Shaping the Post-War World: Employment and Commodities* (Cambridge: Macmillan/Cambridge University Press for the Royal Economic Society, 1944), 385–88; Friedrich Hayek, "The Keynes Centenary: The Austrian Critique," in *The Essence of Hayek,* ed. Chiaki Nishiyama and Kurt Leube (Stanford, Calif.: The Hoover Institution Press, 1983), 50; Bruce Caldwell, introduction to *The Collected Works of F. A. Hayek,* ed. Bruce Caldwell, vol. 9, *Contra Keynes and Cambridge* (Chicago: University of Chicago Press, 1995), 45–46.

122. Keynes, 1944. *J. M. Keynes: F. Hayek 28/6/44.*

123. Keynes, 1944. *J. M. Keynes: F. Hayek 28/6/44.*

124. Schumpeter, "Hayek on Liberty," in *Friedrich A. Hayek: Critical Perspectives (1991),* ed. John C. Wood and Ronald N. Wood, vol. 2 (London: Routledge, 1946), 67.

125. Ebenstein, *Hayek,* 353.

CHAPTER 7

1. Donald E. Moggridge, *Maynard Keynes: An Economist's Biography* (London: Routledge, 1992), 465.

2. Jose Harris, *William Beveridge: A Biography,* rev. ed. (Oxford: Oxford University Press, 1997), 449.

3. George Kennan, *Memoirs 1925–1950* (Boston: Little, Brown, 1967), 266–70.

4. David McCullough, *Truman* (New York: Simon & Schuster, 1992), 382.

5. Lord Halifax, "8 September," in *Washington Despatches 1941–1945: Weekly Political Reports from the British Embassy,* ed. Harold Nicholas (London: Weidenfeld and Nicolson, 1945), 616–17.

6. Lionel (Lord) Robbins, *Autobiography of an Economist* (London: Macmillan, 1971), 206–7.

7. Kennan, *Memoirs 1925–1950,* 266–70.

8. Moggridge, *Economist's Biography,* 816.

9. Roy Forbes Harrod, Sir, *The Life of John Maynard Keynes* (New York: Harcourt Brace, 1951), 618.

10. Lord Halifax, "9 June," in *Washington Despatches 1941–1945: Weekly Political Reports from the British Embassy,* ed. Harold Nicholas (London: Weidenfeld and Nicolson, 1945), 576.

11. Halifax, "9 June," 557, 559.

12. Isaac Kramnick and Barry Sheerman, *Harold Laski: A Life on the Left* (London: The Penguin Group, 1993), 497.

13. Robert J. Skidelsky, *John Maynard Keynes: A Biography,* vol. 3, *Fighting for Britain 1937–1946* (London: Macmillan, 2000), 418.

14. Skidelsky, *Keynes,* vol. 3, xv, 8.

15. Robbins, *Autobiography,* 208–9.

16. Skidelsky, *Keynes,* vol. 3, 448, 451.

17. Skidelsky, *Keynes,* vol. 3, 453, 480, 492.

18. Moggridge, *Economist's Biography,* 835–36.

19. Skidelsky, *Keynes,* vol. 3, 471.

20. In Skidelsky, *Keynes,* vol. 3, 472.

21. In Skidelsky, *Keynes,* vol. 3, 471.

22. Harrod, *Keynes,* 644.

23. Mark Blaug, *John Maynard Keynes: Life, Ideas, Legacy* (London: Macmillan, 1990), 26–27.

24. Seymour Harris, "Acknowledgements," in *The New Economics: Keynes' Influence on Theory and Public Policy,* ed. Seymour Harris (London: Dobson, 1947), 1.

25. Robert Clyde, "The Bland Bombshell: No One Ever Calls Him Harold," *Daily Mail,* June 21, 1945.

26. In Ralf Dahrendorf, *LSE: A History of the London School of Economics and Political Science 1895–1995* (Oxford: Oxford University Press, 1995), 365.

27. Peter Clarke, "Keynes in History," *History of Political Economy* 26, no. 1 (1994): 118.

28. Peter Clarke, *Hope and Glory: Britain 1900–1990* (London: Allen Lane/Penguin, 1996), 214–15.

29. In Kramnick and Sheerman, *Laski*, 481.

30. Michael Newman, *Harold Laski: A Political Biography* (Basingstoke, U.K.: Macmillan, 1993), 258–59.

31. Clarke, *Hope and Glory,* 197.

32. David Cannadine, *Aspects of Aristocracy: Grandeur and Decline in Modern Britain* (London: Penguin, 1994), 161–62.

33. Kramnick and Sheerman, *Laski,* 481.

34. In Richard Cockett, *Thinking the Unthinkable,* rev. ed. (London: Fontana, 1995), 92–93.

35. Kramnick and Sheerman, *Laski,* 482.

36. In Tom Driberg, *Beaverbrook: A Study in Power and Frustration* (London: Weidenfeld and Nicolson, 1956), 302–3. Disappointed members at the Conservative Party conference after the election debacle moved to kick Beaverbrook out of the party for his role in the defeat. He denied having anything to do with the speech, and laid the blame at the door of Ralph Assheton and another party official both of whom had approved it.

37. Newman, *Laski*, 263–64.

38. Stephen Brooke, *Labour's War: The Labour Party during the Second World War* (Oxford: Clarendon Press, 1992), 92–97.

39. Kramnick and Sheerman, *Laski*, 483–84.

40. Guy Eden, "Churchill Forces Laski Show-Down," *Daily Express,* July 3, 1945, 1; Winston Churchill, "Churchill: Attlee 3/7/45," *Daily Express*, July 3, 1945, 1.

41. Kingsley Martin, *Harold Laski: A Biographical Memoir* (London: Victor Gollancz, 1953), 173.

42. Paul Addison, *The Road to 1945,* rev. ed. (London: Pimlico, 1994), 266.

43. "Socialist Chance is Remote," *Daily Express,* July 5, 1945, 1.

44. Catherine Kord, "Review of Harold Laski: A Life on the Left," *The Antioch Review* (Summer 1994): 531–32. In fact, a meeting of the principals of the cabinet could have been held in LSE's faculty club. Former LSE teachers included the Prime Minister, Chancellor of the Exchequer, Secretary of State for India, and Minister of State.

45. Harold Laski, "Why I Didn't Make a Good Red Herring," *Picture Post,* August 11, 1945.

46. "Morrison Did a Cowardly Thing," *Daily Express,* July 5, 1945, 1.

47. Kramnick and Sheerman, *Laski,* 489.

48. Laski, "Why I Didn't Make a Good Red Herring."

49. Laski, "Why I Didn't Make a Good Red Herring."

50. Noel Annan, *Our Age: The Generation That Made Post-War Britain* (London: Fontana, 1990), 294–95.

51. Addison, *Road,* 264.

52. Annan, *Our Age,* 282–83.

53. Clarke, *Hope and Glory,* 214–15.

54. Clarke, *Hope and Glory,* 225–26.

55. Addison, *Road,* 274, 283.

56. Dahrendorf, *LSE,* 365.

57. Newman, *Laski,* 307.

58. Newman, *Laski,* 269–70.

59. Kramnick and Sheerman, *Laski,* 515.

60. Clement Attlee, University of Hull, DLA, 13, Attlee: Laski 20/08/45, Kingston-upon-Hull.

61. Kramnick and Sheerman, *Laski,* 574–75.

62. Newman, *Laski,* 346.

63. Kramnick and Sheerman, *Laski,* 501.

64. Kramnick and Sheerman, *Laski,* 566.

65. Newman, *Laski,* 292.

66. Friedrich Hayek, "The Mirage of Social Justice," in *Law, Legislation and Liberty: A New Statement of the Liberal Principles of Justice and Political Economy,* vol. 1, with rev. preface (1976; reprint, London: Routledge, 1982), 113 n.

67. Michael Shelden, *Orwell: The Authorized Biography* (London: Minerva, 1991), 436–37.

68. Ben Pimlott, *The Queen: A Biography of Elizabeth II* (New York: John Wiley, 1996), 84.

69. Martin, *Harold Laski,* 180–81.

70. Harold Laski, "What is Democracy?" *Manchester Guardian,* April 24, 1946.

71. Harold Laski, *The Secret Battalion: An Examination of the Communist Attitude to the British Labour Party,* Pamphlet (London: British Labour Party, 1946). Issued after Exec of BLP decided to reject the campaign for affiliation of the British CP.

72. Harold Laski, "'Try Friendship,' Says Laski to Soviet," *Manchester Evening News,* June 10, 1946.

73. "Bevin's Big Hand," *News Review,* June 20, 1946.

74. Newman, *Laski,* 299.

75. Martin, *Harold Laski,* 195.

76. Kramnick and Sheerman, *Laski,* 124.

77. In the *Newark Advertiser* and the *Daily Express.* Quoted in Kramnick and Sheerman, *Laski,* 486–87.

78. Newman, *Laski,* 273–74.

79. "Laski Libel Ruling, No Imputation of Treason: No Evidence of Malice," *Manchester Guardian,* November 30, 1946.

80. Newman, *Laski,* 115.

81. Kramnick and Sheerman, *Laski,* 517.

82. Royal Courts of Justice, *Laski v. Newark Advertiser and Parlby* (London: 1947), 72–73.

83. Harold Laski, *The State in Theory and Practice* (New York: Viking Press, 1935), 164–65.

84. Annan, *Our Age,* 246.

85. Dahrendorf, *LSE,* 367.

86. Quoted in Addison, *Road,* 232.

87. Newman, *Laski*, 278.

88. Dahrendorf, *LSE*, 367.

89. Newman, *Laski* 280.

90. Dahrendorf, *LSE*, 367.

91. Harold Laski, University of Hull Library, Laski, DLA, File: 34/38, Laski: Frida Laski 27/11/45, Kingston-upon-Hull.

92. C. Northcote Parkinson, *Left Luggage: A Caustic History of British Socialism from Marx to Wilson* (Boston: Houghton Mifflin, 1967), 128.

93. Kramnick and Sheerman, *Laski,* 546.

94. Kramnick and Sheerman, *Laski,* 509.

95. Martin, *Harold Laski*, 202–3.

96. In Newman, *Laski,* 302.

97. In Martin, *Harold Laski,* 201.

98. Martin, *Harold Laski,* 226.

99. Kramnick and Sheerman, *Laski,* 570–71.

100. Harold Laski, *The American Democracy: A Commentary and an Interpretation* (New York: Viking Press, 1948), 754.

101. Laski, *The American Democracy*, 735.

102. Laski, *The American Democracy*, 737.

103. Laski, *The American Democracy*, 738.

104. Laski, *The American Democracy*, 761.

105. Laski, *The American Democracy*, 69.

106. Newman, *Laski*, 347.

107. Kramnick and Sheerman, *Laski,* 562–64.

108. Harold Laski, "Fabian Socialism," *The Listener,* February 19, 1948.

109. Orwell: Rees 17/5/49. In *The Complete Works of George Orwell,* vol. 20, *Our Job Is to Make Life Worth Living, 1949–1950*, ed. Peter Davison with Ian Angus and Sheila Davison (London: Secker and Warburg, 1998).

110. The statement was put out by the "Freedom Defence Committee" and appeared in the *Socialist Leader* on August 21, 1948. Cf. letter by Christopher Hitchens to *The London Review of Books,* January 6, 2000, 4–5.

111. Martin, *Harold Laski,* 247–52.

112. Harold Laski, *Trade Unions in a New Society* (New York: Viking, 1949), 161, 178.

113. Kramnick and Sheerman, *Laski,* 577.

114. Isaac Kramnick, "Our Harold," *The New Republic,* December 6, 1993.

115. In Martin, *Harold Laski,* 255.

116. Newman, *Laski*, 353.

117. Kramnick and Sheerman, *Laski,* 577–78.

118. Peter Clarke, "Their Brilliant Careers, Review of the Progressive Dilemma by David Marquand," *New Statesman and Society* 3, no. 136 (February 1, 1991): 37.

119. Newman, *Laski,* 357.

120. Michael Harrington, *The Long-Distance Runner: An Autobiography* (New York: Holt, 1988), 190–91.

121. Lord Halifax, "31 March," in *Washington Despatches 1941–1945: Weekly Political Reports from the British Embassy,* ed. Harold Nicholas (London: Weidenfeld and Nicolson, 1981), 531–35. On Berlin's role, see xiii, xv.

122. Cf. letter to Karl Popper in 1944, quoted in Cockett, *Thinking,* 96.

123. Cockett, *Thinking,* 94–95.

124. Hayek told Stephen Kresge toward the end of his life that he had only met Churchill once at a dinner at LSE, but on that occasion, though Churchill was "stock drunk" and could hardly speak from a surfeit of brandy, he identified Hayek as the author of *The Road to Serfdom.* Hayek recalled, "He said just one sentence: 'You are completely right; but it will never happen in Britain.' Half an hour later he made one of the most brilliant speeches I ever heard." Hayek, "Hayek on Hayek," Oral History Program, Axel Leijonhufvud, Department of Economics, UCLA (London: Routledge, 1994), 106.

125. See Claude Robinson, F. Hayek, 46, 28, Robinson: Hayek 6/6/45, Palo Alto, Calif., Hoover Institution Archives.

126. Friedrich Hayek, "State Boss Makes State Slaves," *The Sunday Chronicle,* June 17, 1945.

127. Cockett, *Thinking,* 94–95.

128. Friedrich Hayek, "Hayek on Hayek," University of Chicago Radio Roundtable on NBC (London: Routledge, April 1945 [broadcast], 1994 [publication]), 110–11.

129. Hayek, "Hayek on Hayek," 121.

130. Albert Hirschman, *The Rhetoric of Reaction: Perversity, Futility, Jeopardy* (Cambridge, Mass.: Harvard University Press, 1991), 111–12.

131. Friedrich Hayek, F. Hayek, 106, 8, April 23, 1945 "The Road to Serfdom" (address to the Economic Club of Detroit on April 23, 1945), Palo Alto, Calif., Hoover Institution Archives.

132. Hayek, "The Road to Serfdom."

133. Loren Miller, F. Hayek, 58, 16, Miller: Hayek 25/4/45, Palo Alto, Calif., Hoover Institution Archives.

134. Friedrich Hayek, F. Hayek, 58, 16, Hayek: Luhnow 3/5/45, Palo Alto, Calif., Hoover Institution Archives.

135. Claude Robinson, F. Hayek, 46, 28, Robinson: Hayek 3/5/45, Palo Alto, Calif., Hoover Institution Archives.

136. Friedrich Hayek, F. Hayek, 46, 28, Hayek: Robinson 19/5/45, Palo Alto, Calif., Hoover Institution Archives.

137. Claude Robinson, F. Hayek, 46, 28, Robinson: Hayek 5/6/45, Palo Alto, Calif., Hoover Institution Archives.

138. Harold Luhnow, F. Hayek, 58, 16, 7 September 1945, Luhnow: Hayek 7/9/45, Palo Alto, Calif., Hoover Institution Archives.

139. Luhnow, Luhnow: Hayek 7/9/45.

140. Friedrich Hayek, F. Hayek, 58, 16, Hayek: Luhnow 9/5/48, Palo Alto, Calif., Hoover Institution Archives.

141. Charlotte Cubitt, *Hayek: An Affectionate Memoir.* Unpublished MSS of Draft of Memoir (Colchester, England, 1999), 84.

142. Quoted in Lord Harris, "The Plan to End Planning," *National Review,* June 16, 1997, 23–24.

143. Claude Robinson, F. Hayek, 46, 28, Robinson: Hayek 9/1/46, Palo Alto, Calif., Hoover Institution Archives.

144. Friedrich Hayek, F. Hayek, 46, 28, Hayek: Robinson 18/1/46, Palo Alto, Calif., Hoover Institution Archives. Finer had left LSE for the University of Chicago by this time, and Hayek would encounter him again in the next decade.

145. Aaron Director, F. Hayek, 58, 16, Director: Crane 3/5/46, Palo Alto, Calif., Hoover Institution Archives; Friedrich Hayek, F. Hayek, 58, 16, Hayek: Luhnow 23/5/46, Palo Alto, Calif., Hoover Institution Archives.

146. In Sara Diamond, *Roads to Dominion: Right Wing Movements and Political Power in the United States* (New York: Guilford Press, 1995), 27–28.

147. Harold Luhnow, F. Hayek, 58, 16, Luhnow: Hayek 6/5/46, Palo Alto, Calif., Hoover Institution Archives.

148. Loren Miller, F. Hayek, 58, 16, 7 May 1946, Miller: Hayek 7/5/46, Palo Alto, Calif., Hoover Institution Archives.

149. Friedrich Hayek, F. Hayek, 58, 16, Hayek: Luhnow 8/5/46, Palo Alto, Calif., Hoover Institution Archives.

150. Hayek, Hayek: Luhnow 23/5/46.

151. Harold Luhnow, F. Hayek, 58, 16, Luhnow: Katz 29/7/46, Palo Alto, Calif., Hoover Institution Archives.

152. Harold Luhnow, F. Hayek, 58, 16, Luhnow: Hayek 6/1/47, Palo Alto, Calif., Hoover Institution Archives.

153. Harold Luhnow, F. Hayek, 58, 16, Luhnow: Hayek 27/1/47, Palo Alto, Calif., Hoover Institution Archives.

154. Friedrich Hayek, F. Hayek, 58, 16, Hayek: Luhnow 5/2/47, Palo Alto, Calif., Hoover Institution Archives.

155. Friedrich Hayek, F. Hayek, 55, 1, Hayek: Nef 22/5/51, Palo Alto, Calif., Hoover Institution Archives.

156. Cockett, *Thinking,* 116–17.

157. Diamond, *Roads to Dominion,* 27–31.

158. Friedrich Hayek, F. Hayek, 58, 16, Hayek: Luhnow 14/10/47, Palo Alto, Calif., Hoover Institution Archives.

159. Aaron Director, F. Hayek, 58, 16, Director: Read 24/11/47, Palo Alto, Calif., Hoover Institution Archives.

160. Friedrich Hayek, F. Hayek, 58, 16, Hayek: Luhnow 8/12/47, Palo Alto, Calif., Hoover Institution Archives.

161. Jacob Viner, F. Hayek, 56, 21, Viner: Hayek 9/6/47, Palo Alto, Calif., Hoover Institution Archives.

162. Friedrich Hayek, Cubitt Archive, Hayek: Robbins 7/3/50, Colchester, England.

163. Friedrich Hayek, F. Hayek, 46, 28, Hayek: Robinson 7/2/48, Palo Alto, Calif., Hoover Institution Archives.

164. Robert Oppenheimer, F. Hayek, 58, 17, Oppenheimer: Luhnow 25/5/48, Palo Alto, Calif., Hoover Institution Archives. Oppenheimer became a cause célèbre because of allegations that he spied for the Soviets. However, though there is clear evidence that the Soviets were intensely interested in recruiting him, there is no evidence that they succeeded in getting him to spy. Joseph Persico, "The Kremlin Connection: Review of *The Haunted Wood* by Allen Weinstein and Alexander Vassiliev," *New York Times Book Review,* January 3, 1990, 6.

165. Hayek, "Hayek: Luhnow 9/5/48."

166. Harold Luhnow, F. Hayek, 58, 16, Luhnow: Hayek 10/6/48, Palo Alto, Calif., Hoover Institution Archives.

167. Friedrich Hayek, F. Hayek, 56, Viner, Hayek: Viner 11/6/48, Palo Alto, Calif., Hoover Institution Archives.

168. Jacob Viner, F. Hayek, 56, Viner, Viner: Hayek 30/7/48, Palo Alto, Calif., Hoover Institution Archives.

169. Alan Ebenstein, *Friedrich Hayek: A Biography* (London: Palgrave, 2001), 174–75.

170. Aaron Director, F. Hayek, 58, 16, Director: Hayek 14/7/48, Palo Alto, Calif., Hoover Institution Archives.

171. Friedrich Hayek, F. Hayek, 58, 16, Hayek: Robbins 26/9/48, Palo Alto, Calif., Hoover Institution Archives.

172. John U. Nef, 58, 16, Nef: Hayek 24/9/48, Palo Alto, Calif., Hoover Institution Archives.

173. Harold Luhnow, F. Hayek, 58, 16, Luhnow: Hayek 29/9/48, Palo Alto, Calif., Hoover Institution Archives.

174. Robert Hutchins, F. Hayek, 58, 16, Hutchins: Luhnow 19/10/48, Palo Alto, Calif., Hoover Institution Archives; Harold Luhnow, F. Hayek, 58, 16, Luhnow: Hutchins 20/10/48a, Palo Alto, Calif., Hoover Institution Archives; Harold Luhnow, F. Hayek, 58, 16, Luhnow: Hayek 20/10/48b, Palo Alto, Calif., Hoover Institution Archives.

175. John U. Nef, F. Hayek, 58, 16, Nef: Hayek 26/10/48, Palo Alto, Calif., Hoover Institution Archives; Robert Hutchins, F. Hayek, 55, 1, Hutchins: Hayek 24/12/48, Palo Alto, Calif., Hoover Institution Archives.

176. Friedrich Hayek, F. Hayek, 55, 1, Hayek: Nef 6/11/48, Palo Alto, Calif., Hoover Institution Archives.

177. Harold Luhnow, F. Hayek, 58, 16, Luhnow: Hayek 14/12/48, Palo Alto, Calif., Hoover Institution Archives.

178. Hayek, Hayek: Robbins 7/3/50.

179. Friedrich Hayek, Cubitt Archive, Hayek: Hella 21/12/48, Colchester, England; Hayek, Hayek: Robbins 7/3/50.

180. Hayek, Hayek: Hella 21/12/48.

181. Hella Hayek, Cubitt Archive, Hella: Hayek 11/3/49, Colchester, England.

182. John Nef, F. Hayek, 39, 39, 18 February, 1949, Nef: Hayek, Palo Alto, Calif., Hoover Institution Archives; John Nef, F. Hayek, 39, 39, Nef: Hayek 7/3/49, Palo Alto, Calif., Hoover Institution Archives.

183. Friedrich Hayek, F. Hayek, 58, 17, Hayek: Luhnow 7/5/49, Palo Alto, Calif., Hoover Institution Archives.

184. Hayek, Hayek: Robbins 7/3/50.

185. Friedrich Hayek, F. Hayek, 39, 39, Hayek: Nef 4/6/49, Palo Alto, Calif., Hoover Institution Archives; John Nef, F. Hayek, 39, 39, Nef: Hayek 26/8/49, Palo Alto, Calif., Hoover Institution Archives.

186. Ebenstein, *Hayek*, 169.

187. Friedrich Hayek, F. Hayek, 39, 39, Hayek: Nef 4/5/50, Palo Alto, Calif., Hoover Institution Archives.

188. Robert Hutchins, F. Hayek, 55, Hutchins: Hayek 12/1/50, Palo Alto, Calif., Hoover Institution Archives.

189. John Nef, F. Hayek, 39, 39, Nef: Hayek 18/1/50, Palo Alto, Calif., Hoover Institution Archives.

190. Lionel Robbins, Cubitt Archive, Robbins: Hayek 28/2/50, Colchester, England.

191. Friedrich Hayek, F. Hayek, 58, 17, Hayek: Luhnow 11/3/50, Palo Alto, Calif., Hoover Institution Archives.

192. Hayek, Hayek: Luhnow 11/3/50, Hayek, "Hayek: Nef 4/5/50."

193. Friedrich Hayek, "Hayek: Luhnow," F. Hayek (Palo Alto, Calif.: Hoover Institution Archives, March 11, 1950), 58.

194. Hayek, Hayek: Luhnow 11/3/50.

195. Lionel Robbins, Cubitt Archive, Robbins: Hayek 14/3/50, Colchester, England.

196. Friedrich Hayek, Cubitt Archive, Hayek: Robbins 17/3/50, Colchester, England.

197. Lionel Robbins, Cubitt Archive, Robbins: Hayek 21/3/50, Colchester, England.

198. Friedrich August von Hayek versus Helen Berta Maria von Fritsch von Hayek, No. 12166 *Divorce Decree* (July 13, 1950), Chancery Court of Washington County, Arkansas: 193–96, book 42. Alan Ebenstein reports that Hayek's royalties never amounted to more than £5,000 ($35,000 in current dollars as of the time of his divorce) in any year prior to receiving the Nobel Prize. Ebenstein, *Hayek*, 209.

199. LSE Assistant Secretary and Accountant, The Hoover Institution, Hayek, December 5, 1949, Record of Salary, Stanford University.

200. Lionel Robbins, Cubitt Archive, Robbins: Hayek 30/10/50, Colchester, England.

201. Lionel Robbins, Cubitt Archive, Robbins: Hayek 23/11/50, Colchester, England; Friedrich Hayek, Cubitt Archive, Hayek: Robbins 8/12/50, Colchester, England.

202. Friedrich Hayek, Cubitt Archive, Hayek: Hella 13/7/50, Colchester, England.

203. Cockett, *Thinking,* 120–21.

204. As to the cause of Helen von Hayek's death, it was listed as follows: a. coronary thrombosis, b. hypertension, c. arteriosclerosis. Death Certificate, Sub-district of Hendon, County of Middlesex, General Register Office, DXZ 577576, no. 131.

205. Cubitt, *Hayek*, 6.

206. John Nef, F. Hayek, 39, 39, Nef: Hayek 12/10/50, Palo Alto, Calif., Hoover Institution Archives.

207. Stephen Kresge, introduction to *Hayek on Hayek: An Autobiographical Dialogue,* ed. Stephen Kresge and Leif Wenar (Chicago: University of Chicago Press, 1994), 22–23; Bruce Caldwell, introduction to *The Collected Works of F. A. Hayek,* ed. Bruce Caldwell, vol. 9, *Contra Keynes and Cambridge* (Chicago: University of Chicago Press, 1995), 46.

208. Hayek, Hayek: Nef 22/5/51.

209. Friedrich Hayek, F. Hayek, 58, 18, Hayek: Cornuelle 21/5/53, Palo Alto, Calif., Hoover Institution Archives.

210. Friedrich Hayek, *Capitalism and the Historians* (Chicago: University of Chicago Press, 1954), 15–17.

211. H. C. Cornuelle, F. Hayek, 58, 17, Cornuelle: Letwin 20/6/52, Palo Alto, Calif., Hoover Institution Archives.

212. Friedrich Hayek, "Hayek on Hayek," from an interview in the Oral History Program, Jack High, Department of Economics, UCLA (London: Routledge, 1994), 143.

213. Hayek, "Hayek on Hayek," Oral History Program, James Buchanan, Center for the Study of Public Choice, Virginia Polytechnic University (London: Routledge, 1994), 103.

Chapter 8

1. Data from Caves and Krause, *Britain's Economic Performance,* cited in Andrew Gamble, *Hayek: The Iron Cage of Liberty* (Boulder, Colo.: Westview Press, 1996), 242.

2. Peter Clarke, *Hope and Glory: Britain 1900–1990* (London: Allen Lane/Penguin, 1996), 333–34.

3. Clarke, *Hope and Glory,* 351; Robert J. Skidelsky, *John Maynard Keynes: A Biography,* vol. 3, *Fighting for Britain 1937–1946* (London: Macmillan, 2000), 508.

4. Clarke, *Hope and Glory,* 352–53.

5. Noel Annan, *Our Age: The Generation That Made Post-War Britain* (London: Fontana, 1990), 453, 472–73.

6. Annan, *Our Age,* 477.

7. Charlotte Cubitt, interview by author, August 8, 1997.

8. Catherine Kord, review of Kramnick and Sheerman, *Laski,* in *The Antioch Review* (Summer 1994): 531–32.

9. Isaac Kramnick and Barry Sheerman, *Harold Laski: A Life on the Left* (London: The Penguin Group, 1993), 587.

10. Kramnick and Sheerman, *Laski,* 211, 350.

11. *New Statesman,* January 17, 1953. Cited in Kramnick and Sheerman, *Laski,* 589.

12. Kingsley Martin, *Harold Laski: A Biographical Memoir* (London: Victor Gollancz, 1953), 180–81.

13. Ralf Dahrendorf, *LSE: A History of the London School of Economics and Political Science 1895–1995* (Oxford: Oxford University Press, 1995), 368–69.

14. The author had the pleasure of taking lectures from Professor Oakeshott at LSE in 1960–1961.

15. Though Peter Clarke notes that monetary manipulation after 1951 became the primary means of propping up the economy—a strategy reminiscent of "the Treasury view"—and that this, nevertheless, came to be labeled "Keynesianism." Clarke, *Hope and Glory,* 244–45.

16. Clarke, *Hope and Glory,* 241–44.

17. Hayek commented in later years that Milton Friedman's *Essays in Positive Economics* was "quite as dangerous a book" as Keynes's *General Theory.* Friedrich Hayek, "Hayek on Hayek," in *The Collected Works of F. A. Hayek,* ed. Stephen Kresge and Leif Wenar, vol. supplement, *Hayek on Hayek: An Autobiographical Dialogue* (London: Routledge, 1994), 144–45.

18. Richard Cockett, *Thinking the Unthinkable,* rev. ed. (London: Fontana, 1995), 122–24, 130–31.

19. Cockett, *Thinking;* Sidney Blumenthal, *The Rise of the Counter-Establishment* (New York: Harper, 1988).

20. Ralph (Lord) Harris, interview by author, Institute of Economic Affairs, London, U.K., May 28, 1997.

21. Margaret Thatcher, *The Path to Power* (New York: HarperCollins, 1995), 254.

22. Cf. Greg Ransom, "The Significance of Myth and Misunderstanding in Social Science Narrative: Opening Access to Hayek's Copernican Revolution in Economics" (paper presented at the 1996 annual meetings of the History of Economics Society and the Southern Economics Association), www.kli.ac.at/theorylab/AuthPage/R/RansomG.html, 2003 [accessed March 10, 2003].

23. Friedrich Hayek, *The Constitution of Liberty* (Chicago: University of Chicago Press, 1960), 87–88.

24. Hayek, *The Constitution of Liberty,* 46–49.

25. Hayek, *The Constitution of Liberty,* 133–34.

26. Alan Ebenstein, *Friedrich Hayek: A Biography* (London: Palgrave, 2001), 308.

27. Hayek did not quite know what to call himself by this time. "Liberal" had acquired unacceptable connotations in America. "Conservative" bespoke privilege and hierarchy. "Libertarian" he found "singularly unattractive." "For my taste it carries too much the flavor of a manufactured term and of a substitute. What I should want is a word which describes the party of life, the party that favors free growth and spontaneous evolution. But I have racked my brain unsuccessfully to find a descriptive term which commends itself." Hayek, *The Constitution of Liberty,* 408.

28. Hayek, *The Constitution of Liberty,* 241.

29. Hayek, *The Constitution of Liberty,* 280.

30. David Felix, *Biography of an Idea: John Maynard Keynes and the General Theory* (New Brunswick, N.J.: Transaction, 1995), 248.

31. Lionel Robbins, "Hayek on Liberty," in *Friedrich A. Hayek: Critical Perspectives,* vol. 2, ed. John C. Wood and Ronald N. Wood (1961; reprint, London: Routledge, 1991), 131.

32. Jacob Viner, "Hayek on Freedom and Coercion," in *Friedrich A. Hayek: Critical Perspectives,* vol. 2, ed. John C. Wood and Ronald N. Wood (1961; reprint, London: Routledge, 1991), 109.

33. Ebenstein, *Hayek,* 196.

34. Ebenstein, *Hayek,* 192. The impression is supported by the memoir of Charlotte Cubitt, his personal secretary, who records a series of disputes and disagreements between the two as they lived out their later years. Charlotte Cubitt, *Hayek: An Affectionate Memoir, Revised Edition.* Unpublished MSS of Draft of Memoir, rev. ed. (Colchester, England, 2000).

35. Ebenstein, *Hayek,* 154, 371.

36. He estimated his pension at $177 per month (1962 dollars—approximately $1,000 per month in current dollars). Friedrich Hayek, J. Nef, 39, 39, Hayek: Nef 14/1/62, Palo Alto, Calif., Hoover Institution Archives.

37. Friedrich Hayek, F. Hayek, 58, 18, Hayek: Volker Foundation 22/7/61, Palo Alto, Calif., Hoover Institution Archives.

38. Ebenstein, *Friedrich Hayek,* 211.

39. Ebenstein, *Friedrich Hayek,* 207.

40. Cockett, *Thinking,* 160, 171–72.

41. Cockett, *Thinking,* 149.

42. Gamble, *Hayek,* 166–67.

43. Royal Academy of Sciences, "The Nobel Memorial Prize in 1974," *Swedish Journal of Economics* 76 (1974): 469–71.

44. Paraphrase appears in Sylvia Nasar, "Dept. of Winning: Why Does the Nobel Prize in Economics Get No Respect?" *The New Yorker,* December 20, 1999, 35–36.

45. Quoted in Cockett, *Thinking,* 173–74.

46. Thatcher, *The Path to Power,* 50–51, 84–85.

47. Thatcher, *The Path to Power,* 51.

48. Annan, *Our Age,* 591.

49. Quoted in Anne Perkins, "Blair Sets Out Vision for 'New Patriotism,'" *The Manchester Guardian,* May 26, 2001, 5.

50. Cockett, *Thinking,* 187, 198–99.

51. Charlotte Cubitt, *Hayek: An Affectionate Memoir.* Unpublished MSS of Draft of Memoir (Colchester, England, 1999), 11.

52. Friedrich Hayek, "Whither Democracy?" in *The Essence of Hayek,* ed. Chiaki Nishiyama and Kurt Leube (Palo Alto, Calif.: Hoover Institution, 1978), 358.

53. Friedrich Hayek, "The Political Order of a Free People," in *Law, Legislation and Liberty: A New Statement of the Liberal Principles of Justice and Political Economy,* vol. 3, with rev. preface (1979; reprint, London: Routledge, 1982), 137–38, 143–44.

54. Thatcher, *The Path to Power,* 50–51.

55. Kramnick and Sheerman, *Laski,* 539.

56. Clarke, *Hope and Glory,* 354.

57. Margaret Thatcher, F. Hayek, 102, Thatcher: Hayek 18/5/79, Palo Alto, Calif., Hoover Institution Archives.

58. Cubitt, *Hayek: An Affectionate Memoir,* rev. ed. (2000), 24–25.

59. Cockett, *Thinking,* 99.

60. Friedrich Hayek, F. Hayek, 102, Hayek: Thatcher 28/8/79, Palo Alto, Calif., Hoover Institution Archives; Friedrich Hayek, F. Hayek, 102, Hayek: Thatcher 24/4/80, Palo Alto, Calif., Hoover Institution Archives.

61. Margaret Thatcher, F. Hayek, 102, Thatcher: Hayek 13/5/80, Palo Alto, Calif., Hoover Institution Archives.

62. Norman Tebbit, F. Hayek, 102, Tebbit: Hayek 29/9/81, Palo Alto, Calif., Hoover Institution Archives.

63. Cited in Cockett, *Thinking,* 254. Cf. Kenneth Hoover, "The Rise of Conservative Capitalism: Ideological Tensions within the Reagan and Thatcher Governments," *Comparative Studies in Society and History* 29, no. 2 (April 1987): 245–68; Desmond King and Kenneth Hoover, "New Right Ideology: A Debate," *Comparative Studies in Society and History* 30, no. 4 (October 1988): 792–803.

64. Hayek, "The Political Order of a Free People," 148.

65. Hayek, "The Political Order of a Free People," 158–59.

66. Hayek, "The Political Order of a Free People," 150–51.

67. Friedrich Hayek, Hayek, 44, Palo Alto, Calif., Hoover Institution Archives, December 9, 1980, Letter and Statement Responding to Pope's Invitation, Stanford University.

68. Cubitt, *Hayek: An Affectionate Memoir,* rev. ed. (2000), 11.

69. Cubitt, *Hayek: An Affectionate Memoir,* rev. ed. (2000), 25.

70. Margaret Thatcher, F. Hayek, 102, Thatcher: Hayek 17/2/82, Palo Alto, Calif., Hoover Institution Archives.

71. Sara Diamond, *Roads to Dominion: Right Wing Movements and Political Power in the United States* (New York: Guilford Press, 1995), 210.

72. Cf. Rowland Evans and Robert Novak, *The Reagan Revolution* (New York: Dutton 1981, 229, and Martin Anderson, *Revolution* (New York: Harcourt Brace Jovanovich, 1988), 164. Quotes available on www.hayekcenter.org/friedrichhayek/hayekquote.htm, April 8, 2001 [accessed March 23, 2003].

73. Ebenstein, *Hayek,* 208.

74. Blumenthal, *Counter-Establishment,* 229.

75. Hayek was not persuaded of the dubious "supply-side" proposition that lower taxes would yield higher revenues due to the speedup in economic activity. Ebenstein, *Hayek,* 300.

76. Clarke, *Hope and Glory,* 371–76.

77. Cockett, *Thinking,* 288.

78. "F. A. Hayek Addresses U.S. Plenary," *International Cultural Foundation Report* March, 2, no. 1 (1984), 2–3.

79. Cubitt, *An Affectionate Memoir,* rev. ed. (2000), 79; Margaret Thatcher, F. Hayek, 102, Thatcher: Hayek 22/5/84, Palo Alto, Calif., Hoover Institution Archives.

Hayek was denied a baronetcy, according to Charlotte Cubitt, because the Queen Mother was perturbed at his divorce. Interview by author, Oxford, U.K., August 8, 1997. Cf. Dr. Anne Bohm, interview by author, London, U.K., unpublished, May 5, 1997. Cf. K. Leube, "Friedrich August von Hayek: A Biographical Introduction," in Nishiyama and Leube, eds., *Essence of Hayek*, xxiv; Cockett, *Thinking,* 120. Even in the postwar era, divorced people were not invited to attend garden parties or other functions at which members of the royalty were present. Ben Pimlott, *The Queen: A Biography of Elizabeth II* (New York: John Wiley, 1996), 201.

80. Lord Dahrendorf, interview by author, Oxford, U.K., March 24, 1997.

81. Friedrich Hayek, "Jobs: The Basic Truths We Have Cast Aside," *Times,* August 7, 1984, 8–10.

82. Robert J. Skidelsky, *John Maynard Keynes: A Biography,* vol. 2, *The Economist as Saviour 1920–1937* (London: Allen Lane/Penguin, 1992), 251.

83. Clarke, *Hope and Glory,* 369.

84. President Ronald Reagan, F. Hayek, 58, 16, Reagan: Hayek Reagan 15/5/86, Palo Alto, Calif., Hoover Institution Archives.

85. Cockett, *Thinking,* 307.

86. Diamond, *Roads to Dominion,* 198–99.

87. Hayek, "Whither Democracy?" 379; Hayek, *The Constitution of Liberty*, chap. 20.

88. Annan, *Our Age,* 601–3.

89. In the preface to *The Fatal Conceit,* Hayek states: "I wish, however, to express my deep gratitude to Miss Charlotte Cubitt, who has served as my assistant throughout the period that this work was in preparation and without whose dedicated help it never could have been completed." Miss Cubitt reports that she was employed by Hayek for fifteen years. She was paid irregularly from small grants and other sources and was left without any provision in the estate for a pension when he died. Hayek's family later provided a supplement to her government pension. Interview by author, Colchester, U.K., August 8, 1997.

90. Friedrich Hayek, "The Fatal Conceit: The Errors of Socialism," in *The Collected Works of F. A. Hayek,* vol. 1, ed. W. W. Bartley III (Palo Alto, Calif.: Hoover Institution, 1988), 7.

91. Phillip Brady, F. Hayek, 102, Brady: Hayek 12/11/91, Palo Alto, Calif., Hoover Institution Archives.

92. Thatcher, *The Path to Power,* 603–4; "Hayek's Victory," *Wall Street Journal,* March 25 1992, editorial, A12.

93. Ironically, Laski and Keynes can also claim a share of Burke: Laski for the early conception of a plurality of institutions in society and Keynes for his sense of persuasion in a climate of "feelings and prejudices" that must necessarily be a part of governance. Donald E. Moggridge, *Maynard Keynes: An Economist's Biography* (London: Routledge, 1992), 164.

94. Hoover, "Rise of Conservative Capitalism," 245–68; King and Hoover, "New Right Ideology"; Kenneth Hoover and Raymond Plant, *Conservative Capitalism in Britain and the United States: A Critical Appraisal* (London: Routledge, 1989), 93–154.

95. George Nash, *The Conservative Intellectual Movement in America Since 1945* (New York: Basic Books, 1979).

96. Hayek, "The Fatal Conceit," 6.

97. Edward H. Crane, "The Fatal Conceit: The Errors of Socialism," *Wall Street Journal,* April 20, 1989, A12.

98. Diamond, *Roads to Dominion,* 29–31, 198–99.

Chapter 9

1. The method of this study is to establish logical congruence. Congruence refers to the connection between developmental turning points and ideological formulations. The logic resides in the pattern of the congruence and the fact that the fit is not contradicted by significant evidence. Both the pattern and the fit may be subjected to the test of evidence, so that the thesis is falsifiable. The objective is not causal explanation per se, but a substantial form of inferential correlation that gives us reason, and direction, in critiquing ideological formulations and in understanding their "social purchase." The phrase is Peter Clarke's in Peter Clarke, *Liberals and Social Democrats* (New York: Cambridge University Press, 1978), 3.

2. Isaiah Berlin, "Historical Inevitability," in *The Proper Study of Mankind: An Anthology of Essays,* ed. Henry Hardy and Roger Hausheer (1953; reprint, New York: Farrar, Straus, and Giroux, 1997), 180.

3. Cf. Kenneth Hoover, with James Marcia, and Kristen Parris, *The Power of Identity: Politics in a New Key* (Chatham, N.J.: Chatham House Publishing, 1997), 1, 330.

4. Cf. Piero Mini, *John Maynard Keynes: A Study in the Psychology of Original Work* (New York: St. Martin's Press, 1994).

5. Erik H. Erikson, *Identity: Youth and Crisis* (New York: Norton, 1968), 32.

6. Identity relations analysis aims to avoid the pitfalls noted by Robert Skidelsky in discussing "psychohistory." Robert Skidelsky, "Psychohistory: A Speech to the South Place Ethical Society, February 12, 1977," in *Interests and Obsessions,* ed. Robert Skidelsky (London: Macmillan, 1993), 410–20, while taking advantage of the empirical extension and confirmation of Erikson's original analysis. Skidelsky objects to psychohistory on three grounds: falsifiability, cultural transferability of psychoanalytic categories, and difficulty of explaining the exceptionalism of great figures by using generic categories. The first problem has been dealt with by remaining with observable aspects of behavior. The second is less of a problem, since all three characters fit broadly within Erikson's own cultural experience—and specifically within Freud's (Austrian, British, and Jewish influences). The third critique targets a different kind of inquiry—the purpose here is not quite to explain greatness per se, but rather the genealogy of ideological behavior and the ways that such behavior finds consonance with political developments.

7. Peter Hall, "Keynes in Political Science," *History of Political Economy* 26, no. 1 (1994): 143.

8. Anna Carabelli, "The Methodology of the Critique of Classical Theory: Keynes on Organic Interdependence," in *John Maynard Keynes: Language and Method,* ed.

Alesandra Margola and Francesco Silva (Brookfield, Vt.: Edward Elgar Publishing, 1994), 142.

9. Roy Forbes Harrod, Sir, *The Life of John Maynard Keynes* (New York: Harcourt Brace, 1951), 184.

10. Robert J. Skidelsky, *John Maynard Keynes: A Biography,* vol. 2, *The Economist as Saviour 1920–1937* (London: Allen Lane/Penguin, 1992), xx–xxi.

11. Skidelsky, *Keynes,* vol. 2, xxiii.

12. Robert J. Skidelsky, *John Maynard Keynes: A Biography,* vol. 3, *Fighting for Britain 1937–1946* (London: Macmillan, 2000), xvii.

13. Michael Holroyd, *Lytton Strachey: A Biography* (London: Penguin, 1971), 243.

14. *Strachey,* 243.

15. Skidelsky, *Keynes,* vol. 2, xviii.

16. Skidelsky, *Keynes*, vol. 2, 517.

17. Skidelsky, *Keynes*, vol. 2, 409.

18. Isaac Kramnick and Barry Sheerman, *Harold Laski: A Life on the Left* (London: The Penguin Group, 1993), 107.

19. Mark DeWolfe Howe, ed., *Holmes-Laski Letters: The Correspondence of Mr. Justice Holmes and Harold J. Laski,* vol. 2, *Holmes-Laski Letters: 1916–1935,* by Oliver Wendell Holmes and Harold Laski (Cambridge, Mass.: Harvard University Press, 1953), 1094.

20. Kramnick and Sheerman, *Laski,* 477.

21. Private communication to the author, Sept. 21, 2001.

22. John Strachey, "Laski's Struggle for Certainty," in *The Strangled Cry and Other Unparliamentary Papers,* ed. John Strachey (London: Bodley Head, 1962), 196.

23. Strachey, "Laski's Struggle for Certainty," 196.

24. Peter Lamb, "Laski's Ideological Metamorphosis," *Journal of Political Ideologies* 4, no. 2 (June 1999): 250–51.

25. Michael Newman, "Harold Laski Today," *Political Quarterly* 67, no. 3 (July–September 1996): 236.

26. Royal Courts of Justice, *Laski v. Newark Advertiser and Parlby* (London: 1947).

27. David Miller, "F. A. Hayek: Dogmatic Skeptic," *Dissent* 41 (Summer 1994): 346. Cf. Margaret Thatcher, *The Path to Power* (New York: HarperCollins, 1995), 84–85.

28. Friedrich A. Hayek, "'Social' or Distributive Justice," in *The Essence of Hayek,* ed. Chiaki Nishiyama and Kurt Leube (1976; reprint, Palo Alto, Calif.: Hoover Institution, 1984), 62–63. Raymond Plant points up the contradiction in making individual choice the fulcrum of morality and then denying that the state has any role in enabling individuals to have meaningful choices, Raymond Plant, "Hirsch, Hayek and Habermas: Dilemmas of Distribution," in *Dilemmas of Liberal Democracies: Studies in Fred Hirsch's Social Limits to Growth,* ed. Adrian Ellis and Krishnan Kumar (London: Tavistock Publications, 1983), 53–63.

29. Michael Freeden, *Ideologies and Political Theory* (Oxford: Oxford University Press, 1996), 303.

30. Charlotte Cubitt, *Hayek: An Affectionate Memoir.* Unpublished MSS of Draft of Memoir (Colchester, England, 1999), 9–11.

31. Alan Ebenstein, *Friedrich Hayek: A Biography* (London: Palgrave, 2001), 107.

32. Friedrich Hayek, *The Constitution of Liberty* (Chicago: University of Chicago Press, 1960), 138.

33. In 1969, a disciple of Hayek's, California Governor Ronald Reagan, signed into the law the first "no-fault" divorce law in the United States. In England the 1937 divorce law that added desertion to adultery as grounds for divorce was only significantly changed in 1969 when the concept of "matrimonial offense" was replaced with the notion of marital breakdown. Peter Clarke, *Hope and Glory: Britain 1900–1990* (London: Allen Lane/Penguin, 1996), 366. Still, however, grounds needed to be specified. It took the Conservative government until 1996 to adopt a no-fault plan in England and then the Labour government declined to implement it. Clare Dyer, "Government Drops Plan for No-Fault Divorce," *Manchester Guardian,* September 2, 2000, 3.

34. The marriage was, of course, contracted in Austria; however, Austria was a Catholic state with notably conservative views about divorce.

35. Friedrich A. Hayek, "Individualism: True and False," in *The Essence of Hayek,* ed. Chiaki Nishiyama and Kurt Leube (1945; reprint Palo Alto, Calif.: Hoover Institution, 1984), 131–59.

36. Hayek, *The Constitution of Liberty,* 62.

37. Hayek discusses this in Friedrich Hayek, "The Political Order of a Free People," in *Law, Legislation and Liberty: A New Statement of the Liberal Principles of Justice and Political Economy,* vol. 3, with rev. preface (1979; reprint, London: Routledge, 1982), 170–71, and comes to no clear resolution. While allowing for the "conscientious and courageous" dissenter from society's moral rules, he also declares that "there can be no excuse or pardon for a systematic disregard of accepted moral rules because they have no understood justification." Cf. Rodney Barker, *Political Ideas in Modern Britain in and After the 20th Century,* 2nd ed. (London: Routledge, 1997), 241–47.

38. Friedrich Hayek, "Hayek on Hayek," in *The Collected Works of F. A. Hayek,* ed. Stephen Kresge and Leif Wenar, vol. supplement, *Hayek on Hayek: An Autobiographical Dialogue,* W. W. Bartley III Audiotape Archive, 1984–1988 (London: Routledge, 1994), 72.

39. Cubitt, *Hayek: An Affectionate Memoir,* 43.

40. Oral History Program, University of California at Los Angeles, *Nobel Prize-Winning Economist Friedrich A. von Hayek,* ed. Arman Alchian (interview took place in 1978: available in 1983). Cf. Ebenstein, *Hayek,* 169.

41. Freeden, *Ideologies and Political Theory,* 300–11.

42. Hayek, *The Constitution of Liberty,* 143.

43. Hayek, "Hayek on Hayek," Oral History Program, Axel Leijonhufvud, Department of Economics, UCLA (London: Routledge, 1994), 108.

44. Cf. Ebenstein, *Hayek,* 75.

45. Rodney Barker draws attention to this ambiguity in his critique of Hayek. Rodney Barker, *Political Ideas in Modern Britain,* 241–47.

46. Ebenstein, *Hayek,* 88.

47. Ebenstein, *Hayek,* 88.

48. Freeden, *Ideologies and Political Theory,* 76.

Chapter 10

1. John Patrick Diggins, *The Rise and Fall of the American Left* (New York: Norton, 1992).

2. James M. Glass, *Life Unworthy of Life: Racial Phobia and Mass Murder in Hitler's Germany* (New York: Basic Books, 1997), 125.

3. Lionel (Lord) Robbins, *Autobiography of an Economist* (London: Macmillan, 1971), 81. Robbins comments that he finds "very little to alter" about this description nearly fifty years after he noted it in his journal. "For the showiness increased and the pure interest in knowledge as such had diminished."

4. Harold Laski, *The Dangers of Obedience and Other Essays* (New York: Harper and Brothers, 1930), 279.

5. Harold Laski, *The American Democracy: A Commentary and an Interpretation* (New York: Viking Press, 1948), 186, 191.

6. Harold Laski, "The Problem of Administrative Areas: An Essay in Reconstruction," *Smith College Studies in History* 4, no. 1 (October 1918): 42–45; Harold Laski, "Can Business Be Civilized," in *The Dangers of Obedience and Other Essays,* 286–87. Cf. Michael Newman, *Harold Laski: A Political Biography* (Basingstoke, U.K.: Macmillan, 1993), 86; Roy (Lord) Hattersley, interview by author, May 22, 1997, the House of Lords, London, U.K.

7. Harold Laski, *A Grammar of Politics* (London: Allen and Unwin, 1925), 507.

8. Ralf Dahrendorf, *LSE: A History of the London School of Economics and Political Science 1895–1995* (Oxford: Oxford University Press, 1995), 230.

9. William Y. Elliott, "The Pragmatic Politics of Mr. Laski," *The American Political Science Review* 18, no. 2 (May 1924): 271. Elliott, as it happens, authored a plan to break up the United States into several commonwealths that would preserve its agrarian society—pluralism but with sovereignty distributed. Cf. Isaac Kramnick and Barry Sheerman, *Harold Laski: A Life on the Left* (London: The Penguin Group, 1993), 234. In 1934, when Laski made his move in the opposite direction, toward Marxism, Elliott was one target for his arguments in *The State in Theory and Practice* (1935). Cf. Kramnick and Sheerman, *Laski,* 359. Elliott published a more extensive attack on Laski in his *The Pragmatic Revolt in Politics* (New York: Macmillan, 1928). Elliott became Laski's daughter's teacher at Radcliffe in 1939, the year that she defied her parents and married her college sweetheart, whom they thought to be too young, while the senior Laskis were on a voyage—acts of defiance that seem to mirror those of her parents. Kramnick and Sheerman, *Laski,* 404.

10. Newman, *Laski*, 86.

11. Cf. Harold Laski, *Lecture: Introduction to Contemporary Politics*, ed. Francis G. Wilson (Seattle: University of Washington Bookstore, 1939), 3–12; Michael Freeden, *Liberalism Divided* (Oxford: Oxford University Press, 1986). However, Laski never abandoned democratic socialism for Soviet-style Marxism.

12. Kramnick and Sheerman, *Laski*, 470.

13. Michael Newman argues persuasively that Laski was in transition from his early pluralist position after the 1917 Boston Police Strike and its consequences for his role at Harvard. He became a Fabian socialist more than a Marxist and more anti-American than anticapitalist for a time. Newman, *Laski*, 56–64.

14. Newman, *Laski*, 232.

15. Newman, *Laski*, 372–73.

16. Bernard Crick, "Two Laskis," Book review, *The Political Quarterly* (1993): 466–74; Norman Birnbaum, "The Elusive Synthesis: Review of Harold Laski: A Life on the Left, by Isaac Kramnick and Barry Sheerman," *The Nation*, June 13, 1995, 838–88.

17. Kramnick and Sheerman, *Laski*, 102–3.

18. Edward H. Crane, "The Fatal Conceit: The Errors of Socialism," *Wall Street Journal*, April 20, 1989, A12.

19. Alan Ebenstein, *Friedrich Hayek: A Biography* (London: Palgrave, 2001), 300.

20. Ebenstein, *Hayek*, 294–95.

21. Ebenstein, *Hayek*, 257, 280.

22. Ralph (Lord) Harris, interview by author, Institute of Economic Affairs, London, U.K., May 28, 1997.

23. Lord Dahrendorf, interview by author, Oxford, U.K, March 25, 1997.

24. Friedrich Hayek, "The Fatal Conceit: The Errors of Socialism," in *The Collected Works of F. A. Hayek,* vol. 1, ed. W. W. Bartley III (Palo Alto, Calif.: Hoover Institution, 1988), 44.

25. Hayek, "The Fatal Conceit," 66.

26. These issues are discussed in the Hayek–Keynes correspondence. See Gregory Christainsen, "What Keynes Really Said to Hayek about Planning," *Challenge* 36, no. 4 (1993): 50–54.

27. Hayek, "The Fatal Conceit," 63–67.

28. Friedrich Hayek, *The Constitution of Liberty* (Chicago: University of Chicago Press, 1960), 138–39.

29. Michael Oakeshott, *Rationalism in Politics and Other Essays* (London: Methuen, 1962), 26. Cf. Friedrich Hayek, "The Principles of a Liberal Social Order," in *The Essence of Hayek,* ed. Chiaki Nishiyama and Kurt Leube (Palo Alto, Calif.: Hoover Institution, 1967), 363–81.

30. Friedrich Hayek, "The Principles of a Liberal Social Order," in *The Essence of Hayek*, ed. Chiaki Nishiyama and Kurt Leube (Palo Alto, Calif.: Hoover Institution, 1967), 368–69.

31. Andrew Gamble, *Hayek: The Iron Cage of Liberty* (Boulder, Colo.: Westview Press, 1996), 15, 75. Cf. John Gray, *Hayek on Liberty*, 3rd ed. (London: Routledge, 1998), 5.

32. Richard Bellamy, "Dethroning Politics: Liberalism, Constitutionalism, and Democracy in the Thought of F. A. Hayek," *British Journal of Political Science* 24 (1994): 429.

33. Ebenstein, *Hayek*, 224.

34. Hayek, "The Principles of a Liberal Social Order," in *The Essence of Hayek* (1967) 367–68; Friedrich Hayek, "The Origins and Effects of Our Morals: A Problem for Science," in Nishiyama and Leube, 318–330.

35. Kenneth R. Hoover, with James Marcia and Kristen Parris, *The Power of Identity: Politics in a New Key* (Chatham, N.J.: Chatham House Publishing, 1997), 73.

36. Cf. Hayek, *The Constitution of Liberty*, 106–14. Hayek acknowledges the transmission of ideas in a democracy but does not deal with the process of deliberation and compromise as a way of fitting together individual views into a considered social policy.

37. I am indebted to Mark Blaug for making this point in his opening remarks to the annual conference of the European Society for Economic History in Graz, Austria, February 2000. Cf. the very insightful analysis of Smith's use of terms in Roger Backhouse, "Competition," in John Creedy, ed., *Foundations of Economic Thought* (London: Basil Blackwell, 1990), 58–86.

38. Harold Laski, *The Foundations of Sovereignty and Other Essays* (New Haven, Conn.: Yale University Press, 1921), ix.

39. Laski, *Foundations*, ix.

40. Friedrich Hayek, "The Political Order of a Free People," in *Law, Legislation and Liberty: A New Statement of the Liberal Principles of Justice and Political Economy*, vol. 3, with rev. preface (1979; reprint, London: Routledge, 1982), 40–50.

41. Hayek, *The Constitution of Liberty*, 41.

42. John Maynard Keynes, "A Tract on Monetary Reform," in *The Collected Writings of John Maynard Keynes*, ed. Elizabeth Johnson and Donald Moggridge, vol. 4, *A Tract on Monetary Reform* (London: Macmillan/Cambridge University Press for the Royal Economic Society, 1971), 36.

43. Cf. Ebenstein, *Hayek*, 234.

44. Gray, *Hayek on Liberty*, 151.

45. David Miller, *Principles of Social Justice* (Cambridge, Mass.: Harvard University Press, 1999).

46. In George Orwell, "Review of *The Road to Serfdom* by F. A. Hayek," in *The Complete Works of George Orwell*, vol. 16, *I Have Tried to Tell the Truth*, ed. Peter Davison with Ian Angus and Sheila Davison (London: Secker and Warburg, 1944), 149.

47. Friedrich A. Hayek, "Individualism: True and False," in *The Essence of Hayek*, ed. Chiaki Nishiyama and Kurt Leube (1945, 1967; reprint, Palo Alto, Calif.: Hoover Institution, 1984), 136.

48. Hayek, "Individualism," 143.

49. Donald E. Moggridge, *Maynard Keynes: An Economist's Biography* (London: Routledge, 1992), 377–78, 417, 449.

50. Moggridge, *Economist's Biography*, 455; Elizabeth S. Johnson and Harry G. Johnson, *The Shadow of Keynes: Understanding Keynes, Cambridge, and Keynesian Economics* (Chicago: University of Chicago Press, 1978), 137–38.

51. John Maynard Keynes, *Rethinking Employment and Unemployment Policy*, vol. 20 of *The Collected Writings of John Maynard Keynes,* ed. Donald Moggridge (Cambridge: Macmillan/Cambridge University Press for the Royal Economic Society © 1980, 1979), 603–4.

52. John Maynard Keynes, *Economic Articles and Correspondence: Investment and Editorial*, vol. 12 of *The Collected Writings of John Maynard Keynes,* ed. Donald Moggridge (Cambridge: Macmillan/Cambridge University Press for the Royal Economic Society © 1980, 1976), 252.

53. Maynard Keynes, Modern Archives, A, 31, 1931, File: 174–192, Draft of "The Pure Theory of Money. A Reply to Dr. Hayek," King's College, Cambridge University.

54. *Letter to G. B. Shaw* (1934) in John Maynard Keynes, *Social, Political and Literary Writings,* vol. 28 of *The Collected Writings of John Maynard Keynes,* ed. Donald Moggridge (Cambridge: Macmillan/Cambridge University Press for the Royal Economic Society © 1980, 1978), 42.

55. John Maynard Keynes, "My Early Beliefs," in *Two Memoirs* (1938; reprint, New York: Augustus M. Kelly, 1949), 97.

56. Moggridge, *The Shadow of Keynes*, 374, 379, 453–55.

57. Moggridge, *The Shadow of Keynes*, 433, 455.

58. Keynes, *Activities 1929–1931*, vol. 20 of *The Collected Writings* (1981), 595.

59. Keynes, *Activities 1929–1931,* vol. 20 of *The Collected Writings* (1981), 598.

60. Moggridge, *The Shadow of Keynes*, 370–71.

61. Robert J. Skidelsky, *John Maynard Keynes: A Biography,* vol. 1, *Hopes Betrayed 1883–1920* (New York: Viking Penguin, 1983), 84–85, 178.

62. Michael Stewart, *Keynes and After* (London: Penguin, 1967), 16.

63. Keynes, "My Early Beliefs," 101.

64. Peter Clarke, "John Maynard Keynes: The Best of Both Worlds," in *After the Victorians: Private Conscience and Public Duty*, ed. Susan Pedersen and Peter Mandler (London: Routledge, 1994), 171–88; interview by author, Cambridge, U.K., April 18, 1997.

65. Clarke, "The Best," 181.

66. Kramnick and Sheerman, *Laski*, 392.

67. Michael Oakeshott welcomed Keynes's appreciation for the nonrational but was disturbed that his account made all that was nonrational seem vulgar, even if potentially valuable. Oakeshott, *Rationalism*, 114–15.

68. Keynes, *The General Theory of Employment, Interest and Money,* vol. 7 of *The Collected Writings* (1936), 162–63.

69. Robert J. Skidelsky, *John Maynard Keynes: A Biography,* vol. 2, *The Economist as Saviour 1920–1937* (London: Allen Lane/Penguin, 1992), 539.

70. Roy Forbes Harrod, Sir, *The Life of John Maynard Keynes* (New York: Harcourt Brace, 1951), 36.

71. Robert J. Skidelsky, *John Maynard Keynes: A Biography,* vol. 3, *Fighting for Britain 1937–1946* (London: Macmillan, 2000), 156.

72. Peter Clarke, *The Keynesian Revolution in the Making, 1924–1936* (New York: Oxford University Press, 1988), 101–2.

73. Cf. Peter Clarke, "Keynes in History," *History of Political Economy* 26, no. 1 (1994): 130–31; Bradley Bateman, "In the Realm of Concept and Circumstance," *History of Political Economy* 26, no. 1 (1994): 99–116.

74. Charles H. Hession, *John Maynard Keynes : A Personal Biography of the Man Who Revolutionized Capitalism and the Way We Live* (New York: Macmillan, 1984); and Piero Mini, *John Maynard Keynes: A Study in the Psychology of Original Work* (New York: St. Martin's Press, 1994). Cf. C. H. Hession, "John Maynard Keynes: A Study of the Psychology of Original Work—Review of Book by Piero V. Mini," *Review of Social Economy* 54, no. 1 (Spring 1996): 109–14.

75. Mini, *Psychology of Original Work,* 9–10.

76. See Hession's reflections on this point in Hession, "Study of the Psychology—Review," 112.

77. Sweezy continues, "The only trouble is—as every Marxist knows—that the state is not a god but one of the actors who has a part to play just like all the other actors." Paul Sweezy, "John Maynard Keynes," in *The New Economics: Keynes's Influence on Theory and Public Policy,* ed. Seymour Harris (London: Dennis Dobson, 1947), 108.

78. Piero Mini, *Keynes, Bloomsbury, and the General Theory* (London: Macmillan, 1991), 197.

79. Harris, "Acknowledgements," in *The New Economics,* 1.

80. Hayek suggested that he avoided government service only because "I cleared out of every country as soon as they started using me for governmental service." He did see brief service on a government committee in Austria; however, he was not wanted in Britain during the second war—a circumstance he blamed on his "ex-alien" status. *Hayek on Hayek,* 94–95.

81. Skidelsky, *Keynes,* vol. 3, 286.

82. John Maynard Keynes, *J. M. Keynes: F. Hayek 28/6/44, The Collected Writings of John Maynard Keynes,* vol. 27, *Activities 1940–1946, Shaping the Post-War World: Employment and Commodities,* ed. Donald Moggridge (London: Macmillan, 1980), 385–88.

83. Cf. Gray, *Hayek on Liberty,* 4.

Chapter 11

1. Max Beloff, "The Age of Laski," *The Fortnightly* 167 (June 1950): 380.

2. Ivor Crewe and Donald Searing, "Ideological Change in the British Conservative Party," *American Political Science Review* 82, no. 2 (June 1988): 378.

3. Crewe and Searing, "Ideological Change," 379.

4. On the shift in Labour rhetoric from egalitarianism to the provision of minimums, see Crewe and Searing, "Ideological Change," 379.

5. Peter Clarke, "Keynes in History," *History of Political Economy* 26, no. 1 (1994): 118. Cf. Peter Clarke, *The Keynesian Revolution in the Making, 1924–1936* (New York: Oxford University Press, 1988), 313–30, for a most persuasive interpretation of Keynes's significance as a political economist and shaper of policy.

6. For a survey, see Peter Hall, "Keynes in Political Science," *History of Political Economy* 26, no. 1 (1994): 142–43. A more complicated discussion of his legacy appears in Paul Diesing, *How Does Social Science Work?* (Pittsburgh, Pa.: University of Pittsburgh Press, 1991), 112–15.

7. John Diggins, *The Rise and Fall of the American Left* (New York: Norton, 1992), 138.

8. Alfred Borneman, "Fifty Years of Ideology: A Selective Survey of Academic Economics in the U.S. 1930 to 1980," *Journal of Economic Studies* 8, no. 1 (1981): 28–29.

9. On Marx, see Terence Ball, "Marxist Science and Positivist Politics," in *After Marx,* ed. Terence Ball and James Farr (Cambridge: Cambridge University Press, 1984), 235–60.

10. Skidelsky goes further: "For some purposes at least, Keynes thought that the distinctions between magic, science, and art were less interesting than the similarities." Robert J. Skidelsky, *John Maynard Keynes: A Biography,* vol. 2, *The Economist as Saviour 1920–1937* (London: Allen Lane/Penguin, 1992), 414.

11. David Felix, *Biography of an Idea: John Maynard Keynes and the General Theory* (New Brunswick, N.J.: Transaction, 1995), 242–43.

12. Elizabeth S. Johnson and Harry G. Johnson, *The Shadow of Keynes: Understanding Keynes, Cambridge, and Keynesian Economics* (Chicago: University of Chicago Press, 1978), 14–15; cf. Donald E. Moggridge, *Maynard Keynes: An Economist's Biography* (London: Routledge, 1992), 374.

13. Quentin Bell, "Recollections and Reflections on Maynard Keynes," in *Keynes and the Bloomsbury Group/The Fourth Keynes Seminar Held at the University of Kent at Canterbury, 1978,* ed. Derek Crabtree and A. P. Thirlwall (London: Macmillan, 1980), 83–85.

14. Anand Chandavarkar, *Keynes and India: A Study in Economics and Biography* (Basingstoke, U.K.: Macmillan, 1989), 142.

15. Cf. Andrew Gamble, *Hayek: The Iron Cage of Liberty* (Boulder, Colo.: Westview Press, 1996), 157.

16. Margaret Thatcher, *The Path to Power* (New York: HarperCollins, 1995), 565.

17. Laski, for example, was more opposed to capitalism than to the market per se. Interview with Michael Newman, London, U.K., April 16, 1997.

18. Michael Freeden, *Ideologies and Political Theory: A Conceptual Approach* (Oxford: Oxford University Press, 1996), 553.

19. Albert Hirschman, *The Rhetoric of Reaction: Perversity, Futility, Jeopardy* (Cambridge, Mass.: Harvard University Press, 1991), chap. 7.

20. Or, one might add after a lifetime spent in such institutions, of universities. For the apposite examples, see Frances MacDonald Cornford, *Cosmographica Academica*, 2nd ed. (Cambridge, U.K.: Bowes and Bowes, 1922).

21. John L. Campbell, "Mechanisms of Evolutionary Change in Economic Governance: Interaction, Interpretation, and Bricolage," in *Evolutionary Economics and Path Dependence*, ed. Lars Magnusson and Jan Ottosson (Cheltenham, U.K.: Edward Elgar, 1997), 10–31.

22. Paul Krugman, *Peddling Prosperity* (New York: Norton, 1994), 197–98.

23. R. E. Lucas, "John Maynard Keynes, vols. 1 and 2, by R. Skidelsky," *Journal of Modern History* 67/4 (December 1995), 914–17.

24. Simon Tormey, "The Vicissitudes of 'Radical Centrism': The Case of Agnes Heller, Radical Centrist *avant la Lettre*," *Journal of Political Ideologies* 3, no. 2 (1998): 147–67.

25. Sir Roy Forbes Harrod, *The Life of John Maynard Keynes* (New York: Harcourt Brace, 1951), 136.

26. Cf. Trudi Miller, "The Operation of Democratic Institutions," *Public Administration Review,* November/December 1989: 519.

27. For further thoughts on these matters, see Hoover, "What Should Democracies Do About Identity" (paper presented to the Nuffield Political Theory Workshop, Oxford University, April, 2000), www.wwu.edu/~khoover/democracy.pdf, 2001 [accessed March 13, 2003].

Index

activism: Kerry and, 25; Laski and, 25–26, 40
Addison, Paul, 133, 167
aestheticism, Keynes and, 13–15, 224
air traffic controllers' strike, 215
Alchian, Arman, 231–32
Alexander, Samuel, 23
Allende, Salvador, 210
altruism, Keynes on, 15
American Democracy (Laski), 179–80
American Enterprise Institute, 207
Annan, Noel, 12–13, 167, 201
anti-communism, 181–83
Apostles, 12–13, 20
appeasement, 103, 122
Armey, Dick, 260, 268
Asquith, Herbert, 33, 61, 72
Asquith, Margot, 124
Assheton, Ralph, 164, 296n36
associations, Laski on, 41–42
Atlantic Charter, 132
Atlas Foundation, 215
Attlee, Clement, 131–35, 138, 140, 143–44; Churchill on, 169; and postwar election, 160, 162, 164–68, 177–78
Austria, 242; Hayek and, 228–29

Austrian Civil War, 108, 116
Austro-Hungarian Empire, 7–9, 29, 47
authoritarianism, Hayek on, 210
Authority in the Modern State (Laski), 42

Baldwin, Stanley, 51, 91–92
Barker, Ernest, 25, 37
Barker, Rodney, 97, 226
Barnett, Henrietta, 107
Bartley, W. W., III, 76, 231
Bartley, William, 216
Beaverbrook, Max, 158, 164–66, 173, 296n36
Becker, Carl, 93
Bell, Clive, 20, 32
Bell, Quentin, 20–21, 32, 60, 264
Bell, Vanessa Stephens, 20, 32, 51, 160
Bellamy, Richard, 243
Beloff, Max, 2, 93, 260
Benn, Tony, 200
Berlin, Isaiah, 184, 220
Bevan, Aneurin, 104, 138, 143
Beveridge, William, 50, 61, 87, 145, 156; and Hayek, 106, 112, 118, 150; and Keynes, 122, 124; and Laski, 62, 68, 101

319

About the Author

Kenneth R. Hoover is Professor of Political Science at Western Washington University. He is the author of six books on identity, ideology, and methodology including *The Power of Identity: Politics in a New Key* and, with Raymond (Lord) Plant, *Conservative Capitalism in Britain and the United States: A Critical Appraisal.* Along with several colleagues, he is currently working on a new book, *The Future of Identity: Centennial Reflections on the Legacy of Erik Erikson.* He and his wife, Judy, who shared in the research for this book, live in Bellingham, Washington.